Sleuthing Ethnicity

Sleuthing Ethnicity

The Detective in Multiethnic Crime Fiction

Edited by
Dorothea Fischer-Hornung
and
Monika Mueller

Madison • Teaneck
Fairleigh Dickinson University Press
London: Associated University Presses

© 2003 by Rosemont Publishing & Printing Corp.

All rights reserved. Authorization to photocopy items for internal or personal use, or the internal or personal use of specific clients, is granted by the copyright owner, provided that a base fee of $10.00, plus eight cents per page, per copy is paid directly to the Copyright Clearance Center, 222 Rosewood Dr., Danvers, Massachusetts 01923. [0-8386-3979-8/03 $10.00 + 8¢ pp, pc.]

Associated University Presses
2010 Eastpark Boulevard
Cranbury, NJ 08512

Associated University Presses
Unit 304, The Chandlery
50 Westminster Bridge Road
London SE1 7QY, England

Associated University Presses
P.O. Box 338, Port Credit
Mississauga, Ontario
Canada L5G 4L8

The paper used in this publication meets the requirements of the American National Standard for Permanence of Paper for Printed Library Materials Z39.48-1984.

Library of Congress Cataloging-in-Publication Data

Sleuthing ethnicity : the detective in multiethnic crime fiction / edited by Dorothea Fischer-Hornung and Monika Mueller.
    p. cm.
Includes bibliographical references and index.
  ISBN 0-8386-3979-8 (alk. paper)
1. Detective and mystery stories, American—History and criticism. 2. American fiction—Minority authors—History and criticism. 3. Detective and mystery stories—History and criticism. 4. Ethnic groups in literature. 5. Minorities in literature. 6. Crime in literature. I. Fischer-Hornung, Dorothea, 1949– II. Mueller, Monika, 1960–
  PS374.D4S58 2003
  813'.087209355—dc21

2003005811

PRINTED IN THE UNITED STATES OF AMERICA

Contents

Introduction
DOROTHEA FISCHER-HORNUNG AND MONIKA MUELLER   11

Part I: Historicizing Ethnicity

Insider Knowledge versus Outsider Perspective in
Early Italian American and African American
Detective Stories
MARINA CACIOPPO   23

Samurai Sleuths and Detective Daughters:
The American Way
THEO D'HAEN   36

Of Sherlocks, Shylocks, and the Shoah: Ethnicity in
Jewish American Detective Fiction
CARMEN BIRKLE   53

Marketing Mystical Mysteries: Rudolfo Anaya's
Mystery Trilogy
ANN-CATHERINE GEUDER   81

Part II: Comparing Ethnic Identities

Detectives, Hoodoo, and *Brujería:* Subverting the
Dominant U.S. Cultural Ethos
CARMEN FLYS-JUNQUERA   97

A Cuban American "Lady Dick" and an African American
Miss Marple?: The Female Detective in the Novels of
Carolina Garcia-Aguilera and Barbara Neely
MONIKA MUELLER   114

CONTENTS

Investigating Newark, New Jersey: Empowering Spaces
in Valerie Wilson Wesley's Detective Fiction
CARMEN BIRKLE 133

From Roots to Routes: Sleuthing Identity in Two
Juvenile Ethnic Detective Novels
SABINE STEINISCH 148

"A Great Space Where Sex Should Be," or "Who's the
Black Private Dick Who's Not a Sex Machine to
All the Chicks?": *Shaft* (2000)
STEPHANIE BROWN 164

The Mystery of Identity: The Private Eye (I) in the
Detective Fiction of Walter Mosley and Tony Hillerman
ALISON D. GOELLER 175

Detecting from the Borderlands: Aimée and
David Thurlo's Ella Clah Novels
KATRIN FISCHER 187

"Crime Spirit": The Significance of Dreams and Ghosts
in Three Contemporary Native American Crime Novels
ESTHER FRITSCH AND MARION GYMNICH 204

Part III: Globalizing Ethnicity

"Here's tae Us, Wha's Like Us": Val McDermid's
Lindsay Gordon Mysteries
SAMANTHA HUME 227

The Hard-Boiled Pattern as Discursive Practice of Ethnic
Subalternity in Jakob Arjourni's *Happy Birthday, Turk!*
and Irene Dische's *Ein Job*
KONSTANZE KUTZBACH 240

Frenchness and Arab Alterity in Jean-Christophe Grangé's
Blood-Red Rivers
DOROTHEA FISCHER-HORNUNG 260

Uncovering Collective Crimes: Sally Morgan's *My Place*
as Australian Indigenous Detective Narrative
RUSSELL WEST 280

Part IV: Interviews

An Interview with Barbara Neely
ALISON D. GOELLER 299

An Interview with Valerie Wilson Wesley
DOROTHEA FISCHER-HORNUNG AND MONIKA MUELLER 308

Afterword
DOROTHEA FISCHER-HORNUNG AND MONIKA MUELLER 320
Contributors 323
Index 327

Sleuthing Ethnicity

Introduction

DOROTHEA FISCHER-HORNUNG
and MONIKA MUELLER

Eᴛʜɴɪᴄ ᴅᴇᴛᴇᴄᴛɪᴠᴇs sᴇᴇᴍ ᴛᴏ ʙᴇ ᴇᴠᴇʀʏᴡʜᴇʀᴇ. Iɴ ɢᴇʀᴍᴀɴʏ, ᴏɴ ᴛʜᴇ ᴛᴇʟᴇᴠɪsɪᴏɴ series *Sinan Toprak—The Incorruptible,* the smart Turkish detective on the German police force is played by the Turkish German former Armani model Erol Sander, an actor whose pseudonym resonates with a touch of Errol Flynn and whose looks suggest Rock Hudson or Cary Grant. Toprak dresses like James Bond and drives a 1972 vintage Mercedes convertible. He speaks impeccable German—without any Turkish accent whatsoever—lives in an apartment that appears to have been designed by Charles Eames and Verner Panton, has a charming blonde German wife, and a daughter with a Scandinavian first name. References to his ethnic background occur only through the occasional well-placed short hint. The television series is advertised by its producers as a first attempt to focus on a representative of the sizable Turkish population in Germany distinct from the stereotype of the Turk as the friendly owner of the Turkish kebab joint or mom-and-pop store. And Toprak certainly does not even faintly recall the more malicious stereotype of the swarthy, small-time criminal. Nevertheless, the figure of Sinan Toprak has met with mixed reactions. Some reviewers have lauded the series as "multicultural and critical of contemporary society" and a good parody of classical detective series like James Bond,[1] whereas others have complained that the detective, a "Turkish-Not-Turk,"[2] seems to be "as ready for violence as a sterilized washrag," and that he is multicultural only in that he represents the bland world of international advertising and modeling.[3]

The example of Sinan Toprak demonstrates that the ethnic detective has moved beyond countries that have a long standing history of immigration, such as the United States and Australia, and has arrived in an increasingly multicultural Europe. It also raises the question of what the term "ethnicity" designates and "how ethnic" a detective stemming from a

12 DOROTHEA FISCHER-HORNUNG AND MONIKA MUELLER

nondominant population group actually has to be in order to represent cultural alterity—or if s/he is even obliged to represent alterity within "mainstream" culture at all.[4] Issues such as these were the primary focus of discussion in our workshop "Sleuthing Ethnicity" at the Second MELUS Europe/First MESEA[5] conference in Orléans, France, in June 2000, and are explored in this collection of essays. With our decision to include a section on ethnic detectives outside the United States in this volume, we want to reflect MESEA's new emphasis on European and even global issues, thereby expanding the scope of critical studies on ethnic detective fiction.

During the last two decades, detective fiction has emerged as a literary field worthy of academic attention. Ethnic detective novels have by now become an accepted subgenre of detective fiction, as recent publications of several monographs and volumes of essays on the subject show. As with academic publications on detective fiction by women (which usually feature more or less hard-boiled female sleuths), critical studies about ethnic detective fiction often address the genre modifications effected by the subgenre. In ethnic detective fiction the importance of the detective's community of origin often supersedes the traditional loneliness of the detective. Sometimes the "ethnic plot," frequently dealing with aspects of the traditional way of life of the community from which the detective derives, also seems to diminish the importance of the detective plot. Furthermore, ethnic detective novels address issues of personal and social identity that reflect the importance of the ethnic community for the particular detective. The intensity of the detective's negotiation of his or her ethnic identity tends to directly correlate with the distance that the detective's particular ethnic group has from "mainstream" society.

The sleuths of Native American detective fiction, for example, usually live on the reservation and actively participate in their tribal tradition. Often they administer justice according to their own understanding of it rather than the letter of the dominant culture's law, as, for example, tribal policeman Jim Chee does in Tony Hillerman's *The Dark Wind* when he disposes of $15 million worth of cocaine without letting anybody know about it. If they have become alienated from traditional society, they often come to realize that they cannot have it both ways—to be Native American and Anglo at the same time. Thus, some Native American detective fiction presents us with detectives who return to their community after having worked for the FBI (for example, Aimée and David Thurlo's Ella Clah and Dana Stabenow's Aleut detective Kate Shugak).

Detectives who are members of ethnic groups that are more assimilated into "mainstream" society are involved in different negotiations of identity, which often seem to pose the question of whether race is more important than culture in constituting identity or vice versa. Thus, Dale

INTRODUCTION 13

Furutani's Japanese American sleuth, Ken Tanaka, goes to Japan, partly in order to solve a crime and partly in quest of racial acceptance in his country of origin, but Tanaka realizes that he will ultimately remain a stranger in Japan, since his cultural affiliation is predominantly American. African American writer Barbara Neely, however, wants to counteract the once brutally forced acculturation of African Americans by having her amateur detective, Blanche White, reclaim her African cultural roots by worshipping in front of an ancestor altar and by developing an increasingly black separatist stance as the Blanche White series progresses.

The essays collected in this volume reflect these established issues of ethnic detective fiction but also move beyond them by focusing on wider topics: the intersection of ethnicity and gender; marketing strategies for ethnic mysteries; juvenile ethnic detective literature; changing sexual politics as reflected in the remake of a classic blaxploitation film series; and historical ethnic crime as mirrored in fictions of detection. The additional focus on recent non-U.S. ethnic detective fiction in this collection of essays redirects attention to questions of authenticity, authority, and stereotyping—like the television series *Sinan Toprak—The Incorruptible* discussed initially.

Among the authors included in the non-U.S. section, only Val McDermid, who alludes to the long-standing cultural conflict between the Scottish and the English in her Lindsay Gordon series, writes from an insider's perspective. All of the other recent novels discussed (with the exception of Australian Sally Morgan's *My Place*, which is fiction of detection but not "classic" detective fiction) are authored by cultural outsiders, who, nevertheless, like the creators of *Sinan Toprak*, carefully attempted to avoid stereotypical references to the ethnicities portrayed in their novels. Arthur Upfield, who from the late twenties until the early sixties wrote his Inspector Bony novels, featuring a detective who is part-Aboriginal, provides an exception to this rule, since his novels still betray instances of inadvertent racialism. The other authors, however, try to be as "ethnically correct" as Tony Hillerman, the Anglo "father" of Native American detective fiction. But unlike Hillerman who, through meticulous anthropological research, succeeded in authoring culturally credible novels featuring Navajo, Hopi, and Zuni detectives,[6] the first generation of European authors of ethnic detective fiction seems to have mostly shied away from extensive research that would enable more than a degree of ethnic authenticity.

Thus, German author Jakob Arjouni (who acquired his Moroccan last name through marriage) elegantly circumvents his lack of knowledge about his detective Kemal Kayankaya's Turkish background by leaving Kemal himself in the dark about his own culture since he was adopted by a German couple as a baby. French author Jean-Christophe Grangé makes his French-Arab detective, Karim Abdouf, a partner to the French star inspector Pierre Niémans and does not devote a lot of attention to Abdouf's background, which is similar to Kemal's in that he was raised in a French orphanage. Like Arjouni, Grangé references ethnicity primarily by means of the discrimination suffered by the ethnic protagonist;[7] moreover, he includes a larger thematic focus on Nazism and eugenic racial engineering. Only German American author Irene Dische, whose novel *Ein Job* (A Job)[8] thematizes the devastating—but ultimately humanizing—cultural confusion that her Kurdish hard-boiled assassin, Alan Korkunç, suffers in New York, seems to have "authenticated" her novel's cultural background through collaboration with Nizamettin Ariç. He is listed as coauthor of the movie script *The Assassin's Last Killing*, on which *A Job* is based. It thus seems that there is still much cultural work left to be done for later generations of immigrants in Europe, who undoubtedly will eventually also contribute to European ethnic detective fiction.

The papers collected in this volume have been divided into three segments: "Historicizing Ethnicity," "Comparing Ethnic Identities," and "Globalizing Ethnicity." In her introductory essay, Marina Cacioppo takes a historical look at early ethnic detectives and investigates how Garibaldi Marto Lapolla, Prosper Buranelli, and Rudolph Fisher have incorporated their own ethnic settings and characters into hard-boiled and classic mystery fiction genres. By supplying an insider's perspective on their neighborhoods, they challenge dominant representations of Little Italies and Harlem as dangerous, atavistic, and exotic. The three writers, moreover, accomplish this reworking of the genres by introducing ethnic detectives whose ethnicity is an essential element of crime solving.

Theo D'haen, in his essay on Asian American detective fiction, calls attention to the fact that in the wake of the massive upsurge in crime writing in the United States, the 1990s have seen the emergence of countless ethnic crime fighters. D'haen also stresses that recent studies on detective fiction call attention to submerged ethnic plots in classic hard-boiled fiction. He compares Asian American detective fictions by three authors: Japanese American crime writer Dale Furutani; Chinese American detective fiction writer S. J. Rozan; and the historical detective fictions writer Laura Joh Rowland, who sets her novels in seventeenth-century Japan although she is Chinese American. Throughout his paper, D'haen concentrates on the intersection of crime, history, nationality, ethnicity, and gender and shows how the three authors work toward a hybridity of Asian traditionalism and American individualism.

Addressing similar concerns about tradition and change in her paper about ethnicity in Jewish American detective fiction, Carmen Birkle argues that Harry Kemelman, Faye Kellerman, and Ed Goldberg represent different forms of Jewishness in their writing. In contrast to Kemelman and Kellerman, who use their fiction to explain Conservative and Orthodox Judaism to Jews and Gentiles alike, Goldberg focuses more on the vanishing relevance of Judaism in his protagonist-detective's everyday life, emphasizing his embeddedness in the multicultural and transculturating society of New York City. All three authors negotiate ideas of self and other, and they reject notions of fixed identities and universalized "Jewishness," but still pose Judaism as determinant in the lives of all the Jewish characters.

Ann-Catherine Geuder introduces an entirely different focus on the significance of ethnicity by discussing the marketing strategies for Rudolfo Anaya's trilogy *Zia Summer, Rio Grande Fall,* and *Shaman Winter,* which combines its ethnic concerns with elements of detective fiction. His texts draw their strength from the traditions of their protagonists' Indo-Hispanic roots, yet at the same time they also captivate his readers' attention with suspense and mystery. Geuder argues that Anaya's publishers have assumed it advantageous to market the novels only as mysteries, stressing this aspect while ignoring the cultural elements. Critics, however, have tried to correct this misrepresentation in their reviews, but their exclusive focus on the cultural and spiritual levels of the novels tends to downplay the mystery aspect.

In her analysis of Chicano/a and African American detective fiction, Carmen Flys-Junquera demonstrates that contemporary ethnic detective writers use the popular genre of detective fiction to subvert the underlying value system of the dominant cultural ethos in the United States. She focuses on the portrayal of different belief systems, particularly that of folk beliefs and so-called superstition, that reveal an alternative worldview. Her article explores the representation of these belief systems as characteristics of ethnic pride and identity in the detective fiction of Rudolfo Anaya, Lucha Corpi, Walter Mosley, Barbara Neely, and Ishmael Reed. She concludes that by writing against the grain, these authors endow the formula of detective fiction with new meanings.

Monika Mueller addresses the intersection of ethnicity and gender in her paper. She argues that even though both Cuban American writer Carolina Garcia-Aguilera and African American author Barbara Neely deal with the relationship of crime, gender, and ethnicity, their works, nevertheless, position themselves in different traditions of detective fiction, reflecting the two writers' diverging personal and social agendas. Garcia-Aguilera rewrites the hard-boiled genre by parodying the hard-boiled mode, yet she ultimately confirms the social status quo by endorsing a male world and a hegemonic capitalist social order through her portrayal of the glamorous lives of wealthy Cuban immigrants in Miami. Neely, however, focuses on domestic mystery plots in her Blanche White novels but finally privileges her commitment to the depiction of gendered and racialized social problems over her detective plots.

Newark, New Jersey, with its specific racial and ethnic history, provides the background for Valerie Wilson Wesley's Tamara Hayle novels. As Carmen Birkle argues, the city essentially becomes an additional character in the series. Birkle investigates the spaces the city provides for Wesley's African American female detective. In contrast to the classic hardboiled portrayal of the city as dangerous and destructive, Wesley stresses that Newark is also a site of empowerment for Tamara Hayle's private and professional life.

Two U.S. juvenile ethnic detective novels are discussed by Sabine Steinisch in the light of postcolonial theories of diasporic identities. She compares how experiences of exile and dispossession, of loss of roots and cultural displacement, are represented in *Thief of Hearts* by Chinese American writer Laurence Yep and in *The Disappearance* by Rosa Guy. Guy immigrated to the United States from Trinidad and writes about a young black man from Harlem in *The Disappearance*. Steinisch concludes that by offering new ways of thinking about ethnic identities, Yep and Guy heighten their young readers' awareness of what it means to live in a hybrid society.

Stephanie Brown's essay explores the revisions of the original *Shaft* films by the recent remake of *Shaft* (2000). She argues that the new film, part remake and part sequel, most notably through its erasure of sexuality, with extreme violence taking the place of sex, offers a substantial revision of the "black private dick who's a sex machine to all the chicks." *Shaft*'s new protagonist is in the tradition of the loner detective hero for whom women are at best a distraction and at worst a threat. But the narrative also harks back to a pre-civil rights-era tradition in African American protest literature, in which an idealized black character is undone by a racist system that accuses him of errant sexual desires vis-à-vis white women and then punishes him for a nonexistent offense. Brown contends that in "postfeminist" America, there is no place for the sexism of the original *Shaft*, even as parody.

Identity formation is the focus of Alison D. Goeller's analysis of Walter Mosley's and Tony Hillerman's detective fiction. She explores how detection takes on existential dimensions for both the African American and the Native American sleuths. In trying to solve the crimes, they are also trying to solve their personal mysteries concerning who and what they want to be in a society where they are essentially invisible and treated as second-class citizens. Both Hillerman's and Mosley's ethnic detectives investigate the

INTRODUCTION

17

immediate, obvious crimes that are solved at the end of the novel and the larger, more pervasive crimes of social injustice that are not resolved.

Katrin Fischer deals with related issues of personal and collective identity in Aimée and David Thurlo's series about Navajo tribal policewoman Ella Clah. By focusing on Clah's intricate personal story, Fischer shows that Aimée and David Thurlo successfully integrate a modern woman sleuth and an age-old culture, and she also demonstrates that the mystery genre can be a device for discussing cross-cultural themes as well as for exploring gender and ethnicity.

According to Esther Fritsch and Marion Gymnich, Native American authors Louis Owens and Sherman Alexie make extensive use of ethnographic detail to modify the genre of crime fiction in order to validate Native American cultures. Both in Owens's *The Sharpest Sight* and *Bone Game* as well as in Alexie's *Indian Killer*, culture-specific concepts play a decisive role in the crimes as well as in their solutions. The detectives are often guided by visionary dreams and by the interference of ghosts; they rely on communal efforts rather than on deductive reasoning and more genre-bound Western investigative methods. The foregrounding of the supernatural has a dual function in these novels: it subverts conventions of traditional crime fiction and lends authority to alternative conceptions of reality.

With her paper on Val McDermid's Lindsay Gordon mysteries, Samantha Hume moves the ethnic detectives presented in this volume away from the United States. She argues that McDermid's series highlights the main elements of Gordon's identity as a socialist lesbian feminist. In addition, Hume discusses how Gordon's Scottish heritage, exemplified by her strong socialist convictions and sense of justice, informs her behavior as a detective. She also focuses on issues typical to the genre, such as the private detective's problematic relationship with the police. Hume's paper concludes with a discussion of how the novel's subversive elements, which result from her detective's "subversive identity," serve to challenge the conventions of the genre per se.

Konstanze Kutzbach compares the identity quest of Germany's first ethnic detective, Jakob Arjouni's hard-boiled Turkish German investigator, Kemal Kayankaya, to that of Irene Dische's Kurdish hard-boiled assassin, Alan Korkunç. She concludes that both men—Kemal, who looks Turkish, but knows little about his culture of origin, and Alan, who completely loses his cultural bearings in New York—use hard-boiled behavior to counteract their cultural confusion. While Kayankaya holds on to his dual identity through a tenuous reconciliation of the conflicting ethnic discourses that constitute his personality, Alan, victimized by a plethora of ethnic and cultural discourses, undergoes a complete personality change from Kurdish assassin to American gas station owner.

In the same vein, Dorothea Fischer-Hornung contends that Jean-Christophe Grangé addresses a similar problem in *Blood-Red Rivers* (2000) by combining the stories of a pair of doppelgänger detectives in two seemingly unconnected investigations after a dismembered corpse is discovered near Grenoble and a child's tomb is desecrated in a small French village. His French-Arab investigator, Karim Abdouf, a dreadlocked, earring-wearing former car thief, is a frustrated police officer who, although he was raised in France and has no connection to the Maghreb but for his appearance, is reduced to his status as the Arab Other. Pierre Niémans, a French detective who is trying to escape from the force of his own uncontrolled violence, also suffers from fundamental alienation from French society. Niémans unearths a diabolical plot to create a superrace using eugenic methods, while Abdouf investigates a seemingly insignificant and unrelated burglary and grave desecration. Eventually, the two cases are joined: alienation and otherness are posited as the major force in the crimes as well as in the detectives' solution of them. Thus, Grangé's novel explores and challenges the interpretive paradigms surrounding the postcolonial situation of Arab alterity in France, while simultaneously "unfixing" the fixity of "Frenchness."

Russell West's concluding essay takes us to Australia, the home of one of the first ethnic detectives, Arthur Upfield's part-Aboriginal detective inspector Napoleon Bonaparte. Taking Upfield's *Bony and the Black Virgin* as a point of departure for his exploration of the indigenous investigator's capacity to read Australian history for traces of crime, West goes on to investigate issues of ethnic detection in the best-selling 1987 autobiographical text *My Place* by the indigenous writer Sally Morgan. He argues that *My Place* records the protagonist's discovery of her Aboriginal identity. His paper reads Morgan's text as a detective narrative that has at its center the historical context of the white government's forced removal of thousands of "half-caste" children from their parents. According to West, *My Place*, using first-person oral narratives, gradually exposes this policy and explores its reverberations in a single family.

The papers collected in this volume reflect a growing tendency to explore a globalized and ethnically mixed world in literature and an expanding and fundamentally changing genre of detective fiction. Popular crime fiction provides entertainment for a wide reading audience and transmits cultural discourses. In the United States, for example, the market for the genre of ethnic detective fiction has boomed in the last two decades; this is evidenced by the growing body of publications in the field. Due to diverse historical situations, the production of ethnic detective fiction has proceeded differently in many countries—rapidly in some and slowly in others—depending on the given history of migration. Often cultural production, not

INTRODUCTION 19

to speak of criticism, lags behind social and cultural development, as can be seen in the relatively rudimentary state of European criticism on ethnic crime fiction. Therefore, with this volume we intend to contribute to a more complex critical discourse on European ethnic detective fiction as well as to enlarge the critical focus on U.S. ethnic crime fiction by looking at the genre through (mostly) European eyes.

NOTES

We would like to express our particular thanks to Katja Beck and Kurt Fischer for their contribution to the cover design of this book.

1. See "Dieser Türke kann kaum Türkisch," *Salzburger Nachrichten*, 8 February 2001. www.salzburg.com/sn/01/02/08/tv-1373.html (24 August. 2001).

2. See "Türke als Nichttürke," *epd Medien*, 21 February 2001. www.epd.de/medien/2001/14kritik.htm (24 August 2001).

3. See "Das Bild des Türken im Fernsehen," *Tagesspiegel*, 15 March 2001. www.tagesspiegel/archiv/2001/03/14/ak-me-2210874.html (23 August 2001).

4. According to an article in *Jungle World*, Erol Sander actually describes both himself and the character that he is playing as "more German than the Germans." See "Der ganz große Coup," *Jungle World*, 21 February 2001. www.nadir/ord/nadir/periodika/jungleworld/2001/09/30b.htm (23 August 2001).

5. At the Orléans conference, the European association MELUS, Europe (Society for the Study of the Multi-Ethnic Literatures of the United States, Europe) moved to form its own independent association, MESEA (Society for Multi-Ethnic Studies: Europe and the Americas), based on an expanded theoretical and geographical concept.

6. Ray B. Browne seems to be the only critic to point out cultural inaccuracies in Hillerman's novels: "Native American experts agree that Hillerman sometimes misses the details of Indian culture. In his introduction to *Talking Mysteries*, Ernie Bulow . . . says . . . that he recognized that . . . the author . . . did not realize that there are not and probably never will be Navajo policemen like Leaphorn and Chee." Ray B. Browne, "The Ethnic Detective: Arthur Upfield, Tony Hillerman and Beyond," in *Mystery and Suspense Writers: The Literature of Crime, Detection, and Espionage,* edited by Robin W. Winks (New York: Charles Scribner's Sons, 1998), 2:[1021]1029–46.

7. A variation of this strategy is used by Dale Furutani in presenting his detective Ken Tanaka's encounter with Japanese locals who identify him according to his Asian physical appearance but who discriminate against him because of his U.S. cultural background.

8. The novel has only been published in German translation from the English original.

Part I:
Historicizing Ethnicity

Insider Knowledge versus Outsider Perspective in Early Italian American and African American Detective Stories

MARINA CACIOPPO

"DR. MICHELLE GORGON WAS JUST A WOP, JUST A PHYSICAL ROTTEN BIT OF LIFE" (Daly 1931, 5). This is how an Italian gangster is presented in *The Third Murderer*, a novel by one of the fathers of the hard-boiled tradition, Carroll John Daly. Crime fiction has always dealt with the fears of its time and its readership: foreign criminals in strange and dangerous neighborhoods threatening the respectable middle class were a constant of early detective fiction. In Britain, at the turn of the century there was an abundance of Italian master villains, most notably Guy Boothby's Dr. Nikola,[1] and Italians were associated with the old stereotypes of secret societies, unusual methods of poisoning, the sorcery of Cagliostro, and Machiavellian cunning. Early American detective fiction went even further, echoing the unsympathetic and often xenophobic representations of foreigners in the popular press, which chose to emphasize the most superficial and sensational aspects of life in ethnic enclaves: the Black Hand, stories of Tong and gang wars, opium smuggling and bootlegging, gambling dens and white slavery. Alerts against the "Pasta Peril" and the "Yellow Peril" reached their zenith as American xenophobia peaked in the 1924 immigration act, and they persisted throughout the American mainstream press of the 1920s, repeated almost daily in newspaper accounts of urban criminality. The most notorious of all the American tabloids was Bernard MacFadden's lurid *New York Evening Graphic* (1924–32). By 1930, as New York's murder rate dramatically increased, crime reportage occupied almost a quarter of the *New York Daily News*'s coverage.

In fiction, such xenophobic representations of ethnic enclaves and communities were made popular by the novels of Sax Rohmer. His depiction of

Chinese characters and settings reached a mass market: two sequels to his popular novel *The Insidious Fu Manchu* had appeared by 1920;[2] his stories were run in *Colliers* and were brought to the screen by Paramount in 1929, and many more appeared in *Detective Story Magazine*. His characterization was to play a major role in influencing the representation of Chinese characters in detective fiction: Fu Manchu's descendants include the sinister Wu Fang and Ming the Merciless, to name just a few.[3] Fiction claimed the right to use and abuse ethnic material. Carl Van Vechten insisted that "the squalor of Negro life, the vice of Negro life, offers a wealth of novel, picturesque material to the artist" (1926b, 219). White America's unprecedented fascination with Black Harlem was reduced to the narrow scope of stereotypes in his best-selling *Nigger Heaven*.[4] His alter ego in the novel, Gareth Jones, says, "Well, the low life of your people is exotic. It has a splendid fantastic quality. And the humor! How vital it is, how rich in idiom! Picturesque and fresh! I don't think the Negro has been touched in literature as yet" (1926a, 107).

In the Prohibition era, as America invented new kinds of crime and criminals, new detective pulps proliferated. These works, from *Black Mask* in 1920 to the new titles *Great Gangster Stories*, *The Dragnet*, *Racketeer Stories,* and *The Underworld* in 1927, moved away from the closed-room mysteries of earlier detective fiction and instead looked for their subjects in the "mean streets" of dangerous American cities (see Panek 1990, 110). As Chandler put it, "Hammett and the new hardboiled writers took murder out of the Venetian vase and dropped it in the alley" (1946, 234), presenting dialogue and the language of the streets in a natural and realistic manner through urban slang and wisecracks. They looked for their subject matter in the real events of urban life and in newspaper accounts rather than dreaming up the elaborately imaginary crimes of the dime novels. But the stereotypes remained: even Hammett created a sinister Fu Manchu-style villain in his Continental Op story, "The House on Turk Street," for *Black Mask* in April 1924.

It was the new hard-boiled stories' emphasis on tough, ordinary detectives and the language of the streets, their attention to the true voices of urban America, and their claims to truth and connections to the "real" that was picked up in the ethnic detective stories discussed here. This new approach made it possible for these writers to reverse the ideological constructions of mysterious and exotic Little Italies and Harlem and to concentrate on realistically portraying their neighborhoods—often excluding outsiders almost completely from their plots, as if to keep negative stereotypes at a distance.

In what follows, I will analyze three works of ethnic detective fiction from the early 1930s and investigate how they adapted the traditional features of the hard-boiled and classic mystery fiction genres to their own ethnic settings and characters. Two of these texts—Garibaldi Marto Lapolla's short story "The Madonna's Crime" and Prosper Buranelli's *You Gotta Be Rough: The Adventures of Detective Fiaschetti of the Italian Squad as Told to Prosper Buranelli*—are by Italian American authors, and the third, Rudolph Fisher's *The Conjure-Man Dies*, is by an African American. All three use conventional detective motifs and structures, but all three adapt or twist them to create a new perspective on their ethnic neighborhood and its criminality from an insider's viewpoint. To accomplish this reworking of the genre, they make their detectives Italian or African American and make their ethnicity an essential element of crime solving. They then undermine the dominant representations of Little Italies and Harlem as dangerous, atavistic, and exotic by providing more realistic and sympathetic views of these communities, by presenting more authentic and varied settings and rounded characters, and by using their vernacular language. The outcome of this reinterpretation of the genre is the production of identifiably new ethnic brands of crime fiction that not only present more realistic and sympathetic portrayals of urban ethnic neighborhoods and communities, but which also critique and challenge, both directly and indirectly, the ways in which these places and people were viewed and portrayed by mainstream America and its popular fiction of the period. To highlight the ways in which such works perform such a reinvention and critique of the genre's standard components, I will compare these texts and contrast them with Sidney Herschel Small's short story "King Cobra," which appeared in *Detective Fiction Weekly* in 1931. Set in an exoticized and deadly Chinatown and featuring a white San Francisco cop, "King Cobra" provides a clear example of the type of fiction and its stereotypes that the ethnic detective fiction writers sought to undermine and alter.

The insider knowledge of the ethnic detective is crucial to solving "The Madonna's Crime." The superficial inferences of the police are less successful than the effective methods of an Italian priest. The novel opens with New York police captain Sorly engaged in the investigation of a mysterious murder in Italian Harlem. A small-time bootlegger, Bardo Naldi, is found with a six-inch steel pike nailed through his heart. In the eyes of this hard-boiled and hostile Irish cop,[4] the Italians are naturally uncooperative: "They knew nothing, had heard no noises, seen no strange person" (Lapolla n.d., 2). For him, everyone is a potential suspect until proven otherwise. Even a twelve-year-old girl is subjected to his aggressive, monosyllabic questioning, and he resorts to trying to shake a confession out of her. Seizing her sharply, he demands to know the whereabouts of her father, reducing the girl, "quivering like a frightened animal," to tears (3). His halfhearted efforts to identify the perpetrator fail miserably and, by the end of chapter 2, the case is officially closed, "placed among the growing number of crimes committed by the increasing number of the new-type brewers and distillers" (9). The plotline literally exhausts itself because Sorly is completely uninterested in, and totally lacks any insight into or inside knowledge of, the mentality of Italian Americans. This break in the narration signifies the impossibility of an outsider ever penetrating the mystery. As the narrator notes, Sorly "was not the sort of officer who assumes that he should be the embodied conscience of the community" (6), a remark that is further elaborated:

> How could a police captain, shrewd and thorough as he may be, whether by the grace of intuition or the accumulated wisdom of experience, have leaped across the boundaries of his habits of mind and jumped to the bold conclusion that only in the detailed history of the past of Bardo Naldi could be found the motives and impulses that culminated in his murder? (23)

In Sorly's mind, the only possible motive for the killing is Angela's hatred for her husband. "After corroborating the story of the wife" (23), he admits defeat, and realizing "the fabric of the tragedy was too thickly woven to permit of simple unraveling," he "shrugged his ponderous shoulders, frowned his vigorous frown, lit another cigar, and placed his bet on Modernity" (23). Instead, the answer to the mystery requires an insider who knows the community and its folklore, who is able to understand and communicate with them, gain their trust, and finally get to the truth.

At this point, a radical change of perspective occurs, as the narrator explores events in the Nardi family back in Villetto, Italy, and the roots of the crime itself, through a series of flashbacks. The purpose of these flashbacks in Villetto is to outline the popular beliefs and rumors that had arisen regarding Nardi's widow: "Early in her life, Angela had acquired not only the name of beauty but the reputation of being favored by the Madonna" (Lapolla n.d., 16). Only little Angela is unafraid when Don Anselmo's mastiff, a "huge and mysterious beast" runs amok in the market; she pacifies the animal "as if the Madonna herself had taken possession of the child's soul" (12). Stranger still, the animal is later found dead, "a wooden spike driven into an eye" (13). The community in Villetto quickly interprets the death of Nardi as a further intercession of the Virgin who once again had rescued Angela, this time from a cruel and violent man.

A self-appointed detective, the local priest (and an old suitor of Angela's), Don Matteo, then travels to New York on an official mission to dispel these superstitions and to unravel the mystery. In a final climactic scene, worthy of Poe, he confronts Angela and her new husband, and just as she is about to confide in him, the truth is suddenly revealed. In the

garden he sees Angela's son, "Salvo, the idiot" (Lapolla n.d., 6), accidentally kill their dog with a wooden spike, the same way he killed Bardo.

Like Don Matteo, Michael Fiaschetti makes good use of his inside
knowledge of Italian Harlem in *You Gotta Be Rough*. Buranelli's main character is based on an actual leader of the legendary Italian Squad set up to
tackle Italian crime in 1905. Throughout this memoir of his police career,
his self-professed ability as a "criminal-catching detective" is grounded in
his privileged understanding of the culture and psychology of Italians. It is
precisely his positive dual identity as both an Italian role model and as an
upright, self-made American that enables him (and him alone) to make
sense of the chaos and mysteries of the ghetto and successfully combat
crime:

> The American police were confronted with a new kind of situation among
> a people with a strange language and strange customs. Victims would not
> talk. They considered squealing disgraceful, and besides, they were des-
> perately afraid to squeal—this all the more so as they saw that American
> laws and authorities could not help them. The way people, from victims to
> bystanders, would keep their mouths shut was fantastic. What could an
> Irish cop do with this unearthly situation? (1930, 82)

Fiaschetti's philosophy that only Italians could deal with Italian crime is
clearly laid out: "In the American cities, Italians enlisted in the police de-
partments, and many became detectives. They were best fitted to deal with
the Black Hand" (83). What makes them so effective at policing their own
communities is their commonality with its residents. Buranelli deliberately
portrays his detective as an average Italian immigrant:

> I had a flat on Grand Avenue Brooklyn, a cold water flat that cost $18
> dollars a month. The water was cold, the rooms were cold, everything was
> cold in that tenement house. . . . I could afford only a few luxuries. I went
> to the Metropolitan Opera House. . . . Every year on my daughter's birth-
> day we had a big fiesta and ate spaghetti and drank wine like millionaires.
> (85–86)

His life does not differ from that of his fellow southern Italians whom he
describes as "plain hard-working people nearly all, who ask for nothing
more than a day's labor. . . . They are very frugal and content with a little.
For revelry, they like a heaped-up table, red wine and singing on birthdays,
at Christenings and at weddings and now and then the opera" (81).

It is precisely Fiaschetti's ordinariness and his roots in the locality that
enable him to solve crimes, above all by gaining the trust of local informers.
He views police work as an inherently localized activity: "The ordinary

detective works for the most part in the limited world of his own precinct. There he organizes his little stool-pigeon system" (Buranelli 1930, 40). Thus, the detective's success is determined by his understanding of that locality and its denizens. He must, in fact, be a member of the community if he is to police it effectively. And it is precisely his membership in that community that, in one episode, provides him with an invisibility that allows him to pass unnoticed as an Italian laborer and thus to befriend and entrap a murderer.

Because he has so much in common with the lower-class inhabitants of Little Italy, Fiaschetti can exploit his inside knowledge of the psychology of Italian criminals. Psychology, he says, "will catch more crooks than a mile of rubber hose" (Buranelli 1930, 73). When he has to extract information from a hardened criminal, Bimbo Vitar, who he knows will never squeal, he uses his knowledge of the concept of honor among Sicilians. Bimbo is the owner of a speakeasy and employs a dozen or so strippers. When the girls are arrested, Fiaschetti has them freed because Bimbo owes him a favor. He knows "the word of a Sicilian—you can trust it to the limit" (54), and so he calls him on the favor. Bimbo, bound by his own word, is compelled to reveal where a body had been concealed.

Another time, Fiaschetti exploits the tradition of vendetta among Sicilians to recruit a betrayed wife as an informer. His knowledge of Italian custom also permits him to uncover a lottery scam because he is aware of the popularity of state lotteries in Naples and Sicily and immigrants' ignorance that such schemes were illegal in America.

For Fiaschetti, as in the hard-boiled tradition, detection is a rough and dirty business: "If you have been all your life, a plainclothes dick dealing with thieves and murderers . . . it won't turn you into any vision of sweetness of light, and it may make you hard-boiled, with a hard-boiled way about you" (Buranelli 1930, 11). He wants to show, more than anything, "how the detective really gets his man, or to hell with Sherlock Holmes" (23). For him deduction has its place, but most detective work is based on informants and surveillance. As he says, "I've never analyzed cigar ashes, but have got a little information" (24–25). More than anything, it is knowledge of the neighborhood and local informers that produces results, not logic or the power of the detective's cognitive faculties. And knowledge, unlike logic, must be extracted from the community, not imposed upon it from the outside, in order to make it intelligible.

Unlike Detective Fiaschetti, Dr. Archer in *The Conjure-Man Dies* does analyze ashes to identify the victim's burned skull, and he utilizes all his scientific and deductive ability to help solve the mystery. This novel, by Harlem Renaissance writer Rudolph Fisher, was the first black detective novel set in a completely black environment, and it draws extensively on the classic "locked-room mystery" genre. Consequently, its reliance on ethnic insider knowledge is less explicitly stated than it is in the previous two hard-boiled works. Fisher simply populates his story with an all-black cast of characters and four different detectives, deliberately challenging, as Stephen Soitos notes, the formula of the all-knowing detective and his assistant (Soitos 1996, 93–124). Each of the four detectives contributes in his own way to solving the mystery, and the knowledge of all four is necessary to make sense of the complexity of Harlem and its mysteries.

Scientific detection is the domain of the middle-class physician John Archer; police procedure and the nature of Harlem criminality is the domain of Perry Dart, "one of the ten Negro members of Harlem's police force to be promoted from the rank of patrolman to that of detective" (Fisher [1932] 1992, 14); street knowledge is the area of expertise of Bubber Brown, the "family detective" who specializes in "cheaters and backbiters," and who grows into a real hard-boiled detective by the end of the novel (48). Finally, N'Gana Frimbo, the conjure-man of the title, is a Harvard graduate and a former African king with a background in mysticism—and like the priest in Lapolla's story, he has a profound knowledge of the community's beliefs. He combines scientific rationality with magic and Western and African traditions, and represents the duality of being African American. These four men are simply brought together by the complexities of the plot. When the conjure-man is found dead, Archer joins forces with Dart to solve what turns out to be the strangest of all cases when Frimbo miraculously returns to life and announces his intention to solve his own murder.

The importance of insider knowledge is represented above all by Bubber Brown. This character provides comic relief, but he also finds the suspects, supplies vital clues, and conducts his own private investigation to prove the innocence of his friend Jinx, the prime suspect. His methods are streetwise and based on common sense, but they work: "I used to figure out jes' what happened the night before by what I found in the ash can nex' morning. If I see a torn nightgown and an empty whiskey bottle" (Fisher [1932] 1992, 195). Apparently, this is the extent of his deductive abilities, but when it comes to Harlem, he knows every corner and everyone. His effectiveness in finding all the witnesses for the police surprises Officer Hanks, who asks him, "You know everybody don't you? Well, I recognized these two in the waiting room there tonight. Anybody that travels the sidewalks o' Harlem much as I do knows them by sight anyhow" (106).

In striking contrast, Jimmy Wentworth in "King Cobra" is a complete outsider in Chinatown. In spite of his knowledge of the Chinese language, he has only one friend in the quarter, Wang. A heinous crime is committed in the elegant area of Nob Hill, "San Francisco's exclusive residence district" (Small [1931] 1991, 46), and it is only by pure chance that he connects it to

30   MARINA CACIOPPO

the ferocious Kong Gai, also known as King Cobra. Chinatown is represented as impenetrable and hostile: Wentworth admits that "[n]o white
man—not even one who knew much of Chinese lore—could hope to solve
the mystery" (51). Unlike in Buranelli, where criminals have a conscience
and depth of character, they are so flat here that they become dehumanized:
King Cobra's voice is "akin to the venomous hiss of a viper"(57), and "his
tentacles were always reaching out" (51). His "evil snake-like eyes" are
described as darting "at the white man venomously" (54). All the criminals
are experts in torture. "We will put the serpent mark on his chest and listen
to his screams" (55), they promise. Even Wang is represented as sadistic, a
behavior incompatible with American morals. Killing is recreation for him:
"Why not let one of our hatchetmen do it? The boys really need exercise.
. . . It seems so silly; you want to catch a man alive, just to be able to hang
him. It is not logical. However, I am your friend. Far be it from me to
criticize your strange customs" (62).

The depiction of the community has a central status in all the works
discussed here. In "King Cobra," which typifies the superficial and lurid
external views of ethnic areas that were so prevalent in pulp and detective
fiction, it is depicted as rotten to the core. As in the opening of "The
Madonna's Crime," new immigrants are seen by the police as totally uncooperative and conniving in crime. "The narrow street, a moment ago filled
with Chinese, was emptied miraculously. Even the blind beggar propped
against a sunny wall opened his eyes and scuttled away. There remained
only the man lying in the street" (Small [1931] 1991, 52). A few pages
later, the implication is made even clearer. The streets are deserted when
Kong Gai attempts to carry out his threat to kill Wentworth's informers, the
Wangs, as if "Chinatown knew what was happening" (65). The entire area
and every inhabitant is seen as a potential threat to Nob Hill, and the
detective's objective is to keep the community under control rather than
defend it from crime. Unlike Lapolla and Buranelli, Small presents an "us
versus them" mentality in which the "us" is the white community (symbol-
ized by Nob Hill) and the "them" is the foreign (Chinese) community, which
is equated with criminality in general. In contrast, Lapolla and Buranelli
make it clear that the "us" is much more inclusive—encompassing the vast
majority of all communities—while the "them" is a small, criminal element that plagues all communities from within, not from the outside.

The depiction of Harlem's population in such superficial terms in Carl
Van Vechten's *Nigger Heaven* was fiercely criticized by W. E. B. Du Bois.
In his scathing review of the book, in the December 1926 *Crisis*, he commented that for Van Vechten, "there are no depths [to Harlem life]. It is the
surface mud he slops about in. . . . Life to him is just one damned orgy after
another, with hate, hurt, gin and sadism" (82). His advice to readers was to

INSIDER KNOWLEDGE VERSUS OUTSIDER PERSPECTIVE   31

"drop it gently into the grate" (81). Fisher, in apparent response to Du Bois, provides a much more carefully observed scene, and offers a gallery of characters from all strata of Harlem society. In a radio interview of 1933, he commented:

> [O]utsiders know nothing of Harlem life as it really is . . . what goes on beneath the skins of Harlem folk—fiction has not found much of that yet. And much of it is perfectly in tune with the best of mystery tradition— variety, color, mysticism, superstition, malice and violence. (Perry 1976, 67)

His desire to become "Harlem's interpreter" is fulfilled in *The Conjure-Man Dies:* The community is brought to life, and the classic formula of the locked-room mystery is bent to achieve this end. It has a voice and language, the street-talk and "the dozens" of Jinx and Bubber Brown. It has a smell, the supper of "pigtails and hoppin'-john" ([1932] 1992, 231), and it resounds with the blues:

> I'll be glad when you're dead, you rascal you,
> I'll be glad when you're dead, you rascal you,
> What is it that you got
> Makes my wife think you so hot?
> Oh you dog—I'll be glad when you're gone!
>
> (3)

These lines are the clue for the actual motive of the murder, the jealousy of an outraged husband. Harlem's streets are full of life—there are scuffles, the weekly Sunday noontime stroll down Seventh Avenue, and detailed, accurate settings. The reader follows Bubber Brown into "Henry Patmore's Pool Room—Fifth Avenue and 131st Street" (95), the "Hip-Toe Club on Lenox Avenue" (101), and "Nappy Shanks Café for supper" (231). Harlem's atmosphere is realistically evoked in passages such as this one:

> It was shortly after midnight and the Avenue at this point was alive. The Lafayette Theatre was letting out somewhat later than usual, flooding the sidewalk with noisy crowds. Cabs were jostling one another to reach the curb. Brightly dressed downtowners were streaming into Connie's Inn next door. Habitués of the curb stood about in commenting groups, swapping jibes. The two friends ambled through the animated turbulence, unaware of the gaiety swirling around them. (314)

Fisher provides the "genial insults which were characteristic Harlem greetings" offered to Bubber:

32 MARINA CACIOPPO

"What you say, blacker'n me?"
"How you doin', short-order?"
"Ole Eight-Ball! Where you rollin', boy?" (187)

There is even a whole subplot devoted to "numbers running" (the popular illegal lottery), involving one of the suspects, Spider Webb, who collects for "Harlem's well known policy-king, Sir Brandon" (54).

In *The Conjure-Man Dies*, lower-class Harlemites are three-dimensional characters with depth and development. Bubber is such an example, and so is Arimintha Snead, interviewed because she was among those in the "psychist's" waiting room. Through vivid dialogue she first comes across as brusque and diffident towards Dart: "Police detective? 'Taint so. They don't have no black detectives" (Fisher [1932] 1992, 79). But she manages to get us to sympathize with her when she tells him about her personal troubles—a drunken husband who beats her—and explains why she visited the conjure-man, Frimbo: "Everybody know 'bout this man Frimbo—say he can conjure on down. And I figger I been takin' it to the Lord in prayer long enough. Now I'm going to take it to the devil" (81).

In Fisher, the community is a character in its own right. Similarly, community is also a character in Lapolla's short story. The community is initially presented only through dialogue and action, and as passive and undifferentiated from the viewpoint of the rough, hostile, and hard-boiled Irish cop. However, in the Italian sequences, it acquires real agency: "The people of Villetto were more indefatigable than the police of New York" (n.d., 12). A telegram from America announcing the terrible news is read in the piazza of the town and sets off the investigation. "The heavy somnolence of the town gave way to general excitement" (11) as "in some way they knew that the events in the life of the Naldis long before the murder were connected with it" (12). The mystery is then unraveled because "the Villettani continued their gossiping and ferreting out of this and that detail" (23) in Angela's earlier life. Through them, we learn the true parentage of the idiot, Salvo, and his motive for the murder—ill treatment by his stepfather.

Buranelli goes even further in developing the community as a primary element in the story. He not only includes the Italian American community as the context in which the events gain meaning, but also develops it as a certain kind of character, one worthy of esteem and feelings of commonality from mainstream America. Detective Fiaschetti acts as a moral defender of his community in the face of ethnic slurs and prejudices. Italians are characterized as "plain hard-working people" who are given a bad reputation by professional criminals. "Italians came to America to work" (1930, 82), he insists, not to be parasites preying on hardworking, ordinary citizens. He even has a "special grudge against Italian criminals" (86) because they are used by the mainstream culture as the basis for negative stereotypes of all Italian Americans. Fiaschetti also maintains that the Black Hand is not some vast conspiracy of Italians against America, but merely "terrorizing gangs which might disband and come together as leaders arose or disappeared" (83). Further, the Black Hand is only a real threat to the Italian community because it exploits the community directly and stains it with the stereotype of Italians all being criminals. Understanding that the code of silence, *omertà*, is dictated by fear rather than complicity, he guarantees protection and secrecy and respects his deals. The implication here seems to be that Buranelli was responding to theories of anti-American conspiracy, confronting the stereotype that *omertà* was evidence of complicity in crime, similar to the stereotype that is applied to the Chinese in "King Cobra." *Omertà* was not a threat to society, but a sign of the law's failure to protect a part of society. If only Italian Americans were given a chance to cooperate with the law and were protected, he argues, they would collaborate, as is demonstrated by the hundreds of informers Fiaschetti did recruit in his fight against crime in Little Italy.

In conclusion, these books modify the hard-boiled tradition of conspiratorial foreigners in exotic and menacing subcultures brought to justice by solitary, communally disconnected white representatives of American law and order by giving it a sociological twist. The detective's strength derives not from being an isolated loner, as in the standard hard-boiled story, but from being firmly rooted in the community. In fact, the community becomes a main character of these detective stories. Little Italy and Harlem are not like Small's Chinatown, a source of exotic and eroticized elements to titillate the reader. These writers' insider realism provides a counterstory, a sympathetic vision, that debunks negative representations of them by the press and mainstream fiction. Setting the record straight about their neighbors and neighborhood is as important as solving crime in these books. This emphasis on realistic ethnic settings and the creation of ethnic detectives are the marks of the beginnings of distinct African American and Italian American traditions of crime fiction.

NOTES

1. Guy Boothby's sinister Dr. Nikola appeared in five novels: *A Bid for Fortune or, Dr. Nikola's Vendetta* (1895), *Doctor Nikola* (1896), *Lust of Hate* (1898), *Dr. Nikola's Experiment* (1899), and *Farewell, Nikola* (1901). An online version of *A Bid for Fortune or, Dr. Nikola's Vendetta* is also available at www.heliograph.com/ff/game/ff6/fortune.htm (15 July 2001).

2. Sax Rohmer published the following novels featuring Fu Manchu before 1920:

34   MARINA CACIOPPO

The Mystery of Dr. Fu Manchu (1913) and its American version, *The Insidious Dr. Fu Manchu* (1913); *The Return of Dr. Fu Manchu* (1916) and its British version, *The Devil Doctor* (1916); *The Si-Fan Mysteries* (1917); and *The Hand of Fu-Manchu* (1917).

For a list of Fu Manchu's clones see www.google.com/search?q=cache:6Pmuc2pcINc: www.njin.net/~knappclones.htm+Fu+Manchu+clones+knapp&hl=en (5 August 2001).

3. See also James de Jongh, *Vicious Modernism: Black Harlem and the Literary Imagination* (1990, 31–32), and Gilbert Osofsky, *Harlem: The Making of a Ghetto* (1966).

4. This stereotype of the Irish American cop was not unfounded, as the New York Police Department remained a largely Irish American organization up to 1930, despite the first large infusion of other ethnic groups: Italian Americans, German Americans, Polish Americans, and African Americans (as numbers swelled to 10,000 from an initial 7,500 cops three decades earlier). See www.nyc.gov/html/nypd/html/3100/retro.html (12 August 2001).

WORKS CITED

Boothby, Guy. 1895. *A Bid for Fortune or, Dr. Nikola's Vendetta.* London: Ward Lock and Co.

———. 1896. *Doctor Nikola.* South Yarmouth, Mass.: Curley.

———. 1898. *Lust of Hate.* London: Ward Lock and Co.

———. 1899. *Dr. Nikola's Experiment.* New York: D. Appleton.

———. 1901. *Farewell, Nikola.* London: Ward Lock and Co.

Buranelli, Prosper. 1930. *You Gotta Be Rough: The Adventures of Detective Fiaschetti of the Italian Squad as Told to Prosper Buranelli by Michael Fiaschetti.* New York: Doubleday.

Chandler, Raymond. 1946. "The Simple Art of Murder." In *The Art of the Mystery Story*, edited by Howard Haycraft, 222–37. New York: Simon and Schuster.

"The Clones of Fu Manchu and Sumuru."www.google.com/search?q=cache:6Pmuc2pcINc: www.njin.net/~knapp/clones.htm+Fu+Manchu+clones+knapp&hl=en (22 August 2001).

Daly, Carroll John. 1931. *The Third Murderer.* New York: Farrar and Rinehart.

de Jongh, James. 1990. *Vicious Modernism: Black Harlem and the Literary Imagination.* Cambridge: Cambridge University Press.

Du Bois, W. E. B. 1926. Review of *Nigger Heaven*, by Carl Van Vechten. *The Crisis*, December, 81–82.

Fisher, Rudolph. [1932] 1992. *The Conjure-Man Dies: A Mystery Tale of Dark Harlem.* Ann Arbor: University of Michigan Press.

Lapolla, Garibaldi Marto. n.d. "The Madonna's Crime." Balch Institute for Ethnic Studies, Philadelphia. Typescript.

Osofsky, Gilbert. 1966. *Harlem: The Making of a Ghetto.* New York: Harper.

Panek, Leroy Lad. 1990. *Probable Cause: Crime Fiction in America.* Bowling Green, Ohio: Bowling Green State University Press.

Perry, Margaret. 1976. *Silence to the Drums: A Survey of the Literature of the Harlem Renaissance.* Westport, Conn.: Greenwood Press.

Rohmer, Sax. 1913a. *The Insidious Dr. Fu Manchu.* New York: McBride.

———. 1913b. *The Mystery of Dr. Fu Manchu.* London: Methuen.

———. 1916a. *The Devil Doctor.* London: Methuen.

———. 1916b. *The Return of Dr. Fu Manchu.* New York: McBride.

———. 1917a. *The Hand of Fu Manchu.* New York: McBride.

———. 1917b. *The Si-Fan Mysteries.* London: Methuen.

Small, Sidney Herschell. [1931] 1991. "King Cobra." In *It's Raining Corpses in Chinatown*, edited by Don Hutchinson, 46–67. Mercer Island, Wash.: Starmont House.

Soitos, Stephen. 1996. *The Blues Detective: A Study of African American Detective Fiction.* Amherst: University of Massachusetts Press.

Van Vechten, Carl. 1926a. *Nigger Heaven.* New York: Knopf.

———. 1926b. "The Negro in Art: How Shall He Be Portrayed?" *The Crisis,* March, 219–20.

Samurai Sleuths and Detective Daughters: The American Way

THEO D'HAEN

ANALYSES OF CLASSIC DETECTIVE fICTION PAY LITTLE OR NO ATTENTION TO ISSUES of race or ethnicity. This holds true also for most major works on American crime fiction, hard-boiled or not. In fact, just as attention to issues of gender has mostly been confined to books dealing specifically with crime fiction written by women, so also attention to issues of race has mostly been limited to books dealing with African American crime writers (Bailey 1991; Soitos 1996), or to occasional essays in collective volumes (Kennedy 1997). The proverbial exception that proves the rule is Andrew Pepper's very recent *The Contemporary American Crime Novel: Race, Ethnicity, Gender, Class* (2000). As its title suggests, though, this last book confines itself to the "multicultural" present. Yet, if there is one point that emerges clearly from Sean McCann's equally recent *Gumshoe America: Hard-Boiled Crime Fiction and the Rise and Fall of New Deal Liberalism* (2000), it is that questions of ethnicity and race have played a major role in the emergence and development of the genre that holds McCann's interest. Indeed, since McCann is primarily concerned with how hard-boiled crime fiction participates in the period's ongoing debate as to the role government should play in the United States and the form its society should take, ethnicity is an intimate part of the debate. This holds true for the *Black Mask* stories of Carroll John Daly and Dashiell Hammett in the twenties, the latter's novels, the stories and novels of Raymond Chandler from the thirties through the fifties, Mickey Spillane's, Ross Macdonald's, Jim Thompson's, and Charles Willeford's fiction of the forties and fifties, and Chester Himes's novels of the fifties and sixties. As the buyers of hard-boiled fiction at least initially were primarily white working-class men, it is not surprising that their interests—as mediated through the figure of the hard-boiled hero—are also at the heart of the genre. Implicitly, then, what is metaphorically at stake in hard-boiled fiction is the "common man" and his position in the nation's economic, social, and political realm.

McCann sees the earliest *Black Mask* stories of Daly and Hammett, and therefore the very origins of the hard-boiled genre, as explicitly countering the ideology of the Ku Klux Klan, then one of the fastest growing movements in the United States and one fostering the ideal of a homogeneous brotherhood of like-minded citizens, united by race (white, Northern European) and religion (Protestant). Instead, Hammett especially propagates the liberal idea of the freedom of the individual, any individual. Later, especially the early Chandler will take up the ideals of the New Deal: that of a brotherhood of workers, regardless of race or creed, united against the idle rich that are out to exploit them and cripple the workings of the state.

After World War II, hard-boiled fiction portrays the breakdown of New Deal social solidarity under the pressures of 1950s consumerism. McCann (2000) invokes the term "minorities rule," coined by the contemporary political scientist Robert Dahl in his *A Preface to Democratic Theory* (1956), to describe the change from a political system where the state supposedly directs things for the benefit of all, to one whereby the state limits itself to being the arbiter between various constituencies vying for the same wealth. By the same token, the common workingman was displaced from that American center he had occupied under the New Deal. Minority rule, moreover, not only pitted classes against one another, but did the same with ethnicities or races. Consequently, Chandler's later fiction, such as *The Long Goodbye* (1952), becomes increasingly racialized. Thompson casts the ordinary American man as loser. Ross Macdonald has the white common man emancipate himself by getting an education and an inner life, and thus enter the middle class. Spillane's remedy is to have that same common white man take the law in his own hands in acts of indiscriminate and violent revenge. Himes, from the other end of the racial divide, throughout a series of novels featuring his two Harlem police detectives, Coffin Ed and Grave Digger Jones, tries to negotiate between the ideal of a society unified in its legal system and the reality of that same society split along racial lines. In *Plan B*, the final and unfinished novel of the series, he gives up on this idea and accepts that there is no hope for blacks under a white system of law, ending the novel in a horrific explosion of violence (see Fabre and Skinner 1993, xxx).

For McCann (2000), then, the early history of the hard-boiled genre is rooted in antiracist attitudes and ideals. Still, the racial stereotypes to be found in the work of Hammett or the early Chandler can easily lead to opposite conclusions. At first sight, the latter view seems to be shared by at least one present-day practitioner of the genre—not coincidentally an "ethnic" detective writer himself.

38   THEO D'HAEN

In *Death in Little Tokyo* (1996), the first of the Ken Tanaka mysteries, Dale Furutani has his hero describe himself as follows:

> I looked at myself in the large mirror I had propped up against the wall and decided I still cut a pretty dashing figure. I figured I looked like a worthy recipient of the Silver Dagger trophy for unraveling the L. A. Mystery Club's phony murder.
>
> I was dressed in a tan trench coat and a gray hat. The props helped to compensate for my small frame and delicate features . . . two curses for someone who secretly aspired to be a 1930s hard-boiled detective. Of course, my being a Japanese-American from Hawaii is also an impediment to this aspiration. The only Asian detectives I remember from old movies were Werner Olan doing his Charlie Chan bit or Peter Lorre doing an incredibly campy Mister Moto. At least Charlie Chan was from Honolulu, although nobody I've ever met from Hawaii actually looked and talked like Werner Olan did.
>
> My face is round with a slightly squared jaw. My eyes are more deeply set than the Asian stereotype, but many Asians, particularly in Japan or Southeast Asia, have deep set eyes. I have the epicanthic fold that characterizes Asians everywhere, and of course my eye color is deep brown and I have black hair. (1996, 7–8)

Obviously, Tanaka, and Furutani through him, is participating in an elaborate discourse on the tradition of the private eye in fiction as well as the movies. Everything he sums up leads him to stress that he is different from the generic norm, that is to say, the white male detective. However, the difference also holds with regard to the racially stereotyped representative of Asian Americanness and the most famous of Asian movie private eyes, Charlie Chan. Tanaka is a true Asian, whereas Chan as played by Olan is not. Of course, neither is Mr. Moto as played by Peter Lorre. The same Peter Lorre impersonates another "Asian" in the guise of the Cypriot criminal in the famous movie version of Hammett's *The Maltese Falcon*, starring Humphrey Bogart as Sam Spade. It is this same novel and movie that Tanaka uses as inspiration for the detective game he is orchestrating for a Los Angeles mystery club. The difference between "the real thing" as private eye from a thirties' hard-boiled fiction or its screen adaptation and "the real thing" as an Asian American, therefore, is further underlined when Tanaka, in a passage immediately following upon the one quoted earlier, tries to impersonate none other than Humphrey Bogart as Sam Spade:

> The tan Burberry coat was a good fit, but somehow the felt fedora just didn't look right. I pulled it low over my eyes, but that just blocked my vision. I pulled it off and tried placing it on my head at a rakish angle, but a shock of black hair peeked out and the effect was just goofy. I put it

SAMURAI SLEUTHS AND DETECTIVE DAUGHTERS

squarely on my head and tried bending down the brim a little. Then I sighed. It wasn't perfect, but it was the best of all variations I had tried. I guess I just wasn't used to seeing myself in a hat.

I walked over and took off the trench coat. It was a hot August in Los Angeles, and hats and trench coats were definitely not the attire that suited the weather, especially in an old office building with marginal air-conditioning. (8)

Here, again, Tanaka (and hence Furutani) is invoking the performative conventions of the hard-boiled genre to show how ill they fit a character like himself, and vice versa. The irony, however, is that after having first questioned the stereotypes of both the hard-boiled detective as "white man" and as "Europeanized Other" and the possibility of himself as accommodating either one of these, Tanaka goes on to become a real private eye after all. In other words, he does so based on his own premises, and as a true Asian American. Furutani thereby turns the very racial premises the genre traditionally has been built upon against themselves.

These premises are even further undermined, not just with regard to the hard-boiled fiction genre but also, and primarily, with regard to the society this fiction originally emanated from, by the outcome of Tanaka's investigations. True to *The Maltese Falcon* antecedents of *Death in Little Tokyo*, a woman comes to visit Tanaka in the shoddy office he has rented as part of his mystery club private eye ploy. She wants him to deliver a package for her. At first, Tanaka assumes that some other members of the club are playing a prank on him, trying to outsmart him at his own game. He decides to play along. However, Tanaka finds himself implicated in a real murder when the Japanese man from whom he had collected the package is found dead. Eventually, both the victim and his killer turn out to be Japanese Americans; both had been interned in a "relocation camp" for Japanese American citizens during World War II. The conflict that eventually leads to the murder originates in the sharp division between those Japanese Americans that took the oath of loyalty imposed upon them by the United States government and those that refused to do so. Finally, then, it is white racial prejudice and bigotry that are to blame for setting two members of one ethnic community against each other.

Although the resolution to *Death in Little Tokyo* underlines that during World War II there was at least one ethnic group that was not allowed to participate in the brotherhood of man promulgated by the New Deal and, in McCann's view, by the hard-boiled fiction of the thirties and early forties, various other discursive passages in the novel—spoken by Tanaka but presumably also reflecting Furutani's feelings—make the same point with regard to present-day multicultural America. Fairly early on in the novel, for instance, Tanaka muses on his own immediate past. He is in his early

40   THEO D'HAEN

forties and has his first marriage, to a Caucasian, behind him. He has also
recently been laid off as a software engineer. His girlfriend, Mariko, is in
her thirties, and she too went through a failed first marriage to a Caucasian.
Mariko is an aspiring actress, though her career does not seem to be going
anywhere. Both Tanaka and Mariko wonder whether race has anything to
do with their misfortunes. Tanaka's conclusion is crystal clear:

> I used to think that the world is color-blind. Maybe that's my Hawaiian
> upbringing. Lately I've come to the frightening conclusion that race is be-
> coming the defining factor of our lives. Maybe this is because I live in Los
> Angeles, which has degenerated into a collection of ethnic tribes instead of
> a community. Here all the racial groups are in deadly competition. Liter-
> ally. This has consequences for all of us, no matter what our race is. (Furutani
> 1996, 54)

This competition most immediately translates into wrangles about who has
the right to call himself an "American":

> In my own country I've been called a gook, a chink, a Jap, and a slope. I
> think "gook" was first applied to Korean, "chink" to Chinese, "slopes" to
> Vietnamese, and "Jap" is both obnoxious and obvious. Asians in the U.S.
> get to learn the full range of ethnic slurs, no matter what their real ethnicity
> is. I've also been told to go back to my own country, even though America
> has been home to my family since 1896. (55)

Death in Little Tokyo, then, can be read as a reflection, from a "minority"
point of view (see Deleuze and Guattari 1975), upon America's social, political, and economic system, as well as in many ways an indictment of that
system. That the matter does not rest there, however, is demonstrated in
The Toyotomi Blades (1997). At the outset of this novel, Tanaka is invited
to Japan, there to appear on a television talk show to expatiate on the case
he solved in *Death in Little Tokyo*. For Tanaka, this is the country of his
ancestors offering him the recognition his native country withholds. In Japan, though, it soon becomes clear that there were ulterior motives for
inviting Tanaka. Specifically, there is great interest in the ancient samurai
sword Tanaka picked up sometime before at a Los Angeles garage sale and
that, displayed on the wall of his living room, featured in a photograph of
him that appeared in the Japanese press. It is one of six such swords—the
Toyotomi blades referred to in the novel's title—that together turn out to
reveal the location of a fabled treasure. When Tanaka finally succeeds in
locating the treasure, he finds that ancient robbers had been there before
him. They had been followed more recently by the Japanese traditionalists
who were after the blades, including Tanaka's, and the treasure from the

onset. In the end, though, all proves useless, as the ancient treasure turns out to consist of bales of silk and brocade—priceless at the time they were hidden away, but that had now turned to dust.

The Japanese traditionalists had hoped to rejuvenate traditional Japanese culture with the hidden treasure. For Tanaka, the decayed treasure is analogous to his failure to find the cultural roots and the racial acceptance in Japan he feels are denied to him in the United States. As in *Death in Little Tokyo*, the failure of both these quests has been prefigured all along in passages explicitly reflecting upon Tanaka's relationship both to the United States and to Japan. One such passage has to do with the same issue of race that also featured prominently in the earlier novel:

> Junko would be able to blend into this street scene as easily as I would, but in Japan she was an alien. I was used to standing out based on my Asian looks, and I associated racial prejudice with looking different. When I was in the army during the Vietnam War, I was once sitting on the ground with a large number of recruits early in my stint in basic training. A grizzled sergeant came up to us and barked, "Tanaka! Stand up!" I didn't know what I had done wrong, but I scrambled to my feet as ordered. "Okay, you recruits, look at Tanaka. Take a good look, because this is what a gook looks like, and gooks are the enemy!" My face burned, but I was nineteen and in the midst of the most frightening and unsettling experience of my life and didn't know what to do. All I could do was stand there humiliated as the other recruits laughed. What was especially disturbing was this sergeant was African American, and he must have known what it was like to be singled out because of your race. Unfortunately, whatever life experiences he had along these lines didn't teach him empathy, only mimicry.
>
> Junko looked just like the people walking around on the street below me. Yet despite looking, acting, and sounding like everyone else, she was a minority because her ancestors were born in Korea. It's a strange world, and one we make unnecessarily stranger by dividing people up into different types of minorities. (Furutani 1997, 52)

The empathy Tanaka here demonstrates with Junko is obviously based on the similarity in the position they themselves occupy as representatives of minorities in their respective countries of birth and of citizenship. Yet how easily such positions shift is demonstrated later on in the novel, when Tanaka suspects Junko of being connected to the Yakuza, the Japanese variant of the Mafia. As it turns out these suspicions are totally ungrounded, and Tanaka has to confess:

> I found myself just as prejudiced as the Japanese majority. I thought [Junko] had a Yakuza connection because she was Korean. It was stupid. I get outraged when I encounter this type of thinking back in the States, especially

42   THEO D'HAEN

> when it's directed at Asians, but as soon as I found myself in the majority,
> I slipped into the ready comfort of a stereotypical prejudice. It was a sober-
> ing lesson, and one I'm not proud to admit. (209)

In other words, just like the grizzled African American sergeant he shrank
from during boot camp, Tanaka himself switches effortlessly from empathy to mimicry, depending upon whether he identifies with a minority or
with the majority in a given society. The difference is that Tanaka is conscious of the mechanism he himself has fallen victim to. Moreover, the
terms in which he had previously explained his coming to terms with his
own ancestry, his family's country of origin and his country of citizenship,
already signaled the dawning of such consciousness. Tanaka and Mariko
are taking a Japanese hot water bath, and he complains that he feels like "a
featured dish in a Louisiana crab boil." When Mariko tells him that he is
"supposed to like it. It's cultural," Tanaka's rejoinder, and the musings this
leads him to, are revealing:

> "In case you haven't noticed, culturally I'm American, not Japanese."
> As soon as I said that I realized that I meant more than just my prefer-
> ences in bath water. From the moment I came to Japan, when the customs
> agent spoke Japanese to me, I was trying to sort out what it meant to return
> to the land of my ancestors. I felt strangely comfortable in Japan. Sights,
> sounds, customs, and the faces of the people had a resonance with me that
> reminded me I came from Japanese stock. But this was an ease that came
> from preserved memories, not from actually fitting in. Foundations of cul-
> ture transcend race, and I realized that my culture is American.
> . . . No matter how uncomfortable I may sometimes feel in America as a
> minority, I will never fit in better elsewhere, even in Japan, where I'm part
> of the racial majority. (179)

By positing that "foundations of culture transcend race," Tanaka takes a
stand against the Japanese sense of identity as rooted in racial prejudice.
By defining his own culture as "American," and by implying that it is this
same culture that in fact leads him to posit that "foundations of culture
transcend race," Tanaka at the same time reaffirms the ideal of an American identity as rooted in shared ideals and goals rather than in any kind of
racial or ethnic essentialism. Couched in terms and situations appropriate
to the 1990s, this, in fact, takes Furutani close to the position Sean McCann
saw Furutani's original hard-boiled predecessors adopting for their own
period. It is fully appropriate, therefore, that at the end of *The Toyotomi
Blades* Tanaka, who until then has been merely an amateur sleuth, announces, "[W]hen I get back to California, I'm going to investigate what it
will take to make me a licensed private investigator" (212). Mystery-Club-
Sam-Spade Tanaka is about to turn into the real thing after all. Furutani's

Tanaka novels, then, instead of angrily condemning American hard-boiled fiction and cinema for reasons of racial stereotyping, in reality conduct a complex debate with the origins and ideology of the genre and finally re-fashion it in a form, and with a set of characters and concerns, commensurate with our present age. Specifically, they foreground the ideal of a truly multicultural America.

In their often very different ways, the other detective fiction authors that I will deal with in the remainder of this essay all share Furutani's concerns with multiculturalism, particularly in the way it affects Asian Americans. As these authors are all women, they are also specifically concerned with the position of women in society. Detective writing ever since the 1980s has been marked by a massive influx of women writers. The authors I will deal with—S. J. Rozan, Sujata Massey, and Laura Joh Rowland—are all part of a highly successful generation of writers joining this trend in the 1990s. Like their immediate predecessors of the 1980s—Marcia Muller, Sara Paretsky, Sue Grafton, and Karen Kijewski, to name just a few of the more obvious examples—Rozan, Massey, and Rowland are all very much concerned with issues of female agency (see Walton and Jones 1999). As "minority" writers, moreover, they are obviously also very much concerned with issues of ethnic agency. These issues are most immediately reflected in S. J. Rozan's Lydia Chin/Bill Smith novels. Lydia Chin first appears in *China Trade* (1994), where she is hired to unravel a case involving a collection of rare Chinese porcelains stolen from a New York Chinatown museum.

In addition to their plots, which are interesting in themselves, what really holds the reader's attention in *China Trade* and its sequels, *Concourse* (1995), *Mandarin Plaid* (1996), *No Colder Place* (1997), *A Bitter Feast* (1998), and *Stone Quarry* (1999), is, on the one hand, the relationship between Lydia Chin and her partner Bill Smith, and, on the other hand, her relationship to her native community of Chinese Americans.

Rozan, who has no Asian American roots whatsoever, alternates between Lydia Chin and Bill Smith as protagonists and narrators; odd-numbered novels in the series are narrated by Lydia and even-numbered novels by Bill. Regardless of who the narrator is, though, in all novels it is clear that Lydia and Bill are strongly attracted to each other. What keeps them apart is Lydia's hesitance to fully commit herself to a white man from a background obviously so very different from her own. At the same time, her reluctance also has a lot to do with her uncertainty as to whether Bill actually takes her seriously enough professionally. Even as late as *Stone Quarry*, the sixth novel in the series and told from the point of view of Bill Smith, Lydia still is not fully certain as to where she stands professionally with Bill. Bill, in contrast, never doubts Lydia.

However, Lydia not only feels she has to continually prove herself to Bill; she has the same problem with her own community. In fact, in *China Trade* she is hired initially only through the intervention of her older lawyer brother, and it turns out that this in fact was merely part of a ploy—she was never expected to come up with any real results. Though her community eventually comes to feel a grudging kind of respect for her, initially she has to surmount prejudices connected to race, and even more particularly sex, before being taken seriously as a private investigator. Not surprisingly, some of this initial reserve is based on the clichés we know from the hard-boiled genre. When in *China Trade* Lydia goes to see a hoodlum and introduces herself as a private investigator, his rejoinder, echoing Furutani's description of the performative, clichéd nature of Tanaka's PI identity, is: "'What? No kidding!' He laughed. 'You kidding. Private eye. Got no trenchcoat, got no gun'" (Rozan 1994, 27).

In many ways, nevertheless, Lydia's worst opponent is her mother. Though in her late twenties, Lydia continues to live with her mother in a small Chinatown apartment. As a dutiful Chinese daughter, she is expected to be home for dinner, or at least to call if she is not going to make it on time, to do at least part of the shopping, and to generally behave, including making herself attractive to the prospective husbands and providers her mother keeps pushing on her. Needless to say, Lydia's mother strongly disapproves of her daughter's profession. Lydia also has the feeling that her mother dislikes Bill and generally blames him for her daughter's foolish persistence in wanting to be a private detective—a feeling that is shared by Bill himself. In fact, the impression one gets is that Lydia's mother sees Bill as largely responsible for her daughter's drifting away from her Chinese roots and for joining the outside world of mainstream America. The result is constant ethnic and generational tension throughout these novels, with Lydia's dilemma as to where and how she belongs neatly personified in the opposing figures of her mother and Bill.

Obviously, it is in the novels narrated by Lydia herself that the tension this contest for her loyalty causes comes out strongest. In all of Rozan's novels, though, Lydia finally emerges as a modern American woman, fiercely jealous of her independence and her individual and professional integrity, regardless of the fact that she also tries to live up to her mother's and her ethnic community's expectations. In fact, at the end of *A Bitter Feast*, when Lydia has succeeded, with Bill's help, in solving a case that threatened the very stability of Chinatown's social and economic fabric, even Lydia's mother—in one of the telephone conversations with her Cantonese women friends about their respective daughters' merits or demerits—obliquely admits that she is proud of Lydia's achievements as a detective.

SAMURAI SLEUTHS AND DETECTIVE DAUGHTERS

Lydia's mother here joins her daughter in being more responsive to the realities of life in multicultural America than most of the Chinese males in the Lydia Chin/Bill Smith novels. These males in general either try to hang on to the power they traditionally have within their own community, or they try to muscle in on it by criminal means. In either case, they organize strictly not only along Chinese ethnic lines, but even along lines of regional origin in China itself. In *A Bitter Feast*, for instance, part of the plot is powered by the rivalry between the earlier immigrant Cantonese and Fukien newcomers.

It is Lydia's intervention as a detective that not only reestablishes stability within the community of Chinatown, but will also make room for necessary renewal, change, and integration within that community and in the wider world. Lydia, so to speak, acts as an interface between her ethnic community and America at large. As with Furutani's Tanaka, Lydia can do so because with her, too, "foundations of culture transcend race," and Lydia's "culture" is first of all "American." The point is made symbolically at the end of *A Bitter Feast*, and given the fact that in this novel Lydia had to go undercover as a waitress in a Chinese restaurant for a time, it is made by way of food. In the course of the investigation, Bill has had to have quite a few meals at the restaurant Lydia worked at. To her surprise, he had shown himself not only quite appreciative, but even quite knowledgeable about Chinese food. Now, to celebrate their rounding off the case, Bill has invited Lydia to dinner. Instead of taking her out, though, as Lydia expected, Bill has cooked himself:

> "You cooked?" I shrugged off my jacket and tried to deal with this concept. "You cooked what?"
> "Meat loaf. Mashed potatoes, steamed carrots, salad, bread. Apple pie for desert."
> "You baked apple pie?"
> "Of course not," he said, as though that idea was ridiculous but the rest of this was not. "I bought it at Greenberg's."
> An apple pie from Greenberg's was not to be sneezed at.
> Still, I said, "I have to tell you I'm suspicious."
> "Of my motives?"
> "Not more than usual. But of your cooking."
> "Fear not. It's meat loaf, food of my people." (Rozan 1998, 305–6)

As with Furutani's Tanaka, Rozan's ethnic detective here too shows the same prejudice he or she usually blames the majority for: Lydia cannot believe that Bill, a white male, could possibly be a competent cook. Bill's only half-ironic "food of my people" ably counters Lydia's prejudice by invoking the very ground upon which ethnics traditionally rate their own

46 THEO D'HAEN

cuisine a couple of cuts above that of the "average" American. Interestingly, Lydia's initial suspicion is already partially overcome by the apple pie from Greenberg's, in itself a multicultural mix—America's proverbial favorite dessert from what is probably a Jewish baker. The very un-Chineseness of what Lydia is served at Bill's is underlined when her comment upon having "room-temperature Brie with three kinds of crackers" is that "[her] mother would have a cow if she saw [her] eating this" (307). In the end, "[t]he tomato-glazed meat loaf filled the room with savory scents. Bill began tossing the salad with a dark dressing full of herbs, and I started to look forward to dinner" (308). What first announced itself as a drab meal has metamorphosed into a superb dinner combining the best of all kinds of European cooking, and Lydia is ready for another slice of multicultural America.

I will finish with two series set in Japan, rather than in the United States. Sujata Massey's Rei Shimura series features a Japanese American returning to the land of her forebears (actually, only her father) to do some (amateur) sleuthing there. Massey herself is of mixed Indian German descent, born in England, and educated on the East Coast of the United States, where she now again resides after an extended stay in Japan. In the novel initiating the Rei Shimura series, *The Salaryman's Wife* (1997), she introduces us to the protagonist on a Japanese train:

> It was dark outside, turning the train's door glass into a mirror. I saw myself as I always appear: small, Japanese-American, and with the kind of cropped haircut that's perfect in San Francisco but a little too boyish for Japanese taste. (1997a, 2)

The difference here is not with the putative homogeneity of the American ideal, but with the Japanese norm. Through her physique, or her self-description of it, Rei expresses not an unease with her specific slice of multicultural America, but rather, like Furutani's Tanaka, with the thrust for uniformity of Japanese identity. Regularly throughout the series Rei alludes to the fact that she is perceived as a half-blood by the true Japanese and that this is held against her. What is also held against her is her sex, specifically when she acts as an amateur sleuth. In fact, the sequence of novels from *The Salaryman's Wife*, via *Zen Attitude* (1997), to *The Flower Master* (1999), chronicles how Rei increasingly succeeds in gaining acceptance in Japan on her own terms, that is to say, those of a modern, young, and liberated American woman. Nowhere is this demonstrated better than in *The Flower Master* and specifically in Rei's relationship to her aunt, Norie, her father's sister and Rei's self-appointed guardian in Japan. Aunt Norie is much concerned with the proprieties of Japanese life, and she constantly tries to make Rei behave the proper Japanese way. This leads Rei at a given moment to explode:

> "Do you treat your own children this way, or do you do this because I'm the outsider? The one who doesn't know enough to take care of herself, despite her pathetically advanced age?"
>
> "Don't talk that way." Aunt Norie was trembling against the door, as if I were liable to attack her.
>
> "You want to take away my freedom of speech along with everything else? Well, I won't let you." (Massey 1999, 214)

Nothing could be more American than Rei's appeal to "freedom of speech." That Rei gains this particular freedom, along with a number of other contemporary American freedoms, such as the right to choose her own partner and her own profession, becomes clear at the end of *The Flower Master*. In this novel Rei has to clear Aunt Norie of the suspicion of murder, thereby proving her worth as an amateur detective. In the course of the novel Rei also gives up on her erstwhile Scottish lover, originally based in Japan but meanwhile returned to Scotland, and instead acquires a Japanese lover, Takeo, son of the flower master after whom the book is named. She thus proves her acceptability as a possible partner not just to Americans and Europeans, but also to native Japanese. In the final scene of the novel Aunt Norie catches Rei and Takeo kissing in her garden:

> "*Gomen nasai!* Excuse me for interrupting!" she called out, the tone of her voice belying the words.
>
> Feeling strangely unembarrassed, I turned my head to smile at my aunt. "We'll get back to work in a minute. After we're through getting reacquainted."
>
> Norie clucked her tongue, but when I looked at her, she was smiling. I radiated my happiness back to her, then returned to Takeo and our wonderful work in progress.
>
> It was going to take a while to plant Norie's new garden.
>
> I had the time. (375)

Obviously, Rei's independence of mind has overcome her aunt's initial resistance. In other words, American virtues carry the day also in Japan. The passage in question, though, has much more profound implications. This becomes clear if we stop to consider that in many ways Takeo is a very "American" scion of an otherwise very traditionally Japanese flower-arranging family. His desire for experimentation, for the rejuvenation of the venerable tradition he was raised in, mark him off both from his family and his national background. He even gives up his cushioned future as his father's successor rather than forsake his commitment to his environmental ideals. Though in an intellectual rather than a physical sense, Takeo is as independent of mind, and as much of a "hybrid," then, as Rei Shimura.

For the European reader it is a sobering thought that the political and economic marching order foreshadowed in the foreseeable future union of Rei and Takeo apparently is a strictly trans-Pacific affair. In the earlier novels in the series Rei still had a very passionate affair with a Scottish lawyer, Hugh Glendinning. This relationship was always wrought with cultural tensions, though, and by the end of the second novel in the series, *Zen Attitude*, Rei and her Scottish lover are heading for a breakup. In *The Flower Master* Hugh Glendinning is definitely past history, and Europe with him. All hopes, all expectations, now are pinned on a Japanese American understanding. From the point of view of female agency, it is crucial that the catalyst in bringing about such an understanding is herself a Japanese American woman.

But such issues need not only be addressed in the present, they can also be explored in a novel set in the past. The detective series that Laura Joh Rowland, granddaughter of Chinese and Korean immigrants to the United States, has been developing since 1994 is set in late-seventeenth-century Japan but nevertheless touches on many concerns of contemporary ethnic crime fiction. *Shinju* (1994) introduces us to Sano Ichiro, student of history and master of arts schooled in the martial arts school of his samurai father in Edo, the ancient name of Tokyo before the Meiji Restoration of 1868. Sano is a *yoriki* or policeman. In *Shinju* he succeeds not only in solving a double murder masked as suicide, but also in rendering a good service to the shogun, or military ruler of Japan. In the next novels in the series, *Bundori* (1996), *The Way of the Traitor* (1997), *The Concubine's Tattoo* (1998), and *The Samurai's Wife* (2001), Sano rises to become the shogun's chief investigator or *sosakan-sama*.

Rowland's novels give us a detailed picture of life in Japan at a time when the country was closed to any outside influence and when court intrigue ruled. What is remarkable, though, and what makes of the Sano Ichiro novels a very American detective series after all, is that Sano's success as an investigator is rooted not in his obeisance to the iron rules of etiquette and hierarchy, but rather in his independence of spirit and action. One way in which this independence shows itself is in the trust Sano puts in Dr. Ito, the chief physician of Edo's morgue and a noted *rangakusha* or "scholar of Dutch learning," that is, the scientific knowledge imparted to the Japanese by the Dutch in the brief period in which this was possible. As such, Sano shows an openness of mind that stands in sharp contrast to the regime's limitation in terms of politics, economics, and culture. Yet, it is precisely Sano's unorthodox methods—at least in the eyes of the regime he serves—

SAMURAI SLEUTHS AND DETECTIVE DAUGHTERS

that repeatedly allow him to save that same regime, in the form of its undisputed figurehead and ruler, the shogun. Most of all, though, Sano's intelligence and independence of mind are reflected in his dealings with women.

In the second novel in the series, *Bundori*, Sano enters into an arranged engagement with Reiko, an upper-class girl. At first Sano is very hesitant about the arrangement. What finally persuades him to go through with it is Reiko's unorthodox upbringing and behavior. Raised as the only child of a prominent magistrate early widowed, she has received the kind of education traditionally reserved for men rather than women. As a result, she shows an independence of spirit and action very much akin to Sano's. Reiko, in turn, only agrees to become engaged to Sano when she perceives these very same qualities in him. Over the next few novels Reiko gradually comes to share center stage with Sano. It is her aristocratic lineage in *The Concubine's Tattoo* that allows her to go and visit, and in the process subtly question, some of Japan's noblest families, when Sano finds himself barred from doing the same. Moreover, as a woman, Reiko is able to tap into different sources of information than Sano. What surprises Sano most, though, is that Reiko proves herself a match for any man when it comes to wielding a sword.

In *The Samurai's Wife* it is Reiko who uncovers the most meaningful clues to the crime Sano has been sent to investigate in Miyako, the ancient name for Kyoto, the capital of Japan before the rise of the shogunate and the official residence of the Japanese emperor. Indeed, in *The Samurai's Wife* the "agency" of detection can truly be said to pass—at least partially—from Sano to Reiko. Whereas in *The Concubine's Tattoo* Reiko's interventions were largely limited to the female sphere of the household, and of women's life, in *The Samurai's Wife* she ventures into the typically "male" detective territory of undercover operations and reconnoitering raids. The change of roles between Sano and Reiko is underlined, for example, in the following passage in which Reiko reveals to her husband that she has sneaked into a suspect's house:

> She spoke as if she'd done the most reasonable thing in the world. Sano stared, dumbstruck. "And guess what I found!" Animated with excitement, Reiko described an arsenal of weapons and a gang of samurai, gangsters, peasant ruffians, and an armed priest. Sano was too upset by her daring to think about the implications of her discovery. He shouted, "I can't believe you did that! You could have been killed! That was the most stupid, reckless, thoughtless, dangerous, foolhardy...." "And the most important piece of evidence yet," Reiko said. (Rowland 2000, 196)

Reiko's discovery will eventually enable Sano to prevent civil war from breaking out in Japan.

On the grand scale of nation, then, Rowland's *sosakan-sama* Sano Ichiro and his female partner, Reiko, do what Massey's amateur sleuth, Rei Shimura, does on the micro level of Aunt Norie's garden and what Rozan's Lydia Chin does for her Chinatown community: to a body about to collapse from the corruption seething under the façade of purity and tradition, they apply the very "American" cure of individualism, enterprise, independence, and inventiveness, or what Furutani sees as "American culture." Here "culture" (or call it nurture) triumphs over "nature"—in other words, in the final analysis all these protagonists prevail because of their American culture rather than their ethnic nature. If Sean McCann is right in his interpretation of classic hard-boiled American fiction, should Furutani's, Rozan's, Massey's, and Rowland's hard-boiled predecessors come to life, they would have no problem underwriting such a remedy.

In an age of multiculturalism, it should come as no surprise that, alongside African and Native American detectives, we should also meet Asian American ones. Nor should it surprise us if, after several decades of feminism, some of these Asian American detectives are women. As I hope to have demonstrated in the foregoing pages, though, the use to which Furutani, Rozan, Massey, and Rowland put their protagonists goes beyond the merely topical. In fact, I would argue that they not only add to the multicultural and gender agenda, but that they actually reflect on it. Their protagonists are very much aware of the stereotypes they are constantly being compared to, both in the history and literature of their adoptive country or countries—which, as Furutani's Tanaka points out with regard to the United States and his own family history, may actually be their "native" country, but in which they are still, even after several generations, perceived as "immigrants," or Others—and in those of their "native" country—which, as Massey's Rei Shimura points out with respect to Japan and her own relation to it, may actually be their "adoptive" country.

These novels even play off these stereotypes one against the other: they are the faithful samurai and the dutiful daughters "Western" readers expect to find in historical or other fictions about China or Japan, or in much contemporary Asian American "high" literature; yet at the same time they are also the fiercely and fearlessly independent "Americans" that readers around the world, not least in the United States itself, expect to find in "American" literature. If such a combination can be seen as the key to commercial success—and all these series are undeniably successful—it can at the same time also be seen as implying a recipe for social success.

All detectives concerned start from marginal positions in their respective societies; all succeed in integrating themselves in these same societies by applying an appropriate mix of "self" and "Other," whereby these terms can occupy shifting positions with regard to where, in which company or country, the detective in question finds himself or herself at any given moment. This may well prove a chastening corrective to the tendency toward essentialism often noted in contemporary multicultural "high" literature. In its advocacy, then, of what we could call "hybridity," I see the ethnic detective fiction of Furutani, Rozan, Massey, and Rowland as performing "cultural work" comparable to what McCann saw the 1920s to 1950s hard-boiled detective novel do: as a form of popular literature it mediates the (often unspoken) aspirations of a particular population group in the United States. If these aspirations include the preservation of at least part of the Asian cultural heritage, they obviously also include a powerful wish to "become American" in the full sense of the word, with all that implies in terms of adaptation to "American" patterns of life and freedom of thought, even if these patterns may have originated historically with America's "white" or "Caucasian" population. In sum, it is probably not exaggerated to see the protagonists of Furutani, Rozan, Massey, and Rowland as articulating and living the same recipe that has led to the increasing empowerment of Asian Americans, and Asian American women, in the economic, intellectual, and in the future perhaps also the political life of the United States.

Works Cited

Bailey, Frankie Y. 1991. *Out of the Woodpile: Black Characters in Crime and Detective Fiction*. New York: Greenwood Press.

Bhabha, Homi K. 1994. *The Location of Culture*. London: Routledge.

Chandler, Raymond. 1953. *The Long Goodbye*. Boston: Houghton Mifflin.

Dahl, Robert. 1956. *A Preface to Democratic Theory*. Chicago: University of Chicago Press.

Deleuze, Gilles, and Félix Guattari. 1975. *Kafka: Pour une littérature mineure*. Paris: Minuit.

Fabre, Michel, and Robert E. Skinner. 1993. Introduction to *Plan B*, by Chester Himes. Jackson: University Press of Mississippi.

Furutani, Dale. 1996. *Death in Little Tokyo*. New York: St. Martin's Press.

———. 1997. *The Toyotomi Blades*. New York: St. Martin's Press.

Geherin, David. 1982. *Sons of Sam Spade: The Private Eye Novel in the '70s*. New York: Frederick Ungar.

Hagemann, E. R., ed. 1982. *A Comprehensive Index to* Black Mask, *1920–1951*. Bowling Green, Ohio: Bowling Green State University Popular Press.

Hammett, Dashiell. 1930. *The Maltese Falcon*. Harmondsworth, U.K.: Penguin.

Irons, Glenwood, ed. 1995. *Feminism in Women's Detective Fiction*. Toronto: University of Toronto Press.

Kennedy, Liam. 1997. "Black Noir: Race and Urban Space in Walter Mosley's Detective Fiction." In *Criminal Proceedings: The Contemporary American Crime Novel*, edited by Peter Messent, 42–61. London: Pluto Press.

52 THEO D'HAEN

Massey, Sujata. 1997a. *The Salaryman's Wife*. New York: HarperCollins.

———. 1997b. *Zen Attitude*. New York: HarperCollins.

———. 1999. *The Flower Master*. New York: HarperCollins.

McCann, Sean. 2000. *Gumshoe America: Hard-Boiled Crime Fiction and the Rise and Fall of New Deal Liberalism*. Durham, N.C.: Duke University Press.

Pepper, Andrew. 2000. *The Contemporary American Crime Novel: Race, Ethnicity, Gender, Class*. Edinburgh: Edinburgh University Press.

Rowland, Laura Joh. 1994. *Shinju*. New York: HarperCollins.

———. 1996. *Bundori*. New York: HarperCollins.

———. 1997. *The Way of the Traitor*. New York: HarperCollins.

———. 1998. *The Concubine's Tattoo*. New York: St. Martin's Press.

———. 2000. *The Samurai's Wife*. New York: St. Martin's Press.

Rozan, S. J. 1994. *China Trade*. New York: St. Martin's Press.

———. 1995. *Concourse*. New York: St. Martin's Press.

———. 1996. *Mandarin Plaid*. New York: St. Martin's Press.

———. 1997. *No Colder Place*. New York: St. Martin's Press.

———. 1998. *A Bitter Feast*. New York: St. Martin's Press.

———. 1999. *Stone Quarry*. New York: St. Martin's Press.

Soitos, Stephen F. 1996. *The Blues Detective: A Study of African American Detective Fiction*. Amherst: University of Massachusetts Press.

Tompkins, Jane. 1985. *Sensational Designs: The Cultural Work of American Fiction, 1790–1860*. New York: Oxford University Press.

Walton, Priscilla L., and Manina Jones. 1999. *Detective Agency: Women Rewriting the Hard-Boiled Tradition*. Berkeley and Los Angeles: University of California Press.

Of Sherlocks, Shylocks, and the Shoah: Ethnicity in Jewish American Detective Fiction

CARMEN BIRKLE

HISTORIANS, SOCIOLOGISTS, AND LITERARY CRITICS HAVE DESCRIBED THE HISTORY of Jewish Americans as assimilationist because of their desire to belong to so-called mainstream America through "upward mobility" (see Siebald 1998). Abraham Cahan, Anzia Yezierska, and Mary Antin are usually presented as early examples of authors subscribing to this tendency in their fiction. Recently, this categorization of early Jewish American authors has increasingly been questioned. With pressures of growing multicultural American and European societies, more precise theories have been developed to describe the life of multiple cultures in cultural contact zones. Some critics have even concluded that complete assimilation or melting, as in Israel Zangwill's idea of the melting pot, is never possible; neither is a clear-cut cultural pluralism, as suggested by Horace Kallen in the early twentieth century, a viable alternative. Recently, critics such as Mary Louise Pratt (1992, 1996), Diana Taylor (1991), and Wolfgang Welsch (1999) have developed the concept of transculturation and transculturality to explain the preservation of ethnicities, on the one hand, and their mingling, on the other hand; they offer countertheories to the rejection of so-called cults of ethnicity, which, for example, Arthur Schlesinger Jr., in his *The Disuniting of America*, considers threatening to the American project of e pluribus unum. This phenomenon of (re)ethnicization or localization, I argue, goes hand in hand with and even reacts to the phenomenon of globalization. To describe the new space that is created in transculturation, Edward Soja coined the word "Thirdspace" (1996), and Homi Bhabha terms it "Third Space" (1990).

Detective fiction has boomed over the last decades, particularly women's

54 CARMEN BIRKLE

detective fiction, and U.S. detective fiction has spread all over the world, translated or untranslated, and has thus become one of the "global players." While critics such as David Hollinger argue that affiliations to (ethnic) groups can be chosen (1995, 3) and thus are no longer arbitrarily fixed, critics have also noticed a renewed interest in ethnic fiction and ethnic detective fiction that reveals the need for stability and for identity through identification with a particular ethnicity. I argue with Kathleen G. Klein that "detective fiction as popular literature is more a commodity produced for mass consumption" and that therefore "the product is usually responsive to society's demands" (1988, 5).

Mary Louise Pratt, in her study *Imperial Eyes: Travel Writing and Transculturation* (1992), and more explicitly in her essay "Arts of the Contact Zone" (1996), has coined the term "contact zone," which refers "to social spaces where cultures meet, clash, and grapple with each other, often in contexts of highly asymmetrical relations of power, such as colonialism, slavery, or their aftermaths as they are lived out in many parts of the world today" (1996, 530). Pratt sees the major element of these contact zones as the process of transculturation, a term originally coined by the Cuban sociologist Fernando Ortiz in the 1940s. According to Pratt, the term was meant to "replace overly reductive concepts of acculturation and assimilation," which implies a complete integration and thus a dissolution of the dominated culture(s) into the dominant one. In contrast, transculturation ascribes agency to the dominated culture(s). As an example of this process of transculturation, Pratt considers the writing of autoethnographic texts, which, according to her, are not "autochthonous forms of expression or self-representation. . . . Rather they involve a selective collaboration with and appropriation of idioms of the metropolis or the conqueror" (1996, 531). Therefore, transculturation and autoethnography as its literary expression mean for Pratt the active engagement of the dominated groups with the dominant ones as well as the former's acquisition and integration of cultural elements into their own culture (see also Taylor 1991; Lionnet 1989).

While Pratt's contact zone is decidedly embedded in a theory of colonialism, I argue that her concept of contact zones can also be applied to Jewish American detective fiction of the late twentieth century and, in a different sense, to the category of gender, because here, too, dominant and dominated cultures clash ideologically and sometimes physically. Assimilation through encounters with mainstream America, the loss of a specifically Jewish identity, and the need for and/or practice of the preservation of a Jewish culture, in both religious and nonreligious terms, is constantly negotiated in these texts. Autoethnography is used to discuss and present Jewish culture(s) to Jewish and non-Jewish readers alike and to affirm

OF SHERLOCKS, SHYLOCKS, AND THE SHOAH 55

Jewishness. Yet, these texts also show the inevitability of gradual changes, not in the form of assimilation but as transculturation, as development and progress through the interaction with other cultures, which in turn experience changes through these contacts as well.

According to Wolfgang Welsch, transculturation as a concept has the advantage that it combines both globalization, on the one hand, and processes of mixing and ethnicization, on the other (see 1999, 60). However, I argue that depending on where the emphasis is put, new power structures might emerge in order to control the process of transculturation, particularly if strong forces of ethnicization and assimilation clash. In his theoretical concept of transculturation, Welsch underestimates the relevance of human beings' desire for power and for belonging. Consequently, most Jewish American detective fiction contains a more essentialist definition of Jewishness, which clearly contrasts with David Hollinger's "postethnic perspective." This perspective

> favors voluntary over involuntary affiliations, balances an appreciation for communities of descent with a determination to make room for new communities, and promotes solidarities of wide scope that incorporate people with different ethnic and racial backgrounds. A postethnic perspective resists the grounding of knowledge and moral values in blood and history, but works within the last generation's recognition that many of the ideas and values once taken to be universal are specific to certain cultures. (1995, 3)

The process of assimilation, which rejects any grounding in blood and history, happens as a reality, but it can never completely erase differences, according to writers such as Kemelman and Goldberg. However, assimilation does not recognize the cultural specificity of ideas and values, but postulates one culture as universal. In Jewish American detective fiction, beginning with Kemelman, Jewishness will always be a presence and cater to the needs, and perhaps fears, of a loss of Jewish identities in Jewish communities. Choice and voluntary affiliation are possible, but only within Jewish groups. Thus, someone Jewish but not raised Jewish can choose to become a Conservative, Orthodox, or Reformed Jew, but for a non-Jew it would be nearly impossible or at least extremely difficult to become Jewish. Jewish American detective fiction, therefore, does not so much consider transculturation, but negotiates developments that oscillate between assimilation and ethnic segregation in a new cultural Thirdspace, "a strategic location from which to encompass, understand, and potentially transform all spaces simultaneously" (Soja 1996, 68). But this Thirdspace does not, as in Homi Bhabha's understanding, displace "the histories that constitute it . . ." (1990, 211). Soja's Thirdspace encourages a stabilization of

56   CARMEN BIRKLE

ethnicities, but within and together with so-called mainstream cultures, as well as a gradual subversion of the latter toward a democratization of cultures.

Since the 1960s, Jewish American literature and, as a subgenre, Jewish American detective fiction have reflected these cultural debates,[1] beginning with Harry Kemelman's Rabbi Small novels in the 1960s and 1970s, in which he contrasts the assimilationist desires of a small-town Jewish community to Rabbi Small's insistence on the adherence to Conservative Judaism and the Talmud's teachings.[2] In the late 1980s and 1990s, Faye Kellerman's Lina Lazarus and Peter Decker novels emphasized the necessity of critically affirming Jewish Orthodoxy. In the late 1990s, authors such as Ed Goldberg and, similarly, Kinky Friedman created rather transculturated (alter ego) characters whose Jewishness appears almost as a decoration only. Their characters cannot ignore that their Jewish backgrounds shape their identities and thus their lives, but they do not adhere to any religious rituals or practices. While Kemelman and Kellerman argue for a consciously lived Judaism, Goldberg considers his protagonist the site of multiple ethnic influences that turn him into a transculturated subject. In the novels of all three authors, however, the detectives' Jewishness is essential for the unfolding and the subsequent solution of the crimes.

Judaism in all three authors' novels is not just a religious belief; it is a lifestyle, a culture, and an ethnicity—although in various degrees—that determines every aspect of its members' lives. But Judaism is not and has never been a homogeneous concept, even if, for example, Nazi ideology may have presented it as such. Within Judaism, different strands are constantly questioning each other. The main difference lies in their respective attitudes toward gender, progress, and change. Reform Judaism, which is not represented in any of the novels, except for the fact that Goldberg goes far beyond it, was established as the Reformed Society of Israelites in Charleston, South Carolina, in 1824 (see Freese 1992, 116). They adjusted their belief to the *Zeitgeist* and rejected belief in the "Oral Laws, that is, the commentaries on the legal portions of the Scriptures, as neither derived from God nor as binding in any absolute sense . . ." (Freese 1992, 116). Therefore, they adapted to the customs and manners of the respective host-countries. In contrast, Orthodox Judaism declared itself as the preserver of traditional Jewish belief as recorded in the Written and Oral Laws and their commentaries. They accept the halakah, the law, in its entirety (see Freese 1992, 116). Conservative Judaism

> sought to establish some sort of middle position. This position, which arose in Germany in the middle of the nineteenth century as a counter-movement to Reform [Judaism] and was also known as the "positive-historical school," attempted to combine preservation and progress by maintaining

OF SHERLOCKS, SHYLOCKS, AND THE SHOAH   57

the essential aspects of traditional Judaism and allowing a certain measure
of freedom in the interpretation of Jewish doctrine. (117)

But Conservative Judaism adhered to "the Hebrew language in the liturgy,
the observance of *kashruth*, that is, the body of dietary laws, and the holi-
ness of the Sabbath . . ." (Freese 1992, 117).

Kemelman, Kellerman, and Goldberg represent three different manifestations of Jewish ethnicity in Jewish American detective fiction. While
Kemelman and Kellerman use their fiction in order to explain Conservative and Orthodox Judaism, respectively, to Jews and Gentiles alike, and
thus emphasize Jewish ethnicity, Goldberg focuses more on the vanishing
relevance of Judaism in his protagonist detective's everyday life and emphasizes his embeddedness in a multicultural and transculturating New York
City society. Nevertheless, the Jewish past in the form of the Holocaust
reemerges in Goldberg's novel and confronts the detective with his own
ethnicity and past.

Harry Kemelman

Harry Kemelman traces Rabbi David Small's development from his arrival at Barnard's Crossing, a small New England town near Boston,[3] via
constant troubles and crimes[4] to his final resignation from the job as a rabbi
of a congregation[5] in order to become professor of Judaic philosophy at
Windemere College.[6] Because of the success of the first few Rabbi Small
novels, Kemelman became a full-time writer in 1970 (see Freese 1992,
98).

With his rabbi novels, Kemelman picks up on a tradition of detective
novels with priests as amateur detectives. Gilbert Keith Chesterton's (1874–
1936) Father Brown[7]—as probably the most well-known example—or
William F. Love's Bishop Francis X. Regan make manifest the variety of
different types such as the "priest as protector" or the "priest as persecutor"
(Sipe and Lamb 1994, 59).[8] It is more unusual, however, to find a rabbi "in
this somewhat Catholic-Protestant-dominated area of writing" (Schlagel
1983, 101). The creation of Rabbi David Small was, according to Kemelman,
a pure accident, as he comments in an interview:

My use of the rabbi as a detective is purely accidental. I had written a book
about the building of a new temple and my editor objected to it on the
grounds that it was too low-keyed. He suggested jokingly that it might
liven it up if I were to get some of the Nicky Welt[9] business into it. On my
way home, I passed the local temple and it occurred to me that the large
parking lot in front of it would be a good place to deposit a body. That's

how I happened to write *Friday, the Rabbi Slept Late* [the first of his Rabbi Small novels]. (Peters et al. 1990, 130)

In this sense, Kemelman uses his Jewish detective figure didactically in order to teach and explain Judaism to Jews and Gentiles (see Peters et al. 1990, 130) and thus to make the crime novel a means for providing "condensed, standardized, specialist knowledge in innumerable fields of human endeavours . . ." (Mandel 1984, 78). But Yaffe criticizes Kemelman's novels in which "Judaism seems to have no faults, no limitations; any troubling questions it may raise are always explained away" (1990, 27).

Harry Kemelman's Rabbi David Small novels are manifestations of the tension between Rabbi Small's Conservative Judaism and his community's assimilationist tendencies. Central to the novels is Rabbi Small's position as a rabbi within the Jewish community, his talmudic learning as well as his rational and logical way of thinking, which he applies to the solution of the crimes. All novels are situated in or originate from the small town of Barnard's Crossing north of Boston with its small Jewish community and temple recently founded by the first-generation immigrant Jacob Wasserman, who established Conservative Judaism in the congregation. Neither this Jewish community nor the surrounding multiethnic Gentiles are in any way homogenous groups, and both tension and tolerance are characteristic of this town. According to Peter Freese, the rabbi's "name is doubly programmatical, because it announces both his Judaism (David) and his deceptive outward appearance (Small). Moreover, it foreshadows that, although only a small David, he will fearlessly take on the Goliath of public opinion" (1992, 138).

Tuesday the Rabbi Saw Red (1973) can be considered as representative of the rabbi series, because in this novel the rabbi not only has to confront his own Jewish congregation, but also takes on the job of a college teacher teaching a course on Jewish thought to highly critical, ignorant, and resistant Jewish and Gentile college students. The novel is set at Barnard's Crossing and at Windemere College in Boston, featuring Dean Millicent Hanbury, whose favorite pastime is knitting, undermining and simultaneously affirming gender stereotypes. Tension is thus produced on three levels: on the religious level of Judaism between Rabbi Small and his congregation, and between the rabbi and his students; on the gender level in the character of Millicent Hanbury and her relationship with several other characters; and on the crime level, which combines levels one and two. In my discussion of the novel, I will look at how Judaism is presented and at gender roles and their affirmation or subversion in the context of detective fiction, and will tie these two strands together in Rabbi Small's detective work.

The novel begins with the preparation for Edie Chernow and Roger

OF SHERLOCKS, SHYLOCKS, AND THE SHOAH   59

Fine's wedding and Edie's dispute with both her parents and Rabbi Small about the nonkosher catering company she has hired instead of the traditional Jewish one. Rabbi Small remains resolute in his rejection of the company, because the temple's kitchen is kosher (Kemelman [1973] 1985, 16). It is only a brief episode, but it serves as an introduction to Rabbi Small's unobtrusive outward appearance: "He was of medium height, but thin and pale. He held his head forward in a scholarly stoop and peered near-sightedly through thick-lensed glasses. . . . [H]is shoes were dusty and . . . his tie, inexpertly knotted, was slightly askew" (14). This rather unassuming appearance, however, is contrasted with his firm position in religious matters, as a preserver of Jewish religious traditions (15), and it underlines his ignorance of strategic behavior, since he is employed by the members of the temple and needs their votes for his employment. While other members of the board of directors of the temple criticize the rabbi, Jacob Wasserman, the first president of the temple, explains his behavior as in agreement with the position of the rabbi as a teacher, "the teacher . . . [as] the boss" in "the old country" (19). This basic tension between Rabbi Small's Conservative Judaism and many members' Reform Judaism serves as the underlying structure of this novel, as well as in all other Rabbi Small novels. It shows how Judaism, because of its cultural encounters with non-Jewish Americans in cultural contact zones, is constantly questioned from within these groups. It is a question of assimilation or separation and thus of Jewish identity and "the end of the 'melting pot' model of American life . . ." (King and Hershinow 1978, 86). Rabbi Small himself frames this tension as a result of this change:

> My grandfather was the rabbi of a small Orthodox congregation. He didn't make little speeches to bar mitzvah youngsters. He didn't get up to announce the page in the prayer book during holiday services. He spent his time largely in study. When anyone in his community had a question that involved their religion, they came to him and he researched it in the Talmud and answered it. When there was a dispute between two or more members of the community, they came to him and he heard all sides and passed judgment. And they abided by his verdict. He was doing the traditional work of a rabbi. . . . My father was a Conservative rabbi. His congregation is old and established. They have a feeling and understanding of the function of the rabbi, and they trusted him implicitly. They didn't go to him for judgment and they had no great concern for the kind of questions that my grandfather passed on. But they cared about their Judaism and they relied on my father to guide them in it. (Kemelman [1973] 1985, 214–15)

The actual story begins "in mid-September, right after the High Holydays [Rosh Hashannah and Yom Kippur]" (19), when the rabbi is asked to teach

60   CARMEN BIRKLE

a course in Jewish thought and philosophy at Windemere College in Boston. When he agrees, he meets Dean Millicent Hanbury, whose unmarried status is emphasized by the local chief of police, Hugh Lanigan. Rabbi Small encounters her as a woman who loves to knit, a traditionally female occupation in the private sphere. She introduces him to Professor Hendryx, with whom he is supposed to share an office.

When, in his first class, the rabbi explains Jewishness as "[i]f you're born a Jew, you're a Jew" and says that "by rabbinic law, only one born of a Jewish mother—note, mother, not father—is a Jew" (Kemelman [1973] 1985, 50), he initiates a discussion about the roles and position of Jewish women in their congregation. He contrasts Conservative Judaism with Orthodoxy and emphasizes the former's adaptation of changes as well as the equality of the sexes. Kemelman uses the ignorance of the students as a pretext for a basic explanation of Judaism, for a deconstruction of frequent stereotypes and clichés about Jewish belief, and even for an analysis of Israeli-Arab relations. When a bomb explodes and Professor Hendryx is found dead, Rabbi Small is challenged to combine his talmudic reasoning with his curiosity and knowledge of human behavior. According to King and Hershinow, "It is precisely the rabbi's ability to apply the general principles of the Talmud to present-day situations, using Talmudic logic, that unites the mystery elements of the books with the Jewish subject-matter" (1978, 90; see also Neuhaus 1975, 548).

Kemelman, according to detective fiction tradition since Edgar Allan Poe, presents numerous red herrings, various suspects, the police on the wrong track, and an amateur detective, Rabbi Small, who simply happens to get involved because he is the last one to have seen Professor Hendryx alive. As a consequence, the rabbi is also among the prime suspects. When Bradford Ames, the assistant district attorney, asks Small for his opinion and assistance in the case of bail for the four arrested students, Small refers him to the Talmud and explains that the Talmud deals with "criminal law, and religious law—all the laws by which we were governed. We don't separate them in our religion" ([1973] 1985, 161). According to Yaffe, "There is hardly any aspect of human thought and behavior—and especially of law—that the Talmud does not examine" (1990, 20).

The police continue to notice some incongruities in the stories of several of those questioned about that particular Friday afternoon of the murder, but cannot bring them together into a coherent narrative. The rabbi begins to reason, "and unconsciously he lapsed into Talmudic argumentative sing-song . . ." (Kemelman [1973] 1985, 179). He solves the problem of the many matches used to light Professor Hendryx's pipe, who himself was an expert smoker: "[I]f it took half a dozen matches to light that pipe, or to keep it lit, then it wasn't Professor Hendryx who was smoking it!"

OF SHERLOCKS, SHYLOCKS, AND THE SHOAH   61

(181). In the manner of Sherlock Holmes and Watson, Ames and Small meet several times. In one scene, Rabbi Small, like an armchair detective with Auguste Dupin's powers of deduction and reasoning, is sitting in his chair, "abstracted, gazing off into space" (250), reflecting on what he has just learned about Millicent Hanbury.

Like Poe and Doyle in their stories, Kemelman also finishes his novels with a dénouement scene in which the rabbi discovers and interprets for the police some of the clues that they have misread or not understood. He explains the Talmud's method: "[I]t consisted of examining every aspect of a problem from every possible point of view . . ." ([1973] 1985, 258). He shows them how an empty drawer in Hendryx's apartment points to the existence of a girlfriend who must have come after Hendryx's death to get her clothes. The only one who has an alibi is Dean Millicent Hanbury, and the Rabbi reveals how she could have come to retrieve her private belongings, including a knitting bag, and how she could have pushed the bust with the help of a knitting needle by putting it through the hole in the wall the telephone man had just drilled only a few days before. The motive would be disappointed love, because Hendryx was going to marry Betty Macomber, the college president's daughter.

Gender and gender stereotypes play an important part in the solution of this case. Rabbi Small suspects Millicent Hanbury right from the beginning because she is an unmarried woman who, in Judaism, "is a tragic figure because she has not had the chance to complete her normal life cycle" (Kemelman [1973] 1985, 265). So she and Hendryx decide to get married as soon as he gets tenure and is made head of the department, because then she would have to leave her job because couples are not allowed on Windemere's faculty. This theory makes sense only because of the underlying assumption that an unmarried woman has nothing else on her mind but marriage. Millicent Hanbury's traditional idea of a woman's role in life is underlined by her obsession with knitting. With this traditionally female occupation, she can outwardly affirm her womanhood, which is questionable because of her status as an unmarried woman.

At the end of the novel, Judaism, gender stereotypes, and detective work merge in Rabbi Small's reasoning and lead to the solution of the case and the discovery of the murderer. Both the content and method of the Talmud inspire the Rabbi to apply common sense and logical thinking to the crime. The criminal woman, although she is not even Jewish, adheres exactly to the Judaic expectations for women so that the Rabbi cannot fail in his detection. This fulfillment of gender expectations underlines Judaism's, and here Kemelman's, understanding of its own universalism and its applicability to any situation in human life. As the novel emphasizes, Judaism is not so much a theology as a lifestyle, as well as a belief. In

62 CARMEN BIRKLE

line with Auguste Dupin, Sherlock Holmes, and Father Brown, Rabbi David Small, as an amateur detective, solves his case in an impressive but sexist way. Miriam, Small's wife, appears only in the background and usually only as a highly supportive and protective wife and mother. Although the rabbi "acts as a judge within the Jewish community, [and] . . . also a cultural mediator who defends his congregants against the prejudices of the surrounding Christians" (Freese 1992, 165), he voices very conservative and fixed images of women that stand in contrast to even Conservative Judaism's belief in change. Change, triggered by cultural encounters, seems to be exterior and superficial, while the Talmud and the halakah, the Jewish law, remain fixed forever. Kemelman also becomes the spokesperson of every Jewish community, because "in almost all the Kemelman novels the rabbi's solutions to the criminal mysteries with which he is faced lead not only to the apprehension of the murderer but also to the exculpation of some unduly suspected members of his congregation" (165).

FAYE KELLERMAN

Although Faye Kellerman is a very prolific writer and has published more than ten detective novels, very little is known about her life, and scarce research has been done about her fiction. She is raising four children in Beverly Hills with her husband, Jonathan Kellerman, who is also a mystery writer and who was, according to an interview with Kellerman herself, her major inspiration to write detective fiction: "When I saw my husband write, it gave me the idea that I could do this. . . . I was more the mathematical/analytical type. . . . One of the reasons I write mysteries is that the genre appeals to my logical mind" (Marks 2000, online). While the motivation for writing derives from her love for logical thinking, her subjects are based on her own religion:

> Religion and spirituality are important to me. I'm an Orthodox Jew and wanted that in my work. The idea is not to preach, or anything like that. But it gives the main characters much more dimension and a better read. . . . I like books with ethnic characters. . . . You can present Orthodox Jews in a less stereotypical manner. You can go into their thoughts. You can do the differences in the laws, but the human emotions are the same. (Marks 2000, online)

In all of Kellerman's novels, Judaism plays a role in the solution of the cases, as already implied in the titles, for example, in *The Ritual Bath* (1986),[10] *Milk and Honey* (1990), *Day of Atonement* (1991), *False Prophet* (1992), or *Prayers for the Dead* (1996).[11] Like Kemelman, Kellerman inter-

OF SHERLOCKS, SHYLOCKS, AND THE SHOAH 63

twines religion and faith intricately with detection so that knowledge of Judaism, here particularly modern Orthodoxy, is essential for the solution of the crimes. In order to justify her teaching of Orthodoxy in the novels, she chooses Peter Decker, a Jew at the Los Angeles Police Department who was adopted by a Baptist family in childhood, and only learns in adulthood that he is Jewish. When he meets the Orthodox Rina Lazarus and falls in love with her (in *The Ritual Bath*), he decides to convert to Orthodox Judaism. Logically, Kellerman prompts the readers to learn with her protagonist, makes Rina the actual teacher, and uses her in situations where more profound knowledge of Judaism or even of the Yiddish and Hebrew languages is required. Frequently, Rina has to speak Yiddish to Jews who are involved in the cases, because they consider her "one of them" and trust her more than the outsider Peter Decker.

While all of Kellerman's novels offer interesting insights into Judaism for both Jews and Gentiles, *Sanctuary* ([1994] 1995) comprises a range of Orthodox elements to which Peter Decker is gradually introduced and which even lead him and his wife, Rina, to Israel, a trip that Rabbi Small also undertakes in Kemelman's *Monday the Rabbi Took Off*. In *Sanctuary*, Peter and Rina live together on Peter's ranch near Los Angeles in the San Fernando Valley and are raising Rina's two sons from her first marriage (her husband having died) and their baby daughter, Hannah. While a friend from high school, Honey Klein, a member of the extreme ultra-Orthodox Leibben Chasidic (Hasidic) sect, is visiting Rina with her four children, her husband, a diamond dealer, is murdered in New York City. Honey Klein escapes with her children to Israel. Parallel to this personal case, Peter Decker has to find the murderers of the rich Jewish diamond-dealer couple Dalia and Arik Yalom, whose two sons have disappeared. In the first case, Rina's knowledge of the *agunah* (a Jewish woman trapped in a dead marriage because her husband refuses to grant her a Jewish divorce) is the key to the solution; in the second case, Rina's familiarity with Yiddish and Hebrew as well as with the Tel Aviv and Hebron areas helps Rina and Peter to locate not only the two missing boys but also the culprits.

As in Kemelman's rabbi novels, the wife in the background is a stabilizer for the detective, but in contrast to Kemelman, Rina goes beyond mere support. She breaks the rules set for her as an Orthodox Jewish wife by her belief and by her husband, who tries to protect her and keep her out of his professional life. But Peter Decker is dependent on Rina's knowledge and her courage, which is motivated by her care for her children. Thus, her traditionally feminine roles of housewife, wife, and mother and her role as an Orthodox Jew make her the perfect (detective) companion for her homicide-detective husband. Rina is courageous, caring, and strong, even carrying a gun for her own protection; she resists Peter's constant

64 CARMEN BIRKLE

attempts to tell her what to do and to overprotect her. I will argue that her manner of detection serves to counterbalance the stereotypical view of traditional Jewish women's roles, to underline the necessity and value of Judaism, and to reflect pride and belief in ethnicity and religion. I argue with Laurence Roth that "Kellerman herself, along with multicultural writers of both literary and popular fiction, shares in the contemporary project of recuperating and reshaping images and traditions from the past as models for a meaningful hybrid-American ethnic identity" (1999, 207), but she critically distinguishes ultra-Orthodox sectarian cults from modern Orthodoxy.

In *Sanctuary*, the reader gets glimpses of gender issues in the work relationship between Peter Decker and his non-Jewish partner, Marge Dunn. Peter frequently has to boost Marge's ego because she is not taken seriously by her male boss and some of her male colleagues, but Peter respects her and her work, and she proves to be very well qualified for the job. Although Peter tries to separate his professional and his private lives, his wife, Rina, is constantly drawn into his cases. Between Marge and Rina, however, there is no competition.

When Peter and Marge are called to the Yalom house because the family is missing, Peter notices all the religious objects such as a *mezuzah*, "symbol of a Jewish establishment" (Kellerman [1994] 1995, 271), on the entry hall door frame and a menorah in the bathroom. Peter begins to suspect something is wrong because of the incorrect positioning of two porcelain fighting dogs and because an outside-door *mezuzah* is posted inside and does not contain a parchment with a holy prayer written on it. Rina explains to him that "Yalom" comes from "yaholom" which means "diamond" in Hebrew: *"There probably was a Stein somewhere in his family tree. Peter had been amazed. What's your secret, Sherlock? Stein means stone in German . . . Yiddish. It was probably Hebraized when the family moved to Israel. They do that a lot. Peter's expression was flat. Maybe you should take the case? If you spoke to Bar Lulu in Hebrew, something sub rosa might come out"* (66–67). This passage not only reveals Rina's knowledge of Judaism and her contribution to Peter's cases, but also the tension between the two, because Peter feels inadequate as someone who gradually has to learn his new religion and as someone whose self-confidence based on his job is threatened by Rina's capable intrusion into his professional sphere. This scene is followed by an affirmation of Rina's feminine qualities and her problem with not being able to have any more children:

> Not that she was anxious to get involved in Peter's work. Or any work for that matter. Rina was quite content to stay at home and take care of Hannah— her last baby. One swift cut from the surgeon's knife and she no longer could bear children. . . . At thirty-one, Rina had expected and had wanted more children. She'd always felt that she was born to nurture. Unlike many

women in this modern age, Rina considered childrearing a privilege and not a chore. (67)

This tension between Peter's masculinity, which is threatened by the competent intrusions of his wife into his work, and Rina's femininity, which she feels is reduced by her inability to have any more children, is paired with and triggered by Rina's superior knowledge in religious matters; it is this tension which runs like a leitmotif through all of Kellerman's Peter Decker and Rina Lazarus novels. Peter's masculinity crisis is informed by the traditional hard-boiled images of detectives on the one hand—which he rejects—and the need for assertion in his profession by preventing violence on the other. With Rina's successful intrusions into this male sphere of police work, Peter's definition of himself and of his profession is questioned.[12] Rina is highly intelligent, reading the clues with the tools given to her through the knowledge of Judaism and Jewish habits and community life. Kellerman also makes a point for her feminism when Peter accuses her of "underdeveloped feminist hackles" (322), and she responds: "Peter, where is it written that you can't be traditional and a feminist at the same time? One doesn't preclude the other. . . . I know *who* I am and I'm happy. There are still a few *relics* like me who are proud to be full-time mothers" (323). She continues:

> Besides, it's not the feminists who look askance at us stay-at-home moms. It's everyone else. Especially the *men*. . . . Men today have such unreasonable expectations. . . . It's not *enough* for us poor women to keep house and take care of the kids. . . . We've also got to be beautiful, charming, sexy, physically fit, good cooks—amend that to *gourmet* chefs—. . . . And we also have to work full time and bring in enough money to pay not only our own way, but also help pay for the kids' clothes, the baby-sitters, the groceries. . . . (323)

With marriage to Peter, Rina changes her practice of Judaism as well. She still remains Orthodox, but "in a more modern way" (69). She is reminded of her first marriage to Yitzchak when she meets her high-school friend Honey Klein and her four children and realizes how much she has changed: "Her marriage to Peter had made her more modern, just as her marriage to Yitzchak had made her more Orthodox" (69). Because of her background, she is able to explain to Peter the peculiar situation Honey Klein is in. Honey's husband, a diamond dealer, declared himself a Nazir ("They don't drink wine or alcohol, they don't shave or cut their hair, and they don't defile themselves by contacting dead bodies—" [128]) and refused to have sex with his wife, but also refused to give her a divorce. When Gershon Klein is found murdered in his Manhattan office, Peter begins to see connections to the Los Angeles case. Gradually, historical information about Israel such as army practices becomes relevant when Peter and Marge interview Arik Yalom's Israeli partner, Gold, whose service for the Israeli army leads them to the Israeli context and to the world diamond business in the form of the VerHauten Company and its former director of marketing and sales, Kate Milligan. Rina and Peter finally travel to Israel together in search of the two missing boys of the Yalom family.

In Tel Aviv, Rina wins the sympathies of all Yalom family members because she can communicate with them in Hebrew. Language and cultural understanding open up people's hearts and make them cooperative. Although most people in Israel speak English, Hebrew and Yiddish signify community spirit, cultural belonging, and intracultural solidarity. Only Rina's background and her personality help the two Americans to win people's trust. Language goes beyond its merely linguistic function of verbal communication; it becomes a cultural mediator between the Jews in Israel and the (modern Orthodox) Jews in the United States. Rina feels at home in Israel, because she had lived there for three years (about twelve years previously), but Peter Decker, because he is a recently converted Orthodox Jew, feels torn between belonging and alienation; as a Jew he wants to belong to the people of Israel in the spirit of Zionism, since "Rina had drummed it into him. Every identified Jew alive looked to Israel for sanctuary" (Kellerman [1994] 1995, 292), but as an American Jew, he has an American cultural background that makes him different from Israeli people. He finally sees the "*mezuzah*. The symbol of a Jewish establishment. On every single door. Yes, Decker finally realized they were in a *Jewish* country. It made him feel simultaneously strange and at home" (271). While Peter has consciously decided to become an Orthodox Jew, he experiences the difficulties of this voluntary affiliation in Israel. He sees himself as living in between cultures; yet, he also considers this in-betweenness as a transitory state that he strives to overcome. However, his example shows how religious and cultural affiliations may be disrupted by national affiliations. Peter's recognition of his in-betweenness is also a manifestation of the heterogeneity of Judaism.

Rina decides to follow Kate Milligan when she leaves Tel Aviv. Even Decker has to admit that "Rina was at home in the country. In fact, she knew Israel better than either Milligan or he did. She knew what was dangerous and how to avoid it" (Kellerman [1994] 1995, 277). As soon as she has left, he realizes that "he was in trouble. He couldn't speak Hebrew and Yalom could barely speak English. . . . A stranger in a strange land—a *ger*" (284). Rina follows Kate Milligan to Jerusalem and finally into Hebron. Kellerman uses her chance to elaborate on the Israeli-Arab conflicts. Here, Rina is both a native and a stranger, one of those who is hated (283).

OF SHERLOCKS, SHYLOCKS, AND THE SHOAH 67

Apart from the Arab-Jewish conflict, Kellerman evokes another major danger for Jews, even in Israel, namely that of the Holocaust as a horrible symptom of a worldwide hatred of Jews. Menkovitz, a diamond dealer with whom Milligan does business and who is the grandfather of the two missing Yalom boys, is a survivor of the Holocaust, of the Treblinka concentration camp ([1994] 1995, 286) and comments: "Who needs an excuse to hate Jews?" (288). About Milligan he says: "I don't like the way she acts. She has power and is a bully with it. She would have been a fine Nazi" (290). Kellerman changes the sex of usually male Nazis and turns a powerful and successful but also abusive businesswoman into the epitome of evil. Subtly, she suggests the crime seemingly committed within a Jewish group is the result of a general hatred for Jews, as an extension of the Holocaust. The trip to Israel serves as a means for Kellerman to bring up this issue from the perspective of a survivor. This comparative technique with the Holocaust as a metaphor for suffering and torture in general has been debated in much historical and critical writing about the Holocaust. Israel is the sanctuary for all persecuted Jews from any of the world's diasporas. Ironically, however, Rina has never been in more danger than in Israel, following Kate Milligan until she reaches "*Ma'arat HaMachpelah*— the Tomb of the Patriarchs. The ancient burial place of the holy ancestors" (297).[13] Despite Rina's fluent Hebrew, a young Israeli soldier recognizes her right away as an American who does not belong: "Of course, she was American and that explained everything. What the hell was wrong with these crazy American fanatics? Didn't they know what they were doing to Israel, how they put every soldier—every *Jewish* soldier—in danger with their rhetoric and their stubbornness? Who needed them anyway?" (306). Kellerman makes herself the spokeswoman for heavy Israeli criticism of U.S. intervention in Israel and the Middle East. However, this criticism ignores the support the United States has given to Israel in the Israeli-Palestinian-Arab conflict. Although Kellerman does not question the idea of Israel as the home for all Jews, she disrupts the idea of Jewish homogeneity and the idealized notion of Israel. As an American Jew in Israel, Rina learns that Americanness is not an unquestioned concept. Yet, Rina is overwhelmed by the spirit of the shrine and feels that "[e]very visit to the cave brought [her] that much closer to her ancestral roots" (310).

On her return, Rina tells Peter what she has found out about Kate Milligan, and when Peter in turn lets her know that Honey Klein is probably in Israel, too, they make their way to Jerusalem. En route, Rina explains to Peter what happens if a Jewish man refuses his wife a divorce:

Any man who would blindly refuse to give his wife a *get* [divorce] was under the control of his *yaitzer harah*—his evil impulses. The rabbis considered

68   CARMEN BIRKLE

> it appropriate to beat the *yaitzer harah* out of his soul until he came to
> reason, until he felt the compassion and kindness of his *yaitzer tov*—his
> goodness. (Kellerman [1994] 1995, 324)

Rina and Peter argue about the relativity of cultural and legal practices, whether this practice should be called illegal, which it *is* from the perspective of American and Israeli jurisprudence, but which it is *not* from the point of view of Orthodox Judaism.

At the Or Torah yeshiva in Jerusalem, they finally find Gil Yalom, who has looked for sanctuary there. While Rina is not allowed in the *bais midrash*, the study hall, Peter goes in as a scholar, but again it is Rina who recognizes the one person who does not belong and who, as it turns out, has placed a bomb in the yeshiva:

> Peter, rabbis usually touch the mezuzah with the fringes of their tzitzit,
> then kiss the fringes. Even if they use their fingers, they touch the mezuzah
> with their fingertips only. This guy covered the mezuzah with his entire
> hand and kissed his palm. Someone had schooled him, but not quite cor-
> rectly. And even though he was wearing tzitzit, he didn't use them. Be-
> cause he didn't know what they were for. (Kellerman [1994] 1995, 349)

The same logical reasoning makes them discover Kate Milligan's plan of bombing the stock exchange, where most diamond dealers do their business, as a means to destroy the Israeli diamond business. They find Dov with his other grandparents; Honey shows up and confirms the story of the *agunah*, and finally Rina and Peter can return to the United States. The solution of the private entanglement between the murdered Daliah Yalom and her husband's partner turns out to be a story of the Holocaust again. Gold's mother is Daliah's mother, and Gold was separated from his family in World War II when Nazis took away his family (419). Kate Milligan, the murderer of Arik and Daliah Yalom, once compared to a Nazi, is shot in Syria, but the murderer is never discovered. Yet, Gold comments at the end: "We still hunt Nazis, Detective. Because there are things in this world that are so bad that there is no city of refuge. There is just no sanctuary for pure evil, you understand?" (421).

In *Sanctuary*, Kellerman establishes cultural contact zones in both the United States and Israel and creates Rina Lazarus and Peter Decker as mediators. Peter's gradual learning and conversion to Orthodox Judaism guides the readers, and Rina's explanations to Peter pull them into Judaism as well. Peter and Rina mediate between Jews and non-Jews, and Jews and Orthodox Jews. Cultural and religious habits and artifacts serve as concrete means of mediation and, since it is a detective novel, are used as clues to be read properly for the solution of the two cases, that is, the murder of the Yalom parents and Honey Klein's husband. While the murder of Gershon Klein turns out to be an intra-Jewish act that is justified by the law of the *agunah* used for the well-being of the wife and her children, the murder of the Yalom couple is motivated by economic and political greed and manipulation as well as Arik Yalom's blackmail of the white woman, Kate Milligan, with her black lover, Donald Haas. In both cases, motherhood and the care of children as well as religion and the belief in Israel as sanctuary for all Jews are instrumental in the modus operandi. Both cases are vessels of Jewish culture, history, and politics, and the Holocaust and Arab-Israeli relationships are evoked to give a rounded impression of what Jewish life in the 1990s is like. Knowledge of this past and of culture is the only means for understanding people's motivations. Rina Lazarus, driven by her knowledge of Judaism, her interest in the missing children, and her ability to speak Hebrew and Yiddish as well as English, although not the actual detective in the novel, is the only person who combines feminine and feminist impulses and who is thus able to untangle the web of past and present and ultimately to solve the cases. *Sanctuary* is a lesson in Judaism but also in interculturality and, in its own way, in feminism.

Ed Goldberg

In the 1990s, Portland-based Oregon writer Ed Goldberg,[14] who is of Russian and Rumanian descent, published his first two detective novels, *Served Cold* (1994)[15] and *Dead Air* (1998). He is currently working on a third novel, tentatively entitled *Better Dead*. Goldberg writes about places that he knows best. Therefore, his first novel is set in New York City. After moving to Portland, Oregon, in 1991, Goldberg used a local West Coast radio station as his setting in *Dead Air*. According to my fax interview with the author, *Better Dead* "involves people who were damaged by the McCarthy Era repression, and those who still defend McCarthy and J. Edgar Hoover, who brought us closer to native fascism than ever before." Goldberg is a political writer whose novels are critical of particular phases and attitudes in American history, such as McCarthyism or the practices of Nazis and their collaborators hiding in the United States after World War II. Goldberg was born in the Bronx, was educated at a Hebrew religious school, and read the Torah in the original Hebrew and Aramaic. This early education, however, inspired in him "a thorough disrespect for organized religion" and the desire "to get freedom *from* religion" (Goldberg 2000). After graduation from college in 1972, he moved to Washington, D.C., to work for various consulting firms and "to write features and reviews for a monthly arts and entertainment paper" (interview). He began reading at the age of

70   CARMEN BIRKLE

three "and writing for publication at six" (interview). *Served Cold* was his first finished and published novel, and while it concentrates on Jewish questions, Goldberg, in contrast to Kemelman and Kellerman, is not preaching Judaism to his readers. His main concern is "[s]imple friendship, kindness or tolerance," which are "preferable to any religion I ever heard of" (interview). Yet, Jewishness as a cultural more than as a religious phenomenon is important for Ed Goldberg and finds expression in his novels, most prominently in *Served Cold*.

In my interview, Goldberg admits: "I wasn't aware of my own Jewish 'issues' until I started to write. What a surprise! I decided to go with it. My own Jewish background also makes it easier to write about Lenny [his protagonist], than if he were Japanese" (interview). In *Served Cold*, the detective protagonist, PI Lenny Schneider, is of Jewish background, but hardly incorporates it into his everyday life. He is, as he calls himself, "an atheistic, assimilated antireligious Jew" (Goldberg [1994] 1997, 37), and he questions the innateness of Jewishness (quoting Einstein): "We are not Jews because we say so, but because the world says so. We forget this at our peril" (37). He is, however, confronted with anti-Semitism by opponents of his clients, who call him "a fucking Jew bastard" (13), and by Bruno, a bodyguard, who tells him: "My father raised me to hate Jew scum like you. He told me stories about how you poison everything, how you take food out of people's mouths. Everybody hates Jews, even the fuckin' Japs, and they ain't even got any there!" (100). Otherwise, Schneider enjoys doing "what so many Jews in New York did on Rosh Hashanah: having lunch at a Chinese restaurant and going to the track or a ball game" (42). When he is invited to a Jewish household, he admits that he "came from a house where this ritual [the *Shabbas*, the Sabbath] was observed, in its beauty and awesomeness," but that when his "widowed mother remarried, this ritual, along with several other of her finer instincts, was lost" (67). Thus, Lenny Schneider is a cultural Jew who has lost any deeper connections to Judaism as a religion. When he is hired by Lou Goffin to help his uncle Solomon Vishniac, who is a survivor of Auschwitz, Lenny Schneider is confronted with the Holocaust past.

Lou Goffin tells Schneider about his Uncle Solomon's Holocaust experiences:

> Solomon watched the SS kill his whole family, father, mother, uncles, aunts, cousins. They dragged every Jew in the neighborhood out and lined them up outside the buildings. They ridiculed and abused them, especially the orthodox ones with the beards and *payess*, sidecurls. When the Nazis were finished humiliating them, they killed them on the spot. Shot in the street like dogs. Then they looted their houses. Solomon witnessed the whole thing. He escaped because he was returning from late classes and saw the

OF SHERLOCKS, SHYLOCKS, AND THE SHOAH   71

carnage from a distance. He went underground, was shielded for a time by kindly gentiles, and was eventually betrayed to the Nazis by a neighbor. Those who helped him were sent to the camps with him. He survived the camp by killing his soul, becoming as hard as the Nazis, in his way. (Goldberg [1994] 1997, 22)

Solomon developed special hatred for the Nazi Ernst Mueller and his Jewish collaborator Lev Kaminsky. By choosing a Jewish collaborator, Goldberg offers an insight into the complexity of Nazi war crimes and problematizes the question of guilt. By chance, after many years, Solomon sees Mueller in the streets of New York City and now is obsessed with the idea of killing Mueller. As Goldberg states: "I heard of a true incident in New York of a camp survivor who recognized a camp guard on the street and killed him with his bare hands. . . . I needed a vehicle for the action, so I imagined Uncle Sol. He is my version of the real camp survivor. The experience changed him and I like him very much" (Goldberg 2000). With this reminder of the Jewish past, Lenny Schneider suddenly begins to evoke memories of his own childhood as well, triggered by the Yiddish song "Rumenye, Rumenye," which his grandfather used to play for him on a pennywhistle (Goldberg [1994] 1997, 25). Here, cultural memory motivates personal memory and sets in motion a new process of the interrelationship of past and present.

Up until that point, Lenny Schneider—whose name is a pseudonym—has been immersed in the New York City culture of jazz and baseball, has been an avid reader of Sherlock Holmes and Raymond Chandler, and as a result has applied for a private investigator's license. He has considered Jews as one ethnic group among the many populating New York City:

The street I live on is roughly divided by a north-south axis. East of this line is an established community of Latinos, overcrowded and angry. West of the line is a diminishing group of old-line residents, mostly Ukrainians, and a burgeoning of Asians of various nationalities provoking the Ukis. Harmoniousness prevails amongst the groups, as each hates the other passionately. Each group is in complete agreement with the next about the slanders repeated of the others.

The Orientals eye me suspiciously. The Latinos eye me contemptuously. The Ukrainians avert their gazes, muttering ancient curses. The melting pot in action. Sometimes I think about moving to Iceland, where everyone looks alike, has the same names, and the only problems are vicious weather, alcoholism, and suicide. (Goldberg [1994] 1997, 11–12)

He describes the strict separation of ethnic groups and their hatred, but also their various interesting collaborations with and against each other. For him, New York City is not a melting pot of ethnicities, but rather a pluralist

72   CARMEN BIRKLE

society in which ethnic groups live side by side without merging. Food becomes a strong ethnic marker and a means for the preservation of distinct ethnicities, but it also turns into a transethnic commodity, since Lenny Schneider, for example, frequents Chinese, Italian, Russian, and many other ethnic restaurants. In this sense, his body becomes the site of transculturation; he literally swallows ethnicities. In this context, he chooses his ethnic affiliations voluntarily, but the connections remain on a superficial level and do not necessarily imply ethnic understanding. The space Lenny Schneider occupies in New York City is marked by its cultural openness, but also by the reemergence of his own Jewish background and past, which, at least until the solution of the case, take precedence over any other ethnic influences.

With this new case, Lenny becomes "the Hebrew gum shoe, the Shylock of Sherlocks" (Goldberg [1994] 1997, 27–28), in the words of a former professor of physics and computer science who now sells the best frankfurters in Manhattan. Goldberg here evokes Shakespeare's famous character Shylock in *The Merchant of Venice*, who is the prototype of the greedy Jewish businessman but ultimately also the Jewish victim. This evocation points to the fact that Schneider is forced to confront his own Jewishness and the Jewish collective past in order to solve the case. Yet, although Schneider is drawn into this historical context, he largely remains emotionally detached. Schneider's search for Mueller takes him to the Public Library to look for books about Nazis who came to the United States to live underground with new identities, but the books have been removed, a sign of the fear of Nazis still in the 1990s. He remembers seeing Jewish people with concentration camp number tattoos as a constant reminder for American Jews of what they did not experience because they were in the right place at the right time—in short, a reminder of their survivors' guilt. Goldberg feels that "the survivors were a rebuke and a lesson to us. I send money to Simon Wiesenthal, but not enough" (interview). With the help of Professor Feeney, Schneider explores some of the sources tracing Nazis in the United States and learns that both Mueller and Kaminsky entered the United States in 1946. His further research, conducted as an assimilated Jew and therefore as an insider-outsider-in-between figure, guides him as well as the reader through New York City's Jewish institutions such as the Rabbinical Association, which sheds doubts on the authenticity of a Rabbi LeVine who once gave Kaminsky an alibi. LeVine is also revealed to be an abuser of children while working at a center for Holocaust survivors and is recognized by the girl's mother as one of her camp torturers, but she drops dead when she sees him, so readers at that point can only speculate. Confirmation comes much later when Uncle Sol sees the picture, recognizes Mueller, and ventures out on his revenge tour.

OF SHERLOCKS, SHYLOCKS, AND THE SHOAH

In his search for Uncle Sol, Lenny Schneider encounters Lester Farkas, a camp survivor, who leads his own private war against Nazis, just as Gold does in Kellerman's *Sanctuary*, and who is connected to the Jewish Defense League. Farkas kidnaps Lenny and attempts to instill in him survivor's guilt:

> You assimilated Yids are so complacent. You never had to listen to your mother shrieking at night from death-camp nightmares. You never had to put your father to bed when he got too drunk to do it himself, and all the time he's jabbering away in Yiddish about watching his family die and being burnt. At least scum floats on top, Schneider. It doesn't sink, like shit. (Goldberg [1994] 1997, 162)

At the same time, he thus justifies his own crusade for justice against Nazi criminals and his use of Uncle Sol for locating Mueller: "[B]ecause the CIA let in so many Nazi scum, and because Jews like you no longer give a shit, justice has been aborted" (176–77). Schneider is kidnapped again, this time by Louie Carmine aka Lev Kaminsky. Saved by Farkas, he learns that Mueller's concentration camp tattoo was actually an SS tattoo:

> Mueller was SS, right? Well, the SS got a tattoo also: the Lightning SS, on their forearms. After the war, this became a real problem. The SS were war criminals, and they had this distinguishing mark. So, bunches of them faked a camp number, using the jagged esses as fours. You know, just lengthen the line of the S on the right side, and it passes for a four, especially if you aren't looking for it. These fuckers were real clever then, and they still are. (176)

In line with the hard-boiled tradition of American detective fiction, Uncle Sol finally tortures Kaminsky to death with Lenny Schneider as the observer condemning the Old Testament practice of "an eye for an eye." Mueller's intention to kill Uncle Sol when he visits him in the hospital in the disguise of a rabbi is prevented by Schneider.

The result of the novel is justice on all levels, but justice in the form of revenge is also questioned through the protagonist Lenny Schneider. Goldberg unfolds the complexity of the Holocaust and its consequences in various character types such as the Nazi criminal (Mueller), the Jewish collaborator (Kaminsky), the Jewish survivor (Uncle Sol, Farkas), and the assimilated Jews with their survivors' guilt (Schneider). He condemns the crimes of the Holocaust; additionally, he exposes how these crimes are perpetuated in the United States, for example, in Kaminsky's abuse of young girls. The Holocaust becomes the main constituent of memory, a collective memory (see Maurice Halbwachs in Assmann 1999, 34–35) that all share and deal with in different ways. Individual or communicative memory (see Assmann 1999, 50) of those directly affected by the Holocaust is embedded in the larger context of cultural memory in which those who have not experienced the Holocaust personally are forced to participate. Lenny's Jewish background automatically makes him a member of the group of Holocaust survivors. How individual memory can be turned into collective and organized memory can be seen in Uncle Sol, who finds his equivalent in the highly organized Farkas group.

An important element of both individual and collective memory is the camp tattoo with which certain roles and experiences are forever inscribed onto the body. The tattoo as symbol of Jewish suffering is here opposed to the SS tattoo. Tattoos as signs, however, are also subject to manipulation or to a deferring of signification so that Mueller can turn his SS tattoo into a Jewish one. Borders between markers become fluid, unreliable, a means for disguise, and a guide for the misreading of identity. A detective novel, however, depends on the correct interpretation of clues, and thus Lenny Schneider, because of the information received by Farkas, recognizes Mueller in disguise. Just like these visual reminders of the Holocaust, inherited memory is also a determination and cannot be rejected, ignored, suppressed, or manipulated: "Take Farkas. His parents' nightmares informed his life. I don't know what he might have been if he had grown up to typical suburban Jewish life" (Goldberg [1994] 1997, 209).

As in Kemelman's Rabbi Small novels, Goldberg's *Served Cold* depicts women as remaining in the background. Lenny's ex-wife Sue is relevant for the solution of the case, but only as a person who is good for sex and for discussing cases with because "she is smart and intuitive" (Goldberg [1994] 1997, 50). Although Lenny Schneider is not a sex maniac and Goldberg hardly ever portrays sex scenes directly because, as he says, "sex is hard for me to write about. It embarrasses me as I write it" (Goldberg 2000), women are reduced to their physical, sexual function most of the time. But in contrast to the hard-boiled novels by Chandler and Hammett, Lenny does not feel superior to women and has no need to subject them physically. Yet, Goldberg falls into another trap by characterizing women as sex-obsessed and a little crazy (ex-wife Sue), as Jewish mother figures (Melanie, Uncle Sol's grandniece, and Lou Goffin's daughter), and as victims (the abused girl and her mother). Both Sue and Melanie are strong women, but they do not contribute to the cases in any significant way and remain largely flat or, in Sue's case, slightly comic characters. The only female survivor in Goldberg's novel remains a Holocaust victim who dies when she is confronted with her past in the figure of Mueller. Death is also her daughter's choice, while all male survivors choose revenge in the form of actual killings. Goldberg's emphasis clearly lies in the depiction of physical action and of the protagonist as a character between traditional notions of femininity and masculinity.

Lenny Schneider is and simultaneously is not a hard-boiled detective, because he is constantly beaten himself but never really fights back. He needs Bruno as a bodyguard and is not able to defend himself against two amateur criminals who decide to beat him up. In contrast to the classic Chandler hero who tries to overcome his masculinity crisis through violence (Dietze 1997, 9), Lenny Schneider cannot find satisfaction in violence. Yet, violence is a leitmotif in Goldberg's *Served Cold*; corpses can be found in abundance. To alleviate the brutality, Goldberg turns Lenny Schneider into a humorous, sometimes almost "ghetto-humorous" and sarcastic type who has to take things lightly in order not to break down. Like the detectives in contemporary women writers' PI novels, Lenny Schneider is a first-person narrator and not only communicates his views of the cases to the readers but also introduces himself, as in an autobiography, with the words "I am born" (Goldberg [1994] 1997, 1) and "I was a conscientious objector during Vietnam, or at least I tried to be" (1), certainly not the typical introduction of a hard-boiled detective novel. Lenny Schneider continues to demystify his job: "As a private investigator, most of my work is extremely boring. Sometimes, I simply go through court records, or real estate records for my clients. Other times, I stake out buildings and carefully note who enters and leaves. I get to serve a lot of court papers" (3). In contrast, violence comes unexpectedly, is feared by Lenny Schneider, and is portrayed in all its ugliness; it is never idealized; victims have names. Revenge is practiced, but it is rejected by Goldberg as a solution for Holocaust survivors. Violence cannot undo violence, but produces more violence.

One of the final questions addresses the adequacy of the popular genre of detective fiction for the representation of Holocaust-related issues. While fictional accounts of the Holocaust were rejected in famous statements by Theodor Adorno and Elie Wiesel,[16] I argue that writing about the Holocaust serves various functions on both personal and collective levels, such as an individual's coming to terms with, structuring, and remembering but also reliving the past. In Holocaust literature, a community can preserve a shared memory in order to communicate this horrendous event to both Jews and non-Jews. Holocaust writing can also be a reminder of other forms of discrimination and annihilation, such as the destruction of Native Americans in the nineteenth century, and of Armenians in the early twentieth century, and many other atrocities motivated by the fear of and the desire for the destruction of the Other.

While there is a debate about the uniqueness of the World War II Holocaust, there is also a strong argument not to shut our eyes to structural similarities and dangerous developments all over the world. Although writing about the Holocaust in the popular genre of detective fiction implies a participation in what Norman Finkelstein has called the "Holocaust Industry," this genre also helps to confront a wider readership with the injustices of this past and their consequences in the present. Yet, what actually happened to these characters in *Served Cold*, affected by the Holocaust, remains partially hidden, unnamed, and perhaps even unnameable. Only Solomon's story as the witness of his family's murder is told, not by himself but by his nephew. Throughout the novel, Uncle Sol finds it hard to talk about his experiences, heavily ridden by the guilt of the survivor. What he experienced in Auschwitz remains unspoken, but is ultimately transformed into revenge. The woman who dies when confronted with her past never gets a chance to break the silence; her story remains untold. She even passes the status of victim on to her daughter, who, however, chooses to break the silence by communicating the guilt she felt, in believing she had caused her mother's death, by writing a suicide note (Goldberg [1994] 1997, 46). By naming the dangers of silence about Holocaust experiences, *Served Cold* thematizes and, at the same time, breaks this silence and awakens all those who deny the relevance of this historical event: "The memory of the Holocaust must be an illness, a mental disorder that we never cease to suffer from. Not only because of the crimes committed against the Jews, but because genocide will remain forever a possibility" (Ankersmit 1997, 62).

CONCLUSION

As the discussion of examples of Jewish American detective fiction has shown, this genre has few but nevertheless diverging and emerging proponents using autoethnography in order to dissolve the identification of Jews as Other. The historical image of Jews as victims is erased in all the novels discussed and is only evoked in passing by Goldberg when he calls his protagonist "the Shylock of Sherlocks" and when he describes the fate of the female Holocaust survivor. While both Kemelman and Kellerman use their novels for didactic purposes disguised as crime fiction, Goldberg is more concerned with the cultural-historical relevance of Judaism. For him, transculturation is a logical development for Jews within the cultural contact zone of New York City. At the same time, collective/cultural and individual memory prevents people from ever ignoring past aspects of their identities. While Kemelman does not address the Holocaust in any of his novels, it gradually emerges in the novels of Kellerman and Goldberg, parallel to the rise of Holocaust literature in general, particularly in the United States.

Gender and the distribution of gender roles are important in all three authors' novels. While Kemelman's amateur rabbi detective is married in order to make him free from any association with the loner in hard-boiled fiction and distinctly Jewish as opposed to the Catholic priest detectives, Kellerman's Peter Decker and Rina Lazarus struggle with the modern problems of a relationship based on equality; Goldberg's Lenny Schneider becomes the almost-loner who maintains family and other relationships but on an infrequent and loose basis. In the novels of the 1990s, gender is shown to be in transition; masculinity defined by violence is rejected; femininity is not restricted to the private and nurturing sphere. A transition can be noticed from the traditional image of the rabbi as a learned Jewish man via a homicide detective fighting violence but also the protector of womanhood to the PI loner, abhorring violence, loving sex, but unable to build lasting relationships. While women in Kemelman's and Goldberg's novels do not have an independent story to tell, Kellerman's Rina Lazarus does. Gender and Jewishness intermingle in all of the novels. They negotiate ideas of self and other, and reject notions of fixed identities, but still pose Judaism in its various manifestations as determining all Jewish characters' lives. Jewish ethnicity is clearly demarcated by its encounters with non-Jewish groups as well as by the interactions of the various branches of Judaism in cultural contact zones. Cultural encounters lead to the recognition of the relevance of gender and ethnicity as the only means for the solution of the crimes. Cultural knowledge informed by gender and Judaism is instrumental for an understanding of human behavior in both criminal and noncriminal terms.

Notes

In my essay I will not enter into the debate about the definition of Jewish American literature. I have chosen American detective fiction writers who are Jewish and who use Judaism in their novels not as background but as a vital and highly instrumental means in the solution of crimes. For a discussion of what Jewish literature is, see Wirth-Nesher (1994).

1. Before the 1960s, there was hardly any Jewish American detective fiction. In his article "Is This Any Job for a Nice Jewish Boy? (Jews in Detective Fiction)," Yaffe points out the Jewish detective Moe Finkelstein in Claire Boothe's 1940 play *Margin for Error* as the "first fullfledged Jewish detective" (1990, 23).

2. Roughly at the same time, Jerome Charyn writes detective novels in which he uses his "experience of a Jewish childhood in New York" as "a rich source of regional particularity," which serves "to root the rootlessness of his protagonists within a dense and concrete location" (Woolf 1988, 133). In his novels, Jewishness, however, is not instrumental in the solution of the crimes. Neither does it contribute to crime solution in Richard Lockridge's New York City novels with the Jewish detective Lieutenant "Nate" Shapiro (see Paul 1991, 203). The same is true for Arthur Lyons's novels (see Geherin 1985, 183). One of the earliest British American Jewish detective fiction (among other genres) writers was Israel Zangwill

(1864–1926) with his *The Big Bow Mystery* (1891) (see Priestman 1991, 106–11). Yaffe (1990) argued that for most Jewish detectives, their Jewishness does not play a major role and enumerates a large number of relevant authors.

3. In *Friday the Rabbi Slept Late* (1964).

4. In *Saturday the Rabbi Went Hungry* (1966), *Sunday the Rabbi Stayed Home* (1969), *Monday the Rabbi Took Off* (1972), *Tuesday the Rabbi Saw Red* (1973), *Wednesday the Rabbi Got Wet* (1976), *Thursday the Rabbi Walked Out* (1978), *Someday the Rabbi Will Leave* (1985), *One Fine Day the Rabbi Bought a Cross* (1987).

5. In *The Day the Rabbi Resigned* (1991).

6. In *That Day the Rabbi Left Town* (1996). Another series by Joseph Telushkin features the rabbi-detective Daniel Winter (*The Unorthodox Murder of Rabbi Wahl* [1987], *The Final Analysis of Dr. Stark* [1988]).

7. *The Innocence of Father Brown* (1911) is the first short-story collection with the detective Father Brown (see Binyon 1990, 64–65).

8. See Schlagel: "G. K. Chesterton introduced the prototype, Father Brown, to the genre in 1911. This tradition is still to be found in contemporary crime fiction: Ralph McInerny's parish priest, Father Roger Dowling of suburban Chicago; William X. Kienzle's Catholic priest, Father Robert Koesler of Detroit; and Charles Merrill Smith's Reverend Randolph of the Church of the Good Shepherd of San Francisco and Chicago" (1983, 101). Matthew Head's missionaries Dr. Mary Finney and Emily Collins as well as Leonard Holton's Father Joseph Bredder and Jane Dentinger's ex-Catholic Jocelyn O'Roarke could be added to the list. Ishmael Reed's hoodoo priest PaPa LaBas is only loosely connected to the amateur detective tradition.

9. Nicholas Welt is a professor of English and literature. He was "born" during a class Kemelman taught on style at a college. He attempted to show his students what kind of and how many logical conclusions could be drawn from one sentence. Yet, it still took Kemelman fourteen years to write his first Nicky Welt story published by *Ellery Queen's Mystery Magazine*. All of the Nicky Welt stories were collected in 1967 in *The Nine Mile Walk* published by Putnam's Sons.

10. See Yaffe's analysis of this novel (1990, 28–30).

11. Her nonfiction book *The Quality of Mercy* (1989) has allegedly been plagiarized by the producers of the movie *Shakespeare in Love*. Kellerman has a lawsuit pending. *Jupiter's Bones* (1999) deals with the return of a brilliant astrophysicist as the leader of a religious cult. *Stalker* (2000) features Decker's daughter Cynthia as a police officer.

12. Peter's crisis is different from that which Gabriele Dietze describes for the detective in hard-boiled novels: he who needs to assert himself through the submission of and domination over women (see Dietze, "Gender Topography of the Fifties," 1998, and *Hardboiled Woman,* 1997).

13. Kellerman uses every opportunity to convey historical, political, and religious information. She explains the transformations of the shrine from a Jewish shrine, to a Christian church, to a Muslim mosque. Today, it is a monument for all three religions (see Kellerman [1994] 1995, 308).

14. Another writer who should be introduced in this context is Kinky Friedman, a Jewish songwriter from Texas and author of numerous detective novels set in New York City on Vandam Street in Greenwich Village. Among his many novels are *Greenwich Killing Time* (1986), *Musical Chairs* (1991), *Blast from the Past* (1998), and *Spanking Watson* (1999), featuring the detective and first-person narrator Kinky, retired country music performer turned detective.

15. Winner of the 1995 Shamus Award for best original paperback fiction.

16. Elie Wiesel: "[T]here is no such thing as Holocaust literature—there cannot be. Auschwitz negates all literature as it negates all theories and doctrines; to lock it into a

OF SHERLOCKS, SHYLOCKS, AND THE SHOAH 79

philosophy means to restrict it. To substitute words, any words, for it is to distort it. A Holocaust literature? The very term is a contradiction" (1978, 197). Theodor Adorno: "Den Satz, nach Auschwitz noch Lyrik zu schreiben, sei barbarisch, möchte ich nicht mildern ..." (1974, 422).

WORKS CITED

Adorno, Theodor. [1974] 1998. *Noten zur Literatur*. Frankfurt am Main: Suhrkamp.

Ankersmit, F. R. 1997. "Remembering the Holocaust: Mourning and Melancholia." In *Reclaiming Memory: American Representations of the Holocaust*, edited by Pirjo Ahokas and Martine Chard-Hutchinson, 62–86. Turku: University of Turku.

Assmann, Jan. [1997] 1999. *Das kulturelle Gedächtnis: Schrift, Erinnerung und politische Identität in frühen Hochkulturen*. München: Beck.

Bhabha, Homi. 1990. "The Third Space: Interview with Homi Bhabha." In *Identity: Community, Culture, Difference*, edited by Jonathan Rutherford, 207–21. London: Lawrence and Wishart.

Binyon, T. J. 1990. *"Murder Will Out": The Detective in Fiction*. Oxford: Oxford University Press.

Dietze, Gabriele. 1997. *Hardboiled Woman: Geschlechterkrieg im amerikanischen Kriminalroman*. Hamburg: Europäische Verlagsanstalt.

———. 1998. "Gender Topography of the Fifties: Mickey Spillane and the Post-World War II Masculinity Crisis." *Amerikastudien/American Studies* 43, no. 4:645–56.

Finkelstein, Norman. 2000. *The Holocaust Industry: Reflections on the Exploitation of Jewish Suffering*. London: Verso.

Freese, Peter. 1992. *The Ethnic Detective: Chester Himes, Harry Kemelman, Tony Hillerman*. Essen: Die Blaue Eule.

Geherin, David. 1985. *The American Private Eye: The Image in Fiction*. New York: Frederick Ungar.

Goldberg, Ed. [1994] 1997. *Served Cold*. New York: Berkeley Prime Crime.

———. 2000. Interview with the author. 10 January.

Hollinger, David A. 1995. *Postethnic America: Beyond Multiculturalism*. New York: Basic Books.

Kellerman, Faye. [1994] 1995. *Sanctuary*. New York: Avon.

Kemelman, Harry. [1973] 1985. *Tuesday the Rabbi Saw Red*. New York: Fawcett Crest.

King, Margaret J., and Sheldon J. Hershinow. 1978. "Judaism for the Millions: Harry Kemelman's 'Rabbi Books.'" *MELUS* 5, no. 4:83–93.

Klein, Kathleen Gregory. 1988. *The Woman Detective: Gender and Genre*. Urbana: University of Illinois Press.

Lionnet, Françoise. 1989. *Autobiographical Voices: Race, Gender, Self-Portraiture*. Ithaca, N.Y.: Cornell University Press.

Mandel, Ernst. 1984. *Delightful Murder: A Social History of the Crime Story*. London: Pluto Press.

Marks, Jeffrey. 2000. "Meet the Author: An Interview with Faye Kellerman." www.mysterynet. com/fayekeelerman/authors.html (9 June 2000).

CARMEN BIRKLE

Neuhaus, Volker. 1975. "Father Brown und Rabbi Small." In *Teilnahme und Spiegelung: Festschrift für Horst Rüdiger*, edited by Beda Allemann, Erwin Koppen, and Dieter Gutzen, 548–69. New York: Walter de Gruyter.

Paul, Robert S. 1991. *Whatever Happened to Sherlock Holmes? Detective Fiction, Popular Theory, and Society*. Carbondale: Southern Illinois University Press.

Peters, Ellis, et al. 1990. "Religious Detective Fiction: A Symposium of Practitioners." In *Synod of Sleuths: Essays on Judeo-Christian Detective Fiction*, edited by Jon L. Breen and Martin H. Greenberg, 127–36. Metuchen, N.J.: Scarecrow Press.

Pratt, Mary Louise. 1992. *Imperial Eyes: Travel Writing and Transculturation*. London: Routledge.

———. 1996. "Arts of the Contact Zone." In *Ways of Reading: An Anthology for Writers*, edited by David Bartholomae and Anthony Petrosky, 528–42. Boston: St. Martin's Press, Bedford Books.

Priestman, Martin. 1991. *Detective Fiction and Literature: The Figure on the Carpet*. New York: St. Martin's Press.

Roth, Laurence. 1999. "Unraveling 'Intermarriage' in Faye Kellerman's Detective Fiction." In *Multicultural Detective Fiction: Murder from the "Other" Side*, edited by Adrienne Johnson Gosselin, 185–211. New York: Garland.

Schlagel, Libby. 1983. "Today the Rabbi Gets Looked At." *The Armchair Detective* 16, no. 1:101–9.

Schlesinger, Arthur M., Jr. [1991] 1998. *The Disuniting of America: Reflections on a Multicultural Society*. Revised and enlarged edition. New York: Norton.

Siebald, Manfred. 1998. "Jüdisch-amerikanische Literatur im 20. Jahrhundert zwischen *upward mobility* und *ancestral grief*." In *Jüdische Literatur und Kultur in Großbritannien und den USA nach 1945*, edited by Beate Neumeier, 95–121. Wiesbaden: Harrassowitz.

Sipe, A. W. Richards, and B. C. Lamb. 1994. "Divine Justice: William F. Love's Bishop Regan and Harry Kemelman's Rabbi Small." *The Armchair Detective* 27, no. 1 (winter): 58–61.

Soja, Edward W. 1996. *Thirdspace: Journeys to Los Angeles and Other Real-and-Imagined Places*. Cambridge, Mass.: Blackwell.

Taylor, Diana. 1991. "Transculturating Transculturation." In *Interculturalism and Performance: Writings from PAJ*, edited by Bonnie Marranca and Gautam Dasgupta, 60–74. New York: PAJ Publications.

Welsch, Wolfgang. 1999. "Transkulturalität: Zwischen Globalisierung und Partikularisierung." In *Interkulturalität: Grundprobleme der Kulturbegegnung*, edited by Studium generale der Johannes Gutenberg-Universität Mainz, 45–72. Mainz: Universität Mainz.

Wiesel, Elie. 1978. *A Jew Today*. Translated by Marion Wiesel. New York: Random House.

Wirth-Nesher, Hana, ed. 1994. *What Is Jewish Literature?* Philadelphia: Jewish Publication Society.

Woolf, Mike. 1988. "Exploding the Genre: The Crime Fiction of Jerome Charyn." In *American Crime Fiction: Studies in the Genre*, edited by Brian Docherty, 131–43. Houndmills, U.K.: Macmillan.

Yaffe, James. 1990. "Is This Any Job for a Nice Jewish Boy? (Jews in Detective Fiction)." In *Synods of Sleuths: Essays on Judeo-Christian Detective* Fiction, edited by Jon L. Breen and Martin H. Greenberg, 19–55. Metuchen, N.J.: Scarecrow Press.

Marketing Mystical Mysteries: Rudolfo Anaya's Mystery Trilogy

ANN-CATHERINE GEUDER

> The reader wants story and you're talking message; the reader may
> quickly leave you.
>
> —Rudolfo Anaya

W HEN ANAYA PUBLISHED HIS fiRST MYSTERY NOVEL IN 1995, IT WAS REGARDED AS a "radical departure from his previous publications" (Ponce 1998, 50). Ten years earlier he had dismissed this type of literature as boring (see Anaya and Nichols 1982, 77) and had rejected what he perceived as a retreat to formulas (see Anaya 1988, 197). Ever since his groundbreaking first novel *Bless Me, Ultima*, Anaya's fiction has been known for its mythopoesis and lyrical language. Indebted to C. G. Jung's emphasis on the collective unconscious, myths and symbolic references to American Indian, Asian, and Hispanic cultures underlie the action. The novels' protagonists go on a mystical journey and, in a rite of passage, find what Anaya calls their "authentic selves." These narratives of a spiritual bildungsroman are embedded in a New Mexican setting with lyrical descriptions of the landscape, drawing their strength from the traditions of their protagonist's Indo-Hispanic ancestors. Why, then, does Anaya decide to enter a formula genre that, especially in the U.S. tradition, is still famous for its hard-boiled protagonists and rough language? What effects does the mystery genre have on Anaya's writing?

In an attempt to answer these questions, I will focus on Anaya's novels *Zia Summer* (1995), *Rio Grande Fall* (1996), and *Shaman Winter* (1999). Since Anaya's new approach to genre could be a response to a modified attitude toward the role of the writer and his or her responsibilities in society, I will also explore his changing perspective as expressed in various interviews.

82 ANN-CATHERINE GEUDER

To engage in writing in a new genre not only entails changes for the author and his or her own style but also demands new publishing strategies. Publishers may have to promote the book differently; critics may have to adjust their evaluation criteria; and the new genre will have to appeal to an author's audience. How do publishers and critics deal with the fact that the author is already well known as an "ethnic writer" but is now placed in the market as a "mystery writer"? In which way do they mediate the novels to the final addressees—the readers? These interventions are significant for the texts' reception, because the perception the readers have of a book will not only determine whether they buy and read it but will also influence their reading experience.[1] Therefore, it will also be necessary to examine the publishers' advertising[2] of Anaya's novels, as well as the critics' reviews of the books.

MYSTERY, CULTURE, AND SPIRITUALITY

Zia Summer, Rio Grande Fall, and *Shaman Winter* form a trilogy, sharing the same setting (Alburquerque, using its historical spelling) and main characters. In addition, the battle of the protagonist against his archenemy continues throughout all three novels. As some of the mysteries in each novel remain unresolved, the reader has to turn to the sequel to find out how the mystery is ultimately resolved. But since the narrator summarizes the events of the previous book at the beginning of each subsequent book, the reader can understand each novel independently.

Each novel has a multilevel plot system. At the first level, there is the detective story, the murder cases that private eye Sonny Baca has to resolve; yet there is always a more complex crime that has national or international significance. At a second level, Sonny's spiritual coming of age is developed. The protagonist, a thirty-year-old Chicano, has lost contact with his cultural traditions and is finding his way "back home." Moreover, Sonny is in the process of discovering and accepting his shaman identity: he increasingly realizes that it is his duty to fight evil in the shape of Raven, the sorcerer. At a third level, the author offers cultural and historical information about the Nuevo Mexicanos. These three levels, although closely intertwined, are developed differently in each novel. While Sonny is trying to resolve his cases, he is also learning more about the spiritual world, especially the spiritual power within himself. The protagonist learns that the battle he is fighting on the detective level is connected with the archetypal battle—good versus evil—on the spiritual level. Therefore, his struggle against Raven has less and less to do with common crime. While Sonny is searching for clues, he reflects on the living conditions of the inhabitants of the Rio Grande valley and the changes that have come about in this area in the last decades. Through conversations with friends and neighbors he not only manages to solve the mystery cases, but also learns about the traditions of the Nuevo Mexicanos. In contrast to the protagonist of the classical detective novel, PI Sonny is not a loner who solves the mysteries by means of rational analysis; he also relies on his friends' spiritual advice. Without the help of his community he would not be able to solve his cases.

Zia Summer opens with the murder of Sonny Baca's cousin Gloria. She is found on her bed with her blood drained and a Zia sign inscribed around her navel. A sacrificial death? Since Gloria's mother does not trust the police, she puts Sonny in charge of the case. Soon, the PI realizes that more is involved than just a simple crime. Raven, the leader of the Zia sun cult, threatens to blow up a truck loaded with nuclear waste on its way to a storage site. On the sociopolitical level, this threat leads to reflections on the risks of producing nuclear waste. At the same time, on the detective level and on the spiritual level, Raven becomes the dangerous enemy that Sonny has to fight in order to save his life and, in the end, even the entire world. The community warns Sonny that Raven has more power than an ordinary man, that he is a sorcerer. Even though Sonny has some difficulty accepting this seemingly irrational viewpoint, he listens to his friends, reflects on their lessons, and learns to interpret their perspective in the sequels.

In the novel's finale, Sonny and his girlfriend, Rita, stop Raven from blowing up the truck, and Raven plunges into the canyon. His body, however, is never found, and he resurfaces in *Rio Grande Fall*. The novel opens at the traditional Balloon Fiesta in Alburquerque, where two people are murdered to divert attention from a major drug deal. The evidence points not only to Raven, but also to several CIA and FBI agents. On the sociopolitical level, the problem of drug trafficking and its connection to U.S. secret services is explored, and the problem of U.S. interference in the politics of Central America is addressed. Through Sonny's conversations with a Colombian journalist and with his friend Howard, the reader comes to understand that representatives of the U.S. government including FBI and CIA agents are involved in the drug business because they want to keep minorities under control: "Give the colored people enough crack to keep them poor and in misery. Fill the jails with them and convince the whites that all people of color are their enemies. Their object is to divide and conquer. Keep the colored people separated from the white world" (Anaya [1996] 1997, 288). At the same time, the CIA agents' involvement in narcotics traffic offers the narrator the chance to discuss U.S. involvement in the Central American civil wars of the 1980s.

After risking his life several times, Sonny finally discovers the murderers, only to fall into Raven's trap again. They torture him with a heart stimulator, and Sonny survives only with the help of his *Nagual*, his animal guardian spirit. On the spiritual level, Sonny has learned to summon his *Nagual*, a coyote, and to use its power. He has accepted his shaman power and wants to develop it so that he can fight Raven on the spiritual level as well.

Only several weeks have passed between the events of the second and the third novel, *Shaman Winter*. Sonny is confined to a wheelchair, still suffering from the effects of the torture. But his fight with Raven is not over: Raven enters Sonny's dreams and in this dreamworld kidnaps one of his female ancestors. At the same time, in the "real world," several young girls disappear, with all clues pointing to Raven. Sonny's spiritual guides warn him that Raven can kill him by erasing his history. In order to do this, he only needs to capture four of his female ancestors in the dreamworld and four young girls in the real world. To meet this challenge, Sonny learns how to create and control his dreams and begins to immerse himself more deeply in the history of the Nuevo Mexicanos. Implicit in this plot level is a critique of the official historiography that has only recorded the history of the conquerors and repressed the indigenous perspective.[3] Having developed his skills as a shaman, Sonny finally manages to fight Raven successfully in the dreamworld.

Raven is the ally of an ultra right-wing group, the Avengers, who plan to take over the government of the United States with the help of an atomic bomb they are attempting to build. The FBI and CIA are involved; nobody can be trusted. In contrast to the common fear that eastern countries might terrorize the U.S. with such a bomb, Anaya turns the threat inside out—the danger may also lurk within the United States:

> They've created a race war in this country. Whites are afraid of dark-skinned people, and the Blacks do not trust the whites. Now it's a population war, fed by fear of a mass migration from Latin America. In twenty years the majority population of this country is going to be colored, not white. But there's a check on the people promoting race war. The system they despise so much still works. They want to bring down the government, but democracy still works. People are smart enough to know they do not want white supremacists running the country, turning people into addicts. That fed into the class war they created. Now it's the bomb, viruses. (Anaya 1999a, 297)

Again, there is no real solution at the end of the novel. Raven has disappeared with the plutonium core of the bomb, and the Avengers go on with their plans. Sonny, however, has finally decided to settle down, marry Rita, and come to terms with what he has learned in the span of the three novels.

While the plot of *Zia Summer* integrates the mystery level with the sociopolitical, cultural, and historical levels successfully, the sequels increasingly lose sight of the mystery elements, and the cultural dimension remains relatively isolated from the main story. Especially in *Shaman Winter*, the structure of the three levels is less tight and thus is not as convincing as in the other novels. There is no murder in the real world, just in the dreamworld. The key to the mystery lies at this spiritual level. In fact, there is no real mystery, because from the very beginning Sonny's spiritual guides explain everything to him (and the reader). The battle between good and evil on the spiritual level has become the focus of attention. *Shaman Winter* deviates from the classic mystery plot that depends on the solving of a puzzle, thus forgoing the murder or detective mystery formula while retaining some elements of the suspense novel.

In addition, on the sociopolitical level the novel resembles a political thriller, where terrorist groups are trying to gain power while risking the safety of the whole world. This thriller formula adds elements of aggressive action to the mystery and helps to create tension (Landrum 1999, 27). Because of the overwhelming extension of evil, of corruptive forces that infiltrate the government and the secret services, the PI has no chance to actually solve his case and restore order. A political solution for national or even international problems is never offered. The resolution is on the spiritual level: Only if the people are in touch with their tradition and their community can the evil be fought and the universe kept in balance (see Anaya [1995] 1996, 184 and 322, and Anaya [1996] 1997, 313).

In emphasizing the cultural and spiritual elements of the novels and neglecting the mystery formulas, Anaya has not authored mysteries with an "ethnic touch" but ethnic novels with a "mystery touch." Ethnicity is performed on all three levels: in the description of the Nuevo Mexicanos' culture, the presentation of the spiritual worldview based on Native American and Mexican mythologies, and the solution of mysteries based on cultural and spiritual knowledge. Sonny's spiritual guides embody these factors, which help him to solve his cases on the detective as well as on the spiritual level.

In addition to their mentoring function, these guides represent the spiritual dimension of the Nuevo Mexicano community. Don Eliseo is a bearer of cultural traditions and spiritual knowledge, the collective identity of the Nuevo Mexicanos. The *curandera* Lorenza, another mentor, gains importance in the second and third novels, representing female spirituality, whereas Rita, Sonny's girlfriend and later wife, represents female physicality. Rita not only makes love to him, but nurses and feeds him without ever considering her own needs. Both Rita and Lorenza typify the narrator's

86 ANN-CATHERINE GEUDER

ideal of the Nueva Mexicana—wise, strong, beautiful, and absolutely giving:

> Daughters of the old Hispanos, Mexicanos, and Indians of the valley, a blend of genes that over the centuries had produced what Sonny thought were the most beautiful women on earth. The full-bodied, brown-skinned Nueva Mexicana woman, a mestiza with the beauty of the earth and sky in her soul. (Anaya [1996] 1997, 5)

Women play a central role in the trilogy, as Sonny continually seeks help and advice from them. But they remain one-dimensional types.

Another essential feature of Nuevo Mexicano culture is marked by Anaya's use of Spanish, especially in Sonny's thoughts and his communication with the Nuevo Mexicano community. Most of these entries are short, so that the hegemony of the English language is never truly challenged and the text can be comprehended by those who do not understand Spanish. These entries not only serve as "ethnic markers" but also to increase the suspense for monolingual readers: "[T]heir disorientation functions as an element in creating suspense; if they knew Spanish, the text would not be half as intriguing" (Rudin 1996, 216).

THE PRIMACY OF COMMUNICATION:
ANAYA ON HIS ROLE AS A WRITER

When Anaya's first novel, *Bless Me, Ultima,* won the "Premio Quinto Sol" prize in 1971, the critics' reactions were divided between those who praised it for its "fine storytelling, superb craftsmanship, and the artistic and philosophic dignity that it brought to Chicano literature" (Márquez 1982, 36) and those who criticized it for having no bearing on the issues of the Chicano Movement and no answers to the problems the Chicanos face (see Monleón 1981, 13). Anaya rejected any demands to write politically motivated literature. For him writing is a way of connecting to the subconscious collective memory from which he draws his creativity. Any conscious attempt to write politically motivated fiction would disturb the creative act (see Anaya [1979] 1990, 424; Anaya 1975, 4; and Anaya 1980, 191–92).

During the 1980s, Anaya's attitude toward the relation between literature and politics changed. He now regarded it as the writer's responsibility to discuss issues concerning the Chicano community: "I think probably the only way we respond to some of these questions, critical questions if we're going to exist as a culture, is in novels that carry that social-political impact and perhaps allow the public to think on those questions that are crucial" (Anaya [1986] 1990, 62). He became concerned with the question of

MARKETING MYSTICAL MYSTERIES 87

how to communicate with people outside academia as well as how to convey political issues without putting the reader off: "The reader wants story and you're talking message; the reader may quickly leave you" (62).

He has since focused primarily on two goals: to preserve the Nuevo Mexicano culture and to teach his community, especially the younger generation, the traditions and values of their culture (see Anaya 1990, 62; and Anaya 1999c, 64). In order to start a discussion about solutions for global problems (Anaya [1995] 1998, 168), he feels obliged to transmit his spiritual values to others. In the face of growing global violence and disorder, he strongly believes in the healing power of spiritual awareness. Thus he suggests liberating "people by having them become their most true selves, their authentic selves, to find their deepest potential" (Anaya 1992, 248–49).

Exchanging ideas and experiences as well as transmitting values, customs, and beliefs are the central function of storytelling. In the modern world, the writer has become the storyteller for the reading community. Anaya sees himself as one of these storytellers, similar to don Eliseo, as a bearer of collective memory. The writer can also be compared to a shaman, who in a process of mediation, creates a vision, a story, to heal the people (see Anaya 1999b, 159 and Anaya 1989, 231).

The primacy of communication (apart from economic and other reasons) might have been his motivation for choosing a major publishing house. But the question of why he decided to write mystery novels still remains. Years before their publication, Anaya talked about the three novels discussed above, but did not refer to them as mysteries. Instead, he grouped them together with *Alburquerque* as a quartet "based on the city of Alburquerque" (Anaya [1992] 1998, 152). Only after publishing *Zia Summer* did he refer to the novel as a murder mystery and announce a series on Sonny Baca (see Anaya [1995] 1998, 175; Anaya [1997] 1998, 178; and Anaya 1999b, 153). Therefore, his publisher may have suggested labeling the Sonny Baca novels murder mysteries, probably calculating that they could promote and sell the book better in the mystery sector. Because the mystery sector is provided with a well-oiled infrastructure (bookstores, clubs, newsletters, and so on), advantages arise from positioning a title in this specialized niche. Anaya tolerated the promotion of his books as mysteries, but later he felt forced to stress that he never intended to write a perfect murder mystery in the first place and therefore to restrict himself to its generic formulas. Instead, he chose to use the genre for his own purposes: "I didn't think so much of following the prescriptions of the detective genre. I was in part learning what the murder mystery is all about, but was more interested in conveying a cultural context, a tradition, a history" (Anaya [1997] 1998, 178). Which role, then, did the publishers play in positioning the three novels?

Introducing Anaya into the Mystery Field: The Publishers

In the early 1990s, Warner Books offered Anaya a six-figure book contract and in 1994 reissued *Bless Me, Ultima* and *Alburquerque* in mass market paperback editions. With *Zia Summer*, for the first time Warner Books not only published an Anaya novel in a first edition and introduced it to the market, but they also ventured into a new sector of the market. Since the publishers categorized *Zia Summer* as "mystery/general," they had to build up a new audience as well as reassure the former readers that they would not be disappointed by the new direction Anaya's writing had taken.

Warner Books's website on Anaya only offers scant information on the author.[4] Remarkably, the biographic text does not refer directly to Anaya's ethnic or regional origin. The only clues given are the site of his university (Albuquerque) and his first award, the Premio Quinto Sol National Chicano Literary Award. Readers who want more information about the different titles can click specific links, but will fail to find more substantial information if they do so. The main objective of the publisher is to position Anaya as a successful, critically acclaimed author who offers something very specific, namely a portrait of the Hispanic Southwest—more specifically, New Mexico. The book covers convey the image of a very successful author with a special flavor; this is supported by an endorsement from the acclaimed mystery writer Tony Hillerman, who hails Anaya as the "godfather and guru of Chicano literature."

But the publishers have to convince Anaya's former readers that his literary reputation remains unchanged. Thus, for example, they cite the *Denver Post*, which promises that his mysteries "won't disappoint fans" (back cover of *Zia Summer*). The Internet presentation of the first mystery novel starts with a comparison of Anaya to Hillerman and is very similar in approach: "Rudolfo Anaya's *Zia Summer* will be to Nuevo Mexicanos what Tony Hillerman's novels are to the Pueblo Indians."[5] The comparison is tempting because it implies authentic ethnic depiction (even though Hillerman's significance to the Pueblo community is not clarified). However, the publishers do not want to promote Anaya as ethnic or representative of a minority, because that might weaken his mainstream position. Therefore, they promote him as an author who adds an ethnic or Southwestern touch to mainstream stories.

Ethnicity is emphasized even less in the publishers' advertising for the novels. The cultural background is just that—background. Except for the place (Alburquerque) and the ethnic origin of the protagonist (Chicano), the cultural context of the novel is not mentioned. Ethnicity is just an ingredient adding a bit of spice to the mystery.

MARKETING MYSTICAL MYSTERIES

To get the potential readers' attention, the publishers emphasize a whole range of ominous elements: black magic, drugs, corruption. They all threaten to destroy not only Sonny, but also Alburquerque and perhaps even the entire world. The spiritual world is presented as a threat ("bad blood," "black magic," "evil witches") and thus described in notable contrast to the positive image of Nuevo Mexicano spirituality that Anaya renders throughout his novels. While he illustrates Sonny's spiritual quest for self and, simultaneously, his own spirituality, the publishers' text reduces the mythical content to superstitious fears and bizarre cults.

The publishers changed their publication strategy with the publication of *Shaman Winter*. Officially, it is still marketed as a mystery novel—both the front and the back cover even announce Anaya's "most exciting mystery yet." But in the summary on the book's cover and in the online catalog, the spiritual level of the novel is the primary focus, while the cultural and mystery levels get no attention. Expectations are aroused by reference to the dangerous battle that Sonny has to fight against Raven and other supernatural elements—a New Age fantasy novel instead of a mystery.

One can ultimately conclude that the publishers are promoting the books as "mystical mysteries," silencing the cultural elements of the texts and distorting their spiritual worldview. Political elements that are mentioned on the cover of the first novel are excluded in the sequels' descriptions. In promoting *Zia Summer* the tension between mystery and mysticism is resolved in favor of the mystery aspect; in *Shaman Winter* it is resolved in favor of mysticism, a mysticism that is presented without reference to its Mexican and Pueblo Indian cultural background. Thus, even though the publishers are trying to sell the trilogy by emphasizing its specific ethnic character, the "flavor of Hispanic New Mexico," they exclude the ethnic elements from the description of the book and reduce the trilogy to a series of "mystifying-and mystical-adventure[s]."[6]

MEDIATING BETWEEN BOOK AND READER: THE REVIEWS

Although the publishers try to guide the critics' judgment by means of promotional materials, so the first impression a critic gets of a book is the publishers' blurb, reviewers seem remarkably unimpressed by these strategies. Reviewers of *Zia Summer* highlight the aspects they are familiar with from Anaya's former writing, expecting to find them again in his new novel. Thus, they do not read the mystery novel in the context of the mystery genre but in the context of the author's reputation. And this author is famous for his "trademark spirituality" (Niño 1995) or "trademark alchemy" (*Publishers Weekly* 1995)—as if he were producing a brand-name product.

In several of the reviews, no information is given about the author and his previous fiction. Usually, the critics position the author as a leading Chicano writer, emphasizing his ethnic background with reference to Indo-Hispanic spirituality or by using the occasional Spanish expression. *Publishers Weekly* (1995), for example, refers to the blending of "Spanish, Mexican and Indian cultures to evoke the distinctively fecund spiritual terrain of his part of the Southwest."

In the majority of the favorable reviews, the mystery plot is only perceived as a pretext for the "real" story that takes place on the cultural and spiritual levels (see Stasio 1995, 15; Barrientos 1996, 3). Often, the mystery novel is understood as a strategy to transmit a cultural or political message. It seems that these critics often use the novel to voice and impose their own cultural or political viewpoint. Thus, they do not evaluate the text in a literary but in their own political and cultural context (see Johnston 1996, 64–65; Davis-Undiano 1999, 106). Some critics even openly admit that they would trash the novel if it were not for its strategic or documentary value. "Nevertheless, in spite of the books' series of plot inconsistencies, obvious conclusions, and usual menagerie of bad syntax and grammar, Anaya's cultural and historical survey of Albuquerque is rewarding" (Streng 1997, 179; see also *Publishers Weekly* 1996, 73). Others, who have read the novels in the context of Anaya's former literary production, give unfavorable reviews because of their changed style and recommend reading Anaya's former books instead (see Barrientos 1996 and the review of *Shaman Winter* in the *Arizona Republic* 2000 online edition). One of the few critics who analyze *Zia Summer* primarily in a mystery context is Tom Miller from the *Washington Post*. He praises the novel for its likable detective, well-paced action, and convincing dialogues, but criticizes its thriller elements as too predictable. It thus "doesn't work as suspense" (1995, 5).

Only a few critics have praised the novels (especially *Zia Summer*) for their "multidimensional" character and regard the combination of mystery and spirituality as an especially gratifying mixture (see Niño 1995, 1611; Gaughan, 1996, 16; Bellver Saez 1996, 403). But even they prefer to focus on the cultural level of the novel. For example, Pilar Bellver Saez praises *Zia Summer* as an "original contribution to the murder-mystery genre," because she regards the deviations from the genre formula as an enrichment. She does not judge the novel by using criteria of the mystery genre, but situates it in the context of Chicano literature: "Anaya skillfully transforms the traditional detective novel into a novel that addresses the broader question of Mexican-American identity" (1996, 403).

Interestingly, many critics do not even consider *Shaman Winter*, the last novel of the mystery trilogy, a murder mystery but rather a mystical fantasy or science fiction (see *Kirkus Review* 1998; *Arizona Republic* 2000). They reject the mystery classification by the publisher as a "plain-vanilla label" that does not account for the fantasy elements (*Arizona Republic* 2000) and try to correct the genre categorization.

CONCLUSION

In a 1997 interview, Anaya quotes his wife as saying: "You really are not writing murder mysteries, you're kind of using the elements of the genre to do what you have always done" (Anaya [1997] 1998, 178). In fact, it might make more sense to classify the novels as spiritual bildungsromans, primarily using the suspenseful elements of the mystery genre to ensure the readers' attention. In doing so, Anaya wants to address general issues that he regards as crucial, such as environmental, sociopolitical, and cultural concerns. In addition, he tries to teach the younger generation of Nuevo Mexicanos about their traditions and values, seeking to transmit his spiritual philosophy of life in order to help people find their "authentic selves" and achieve "harmony of the soul" (Anaya 1999a, 407). Because Anaya presumes that the readers do not want to be preached to, he tries to captivate their attention by using suspense and mystery elements. Publishers, however, who assume that it is to their advantage to tout the novels as mysteries, stress the mystery level while ignoring the cultural elements and misrepresenting the novels' spirituality. Many critics try to correct this misrepresentation in their reviews, but since they focus on the cultural and spiritual level, they tend to neglect the mystery character. These contradicting presentations may affect the reader's initial perception of the novels. Yet, ultimately, it will be the quality of the reading experience that decides whether or not Anaya has successfully combined suspense with content.

NOTES

1. See Philippe Lejeune (1994), whose concept of a pact between author and reader helps to explain the dynamics of the author-reader relationship. See also Gérard Genette's *Paratexte*, which serves as a theoretical basis for this text. A paratext is the author's and/or publisher's text that surrounds the main text and transforms the text in a book. This "appendage" is a zone of transaction, where author and publisher can have an effect on the reader and his or her mode of reception (1992, 10).

2. The texts of the book covers and of the online catalog serve as my sources.

3. This critical point of view is reflected in conversations between Sonny and Lorenza. In these conversations and in the dream sequences, the novel retells New Mexican history

from an indigenous and female perspective, emphasizing the value of oral tradition. Official history is refuted and an alternative historiography is proposed as a strategy of resistance.

4. The following information was taken from www.twbookmark.com/authors/45/936.html (28 October 2000).

5. This information was obtained from the website of *Zia Summer*, mass market paperback edition: www.twbookmark.com/books/71/0446518433/index.html (28 October 2000).

6. This information can be obtained from the website of *Rio Grande Fall*, mass market paperback edition: www.twbookmark.com/books/2/0446604860/index.html (28 October 2000).

Works Cited

Anaya, Rudolfo A. [1972] 1973. *Bless Me, Ultima*. Berkeley: Quinto Sol.

———.1975. "Plática con Rudy Anaya." Interview. *Caracol* 1, no. 7:3–4.

———. [1979] 1990. "Myth and the Writer: A Conversation with Rudolfo Anaya." By David Johnson and David Apodaca. In *Rudolfo A. Anaya: Focus on Criticism*, edited by César A. González-T., 414–38. La Jolla, Calif.: Lalo Press.

———.1980. Interview with Juan Bruce-Novoa. In *Chicano Authors: Inquiry by Interview*, edited by Juan Bruce-Novoa, 183–202. Austin: University of Texas Press.

———. [1986] 1990. Interview by John F. Crawford. In *This Is About Vision: Interviews with Southwestern Writers*, edited by William Balassi, John F. Crawford, and Annie O. Esturoy, 83–93. Albuquerque: University of New Mexico Press.

———.1988. "The Myth of Quetzalcoatl in a Contemporary Setting: Mythical Dimensions/Political Reality." *Western American Literature* 23, no. 3:195–200.

———.1989. "Aztlán: A Home without Boundaries." In *Aztlán: Essays on the Chicano Homeland*, edited by Rudolfo A. Anaya and Francisco A. Lomelí, 230–41. Albuquerque, N. Mex.: Academia/El Norte Publications.

———.1992. Interview by Feroza Jussawalla. In *Interviews with Writers of the Post-Colonial World*, conducted and edited by Feroza Jussawalla and Reedway Dasenbrock, 245–55. Jackson: University Press of Mississippi.

———. [1992] 1994. *Alburquerque*. New York: Warner Books.

———. [1992] 1998. "Interview with Rudolfo Anaya." By R. S. Sharma. In Dick and Sirias 1998, 142–52.

———. [1995] 1996. *Zia Summer*. New York: Warner Books.

———. [1995] 1998. "A Conversation with Rudolfo Anaya." Interview by Laura Chavkin. In Dick and Sirias 1998, 164–76.

———. [1996] 1997. *Rio Grande Fall*. New York: Warner Books.

———. [1997] 1998. "An Interview with Rudolfo Anaya." By Bruce Dick and Silvio Sirias. In Dick and Sirias 1998, 177–85.

———.1999a. *Shaman Winter*. New York: Warner Books.

———.1999b. "*Bless Me, Ultima* at Twenty-Five Years: A Conversation with Rudolfo Anaya." By Robert C. Dash et al. *The Americas Review* 25:150–63.

———.1999c. "A Passion for History." Interview with Rudolfo A. Anaya. By Martha Espinoza. *Hispanic,* September, 64.

MARKETING MYSTICAL MYSTERIES 93

Anaya, Rudolfo A., and John Nichols. 1982. "A Dialogue: Rudolfo Anaya/John Nichols." *Puerto del Sol* 17:61–85.

Barrientos, Tanya. 1996. "Rudolfo Anaya's Simmering Mystery Is a Recipe That Failed." Review of *Rio Grande Fall,* by Rudolfo Anaya. *Chicago Tribune,* 25 September, CN-3.

Bellver Saez, Pilar. 1996. Review of *Zia Summer,* by Rudolfo Anaya. *World Literature Today,* spring, 403.

Davis-Undiano, Robert Con. 1999. Review of *Shaman Winter,* by Rudolfo Anaya. *Hispanic,* January, 106.

Dick, Bruce, and Silvio Sirias, eds. 1998. *Conversations with Rudolfo Anaya.* Jackson: University Press of Mississippi.

Gaughan, Thomas. 1996. Review of *Rio Grande Fall,* by Rudolfo Anaya. *Booklist,* 1 September, 16.

Genette, Gérard. 1992. *Paratexte.* Frankfurt: Campus.

Johnston, Beatriz. 1996. Review of *Zia Summer,* by Rudolfo Anaya. *Hispanic,* March, 64–65.

Landrum, Larry. 1999. *American Mystery and Detective Novels: A Reference Guide.* Westport, Conn.: Greenwood Press.

Lejeune, Philippe. 1994. *Der autobiographische Pakt.* Frankfurt: Suhrkamp.

Márquez, Antonio. 1982. "The Achievement of Rudolfo A. Anaya." In *The Magic of Words: Rudolfo A. Anaya and His Writings,* edited by Paul Vassallo, 33–52. Albuquerque: University of New Mexico Press.

Miller, Tom. 1995. "Bad Blood in New Mexico." *The Washington Post,* 14 May, 5.

Monleón, José. 1981. "Mitólogos y Mitómanos: Mesa redonda con Alurista, R. Anaya, M. Herrera Sobek, A. Morales, y H. Viramontes." *Maize* 4, no. 3–4:6–23.

Niño, Raúl. 1995. Review of *Zia Summer,* by Rudolfo Anaya. *Booklist,* 15 May, 1610–11.

Ponce, Mary Helen. 1998. "Latino Sleuths: Hispanic Mystery Writers Make Crime Pay." *Hispanic,* May, 44–52.

Review of *Rio Grande Fall,* by Rudolfo Anaya. 1996a. *Kirkus Reviews,* 15 July, 1004.

Review of *Rio Grande Fall,* by Rudolfo Anaya. 1996b. *Publishers Weekly,* 29 July, 73.

Review of *Shaman Winter,* by Rudolfo Anaya. 1998. *Arizona Republic.* www.elibrary.com (6 April 2000).

Review of *Shaman Winter* by Rudolfo Anaya. 1998. *Kirkus Reviews,* 1 December, 1696.

Review of *Zia Summer,* by Rudolfo Anaya. 1995. *Publishers Weekly,* 10 April, 56.

Rudin, Ernst. 1996. *Tender Accents of Sound: Spanish in the Chicano Novel in English.* Tempe, Ariz.: Bilingual Press/Editorial Bilingüe.

Stasio, Marilyn. 1995. Review of *Zia Summer,* by Rudolfo Anaya. *New York Times Book Review,* 2 July, 15.

Streng, R. L. 1997. Review of *Zia Summer,* by Rudolfo Anaya. *Western American Literature* 32, no. 2:179.

Warner Books "*Rio Grande Fall,* mass market paperback edition." Online catalog. www.twbookmark.com/books/2/0446604860/index.html (28 October 2000).

Warner Books "Rudolfo Anaya." Online catalog. www.twbookmark.com/authors/45/936/index.html (28 October 2000).

Warner Books "*Shaman Winter,* hardcover edition." Online catalog. www.twbookmark.com/books/8/0446523747/index.html (28 October 2000).

Warner Books "*Shaman Winter,* mass market paperback edition." Online catalog. www.twbook mark.com/books/20/0446608017/index.html (28 October 2000).

Warner Books "*Zia Summer,* mass market paperback edition." Online catalog. www.twobook mark.com/books/71/0446518433/index.html (28 October 2000).

Part II:
Comparing Ethnic Identities

Detectives, Hoodoo, and *Brujería:* Subverting the Dominant U.S. Cultural Ethos

CARMEN FLYS-JUNQUERA

WORKS OF FICTION CAN REPRESENT BOTH THE IDEOLOGICAL POSITION OF AN ARTIST in relation to the cultural traditions of his or her ethnic, racial, and national community as well as the imaginative strategies for resolving real conflicts and problems in that community. They are, therefore, in the case of artists committed to their community, essential to the reinvention and celebration of the repressed history and culture of minority groups. Many artistic productions also reveal the creative syncretism of combining cultures and endowing old images with new meanings, subverting oppressive systems and creating new metaphors as part of the emancipatory cultural expression and struggles of a group. Therefore, it is only logical that Peter Freese, in his study of ethnic detective fiction, would claim that when the detective belongs "to a community whose history, values, and way of life differ from those of the so-called mainstream, his or her story inadvertently turns into . . . a comment on the challenges of everyday life in a 'multicultural' society" (1992, 9–10). The detectives and, of course, their creators become cultural mediators. It is in this light that I wish to examine the elements of hoodoo and *brujería* in contemporary African American and Chicano detective fiction, focusing on the portrayal of alternative belief systems, particularly that of folk beliefs and so-called superstition that reveal a different worldview.

The traditional detective genre, both the classical armchair and the hard-boiled version, portray the European American worldview based on the Judeo-Christian tradition. As many anthropologists have noted, throughout the centuries each culture and civilization has developed its own distinctive religious practices, often adding to a common foundation those customs, rites, and practices that harmonize with their peculiar view of the universe and the supernatural. Anthropologist Margaret Murray, in *The God of the Witches,* argued that the appearance of witches and other versions of the occult in Europe were the result of the lingering adherents of diverse pagan religions being displaced by Christianity. When a new religion took root, the gods of the old faith became the devils of the new. Similarly, when two different cultures came into contact, the gods of the conquered or colonized peoples were often repressed and demonized by the dominating culture. Yet, as history has illustrated time and time again, the old mixes with the new, and different groups of people develop syncretic beliefs that combine elements of the cultures in contact.

This is clearly the case in hoodoo, a New World transformation of religious elements from many African sources. Although the most visual and well-known features of hoodoo are its ceremonial arts, John Roberts emphasizes the web of intercontinuity in hoodoo as being composed of important philosophical worldviews shared by African Americans. Roberts points out that among these elements is the recognition of a higher power: belief in ancestralism, divination, and animism; belief in a hierarchical chain of existence centered on the human being and in the importance of a full metaphysical attitude for happiness (1989, 76). Likewise, when the Spanish culture came into contact with the diverse Indian cultures of the New World, other syncretic combinations took place, giving way to the traditions of *brujería* and *curanderismo*. Simmons argues that although many of the details in the practice of witchcraft came from Europe, the "belief in the craft itself is aboriginal" (1974, 12). These folk beliefs, as Trotter and Chavira point out, have roots in Judeo-Christian beliefs; early Arabic medicine combined with the Greek humoral medicine, which was revived during the Spanish Renaissance; medieval European witchcraft; and Native American religious beliefs and herbal lore. Simmons points out that one of the ways in which the Hispanic and Indian cultures, which had intermingled, coped with "the aggressive intrusion of 'Anglos'" was through witchcraft and supernaturalism, which were disparaged by the invaders (Trotter and Chavira 1981, xii). Although elements of the European beliefs of the dominant peoples can be found at the origin of both hoodoo and *brujería*, the other aspects that pertained to the specific cultural elements of the African slaves or the Native American population and that represented their religious and sociophilosophical view were precisely those not accepted by the colonizing class. These beliefs were either repressed, declared heretical, or ridiculed as witchcraft or superstition.

This rejection by the dominant Eurocentric tradition of the United States still holds and is very often one of the first elements discarded in the process of acculturation. Acceptance of the Judeo-Christian tradition as well as of the rational, empirical, and scientific methods becomes synonymous with education, assimilation, and, finally, Americanism. What this paper explores, then, is the representation of these alternative belief systems as characteristics of ethnic pride and identity in the detective fiction of a number of African American and Chicano writers. The inclusion of hoodoo, *brujería,* or *curanderismo* is found to varying degrees in many of the writers of ethnic detective fiction. For my purposes here, I am defining African American hoodoo or the Chicano belief in *brujería* and *curanderismo* as the combination of folk beliefs of each ethnic group, including but not limited to religious rites and practices, witchcraft, folk healing, animism, ancestralism, belief in spirits, clairvoyance, dream visions, and conjuring.[1] My intention is not the precise definition or description of these folk beliefs, but their portrayal in the detective fiction discussed. I will center the discussion on the African American writers Walter Mosley, Barbara Neely, and Ishmael Reed and the Chicano writers Lucha Corpi and Rudolfo Anaya.

In the detective novels of these five writers we can find many subversive interventions, some of which have been studied in isolated texts. To the best of my knowledge, no comprehensive or comparative study has been published.[2] Many of the deviations from the traditional hard-boiled formula affect the character of the detective persona. Among them, we can note, for example, the manifest racial or ethnic pride that results in frequent denunciation of racism, discrimination, stereotyping, or calling for ideological/political involvement; ecological awareness; the feminist point of view in Neely and Corpi; the use of vernacular language and cultural customs, foods, and music; the rewriting of history; the alteration of the narrative pace; the special use of retardation and digression to subvert the primacy of the criminal plot; the deliberate resistance to narrative expectations that produce readerly "incompetence"; the openness of the ending, resisting the conventional neat resolution and hinting that problems and injustice will continue; and the subtle questioning of the comfortable detachment found in an isolated and ritualized murder and its legal solution.

The cultural ethos portrayed by the classic hard-boiled detective novel is that of the dominant Anglo middle-class urban society. Detective fiction, according to Porter, projects the image of a given social order and its implied value system. It reinforces the need for policing, law, and order. It is structured on binary oppositions of good and evil, asking the reader to side with the good one. In doing so, the genre promotes the heroization of the agent of surveillance of the culture, the police or the private investigator. Hühn points out that the crime, which the police cannot solve, acts as a "destabilizing event, because the system of norms and rules regulating life in the community has proved powerless" (1987, 452). Often the genre, particularly the hard-boiled version, reveals widespread corruption, both of society, politicians, and the police force, but the detective becomes the moral barometer, the individualistic loner who will restore the established societal order. It is precisely the detective narrative, by restoring the disrupted social order, that "reaffirms the validity of the system of norms" (1987, 452). As Svoboda states in his study of the conventional American detective hero, both the detective and the cowboy act as redeemers "who can tip the balance between good and evil" (1983, 560). Thus, whether it is the cowboy in the Western or the detective in the city, these popular heroes and genres reveal the myths and worldview of the dominant majority.

However, as Porter also points out, the popularity and longevity of the genre is due to the possibility of "grafting contemporary fears onto an endlessly repeated formula" (1981, 127). In doing so, the hard-boiled school subverted the ethos of the classic and elitist British version. Likewise, the rise in women's and multiethnic detective fiction reveals contemporary concerns, and the genre is used to subvert the previous white male ethic. If we look, then, to these novels, we will find significant alterations of the detective persona that imply a different value system.

Looking at the detectives created by these writers, we find that they only partially conform to the formula of the "tough guy," a middle-to-lower-class loner, survivor of the urban jungle, prone to wisecracks, and a womanizer, one who is analytical but also, according to the hard-boiled formula, gets involved, usually through fistfights (see Cawelti 1976, 142). We know very little about the traditional private eye, nothing about his family, and the character, throughout the series, is a fixed motif which does not evolve (see Knight 1980, 16).

Walter Mosley's Easy (Ezekiel) Rawlins is an amateur detective who, despite his intentions of keeping out of things, gets involved in crimes, either because the police or some shady character forces or lures him, often for money, or because the corpse happens to get in his way. In the first novels he poses as a janitor, although he is the owner of the building; later he appears as the supervising senior head custodian in a school. Easy is a war veteran with a drinking problem as well as a history of womanizing and violence that he tries to fight off; he is very streetwise and an active member of his community. He avoids any political involvement or dealings with the law. In fact, if he can avoid the law, for example by manipulating tax returns, he does. Throughout the series of novels, we find that he unofficially adopts two children; his wife abandons him, taking his biological daughter, and in the last of the series published, he seems to be settling down with a new woman with a shady past. Easy appears in *Devil in a Blue Dress* (1990), *A Red Death* (1991), *White Butterfly* (1992), *Black Betty* (1994), *A Little Yellow Dog* (1996), and the prequel to the series, *Gone Fishin'* (1997).

Blanche White is the creation of Barbara Neely and appears in *Blanche on the Lam* (1992), *Blanche Among the Talented Tenth* (1994), *Blanche Cleans Up* (1998), and *Blanche Passes Go* (2000). Blanche is a middle-aged domestic worker by choice, heavyset, streetwise, and an amateur detective. Again, she gets involved because the corpses lie in her way at the houses of her white employers or at a vacation resort. She is very committed to her community and to the racial and social issues that affect it. Although single, she cares for her orphaned niece and nephew. She, too, evades the law—as the title of the first novel indicates—when she has to.

Lucha Corpi's detective, Gloria Damasco, appears in *Eulogy for a Brown Angel* (1992), *Cactus Blood* (1995), and *Black Widow's Wardrobe* (1999). A mother who is widowed early in the series, she is a middle-aged speech therapist who leaves her profession to begin to study for a license as a private investigator. She is a political activist involved in Chicano issues as well as environmental ones. Gloria is very sensitive, insecure, and physically frail. Her sense of justice does not always coincide with the established law and order, particularly on social issues.

Rudolfo Anaya gives us his detective and "alter ego," Sonny Baca (Anaya 1995a, lecture). He outwardly fits the mold as a "tough guy," macho womanizer but is inwardly insecure; he is blundering, has a crisis of impotency, is a devoted son, brother, boyfriend, and neighbor, and is committed to social and Chicano issues and traditions. Sonny is the only licensed private investigator of this sampling and, as such, cooperates, though reluctantly, with the police. He is the protagonist of *Zia Summer* (1995), *Rio Grande Fall* (1996), and *Shaman Winter* (1999).

Finally, PaPa LaBas is Ishmael Reed's unique creation in the novel *Mumbo Jumbo* (1972). He is very old, or actually ageless, eccentric, and outdated. He devotes his life to his daughter, to Haitian hoodoo, loas, and potions as well as being an amateur detective; he is politically involved with African American and social issues, but very distrusting of the law and the establishment.

One might question what these five detectives have in common. Most of them fit the formula character in some aspects, but, as these brief synopses indicate, we know a lot about each one, his or her family, and values. They all have a history and they all evolve through the series and even through each novel. They are certainly not stock characters but rather rounded with a progressive development. There are two main aspects that join them. First, all of them are very involved in their community and family. Family issues appear continuously and condition all of their lives. For the classics, Philip Marlowe or Sam Spade, there is never a family. Similarly, these detectives are part of their community, whether Harlem or East Los Angeles or a barrio in Albuquerque. They are known by the community

102   CARMEN FLYS-JUNQUERA

and are involved in trying to help their neighbors. Community and social issues are very relevant to their lives. They are definitely not the lone vigilantes of the hard-boiled tradition.

Secondly, all of them, to varying degrees, respect and participate in their ethnic traditions and lore. They may have learned to live and work in the dominant Anglo world, but all of them maintain a high degree of ethnic awareness and pride. Within this ethnic identity, the acceptance, respect, and participation in the alternative belief systems, such as hoodoo and *brujería*, are primary features. The degree of participation varies, from the limited experience during the youth of Easy Rawlins and a few more occasional references, on one end of the spectrum, to the complete immersion of PaPa LaBas, on the other. All the detectives have some kind of "power" or sixth sense, from Easy's "inner voice" to Papa LaBas's active hoodoo powers. All of them, except PaPa LaBas, pressured by the dominant culture, feel the need to hide these experiences, especially when trying to explain how they have solved the crime to the police. Often they use the cliché of a "hunch" when there is no other way out. However, part of the development of the character, except in the case of Easy, consists of the increasing inner security and acceptance of their "gifts," beliefs, and traditions, to the extent of deliberately using and trusting them. The same can be said for their varying degrees of participation in rituals or customs belonging to these folk beliefs. Often the detective does not follow a ritual but turns to another character who, in doing so, helps with the crime detection. It is clear, however, that none of these detectives scorns these "superstitions." Moreover, these alternative ways of "knowing" inform the detection process as well as the individual.

Even though the involvement and commitment to the community does not form part of the central theme of this article, it is a significant element in both the alteration of the detective persona and in the presentation of an alternate worldview. For these detectives, protecting an innocent person from the community, even if it means violating the sanctioned social order, is more important than following the law. For example, Easy Rawlins is often involved in criminal activities at the request of a member of the neighborhood. His involvement may be the result of his feelings of guilt about the apparent suicide of his tenant, who was going to be evicted in *A Red Death;* or the unofficial adoption of Jesus, a young Mexican orphan whom Easy had rescued from sexual abuse in *Devil in a Blue Dress;* or the taking in of Feather, an unwanted biracial baby in *White Butterfly;* or being entrusted with a pet in *A Little Yellow Dog.* His dealings with the establishment are always forced, and he often withholds evidence to protect an innocent or not-so-innocent member of his community who is being harassed, as he himself is, by the law. Often he finds hideaways for persecuted com-

DETECTIVES, HOODOO, AND *BRUJERÍA* 103

munity members, for prostitutes running from their pimps, or for old people being evicted.

Blanche White is constantly helping community members; she regularly buys a few items from a neighborhood shop, which is more expensive, just to help the little old lady who has owned it all her life. She gets involved with her nephew in an association against lead poisoning or one that helps integrate ex-convicts into the neighborhood in *Blanche Cleans Up*. She clearly takes a stand on racial and gender issues and tries to educate her niece and nephew with an awareness of social issues. But she is not blind to class divisions within the black community, as *Blanche Among the Talented Tenth* illustrates. However, she, like Easy, is not above hiding evidence from the police if doing so will protect an innocent person, black or white, whether it be herself or, in *Blanche on the Lam,* the white boy Mumsfield, who suffers from Down's syndrome.

In the case of Gloria Damasco, helping illegal immigrants or supporting the grape boycott as a protest against pesticides in *Blood Cactus* is more important than cooperating with immigration officers or the police looking for ecological terrorists. Similarly, she supports the Chicano Movement and is hesitant to trust the police, because the consequences may be to incriminate political activists, as in the demonstration in *Eulogy for a Brown Angel*. However, she, like Blanche, is also willing to go against the elitist Mexican American upper class, who exploit members of the community, as in *Eulogy*, or those who steal art treasures for private collections, or people who use their connections to illegally adopt children, as in *Black Widow's Wardrobe*. Her husband's social involvement as a volunteer doctor for welfare clinics also attests to strong community commitment.

In the case of Sonny Baca we find not only his support of Chicano businesses and the homeless in *Rio Grande Fall*, but issues of nuclear waste and community property rights in *Zia Summer*, drug dealers, CIA contras and illegal animal testing in *Rio Grande Fall*, and Chicano high school dropouts, nuclear bombs, FBI corruption, and Russian sellouts in *Shaman Winter*. When he accepts reward money in *Rio Grande Fall*, it is only to help out a member of the community. Often his work goes unpaid or he prioritizes community needs over FBI demands in *Shaman Winter*. Much of the series is devoted to his increasing awareness of social issues and particularly of Chicano traditions and community needs.

Finally, PaPa LaBas's Mumbo Jumbo Kathedral is a community center specializing in "Fits for your Head" (Reed 1972, 24)—in other words, folk psychiatry and healing. His main preoccupation is helping the community, particularly the youth, giving them a sense of pride in themselves. PaPa also deals with museum thefts and any other issue that attempts to exploit or deprive the community of its material or spiritual wealth. In his sense of justice, the sanctioned law and order deserves very little respect, while the needs of the people are essential.

With regards to the portrayal of folk beliefs, these detective novels could be construed as a continuum, from their minor appearance in the case of Easy Rawlins to a progressively increasing importance in Blanche White, Gloria Damasco, and Sonny Baca, and to the extreme in PaPa LaBas. In the novel *Gone Fishin'* in the Easy Rawlins series, we encounter Mamma Jo and her voodoo practices, complete with potions and dried skulls. Although published last, *Gone Fishin'* actually constitutes a prequel to the series, narrating Easy's youth and relationship to his alter ego, or doppelgänger, Raymond Alexander, known as Mouse. Mamma Jo, whose "especialty is love" (Mosley 1997, 30), had her husband's skull on the mantle: "The skull leaned back with its teeth pushed forward, dried black lips for gums. . . . It was as if the agony of life had followed that poor soul into the after world" (26–27). Easy reluctantly becomes an accomplice to Mouse in killing his stepfather. Mouse uses Mamma Jo's powers for the crime: "'Cause I know I got Reese [his stepfather] by his nuts wit' that doll. He from voodoo country an' a curse gonna tear him up, I know that" (108). These scenes cement the difficult but close relationship between Easy and Mouse. They take place in the bayou country of Louisiana and are the reason Easy had to leave his hometown of Houston, Texas, and settle anonymously in Los Angeles. In the next novel, *Devil in a Blue Dress*, the first of the series, we find that Easy has a kind of sixth sense, a voice that he describes as follows:

> The voice only comes to me at the worst time, when everything seems so bad that I want to take my car and drive it into a wall. Then this voice comes to me and gives me the best advice I ever get.
> The voice is hard. It never cares if I'm scared or in danger. It just looks at all the facts and tells me what I need to do. (Mosley 1990, 104)

The voice appears repeatedly in this novel but not in the others. This intuition, or unreal but rational sense, informs Easy and helps him make the most difficult decisions. There is very little else of this nature in this detective series, which is why I have placed Walter Mosley's novels at the far end of the continuum.

Barbara Neely's detective fiction with her protagonist Blanche White makes significant use of folk beliefs. Blanche clearly speaks of a sixth sense, a kind of extrasensory perception that she describes as follows:

> This was the second or third time this boy had been on her wavelength. This thing with him was beyond her Approaching Employer Warning Sense, which alerted her to the slightest rustling or clinking of a nearing employer.

DETECTIVES, HOODOO, AND *BRUJERÍA*

This was more like the way she always knew when her mother was around, or Ardell, or which one of the children was about to fling open the door and bound through the house. This ability to sense Mumsfield's approach was of the same nature but different. What made it different was the fact that she didn't know this white boy and didn't appreciate having him on her frequency. At the same time it was always those closest and kindest to her whose presence she was able to detect before they came into sight or earshot. (Neely 1992, 45)

This ability, which can be found in all the novels, often warns her and helps her in her detection activity. Likewise, Blanche perceives the aura of people, which often predicts their future. When she meets Hank in the second novel, "He looked in her eyes for the first time. Blanche almost raised her arm to ward off the haint that stared out at her. The term 'living dead' floated across her mind" (Neely 1994, 51). The next day he commits suicide.

Blanche believes in the animated spirit of things, much like Toni Morrison, who believes that nature and objects are inspirited, having feelings and constituting "signs" that "inform [people] about [their] own behavior" (quoted in Ruas 1985, 223). Thus, Blanche, as a domestic worker, reads signs in the houses where she works:

The minute the house sensed she understood it to be a living, breathing, watching creature with a personality and intentions of its own, the house confided in her, directed her attention toward things that told her more about the occupants than she wanted to know. (Neely 1998, 166)

Blanche also believes in ancestralism. She has a small altar in her house for ancestor worship, having rejected any religion that allowed her people to be enslaved. She also turns to a conjure woman to try to interpret her dreams: "Madame Rosa told her she was at a major crossroad in her life and the dream was trying to tell her something about the change that was coming" (Neely 1994, 13). Instructed by Madame Rosa, she performs a cleansing ritual in the ocean. We thus find that Blanche not only respects different aspects of folk beliefs but also partakes fully of them. She takes great pains to explain these beliefs and customs to her niece, conveying the value of these traditions, despite the pressure Taifa is feeling at school to assimilate. These elements are essential to her life and detecting activity and clearly constitute positive aspects, never being associated with ignorance or superstition by Blanche. Undoubtedly, these are things she cannot say to the police, for fear of ridicule.

Following the logic established thus far, we would then come to Lucha Corpi's detective Gloria Damasco. Gloria, like Blanche, senses certain presences as a "blue light" that she will later come to identify. In fact, in the

106 CARMEN FLYS-JUNQUERA

first novel, she senses a "presence, like a sudden gust of blue light brushing [her] arm and swiftly moving away" (1992, prelude). It is the presence of her future partner, whom she will meet eighteen years later and who will be important in solving the crime that was just about to take place. Her mother always said that as a child she had an "impressionable mind" (1992, 26), but it is a feeling she tries to hide. As she reflects:

> Vivid nightmares were not unusual for me. Over the years, I'd had so many that I had learned to free myself from their hold as soon as I opened my eyes. But sometimes I had other kinds of dreams, dreams that triggered visions, fragmented images, and symbols of a larger picture I felt compelled to put together. I dreaded that moment when my visions forced me to act on them. My *dark gift* was a mixed blessing at best, but it was a part of me, a part my reason always tried to deny or control. (1999, 10)

Like Blanche, Gloria also senses the aura of people. When she first meets Detective Kenyon, she feels that "everything seems to be fading in this man" (1992, 25). Days later she learns that he has terminal cancer. After returning to Oakland—the crime had taken place in Los Angeles—a year later, she inexplicably wakes up at three in the morning with "a throbbing pain in the front of my head" and cries all night (117). Her friend calls her later and informs her that Officer Kenyon had died at that hour. Examples of this nature are recurrent in the three novels.

When Gloria first sees the body of the murdered little boy, she has an out-of-body flying experience: "I felt that I was looking down at the child, at Luisa and at myself from a place up above while the action below me rushed, like an old film, over a screen" (Corpi 1992, 18). These experiences affect her physically, making her sick, causing a momentary loss of consciousness, and weakening her. Visions come in flashes and disconnected scenes, and events or items trigger unexpected physical sensations such as a shudder and nausea "every time [she] touched that clipping" (26). Often these visions are fragmented and she cannot explain them—for example, when she dreams that she is suddenly "pursuing the acrobat up a long staircase" (Corpi 1999, 44). Yet later on in the novel those scenes from the vision come back to her:

> My gaze slid down . . . the long staircase. . . . The dream-vision of the acrobat running up a long staircase flashed through my mind, and I wondered as I walked into the room if I was at the place where my visions would start to become real. (93)

Gloria, other than using her own clairvoyance, which she progressively tries to accept and harness to help her, partakes very little of other folk rituals. Nevertheless, many of her close friends and relatives do, something that she accepts and respects. Some have Chicano altars at home, full of plaster saints, herbs, and amulets; she accepts the help of a *curandera,* at her mother's insistence; both her mother and *comadre,* who believe in the folklore learned from their mothers, warn of an impending earthquake: "By reading the *signs,* I remember Mami Julia had been able to predict two minor earthquakes . . ." (Corpi 1995, 149). Moreover, she accepts the possibility of nonrational elements without disdain. Her visions appear, causing time warps and seeing things from a distant past and recurring events in the present. As one of her threatened clients, Licia Lecuona, believes herself to be the reincarnation of the historical and mythical character of La Malinche, Gloria's visions range from the times of Hernan Cortés to the near future. It is essential that she accept this possibility in order to protect Licia and solve the crimes.

Next on the continuum is Rudolfo Anaya's character, Sonny Baca. Sonny is initially unaware of folk beliefs and of his potential powers. In fact, he is quite assimilated into the dominant Anglo culture, and the development of the three novels is precisely one of returning to his cultural roots. In the first of the series, he is affected by *susto* when he sees the body of his cousin, the victim of a cult murder. He feels "the spirit filling the room with its heavy presence." He seems to hear Gloria's voice say "Avenge me." And then he feels "the force of the spirit in the room making him shiver. . . . Something cold and heavy was enveloping him" (1995b, 25–26). This *susto,* a Chicano folk belief, causes his impotence, and until he accepts a *limpieza,* a cleansing ritual at the beginning of the next novel, the effects continue. Sonny is driven throughout the three novels to learn about his history and heritage. Much of the learning, particularly that of the folk beliefs, comes from a *curandera*, Lorenza, and his neighbor, Don Eliseo, whom we discover at the end of the novel to be one of the last *brujos* passing on the torch to Sonny.

Eliseo first teaches Sonny to pray to the sun and the four sacred directions. As he does so, Sonny feels a special energy and realizes that "if he learned the way of his abuelos, he was sure the light would enter his soul" (Anaya 1995b, 204). A significant part of the Chicano worldview is that of harmony with nature. As Sonny learns, the "world of nature is our world. . . . Our nature is linked to that of our ancestors, to their beliefs" (Anaya 1996, 121). As in the case of hoodoo, the importance of one's ancestors is key to Chicano traditions. Sonny's increased harmony with nature allows him to discover and harness the power of his *nagual,* an animal guardian spirit characteristic of the beliefs of Native American tribes of the Southwest. Through his dream visions he learns to enter the dreamworld through a lake and to meet the coyote, his *nagual.* In these visions, he seems to become a coyote: "Their energy flowed to him, filling him with lightness, exuberation. He was running, close to the ground, close to the scents of other animals, running with the coyotes, free, flying" (129). Anaya's choice of *nagual*, the coyote, is highly symbolic on multiple levels. The coyote is an American species, typical of the West, whose name comes from the Nahualt language of precolonial Mexico. In the oral tradition of both Native Americans and Chicanos it is a trickster figure. In Chicano vernacular, a coyote is also a mixed blood, half Mexican and half Anglo. Moreover, those who help illegal immigrants across the border are also called coyotes. Sonny seems to acquire the physical abilities of the coyote—enhanced sense of smell and speed—but also the trickster nature that enables him to outwit his enemy, Raven. The cultural implications of living on the border, so essential to the Chicano identity, are highlighted by this choice of *nagual*.

During this process, Sonny learns to control and direct his dreams and even to act in them. The third novel, *Shaman Winter*, presents time as circular. Actions in the past affect the present and vice versa. The novel shifts from key moments of Chicano history to the present, shifting from the tangible present to dreams in the past. Sonny learns that he must defeat Raven in the past, where Raven has kidnapped his four grandmothers (one for every line of his mixed blood heritage) in order to resolve the kidnappings of four young girls in the present. By threatening Sonny's grandmothers, his bloodlines, Raven pretends to annihilate Sonny himself. The importance of one's ancestors is the key to present life. Sonny, who is being initiated into *brujería*, realizes that the only difference between an evil *brujo*, such as Raven, and a good *brujo* or *curandero* is their own "moral conscience," a very delicate balance that lies at the heart of folk beliefs, as Trotter and Chavira point out (1981, 33). As these anthropologists state, the "biblical theme of the dual worlds of light and darkness, good and evil, health and illness, life and death runs throughout the practice of *curanderismo*" (27). The theme lies at the heart of the Chicano worldview and constitutes the core of all of Anaya's fiction. Thus, on a second level, Sonny and Raven become allegorical figures for the eternal struggle between good and evil.

Finally, the detective most deeply involved in folk practices is PaPa LaBas. I will only briefly mention this character, not only because *Mumbo Jumbo* was written a full twenty years earlier than the other novels, but also because Stephen Soitos has already provided an in-depth study of the hoodoo elements in Ishmael Reed's postmodern and experimental detective novel.[3] LaBas is known in the community as a folk healer who trusts his "knockings" in telling him what to do. He foretells the growth of the spiritual "disease," Jes Grew. In the novel, LaBas's character defies all definition, as the following excerpt illustrates: "PaPa LaBas, noonday

HooDoo, fugitive-hermit, obeah-man, botanist, animal impersonator, 2-headed man, You-Name-It is 50 years old and lithe . . ." (Reed 1972, 45). He is clearly a trickster figure, like Sonny and Raven. He has powers and uses them, never doubting or hiding them like the other detectives. If someone contradicts LaBas, that character feels his powers:

> A little boy kicked his Newfoundland HooDoo 3 Cents and spent a night squirming and gnashing his teeth. A warehouse burned after it refused to deliver a special variety of herbs to his brownstone headquarters and mind haberdashery where he sized up his clients to fit their souls. (23)

The elements of hoodoo are all-pervasive on virtually every page of the novel. As in Anaya, there is a suggestion of timelessness in the novel; LaBas seems to be fifty years old yet is over a hundred at the end. He, like Sonny, seems engaged in the eternal struggle between good and evil, here expressed as the struggle between Osiris and Set, between two concepts of life, represented by LaBas and his alter ego, Hinkle Von Vampton.

The dual nature of most belief systems seems underscored in many of these novels. We find that many of the detectives have an alter ego, or even a doppelgänger.[4] Easy's violent side is represented by Mouse. Eventually, in the last novel, these aspects seem to shift between the two. Sonny is mirrored by Raven and LaBas by Von Vampton. Most of the detectives also have one or more helpers or guides who introduce or reinforce the protagonist's knowledge of folk beliefs. Rather than the traditional sidekick who reads the signs incorrectly, thus emphasizing the admirable abilities of the detective,[5] these partners act more as mediator-guides or protectors for the insecure and doubting detective. Easy is continuously rescued by Mouse, and the mere mention of Mouse is used as a threat by Easy. But Mouse's change of heart in the end also makes Easy reflect on his way of life. In Blanche's case it is her close friend Ardell who perceives her feeling at a distance, and also Madame Rosa. For Gloria it is her poet friend Luisa and later Justin and the *curandera* Rosa. For Sonny, Lorenza and Eliseo's roles as guides are essential. LaBas, too, trusts his friend and occultist Black Herman. Moreover, all these detectives receive help, guidance, and support from their community and family. Without all this help, none could solve the crimes.

Not only, then, do Easy Rawlins, Blanche White, Gloria Damasco, Sonny Baca, and PaPa LaBas have powers, to different degrees, but their acceptance of folk beliefs and rituals is essential to their character and their actions. Hühn points out the "analogy of the detective's activities to sign-interpretation, meaning formation, and story-telling" (1987, 453). Hühn studies the various stories embedded in a detective narrative, as well as the multiple authors and readings of each story. Among these are the story of the crime that took place before the action begins, the process of detection and uncovering the hidden story, the deliberate hiding of the story by the criminal, the erroneous story told by the police or by the sidekick, and so forth. The detective, in order to read the criminal's meaning correctly—in other words, solve the riddle or the crime—has to "disentangle and eliminate the various secondary meanings and stories" (456). In this way, the detective narratives share in the traditional art of storytelling, creating a community of authors and readers. Stories and storytelling become essential elements for the establishment of community and identity. Therefore, the creators of ethnic detectives steeped in folk customs show their respect for and actively participate in the traditional art of storytelling. Moreover, their stories speak not only of the crime, but also of the community itself. In doing so, they reinforce the importance of passing on their legacy of folk beliefs and oral culture in order to achieve a sense of rootedness and community.

The importance of community issues, relationships, and family that these detectives reveal challenges the conventional values of rationalism and individualism, so prevalent in the dominant Anglo tradition of the United States. If Easy, Blanche, Gloria, Sonny, or LaBas solve the crime, it is by relying on faith, on their sixth sense, on powers or folk beliefs, and on help from the community and family. Therefore, we find these novels contesting the heroization of the individual, substituting individual valorization with the primacy of a communal effort. I would agree with Bonnie TuSmith and Priscilla Walton that we need to take into account the ethnic author's position vis-à-vis the community in order to study the mediating functions in the quest for alternative visions of community (Gosselin 1999, 10). Toni Morrison, in "City Limits, Village Values: Concept of the Neighborhood in Black Fiction" (1981), calls attention to the importance of ancestors and community to the African American worldview. Likewise, these values are central to Chicanos. By stressing them in a popular genre, which has a wide audience, these writers are posing alternatives to the dominant value system. These detectives, like their classic counterparts, have their own moral stance, but that stance is shared by their community—they are not lone vigilantes. The fact that these detectives are all portrayed as moral, responsible, and respected persons reinforces their position. But here it is not so much that an individual or the system is corrupt, as in the case of the hard-boiled school, but that the system is unjust per se. They question the dominant sense of justice, not because of the corruption, but because it leaves out too many innocent people, because the laws have been written and interpreted to protect only a privileged few. Thus, by illustrating to the reader an alternative sense of justice they question the dominant system.

In conclusion, what is important about these detective personas is precisely how they challenge the dominant cultural ethos of the United States. Their folk beliefs are usually considered superstition, with all the negative connotations of that word. Mainstream America has accused minorities of ignorance and assigned them low status, frequently basing their argument on these traditions and beliefs. The reader is presented with intelligent ethnic detectives, esteemed by their community and respected, albeit reluctantly, by law enforcement institutions. These detectives not only possess these "gifts," but respect folk beliefs and traditions, using them to aid their very modern, twentieth-century activity of crime detection, solving cases where the legislated powers have failed.

In this way, the authors jar audience expectations, or as Linton states, resist them, creating a kind of readerly "incompetence" that shocks and forces the audience into an outsider perspective (quoted in Gosselin 1999, 6). Ethnic detective fiction, by incorporating subversive interventions as well as elements of the vernacular and folk beliefs, forces the mainstream popular audience of the detective novel into an outsider perspective. If the popular murder mystery deautomatizes signification and makes everyday things "strange" or different, endowing life with a new wealth of potential meanings (see Hühn 1987, 455), this is even more so when the reader is forced to look at the cultural elements of the story from an outsider perspective. Moreover, in this case, the search to find meaning in seemingly trivial events or in assumed everyday attitudes toward people, justice, relationships and so forth, enables the author or narrator to uncover false assumptions. By forcing the mainstream reader into an outsider perspective, the traditional outsider, the member of a minority group, marginal to mainstream culture, is made into an insider, one who understands all the cultural interventions. Thus the ethnic community is empowered as it can enjoy, if only for the time of the reading, the insider perspective. This shifting of perspectives and different levels of readings was identified by Hühn for classical detective fiction. This "readerly incompetence" can, thus, cause inadvertent learning. Echoing Stanley Elkin's claim for Fisher's *The Conjure-Man Dies,* the reader is "drawn through the book by its story, but emerges at last with much more than the story in mind" (quoted in Gosselin 1999, 3). Mainstream readers inadvertently learn about other cultures and beliefs as possible alternatives. Minority readers learn to take pride in their folk beliefs and are therefore empowered.

Walter Mosley, Barbara Neely, and Ishmael Reed clearly incorporate elements of the African American vernacular and hoodoo into their novels, as Lucha Corpi and Rudolfo Anaya incorporate the Chicano vernacular and *brujería* into theirs. Their use of the vernacular, hoodoo, *curanderismo,* and *brujería* clearly attests to a specific cultural ethos and worldview. The importance of these folk beliefs, of the interconnectedness of all things, the importance of the community are all elements that these authors, among others, and the African American and Chicano communities have in common. Moreover, these values are radically different from those portrayed in the classic hard-boiled detective novel. Thus, these writers endow the repeated formula of detective fiction with new meanings, subverting the oppressive mainstream value system. They cause the reader to learn inadvertently, and they develop, through these aesthetic strategies, an emancipatory cultural expression for their respective communities.

NOTES

1. This definition of hoodoo is based on the works of Hurston [1938] 1990, Roberts 1989, and Levine 1977; in the case of Chicano *brujería* and *curanderismo*, it is based on Simmons 1974, Kiev 1968, and Trotter and Chavira 1981.

2. Some aspects of these subversive interventions can be found in Soitos 1996 on African American detective fiction, although he barely addresses that of the nineties, and Gosselin 1999, Walton and Jones 1999, and Flys 2000.

3. See Soitos 1996, chap. 6.

4. For a study of doppelgängers in Mosley, see Nash 1999.

5. For the role of the sidekick or Watson figure in the classic tradition, see Porter 1981, Cawelti 1976, and Hühn 1987.

WORKS CITED

Anaya, Rudolfo. 1995a. "Lecture." Casa de America, Madrid, September.

———. 1995b. *Zia Summer*. New York: Time Warner.

———. 1996. *Río Grande Fall*. New York: Time Warner.

———. 1999. *Shaman Winter*. New York: Time Warner.

Cawelti, John G. 1976. *Adventure, Mystery, and Romance: Formula Stories as Art and Popular Culture*. Chicago: University of Chicago Press.

Corpi, Lucha. 1992. *Eulogy for a Brown Angel*. Houston, Tex.: Arte Publico Press.

———.1995. *Cactus Blood*. Houston, Tex.: Arte Publico Press.

———.1999. *Black Widow's Wardrobe*. Houston, Tex.: Arte Publico Press.

Flys, Carmen. "Writing against the Grain: Rudolfo Anaya's Murder Mysteries." In Gallardo and Llurda 2000, 519–24.

Freese, Peter. 1992. *The Ethnic Detective: Chester Himes, Harry Kemelman, Tony Hillerman*. Essen: Die Blaue Eule.

Gallardo, Pere, and Enric Llurda, eds. 2000. *Proceedings of the Twenty-second International Conference of AEDEAN*. Lleida: Universitat de Lleida.

Gosselin, Adrienne Johnson, ed. 1999. *Multicultural Detective Fiction: Murder from the "Other" Side*. New York: Garland.

DETECTIVES, HOODOO, AND *BRUJERÍA*

Hühn, Peter. 1987. "The Detective as Reader: Narrativity and Reading Concepts in Detective Fiction." *Modern Fiction Studies* 33:451–66.

Hurston. Zora Neale. [1938] 1990. *Tell My Horse: Voodoo and Life in Haiti and Jamaica.* Edited by Henry Louis Gates Jr. New York: Harper and Row.

Kiev, Ari. 1968. *Curanderismo: Mexican-American Folk Psychiatry.* New York: Free Press.

Knight, Stephen. 1980. *Form and Ideology in Crime Fiction.* London: Macmillan.

Levine, Lawrence W. 1977. *Black Culture and Black Consciousness.* Oxford: Oxford University Press.

Linton, Patricia. 1999. "The Detective Novel as a Resistant Text: Alter-Ideology in Linda Hogan's *Mean Spirit.*" In Gosselin 1999, 17–36.

Morrison, Toni. 1981. "City Limits, Village Values: Concept of the Neighborhood in Black Fiction." In *Literature and the Urban Experience*, edited by Michael C. Jaye and Ann Chalmers Watts, 35–44. New Brunswick, N.J.: Rutgers University Press.

Mosley, Walter. 1990. *Devil in a Blue Dress.* London: Pan Books.

———.1991. *A Red Death.* London: Pan Books.

———.1992. *White Butterfly.* New York: Pocket Books.

———. 1994. *Black Betty.* New York: Pocket Books.

———.1996. *A Little Yellow Dog.* New York: Pocket Books.

———.1997. *Gone Fishin'.* London: Serpent's Tail.

Murray, Margaret. 1933. *The God of the Witches.* London: Low and Marston.

Nancy, Jean-Luc. 1991. *The Inoperative Community.* Edited and translated by Peter Connor. Minneapolis: University of Minnesota Press.

Nash, William R. 1999. "'Maybe I Killed My Own Blood': Doppelgängers and the Death of Double Consciousness in Walter Mosley's *A Little Yellow Dog.*" In Gosselin 1999, 303–24.

Neely, Barbara. 1992. *Blanche on the Lam.* New York: Penguin.

———. 1994. *Blanche Among the Talented Tenth.* New York: Penguin.

———. 1998. *Blanche Cleans Up.* New York: Penguin.

———. 2000. *Blanche Passes Go.* New York: Penguin.

Porter, Dennis. 1981. *The Pursuit of Crime.* New Haven: Yale University Press.

Reed, Ishmael. 1972. *Mumbo Jumbo.* New York: Scribner.

Roberts, John W. 1989. *From Trickster to Badman: The Black Folk Hero in Slavery and Freedom.* Philadelphia: University of Pennsylvania Press.

Ruas, Charles. 1985. *Conversations with American Writers.* New York: Alfred A. Knopf.

Simmons, Marc. 1974. *Witchcraft in the Southwest.* Lincoln: University of Nebraska Press.

Soitos, Stephen F. 1996. *The Blues Detective: A Study of African American Detective Fiction.* Amherst: University of Massachusetts Press.

Svoboda, Frederic. 1983. "The Snub-Nosed Mystique: Observations on the American Detective Hero." *Modern Fiction Studies* 29:557–68.

Trotter, Robert T., II, and Juan Antonio Chavira. 1981. *Curanderismo.* Athens: University of Georgia Press.

TuSmith, Bonnie. 1994. *All My Relatives: Community in Contemporary Ethnic American Literatures.* Ann Arbor: University of Michigan Press.

Walton, Priscilla, and Manina Jones. 1999. *Detective Agency: Women Rewriting the Hard-Boiled Tradition.* Berkeley and Los Angeles: University of California Press.

A Cuban American "Lady Dick" and an African American Miss Marple?: The Female Detective in the Novels of Carolina Garcia-Aguilera and Barbara Neely

MONIKA MUELLER

> I asked a lot of questions and started hanging around, and, after I pestered him enough times, Esteban started taking me along to observe his investigations. Eventually I helped him work cases and met his contacts. Even Esteban thought I was just playing around. . . . I wasn't particularly ambitious—it's hard to agonize for long over your future when you live in a huge house in the exclusive Cocoplum section of Miami. If things ever got tight, I figured, I could sell my Mercedes and live off the money for a while.
>
> —Carolina Garcia-Aguilera, *Bloody Waters*

> Twice she'd been caught taking liberties with her employers' space. Both times she'd been in the bathtub. . . . The second time she'd been caught by . . . the brother of her first Farleigh customer. He'd made her pay in a much more painful and private way. She hadn't bothered to report it to the police. Even if they'd believed her and cared about the rape of a black woman by a white man, once it came out that she'd been attacked while naked in her employer's bathtub, she'd never have been employed in anybody's house again. But she still had hopes of fixing that motherless piece of shit one day.
>
> —Barbara Neely, *Blanche on the Lam*

As THE QUOTATIONS SHOW, A WORLD OF DIFFERENCE SEPARATES THE LIFESTYLES of Lupe Solano, the Cuban American private investigator created by Cuban American writer Carolina Garcia-Aguilera, and Blanche White, the black domestic worker turned accidental sleuth invented by African American author Barbara Neely. Both writers are members of nondominant ethnic groups, and they both deal with the conflation of crime, gender, and ethnicity in their novels; but their works, nevertheless, reveal diverging personal agendas and convictions and also reflect different traditions of detective fiction. Yet in spite of the many differences between their gendered ethnic detective fictions, there is no doubt that both writers seek feminist empowerment for their heroines.

Kathleen Gregory Klein has argued in her book *The Woman Detective: Gender and Genre* that female authors of detective fictions have to create strong female characters by virtue of the genre, which demands at least somewhat "heroic" investigators. But a female empowerment within the genre is no easy task, according to Klein, because, in her view, a writer who tries to combine the formula of medium-to-hard-boiled detective fiction with feminist content is facing almost insurmountable difficulties:

> What finally keeps feminism and the detection formula from meshing is the subsequent necessity of creating a female private eye who refuses to play games within a system which seems to exist to support male hegemony. A feminist private eye who is both aware and committed could not be shown subscribing to any social paradigm which dishonestly pretends to uphold a system of values based on a disinterested ethic but actually is grounded in interested power structures, especially as those structures and systems deliberately exclude women. The private motivations of the investigator do not lessen the impact of her bolstering a system which exists, at least in part, to uphold male privilege. . . . Inasmuch as mass-mediated culture, like detective fiction, primarily serves the interests of the relatively small political-economic power elite which sits atop the social pyramid . . . authors trying to create a feminist detective face their own set of necessary compromises. Either feminism or the formula is at risk. (1995, 201–2)

Perhaps not surprisingly, there seems to be a similar conflict between the detective formula and the antihegemonic demands of ethnic fiction. Michelle Stewart, for example, writes about Louis Owens's Native American detective novel *The Sharpest Sight* that the novel "does not fit the rubric of the genre" because of its Native American emphasis on "polyvocalism, circular plots, and . . . on community rather than the individual"—but she concludes, nevertheless, that "Owens creates his own kind of detective fiction simultaneously within and outside of the genre" (1999, 167). Stephen Soitos similarly explains that because Nikki Baker's African American lesbian detective novels mainly deal with her detective's "identity quest" and also because "Baker gives us a black lesbian's viewpoint as she searches for meaning in contemporary American society," they do not have much in common "with the predominantly white male hard-boiled tradition which often relies on the detective's professional status and physical violence for plot construction" (1999, 109). Garcia-Aguilera's and Neely's books illustrate this conflict between formula detective fiction, on the one hand, and feminist and ethnic issues, on the other hand. Garcia-Aguilera prefers focusing on the hard-boiled component rather than the social topics that she also thematizes, whereas Neely neglects hard-boiled content in favor of ethnic and feminist matters. While her fiction does not fit the hard-boiled school of detective novels, it, nevertheless, does show affinities with the tradition of the "classic female detective story" developed by Agatha Christie and "rewrites it with a black difference" (Gruesser 1999, 239).

Ever since Kathleen Klein has argued so provocatively that feminism and the detective formula do not harmonize and that in detective fiction by women "[e]ither feminism or the formula is at risk" (1995, 202), other critics writing about the female tradition in detective writing, most notably among them Sally Munt, Priscilla Walton, and Manina Jones, have taken issue with her thesis. Munt criticizes Klein for basing her indictment of woman-authored detective fiction as complicit with male hegemony on only a handful of novels that "are specifically mainstream" (1994, 200) and neglecting the explicitly feminist texts that "gesture most towards her vision of a feminocentric crime novel" (1994, 200). She rejects Klein's thesis about the incompatibility of the detective novel and a feminist outlook and argues instead for genre modifications (which, as she reasons, Klein also implicitly calls for):

> This paradox illustrates the parameters of this book: despite commonsensical attempts to gender the detective novel as masculine, it could also be argued that whilst the form undoubtedly can foreground masculine and misogynistic structures, there is also an argument for the form being fundamentally friendly to feminists. Whether this compatibility constitutes breaking the form depends on one's initial starting point as to what constitutes the genre in the first place. (1994, 191)

Munt contends that the genre of the crime novel itself might even invite generic change because of its satiric quality. Following the lead of Rick Eden, who "argues . . . for recognizing that *all* varieties of detective fiction are in fact satirical" (1994, 192), she describes a possible direction the genre might take. Both Val McDermid and Amanda Cross use parody as a feminist strategy of debunking gender stereotypes, according to Munt, who therefore concludes, "I have concurred with the common convention that satire, as protest art, suits feminism's desire to parody patriarchal norms and forms" (1994, 197).[1]

Walton and Jones employ a very similar argument by also focusing on the "genre trouble" incurred by women-authored detective novels and the ways in which "women writers of detective fiction strategically talk back to a genre that has often demeaned, trivialized and even demonized women" (1999, 94), but add a fashionable poststructuralist slant to their argument by substituting Munt's insight that feminist hard-boiled novels employ a parodic mode with a Foucauldian notion of the subversive powers of "reverse discourse" as expounded by Teresa de Lauretis:

> Foucault's term *"reverse" discourse* actually suggests something of the process by which a representation in the external world is subjectively assumed, reworked through fantasy, in the internal world and then returned to the external world resignified, rearticulated discursively and/or performatively in the subject's self-representation—in speech, gesture, costume, body stance, and so forth. (quoted in Walton and Jones 1999, 101)

Applying the idea of "reverse discourse" to detective novels by women, Walton and Jones reason that "[i]f the feminist hard-boiled novel is perceived as a reverse rather than a double discourse, then it can be read as producing a critique of a formula by reproducing it with strategic differences, thus redirecting the trajectory of dominant discourse" (1999, 92). In a similar vein, they read the appropriation of hard-boiled manners and appearance by "lady dicks" in terms of Butlerian gender play and performativity (which, of course, is also indebted to Foucault's "reverse" discourse). John Gruesser also theorizes detective fiction authored by African Americans in terms of "repetition with a difference," but instead of turning to Foucault or Butler for his theoretical background, he bases his argument on Henry Louis Gates's notion of "Signifiyin(g)"[2] and writes that "[w]hereas black writers most certainly revise the texts in the Western tradition, they often seek to do so 'authentically,' with a compelling sense of difference based on the black vernacular" (1999, 239). Walter Mosley, for example, "repeats the dominant white detective story with a black difference, illustrating Gates theory of Signifyin(g)" (1999, 240).

Like many other detective novels by lesbian, straight, and "ethnic" female writers, Neely's—and to some extent also Garcia-Aguilera's—novels address issues of "feminist" and ethnic genre modification. As Mary Gerhart proposes in *Genre Choices, Gender Questions*, established genres can change over time because genre is no longer perceived as an immutable category but has come to be understood as a "hypothesis regarding an entire text, relating that single text to one or more texts with similar structures, styles, topics, and effects" (1992, 7). Since it is "both shaping and being shaped by the interpreted object" (7), it is subject to evolution and change. New (sub)genres emerge when "the forced identification" of different fields of meaning "warps both fields" (21). While it might be arguable whether or not ethnic detective novels by women have already created a genre of their own, there is no doubt that contributions by women from nondominant backgrounds have significantly modified the white male tradition of detective fiction.

Garcia-Aguilera's novels powerfully illustrate Munt's point that detective fiction by women often parodies detective fiction by men, but they still present an only somewhat ironic take on the traditionally male-authored hard-boiled novel. Lupe Solano, Garcia-Aguilera's female private detective, is young, attractive, and unattached. She always carries a gun, employs a younger male cousin, a "sexually confused" exercise nut (1999, 27), as her secretary, and has regular lovers who are highly educated, successful white males whom she seems to like because of their "tall, Nordic looks" in Sam's case ([1997] 1998, 52) and abundant wealth in Tommy's. Because she stems from a very wealthy family of Miami-based Cubans, Lupe qualifies as a CAP (Cuban American Princess). Due to her social standing she does not have to face any ethnic discrimination whatsoever. Yet she nevertheless registers sexual and racial discrimination, as her comment about a photograph of the all-white, mostly male mayors of Coral Gables shows: "Maybe I'm too sensitive, but I couldn't help flinching when I saw again that of the twenty-one mayors there, all were white and only one was a woman" (212). Even though Lupe is aware of ethnic and gender-based discrimination, this awareness is often compromised by her unflagging faith in the American Dream of success—she and her close associates all sport a gorgeous Mercedes, BMW, Porsche, or even Rolls Royce along with a beautifully styled body.

For genre-related reasons Solana's PI-persona can neither incorporate overly feminist nor overly conservative notions of female behavior. In order to present an appropriate image of the female private investigator as a sexy loner (just like her male counterpart), Lupe has to reject the traditional Cuban view "that motherhood was and should be every woman's greatest goal in life" (Garcia-Aguilera [1996] 1997, 164) and she also has to present herself as a highly desirable sex object:

> On a good day I clear five feet. I've always thought I had too much figure for my height, but my boyfriends—and there have been plenty—never agree. I wear my long black hair in a very fifties French twist and keep my hands perfectly manicured with blood-red nails.[3] (15)

But in *Havana Heat*, Garcia-Aguilera has Lupe Solano implicitly criticize her ethnic and social background by presenting her "womanliness as masquerade"[4] and her profession as a means toward the end of female empowerment:

THE FEMALE DETECTIVE IN GARCIA-AGUILERA AND NEELY   119

I should have been born a man. I think like one. As a private investigator
for the last eight years, I've worked in a field dominated by men. The men
I've worked with, as well as the men I've been involved with, have always
tried to ascertain who is the real Lupe Solano. Eventually they all discover
that I have two sides: a gentle, feminine veneer that I display when I need
to, and the ruthless heart and soul of a man underneath. (2000, 1)

Just like her self-characterization, which reveals that Lupe ultimately seems
to view her ostentatious femininity as a masquerade of "her true self,"[5] her
description of her sister Lourdes, a "yuppie nun," is also informed by an
almost schizophrenic struggle to both reject and maintain stereotypical
images of femininity. Thus, she wonders whether or not it was the pressure
to conform to the Cuban gender-ideal that "drove Lourdes into the religious life" ([1996] 1997, 164), yet she still presents her as somebody who
religiously adheres to stereotypical notions of female beauty:

My sister was devout and dedicated to her vows, but she wasn't a stereotypical nun. . . . A story had gone around that several years before, Lourdes
had gone to [her beautician's] house hours before Hurricane Andrew hit
south Florida. Lourdes had wanted to look her best in the days to follow,
when Miami would be without electricity and water. In all fairness to
Lourdes, she had vindicated herself by helping the beautician put up storm
shutters—after the critical tweezing. ([1997] 1999, 61)

These few examples show that whenever Garcia-Aguilera seems to have
difficulties in determining whether or not Lupe's "Cuban American femininity" can or even should be reconciled with both a "feminist empowerment" and the generic demands of detective fiction, she has recourse to a
parodic mode that ultimately does not reveal her gender politics. Her novels show a perhaps equally troubling attitude toward ethnicity, but this seems
to have very little to do with ethnic customs running counter to conventions of the detective novel, since the prevalent ethnic group of "white"
Cubans in her novels is highly adapted to the fast and easy living often
presented in detective novels.
    While focusing on the lives of the rich and famous, Garcia-Aguilera
does not shy away from tackling social issues such as class conflicts within
the Cuban community, but she does not present any animosities between
Cubans and other ethnic groups. Her first novel, *Bloody Waters*, features a
plot that is concerned with both gender and ethnicity as it investigates illegal adoption practices between wealthy Miami-based Cuban exiles and
poor pregnant Cuban women. Lupe's involvement in this case is mainly
altruistic—she has been hired by an adoptive couple in desperate need of
finding the birth mother of their illegally adopted daughter who suffers

from a rare genetic disease. In order to help her find the woman in Cuba, Lupe enlists the help of Barbara Perez, a lower-class first-generation immigrant, who escaped by boat from Cuba and who later served as a wet nurse hired by the baby traders. From her very first appearance, Barbara, a poor, obese, and perpetually pregnant mulatto, is described rather unfavorably, especially compared to the aforementioned upper-class Cuban women, as a "homicidal pregnant woman" ([1996] 1997, 231). Thus, Barbara, "her eyes glassy and distant" (230), kills three of the baby traders with a machete and a fishing knife. Lupe explains her actions as the deed of a "savage mother animal. . . . Perhaps Pedro and Tomas had the bad luck to get between a mama bear and her unborn cub—I don't know. Killing is something I've never understood" (234). Even though Barbara herself eventually says, "I just killed three people, Lupe. Maybe you think that's easy for me, that I'm some kind of savage, but it isn't easy" (245), readers of the novel will certainly find it difficult to forget the image of the knife-wielding, bloodsplattered "native" Cuban woman.

While in *Bloody Waters* Barbara Perez, the humongous murderous woman of color, still has to do the dirty work for Lupe, in the following novels Lupe herself becomes more of a hard-boiled character who is ready to kill if necessary. Her private life does not change much, since in order to remain an effective private investigator, willing to take somebody's life if the situation demands it, she apparently has to remain rather unattached. In her second novel, *Bloody Shame*, which is about a corrupt family of Cuban American jewelry dealers, Lupe kills her first thug, albeit in self-defense. Unlike some of her hard-boiled male colleagues, she is quite shaken after the incident, reflecting that "shooting a man was so different from shooting a target at a firing range" (Garcia-Aguilera [1997] 1998, 296) and she also has to be helped out of the unpleasant situation by one of her lovers, the attorney Tommy, who pulls up in his Rolls Royce just in time.

In *Bloody Secrets*, which tells the story of a Cuban immigrant ordeal, Lupe stays true to her hard-boiled self. Luis Delgado, a recent Cuban refugee, hires Lupe Solano because he wants to get back his family's fortune from a wealthy Cuban couple, who allegedly, after they managed to escape—while his family's flight was thwarted—swindled their friends out of mutual funds set aside for a new life in the United States and now, to top it all off, have put a contract out on him. Even though in *Bloody Secrets* Garcia-Aguilera is more critical of the wealthy Cubans "whose snobbery was unparalleled anywhere" ([1997] 1999, 165), she again presents the moneyed Miami Cubans as morally superior to the impoverished recent immigrant, for it turns out that Luis Delgado, rather than the rich Torres, who invested nearly all of their fortune in a fund for Cuban liberation, is the real swindler. Delgado finally meets his well-deserved end at the hands

THE FEMALE DETECTIVE IN GARCIA-AGUILERA AND NEELY   121

of Lupe, who, as Chandler's Philip Marlowe often does with his femme fatale clients, had almost fallen in love with the deceptive Luis—an "homme fatale" in the words of Walton and Jones (1999, 126). Disillusioned and disgusted by his behavior and his continued attempts to seduce her, she pushes him into the ocean, not knowing that Luis, in spite of being a "balsero," a boat person, does not know how to swim.

A Miracle in Paradise, Garcia-Aguilera's fourth novel, chiefly focuses on Cuban religious customs. Lupe is asked by Lourdes's Mother Superior to investigate whether or not the miracle announced by a rival order, predicting that the Virgin of Our Lady of Charity, the patron saint of Cuba, will shed real tears on Cuban Independence Day, is merely a scam. The matter is of utmost importance to Cuban Americans, because the miracle has been announced by a formerly Yugoslavian order and "[i]f this new order could deliver on the promise of this miracle, it would place it at the forefront of all religious orders. Every Cuban woman in Dade County, in the entire United States, would want to be a part of it" (1999, 21). Since the miracle is supposed to take place on 10 October, Cuban unification day, it is of great political significance, because, as Lupe realizes, it calls for reunification of all Cubans: "What I was dealing with here, under the surface, was the concept of Cuban reunification, the bringing together of those on the island and the exiles. Part of me regarded this idea as a great and wondrous thing. But I also knew that reality might be something different" (98).

By dealing with the political dimension that a possible reunification of Cuba might have for both right-wing and left-wing political groups and by investigating the attitudes of second-generation Cuban immigrants, who are torn between their Cuban and American identities, Garcia-Aguilera claims to treat the Cuban American situation in a serious fashion in *A Miracle in Paradise*. Lupe, for example, at one point announces that "[a]lthough I grew up and lived in America, it felt like an accident to me. I was Cuban" (1999, 45), yet she also has to admit that "Cuba might have been in our veins, but we had no reality on which to hang our convictions" (115). Since the parodic tone that Lupe usually employs when referring to gender difference is also applied to Cuban Catholicism and ethnic customs in this novel, it is sometimes difficult to establish whether she seriously intends to uphold Cuban (religious) values or whether she is simply making fun of them. Thus, Cuban Catholicism is ridiculed throughout (for example, the "1-800-MIRACLE" hot line in both Spanish and English), and the detective plot involves the drowning of a nun in holy water and a rather farfetched tale of (non-Cuban) Americans enthralled by Cuban Catholicism and nationalism to the point of arranging the fake miracle. Even Leonardo's sports craze—which involves obtaining an exercise machine that will eliminate "Cuban ass syndrome"—is described in terms of his Cuban identity:

"Leonardo labored with such intensity to reach his personal state of Cuban nirvana that he had actually confessed to me that his goal was a state of psychic control in which he could eat as much fried food as he wished without it reaching his Cuban ass" (140).

The plot of *Havana Heat* harks back to both *Bloody Secrets* and *Bloody Waters.* Lupe is again hired to retrieve Cuban riches that have been lost in the aftermath of the Cuban revolution. As in the Luis Delgado case, she is deceived by her client, who wants to swindle her family out of a valuable work of art, an ancient tapestry displaying a mythical unicorn that is hidden in the basement of the Havana family residence. In the process of doing research for her case, Lupe stumbles upon a dangerous ring of corrupt art dealers, who replace old Cuban paintings in Cuba with fake ones in order to sell the originals in the United States—sometimes even to their rightful owners.

Havana Heat, as Garcia-Aguilera's fifth Lupe Solano novel, does not add much to the ethnicized detective plots of the previous novels in the series. Lupe becomes perhaps even a tad more hard-boiled, suspending her tenuous relationship with the Cuban American lawyer Alvaro Mendoza in order to go on the dangerous trip to Havana to retrieve the tapestry. As in *Bloody Waters*, she depends on Barbara Perez for the boat passage. But this time Lupe herself becomes the knife-wielding, blood-spattered "wild woman," when she kills one of the corrupt art dealers by plunging a carpet knife into his chest—in self-defense, of course. Thus, in *Havana Heat*, issues regarding the interface of ethnicity and class seem to be handled a bit more delicately in that Lupe not only dates a leftist compatriot lawyer, but also becomes Barbara's double by imitating her actions from *Bloody Waters*. She furthermore repeatedly expresses regret over the fact that the Miami social agencies have taken Barbara's children away from her because she lives on a boat. But her classism nevertheless resurfaces in her relationship to the octogenarian household help, Osvaldo and his wife, who in spite of purportedly being regarded as "family" by Lupe and her sisters, are shown to be waiting on the young women hand and foot.

Garcia-Aguilera's often parodic treatment of ethnicity corroborates a point already made above in reference to her presentation of gender: it seems that she often avoids making political statements about controversial topics such as gender and/or ethnicity by hiding behind a highly parodic tone. While it might be possible to read Lupe's gender performance as a type of "gender performativity," a Butlerian interpretation would, however, require a stretch of the imagination, since the Lupe Solano novels otherwise seem to further a very conservative and, ultimately, hegemonic worldview that validates the capitalist lifestyle of the wealthy Cuban exiles in Miami. This endorsement of capitalism can perhaps, at least partly, be

THE FEMALE DETECTIVE IN GARCIA-AGUILERA AND NEELY   123

blamed on generic considerations, since Garcia-Aguilera's novels, even though they are authored by a woman, do qualify as a variant of the classical hard-boiled detective novel and as such—as Kathleen Klein has pointed out—they indeed seem to aim to confirm the societal status quo. It might, therefore, not seem unduly critical to observe that many of Garcia-Aguilera's characters, who, for example, employ less fortunate Cubans over decades as loyal household help,[6] have a strong class—if not race—bias, and that by means of her novels Garcia-Aguilera actively upholds the "interested power structures" of her society, thus stabilizing a capitalist system informed by (white) male interests.

Barbara Neely's Blanche White mysteries, however, seem to run completely counter to this tradition. Blanche, Neely's eggplant-dark domestic worker,[7] has become a mother to her dead sister's children and thus is not unattached and free to operate outside of the law as she pleases. As an accidental sleuth she just happens to stumble upon the murder and mystery cases that she solves. Since she is not a private investigator—or perhaps because she is an exclusively *private* investigator—Neely's characterization is not indebted to any hard-boiled conventions. Thus, Blanche is not overly sexy, does not carry a gun, and also does not have any casual lovers. Instead of using violence to solve crimes, she relies on her own perception of "domestic clues," on ancestor worship,[8] and on a network of fellow domestic workers who have got the lowdown on all of the murderous people she works for, thereby nicely illustrating a point usually made by critics about ethnic detective novels, namely that in these novels the detective's connectedness to his or her community supersedes the individualism of the hard-boiled white male detective (see Reitz 1999, 215; Stewart 1999, 176). Perhaps even more importantly, in all of the four Blanche White novels the detective story is paralleled by an equally important story line dealing with race relations or problems within the black community.

In *Blanche on the Lam* Neely has Blanche solve a case in which a murderous Southern belle kills every male—including her loyal black gardener—who gets in the way of an inheritance scam that she has set up in order to obtain the fortune of her Aunt Emmeline, whom she has also murdered and replaced with an alcoholic African American look-alike who is able to pass for white (the illegitimate offspring of Emmeline's father and a poor black woman). Since in Neely's novels gendered race relations serve as much as a thematic focus as do the crime stories, she continuously presents Blanche's thoughts about her relationship to her haughty white employers. In Neely's first novel, race relations in the New South form the core of the race plot. Blanche's reflections on the relationships of black domestics to their white employers reveal that even in the aftermath of the civil rights movement the power structure has not changed:

Blanche was unimpressed by the tears, and Grace's Mammy-save-me eyes. Mammy-savers regularly peered out at her from the faces of some white women for whom she worked, and, lately, in this age of the touchy-feely model of manhood, an occasional white man. It happened when an employer was struck by family disaster or grew too compulsive about owning everything, too overwrought, or downright frightened by who and what they were. She never ceased to be amazed at how many white people longed for Aunt Jemima. (1992, 39)

Blanche, in her turn, is afraid of succumbing to what she calls "Darkies' Disease" whose most obvious symptom is undue love for one's employer. She, nevertheless, almost infects herself with it when she develops a sort of friendship with her employer's cousin Mumsfield, who is being cheated out of his inheritance by the murderous Grace because he is mildly retarded and thus suffering from the same social invisibility as Blanche. Yet even though there is a connection between the powerless black woman and the retarded white man whom she saves from being seriously wronged by his social peers, Blanche deliberately decides against becoming his caretaker, because she realizes that there still is a line of racial division that she does not want to cross:

> She understood that his Down's syndrome made him as recognizably different from the people who ran and owned the world as she. . . . There was no way she could explain how the last six days had confirmed her constitutional distaste for being any whiteman's mammy. . . . "I understand, Blanche," he'd told her. "I understand." And for two seconds she'd thought that somehow he'd leaped across the gap between them and truly knew what it meant to be a black woman trying to control her own life and stand firm against having her brain vanillaed.[9] (214–15)

As the remark about Blanche's fear of "having her brain vanillaed" indicates, Neely introduces a strategy of reversing the connotations of white equals positive and black equals negative in *Blanche on the Lam*. Thus, she "signifies" on the meaning of "to blackmail" in a very clever and amusing fashion, also confounding the words "mail" and "male":

> She thought the sheriff's solution included paying someone off with money he expected to get from Everett for not telling Grace that Everett was fucking around. Blackmail, in a word. Blanche quickly searched her mind for the other word, the one that began with "ex." She tried not to use words that made black sound bad. When she couldn't find the word she wanted, she settled on "whitemale" and was pleased how much more accurately her word described the situation.[10] (122)

In an article that shows how the novels of Walter Mosley decode the meanings of whiteness, Liam Kennedy argues that "[r]ace functions as a source of psychological and social fantasy for many hard-boiled writers, with blackness often signifying an otherness within the white subject which requires control and mastery" (226). By showing how Blanche fights against having "her brain vanillaed," Neely renders the racialized binary opposition of white and black from a black person's point of view and effectively shows how in Blanche's case "whiteness signifies an otherness within the black subject which requires control and mastery." (The meaning of Blanche's name as "White White" does, of course, provide a very ironic comment on Blanche's otherness.)

Blanche Among the Talented Tenth, Neely's second novel, set in a ritzy African American seaside resort, develops the color theme introduced in *Blanche on the Lam* and focuses even more on "domestic" topics such as Blanche's private life and intraracial problems (class-related snobbery as well as the preference of some blacks for their lighter-skinned brethren and sistren) than on the mysteries: a suicide and what seems to be the murder of a detestable black socialite whose favorite pastime was to reveal her wealthy friends' unsavory secrets to everyone. The murder turns out to have been an accident—one should not keep a radio too close to one's bathtub—but the suicide, as Blanche discovers, was almost a murder, since it had been occasioned by a man's jealousy of his unacknowledged half-brother, whom his father had preferred all of his life. Blanche, who in good detective fiction fashion temporarily falls in love with this man (Robert Stuart, called Stu), finds out that he hated his half-brother, Hank, because his father preferred the brother's darker skin:

> "All my life he was saying things like, 'Boy! Why don't you get some sun,' or, 'Boy, you don't have as much color as a vanilla shake!'" And Hank was his Little Brown Bomber, even though he had hardly qualified as brown, Blanche thought. Another variation on the color fuck-up. (1994, 179)

Stu's attitude toward color, as Blanche subsequently uncovers, had actually set in motion a fatal chain reaction: years ago Stu had inadvertently caused the death of his secret Vietnamese wife. She died of a heart attack because he refused to acknowledge the marriage publicly after he had found out that his father was going to disinherit him if he married "outside the race." The woman who died in her bathtub in the resort had seen him dispose of the body in a garbage dump and subsequently tried to blackmail him. After her accidental death, Stu seized the opportunity of insinuating to his brother that his wife had killed her. In order to save his wife, his brother Hank, already clinically depressed, decided to commit suicide. Also in keeping with the intraracial color plot—which culminates in color-related domestic crime—Blanche, concerned about her daughter Taifa's observation that "if you have dark skin, people laugh at you and say you smell bad and nobody wants to be your friend" (85), continuously struggles to keep her children, who temporarily attend a private school, from turning into snobs who detest dark-skinned blacks.

Blanche Cleans Up, Neely's third novel, follows the same pattern of juxtaposing a mystery plot and a plot about African American community life. Blanche discovers a sex scandal involving politicians of every color, solves a murder her politician employer tried to pin on a friend's (and fellow domestic's) son, and supplies the necessary clue to solve an environmental scandal together with her son Malik. She is very concerned about the upbringing of her children in her rough Boston neighborhood and even becomes a community counselor of sorts, providing the politically correct views on typical problems in the hood such as gang violence, drug dealing, teenage pregnancy, and prejudice against gays. Thus, Blanche often sermonizes on social topics such as, for example, black homosexuality—in this case in a rather heavy-handed educational manner—as the following quotation shows:

> Blanche wished she could tell Mick she was wrong, that no black people had anything against lesbians or gay men, but she knew Mick was right. She'd once heard a black historian say that hatred of homosexuals was taught to African slaves because slave-babies could only be made by female-male couples. (1998, 239)

The rather cumbersome didacticism and more pessimistic vision of *Blanche Cleans Up* also sets the tone for Neely's fourth novel, *Blanche Passes Go*. In Neely's most recent novel, Blanche returns to Farleigh, North Carolina, the setting of *Blanche on the Lam*. This time, Blanche investigates the murder of an attractive young white woman from the wrong side of the tracks who seems to have been involved with David Palmer, the brother of a former employer of Blanche's, who had raped her eight years before. She also becomes reacquainted with Mumsfield, who is about to marry David Palmer's sister, Karen. In keeping with the generally more somber and "separationist" tone of *Blanche Passes Go*, Blanche, by refusing to protect Mumsfield from the racist gold digger Karen, makes an even greater effort to distance herself from her former protégé.[11] In an article on Blanche White as "an *Other* hero," Caroline Reitz has astutely called Blanche a one-woman "contact zone" (2000, 221) for colliding black and white rural and urban worlds (214). While Blanche's interaction with Daisy, the murdered girl's best friend, indicates that to some extent this is also true for *Blanche Passes*

Go, the novel, nevertheless, reinforces the impression that throughout the four novels Blanche moves towards an increasingly Afrocentrist worldview.

Blanche Passes Go introduces a subplot that combines an analysis of gender and race relations at the turn of the millennium by focusing on the difficulties that Blanche experiences in dealing with her lover Thelvin's jealous love for her. At first she views Thelvin's overprotective manner as an attempt to cage her in, asking her friend Ardell, "You never notice how close being protected and taken care of is to being held prisoner?" (2000, 49), but later she attempts to understand his behavior as a reaction to the racism that he has to deal with every day: "Maybe being a black man—the most hated human being in the country—and mostly working jobs where somebody else had all the say had something to do with wanting exclusive ownership of a woman's life. Of course absolutely none of that made it healthy or all right" (250).

Perhaps even more importantly, Blanche also reveals a more pronounced African American focus by repeatedly turning to her ancestors in order to plot her revenge against David Palmer:

> She paused when she was through, trying to decide how to talk with her Ancestors about what she was going through without whining or asking for special favors. She knew she didn't need to explain it to *them*. They knew about rape, they knew about fear, and they hadn't been stopped by either. They'd found ways to fight back—from running away to killing as many slavers as they could, from aborting the slaver's issue to hexing his penis . . . to putting pepper in the slop pot and spit in the soup.[12] They had not run from their enemies, except to rest up and find another way to fight. And there it was. It was as if the answer to last night's question was being whispered in her ear: Find a way to fight back. She was suddenly sure that the ritual she needed to rid her life of David Palmer was to take action against him—not in a legal way or even by getting in his face. (29)

Even though it sounds good to begin with, the advice she assumes to have received from her ancestors turns out to be a mixed blessing at best (since we are dealing with a matter of faith, there is, after all, a chance that the advice might simply be a figment of Blanche's imagination). Because she fails to realize that there is no solid evidence that David Palmer is a murderer on top of being a rapist, she inadvertently becomes an accessory to his murder. By getting her revenge, Blanche develops from an accidental sleuth into an accidental accomplice, thus returning the novel's focus from the "race" to the detective plot during the last chapter. As Kathy Phillips observes, Blanche has fundamentally changed throughout the series: "The Blanche White who appears in her fourth engagement in the newly published *Blanche Passes Go* is not the one who appeared in *Blanche on the*

Lam" (2000, 42), and "One wonders where Blanche has left to go, her anger has escalated so" (43).

In light of the above plot analyses of Neely's novels, one simply cannot help but conclude that Blanche is not your average sexy, gun-toting, Mercedes-driving female private eye. Carolyn Reitz, nevertheless, tries to position Neely's novels in relation to other multicultural detective fiction in the hard-boiled mode:

> Even multicultural detective fiction, which deliberately challenges . . . traditional heroic requirements (white, heterosexual, male), is identified and marketed as a genre of exceptional individuals: an Easy Rawlins or a Pam Nilsen mystery, the latest Kinsey Millhone, V. I. Warshawski, or Tamara Hayle. . . . (1999, 215)

With Blanche White, however, Reitz argues, "Neely alters the tradition of both the hero and the genre, while offering an alternative to the current compromises of contemporary nondominant detective fiction" (1999, 215). While it is certainly true that Neely changes or perhaps even ignores the hard-boiled tradition, it might make more sense to read the Blanche White mysteries as part of another, more woman-oriented tradition of the detective novel, which they also modify by "signifyin(g)" on it with a black difference. The back flap to *Blanche Cleans Up* quotes a review from the *Los Angeles Times* that "[o]ne is tempted to describe Blanche White as a combination of Agatha Christie's Miss Marple and Walter Mosley's Easy Rawlins . . . but it would be a crime to suggest that she is anything less than a truly original creation." And, indeed, in spite of some significant differences, there are quite a few parallels between Neely's novels and Christie's classics. Like Miss Marple, Blanche White relies on the "'feminine' aspects of detection[13] that have been traditionally elided in traditional conceptions of the tough guy PI" (Walton and Jones 1999, 98). Miss Marple, for example, uses "feminine" detection skills when she solves the murder in *The Body in the Library* mainly by simply noticing that the body is that of a lower-class woman dressed up like a socialite, whereas in *Blanche Passes Go*, Blanche, true to her own class background, gathers information by posturing as a window cleaner and a forgetful domestic. In both *4:50 from Paddington* and in *Blanche Cleans Up* unheroic women originally hired to clean houses (a woman named Lucy Eylesbarrow in Christie's novel) find themselves cleaning up whole communities by exposing upstanding pillars of the community as murderers. Long before Neely created her unheroic heroine Blanche, Christie's novels, as Sally Munt points out, "rejected the heroic, preferring instead the permeatic parodic mode first implicated by her female forebears" (1994, 9). In citing Marion Shaw and Sabine Vanacker, Munt maintains that Christie's "women sleuths and

THE FEMALE DETECTIVE IN GARCIA-AGUILERA AND NEELY 129

assistant sleuths . . . appeal to women writers and readers, because in their social roles those women are 'actually the ones who put the pattern together, who restore order to a shaken world'" (1994, 8). The same can be said about Neely's novels, even though there are quite a few necessary differences between Miss Marple's mid-century English villages and Blanche's 1990s U.S. "hoods" and small-town communities. Thus, Miss Marple often complains about "the maids" who "deteriorate in quality" (Hawkes 1998, 208) as modern times start to affect St. Mary Mead. Blanche, however, is the maid.[14] As a distinguished upper-middle-class member of her village, Miss Marple fully trusts the police, whereas Blanche White always has reason to distrust the police; in the first novel she even is on the lam for passing a bad check. And even though, as Munt also indicates, Christie's novels depict "broadly feminist concerns" (1994, 8), there are important differences in the resolution of the novels' gender plots: at the end of Christie's novel, Lucy Eylesbarrow, a bored upper-middle-class mathematician who works as a lady's maid for almost the same reason that Blanche works as a domestic—namely, to maintain a degree of independence[15]—is "rewarded" with a proper husband, whereas Blanche, more true to our fin de siècle sensibilities, remains a single mother who finds it increasingly difficult to trust a man.

This little excursion into the world of Agatha Christie serves to illustrate an important point, namely that Garcia-Aguilera and Neely operate out of different traditions, one male- and the other female-oriented, and that therefore what might come across as Garcia-Aguilera's "political incorrectness" can be explained, if perhaps not condoned, in light of her genre choice. The differences between the Lupe Solano and the Blanche White novels, however, also reflect their authors' personal preferences: Garcia-Aguilera rewrites the hard-boiled genre by parodying many of the stock characters and typical situations of the hard-boiled mode, but she nevertheless confirms the social status quo of the hard-boiled novel by endorsing a "male world" and a hegemonic capitalist social order through her portrayal of the glamorous lives of wealthy Cuban immigrants in Miami. Neely, however, increasingly seems to prefer the gendered and racialized social topics that are of utmost importance to all of her novels over her domestic mystery plots and even supports African American separatism in light of the ubiquitous racism African Americans are confronted with. Her character Blanche proudly accepts her racial identity and social status, whereas Garcia-Aguilera's Lupe, in spite of her pride in her Cuban ethnicity, prefers to "pass" in every possible regard in a white capitalist society. Garcia-Aguilera's and Neely's novels thus address another important aspect of the genre of the ethnic detective novel by illustrating that there still is a difference between ethnicity and race. Differences in social status between more or less "visible" ethnic groups are still "racially" motivated—even within the same ethnicity, as Lupe Solano's attitude toward darker Cubans reveals. The two writers' novels, furthermore, corroborate an important point that Andrew Pepper makes about the social divide between ethnicity and "race" when he argues that even though "[t]erms like race and ethnicity no longer refer to categories that are fixed and stable . . . the temptation to entirely collapse race and ethnicity needs to be resisted" (1999, 243).

NOTES

1. Munt's strategy of appropriating detective fiction for feminist purposes in *Murder by the Book: Feminism and the Crime Novel* also includes looking for ways in which the clichés of crime fiction might empower women: "Perhaps it is more efficacious to examine those specific clichés imbuing crime fiction which, possibly *within an overall conformity*, can be appropriated by feminists for political ends. For example, many a misogynist has filled the need for that staple convention, an 'eminently murderable man'" (1994, 197 [italics in original]).

2. Gates explains that "Signifyin(g) is a uniquely black historical concept, entirely textual or linguistic, by which a second statement or figure repeats, or tropes, or reverses the first. Its use as a figure for intertextuality allows us to understand literary revision without resource [*sic*] to thematic, bibliographical, or Oedipal slayings at the crossroads; rather, critical signification is tropic and rhetorical. Indeed, the very concept of Signifyin(g) can only exist in the realm of the intertextual relation" (quoted in Gruesser 1999, 239).

3. In *A Miracle in Paradise*, Lupe uses her sex appeal to achieve professional goals. Because she cannot afford the "hourly rate of four hundred dollars" (Garcia-Aguilera 1999, 189) that her lover Tommy charges as one of Miami's best defense attorneys, she trades sex for professional help.

4. In her landmark essay "Womanliness as a Masquerade," Joan Riviere argues that many—if not all—women hide their (more positively connoted) "masculinity" (e.g., "active" behavior, professional competence) behind their "womanliness" (e.g., passivity, receptiveness): "Womanliness . . . could be assumed and worn as a mask, both to hide the possession of masculinity and to avert the reprisals expected if she was found to possess it. . . . The reader may now ask how I define womanliness or where I draw the line between genuine womanliness and the 'masquerade.' My suggestion is not, however, that there is any such difference; whether radical or superficial, they are the same thing" ([1927] 2000, 73). The above-quoted passage from *Havana Heat* suggests that Garcia-Aguilera's "lady dick" Lupe Solano seems to agree with this view.

5. As Priscilla Walton and Manina Jones point out in *Detective Agency: Women Rewriting the Hard-Boiled Tradition*, emulations by women writers of the persona of the "hard-boiled dick" have resulted in "critiques of women's practices of hard-boiled writing [which] often condemn these novels as 'drag performances,' in effect using the language of 'queerness' to discredit them" (1999, 99).

6. Neely, who in her novels focuses on the perspective of the household help, sincerely questions the help's loyalty. She thus has Blanche reason in *Blanche on the Lam:* "What she didn't understand was how you convinced yourself that you were actually loved by people who paid you the lowest possible wages . . . who gave you handkerchiefs and sachets for holiday gifts and gave their children stocks and bonds. It seemed to her that this was the real danger in looking at customers through love-tinted glasses" (1992, 48).

THE FEMALE DETECTIVE IN GARCIA-AGUILERA AND NEELY   131

7. Incidentally, as Gruesser points out, the possibly first African American detective was also a female domestic worker: "Two of the earliest black detectives in African American fiction appear in Pauline Hopkins' *Hagar's Daughter* (1901–02) and John E. Bruce's *The Black Sleuth* (1907–09), novels serialized in black periodicals. . . . Hopkins only turns to the mystery genre in the last third of her narrative, when a young, black maid, Venus Johnson, cracks a case that Chief Henson, the head of the federal government's detective agency, has been unable to solve" (1999, 236).

8. As Stephen Soitos observes in "Black Detective Fiction," "Black vernaculars and, to some extent, hoodoo or alternative religious practices are major factors in differentiating black detective texts from other detective novels" (1998, 997).

9. In *Blanche on the Lam* Blanche literally has to force herself to disregard her feelings of "kinship" toward Mumsfield: "For all his specialness and their seeming connectedness, Mumsfield was still a whiteman. . . . Would she always find some reason—retardation, blindness, sheer incompetence—to nurture people who had been raised to believe she had no other purpose in life than to be their 'girl'? Had the slavers stamped mammyism into her genes when they raped her greatgrandmothers? If they had, she was determined to prove the power of will over blood" (1992, 182).

10. Neely also reverses the stereotype of the "dangerous black male" by having Blanche observe about the retarded Mumsfield in *Blanche on the Lam:* "There was an air of harmlessness about him that was puzzling in a white male" (1992, 23).

11. Neely writes about Blanche's attitude toward Mumsfield in *Blanche Passes Go:* "There was no way Blanche could move Mumsfield from the someone-I-know-and-like to the friend category. Karen made that impossible. How could he ever be her friend and not understand this very basic part of who she was? Would he have a friend who chose to marry someone who hated people with Down's syndrome? But, of course, whitefolks in this country are trained to believe they can have it both ways, like stealing the Indian's land while claiming to admire the noble savage" (2000, 238).

12. Blanche uses similar strategies in dealing with her adversaries: in *Blanche on the Lam*, she hexes the penis of a white boy who has insulted her, and in *Blanche Passes Go* she puts a laxative in the drink of a white male party guest who made sexual advances toward a black caterer.

13. Walton and Jones cite "a plodding nature" and "infinite patience" as typically "feminine" skills that also come in handy as detective skills (1999, 98).

14. In his biographical sketch "Agatha Christie," David Hawkes reveals that in this case Miss Marple's concerns are also her creator's concerns: "[Christie's] autobiography contains far more grousing over servant problems than reflection on the author's trade, and she is refreshingly unconcerned with intellectual pretensions" (1998, 196).

15. There is, of course, a difference between the two types of "independence": Lucy Eylesbarrow could choose to work in a different profession, whereas Blanche's lack of other marketable skills precludes her from doing so. Perhaps more importantly, there also is a difference between the two types of "domestic mysteries." Thus, Kathy Phillips complains with reference to *Blanche Passes Go* that Neely modifies the genre too much. She wonders if "the mystery [is] a useful forum for social attack" (2000, 43) and particularly doubts that Neely's preferred subgenre, "the cozy, which rarely takes up matters of social importance" (43), is ready to provide such a forum. Her final evaluation is rather harsh and seems to reject the idea of genre modification through rewriting with an ethnic difference: "In subsuming her plot to her character's attitude, Neely is sacrificing the primary goal of the mystery novel, which is to present a puzzle to be solved by that character and by the reader" (43)

WORKS CITED

Christie, Agatha. [1942] 1992. *The Body in the Library.* London: HarperCollins.

———. [1957] 1995. *4.50 from Paddington.* London: HarperCollins.

Garcia-Aguilera, Carolina. [1996] 1997. *Bloody Waters.* New York: Berkley Prime Crime.

———. [1997] 1998. *Bloody Shame.* New York: Berkley Prime Crime.

———. [1997] 1999. *Bloody Secrets.* New York: Berkley Prime Crime.

———. 1999. *A Miracle in Paradise.* New York: Avon Books.

———. 2000. *Havana Heat.* New York: HarperCollins.

Gerhart, Mary. 1992. *Genre Choices, Gender Questions.* Norman: University of Oklahoma Press.

Gosselin, Adrienne Johnson, ed. 1999. *Multicultural Detective Fiction: Murder from the "Other" Side.* New York: Garland.

Gruesser, John Cullen. 1999. "An Un-Easy Relationship: Walter Mosley's Signifyin(g) Detective and the Black Community." In Gosselin 1999, 235–55.

Hawkes, David. 1998. "Agatha Christie." In vol. I of *Mystery and Suspense Writers: The Literature of Crime, Detection, and Espionage*, edited by Robin W. Winks, 195–216. New York: Charles Scribner's Sons.

Kennedy, Liam. 1999. "Black Noir: Race and Urban Space in Walter Mosley's Detective Fiction." In Klein 1995, 224–39.

Klein, Kathleen Gregory. 1995. *The Woman Detective: Gender and Genre.* 2d ed. Urbana: University of Illinois Press.

———, ed. 1999. *Diversity and Detective Fiction.* Bowling Green, Ohio: Bowling Green State University Popular Press.

Munt, Sally. 1994. *Murder by the Book: Feminism and the Crime Novel.* London: Routledge.

Neely, Barbara. 1992. *Blanche on the Lam.* Harmondsworth, U.K.: Penguin.

———. 1994. *Blanche Among the Talented Tenth.* Harmondsworth, U.K.: Penguin.

———. 1998. *Blanche Cleans Up.* Harmondsworth, U.K.: Penguin.

———. 2000. *Blanche Passes Go.* Harmondsworth, U.K.: Penguin.

Pepper, Andrew. 1999. "Bridges and Boundaries: Race, Ethnicity, and the Contemporary American Crime Novel." In Klein 1995, 240–59.

Phillips, Kathy. 2000. "Mystery Woman." *Women's Review of Books* 27:42–43.

Reitz, Caroline. 1999. "Do We Need Another Hero?" In Gosselin 1999, 213–33.

Riviere, Joan. [1927] 2000. "Womanliness as a Masquerade." In *Psychoanalysis and Woman: A Reader*, edited by Shelley Saguaro, 70–78. Houndmills, U.K.: Macmillan.

Soitos, Stephen. 1998. "Black Detective Fiction." In vol. 2 of *Mystery and Suspense Writers: The Literature of Crime, Detection, and Espionage*, edited by Robin W. Winks, 995–1008. New York: Charles Scribner's Sons.

———. 1999. "Queering the 'I': Black Lesbian Detective Fiction." In Gosselin 1999, 105–21.

Stewart, Michelle Pagni. 1999. "'A Rose by Any Other Name': A Native American Detective Novel by Louis Owens." In Gosselin 1999, 167–211.

Walton, Priscilla L., and Manina Jones. 1999. *Detective Agency: Women Rewriting the Hard-Boiled Tradition.* Berkeley and Los Angeles: University of California Press.

Investigating Newark, New Jersey: Empowering Spaces in Valerie Wilson Wesley's Detective Fiction

CARMEN BIRKLE

In a recent interview, the African American writer Valerie Wilson Wesley stated that she sets her detective novels, featuring the black female PI Tamara Hayle,[1] in Newark, New Jersey, because "I know the city well, in fact my husband grew up in Newark and we live close to it, in Montclair between New York and Newark" (Matter-Seibel 2001, 118; see also Fischer-Hornung and Mueller 2003, 314–15). Wesley continues to explain: "I live close enough so I can drive there and look at corners on Sundays and make notes. I need to get a feeling of the place; that's the reporter in me. In my books the setting is one of the characters" (Matter-Seibel 2001, 119). Wesley reveals in these comments how in her imagination she creates the space(s) in which her PI solves her cases. On the surface, Newark seems to be a real place, located in the vicinity of New York City. But Wesley reads and interprets this place and then translates her own experiences and impressions into language and stories. As Michel de Certeau notes, "Stories about places are makeshift things" ([1984] 2000, 133). This translation process turns the city into one of her fictional characters; thus, Newark in Wesley's fiction is simultaneously real and imagined, fact and fiction, and interacts with Tamara Hayle as a character.

Newark has a publicly known history and also reflects Tamara Hayle's experiences of family and community, of racism and sexism, as well as of private and professional life. Newark here is more than just background; it is what Stephen Soitos calls *"blackground"* that "introduces the reader to varied aspects of African American culture while structurally adhering to the detective story format" (1996, 222). In my paper, I will argue that in a globalizing world, detective fiction, and here particularly that written by

134 CARMEN BIRKLE

Valerie Wilson Wesley, deliberately focuses on a specific locale in which the detective is deeply rooted. Generally, women's detective fiction contributes to this idea of a "New Realism," namely, the tendency toward regionalism and localism (see Keitel 1998, 92). In contrast to the destructive portrayal of the dangerous city in classical hard-boiled detective fiction by authors such as Dashiell Hammett and Chester Himes, Wesley's Newark not only provides her detective with clues for the solution of her cases but also with empowering spaces such as her home and her office. Space and the intimate knowledge of this space in Wesley's fiction are indispensable for the restoration of law and order. Both crime and its solution in Wesley's fiction—which is part of what Evelyne Keitel calls the "New Golden Age" (1998, 7)—depend on and interact with the surrounding geographical and sociopolitical spaces (see Keitel 1998, 89). And it is precisely in this space that Tamara Hayle gains her power as a female African American detective who is also a single mother.[2]

THE CITY IN CLASSICAL HARD-BOILED DETECTIVE FICTION

What we know today as the classical hard-boiled detective genre was inaugurated in the 1920s and '30s in the United States by male writers such as Dashiell Hammett and Raymond Chandler as a reaction to the hitherto dominant genre of the "cosies" by British women writers of the Golden Age of detective fiction such as Agatha Christie and Dorothy Sayers. Writers of the hard-boiled genre were interested in a re-Americanization and a masculinization of the genre (see Dietze 1997, 11). According to Gabriele Dietze, the idea of hypermasculinity was opposed to femininity and "overcivilization" (25) and found its spatial equivalent in the attempt to absolutely separate public/male and private/female spheres, culminating in hard-boiled detective fiction of the early twentieth century. Neither Hammett's Sam Spade nor Chandler's Philip Marlowe were ever shown as private human beings but always in pursuit of criminals in the streets of San Francisco and Los Angeles. Chandler sums it up: "I do not care much about his [Marlowe's] private life . . ." ([1944] 1946, 237). Typical descriptions of the city emphasize its darkness and danger: "San Francisco's night-fog, thin, clammy, and penetrant, blurred the street" (Hammett [1930] 1980, 301), and "Outside the bright gardens had a haunted look, as though small wild eyes were watching me from behind the bushes, as though the sunshine itself had a mysterious something in its light" (Chandler [1938] 1944, 220). In both examples, the city comes across as a frightening and dangerous force that is at the same time oblivious to what happens in its streets. In both Chandler's and Hammett's fiction the setting is more than realistic; it is almost naturalistic in its fixity and hostile indifference. It becomes one of the detective's most dangerous opponents, as Raymond Chandler argues in "The Simple Art of Murder": "But down these mean streets a man must go who is not himself mean, who is neither tarnished nor afraid. The detective in this kind of story must be such a man. He is the hero, he is everything. He must be a complete man and a common man and yet an unusual man" ([1944] 1946, 237).

Chester Himes, the first major African American detective fiction writer, picks up this hostility of the city in his novels, which are frequently set in Harlem, as, for example, in *A Rage in Harlem:*

> Looking eastward from the towers of Riverside Church, perched among the university buildings on the high banks of the Hudson River, in a valley far below, waves of gray rooftops distort the perspective like the surface of a sea. Below the surface, in the murky waters of fetid tenements, a city of black people who are convulsed in desperate living, like the voracious churning of millions of hungry cannibal fish. Blind mouths eating their own guts. Stick in a hand and draw back a nub.
> That is Harlem.
> The farther east it goes, the blacker it gets. ([1957] 1991, 93)

According to Stephen Soitos, Himes creates "a mythical Harlem landscape that offered what he [Himes] often referred to as an absurdist vision of African American existence" (1996, 126) and turns this landscape into a "mirror [of] the disintegrating social fabric of the community . . ." (1996, 223). The private lives of Grave Digger Jones and Coffin Ed, Himes's two memorable detectives, are of no concern to the author or the reader. They are detectives whose enemies are the criminals as well as the city. The city is exposed as a cancerous organism whose illness is gradually spreading and impossible to cure. Poverty, crime, and decay have turned people into creatures constantly engaged in battle for the "survival of the fittest"; survival can be secured only through the destruction of others.

In contrast to Himes, Walter Mosley's detective Easy Rawlins is deeply attached to Los Angeles, and his "personal life and connection to the black community are integral to the progression of the plot" (Soitos 1996, 234). In *Devil in a Blue Dress,* Easy Rawlins's motivation for taking on the job of looking for the mysterious white woman, Daphne Monet, is his lack of money and consequently his fear of losing the small house he has bought in a suburban black neighborhood of Los Angeles. The rest of the city qualifies as "mean streets." Rawlins cannot keep the criminals away from his private property; no personal history connects him to Los Angeles.

Beginning with Dolores Komo's Clio Browne and most prominently continued with Wesley's Tamara Hayle, cities lose the threatening and alien qualities of male hard-boiled detective fiction. Walter Mosley's Easy Rawlins remains a character in between these two trends. By detecting criminals—black and white—black female PIs restore law and order (often taking liberties in the interpretation of the law) and imbue their urban surroundings with human qualities and history.

THE CITY OF NEWARK IN VALERIE WILSON WESLEY'S DETECTIVE FICTION

Newark is a place that many would not think worthy of attracting much fictional attention. Recently, however, Valerie Wilson Wesley has begun to set her detective stories in this city, frequently also considered merely a suburb of New York City. And this may be precisely one of the reasons for Newark's emerging fictional prominence. While New York City is the embodiment of the global city that gathers in its geography people from all over the world and displays architectural symbols of political, military, and financial powers—as unfortunately, the events of September 11, 2001, have shown—Newark has nothing of New York City's global relevance. On the contrary, it has now become a sort of refuge for people trying to escape the noise, high rent, speed, and social and racial conflicts of the "Big Apple." And most recently, as a result of the terrorist attacks, major companies have permanently moved their businesses to Newark. Thus, Newark's relevance has risen from marginality to centrality.

Historically, Newark has witnessed racial conflicts and race riots, and its population consists of a variety of ethnic groups such as African Americans, Hispanics, and people of East European, Italian, and Greek origins. "By 1970 African Americans were 54.2 percent of the [city's] population" (see Mendelsohn, online), and in 1967, just before the outbreak of nationwide race riots, "Newark had the highest percentage of substandard housing, and the second highest crime and infant mortality rates in the country" (Mendelsohn, online). As these figures show, Newark with its "mean streets" could easily qualify as the setting for a traditional hard-boiled mystery. When riots broke out in July 1967 after "an incident of police brutality, the four-day riot left twenty-three people dead and more than $10 million in property damage" (Mendelsohn, online). Even the Newark Coordination Council, the Newark Community Union Project, the New Community Corporation, and the Committee for a United Newark, organized by black writer and activist Amiri Baraka, could neither prevent the riots nor improve the social situation of Newark's population significantly until the

1980s. Thus, the actual upswing, which Valerie Wilson Wesley endorses in her fiction, is currently in progress, but social and racial problems are changing only gradually.

The general history of Newark in Wesley's fiction is connected to Tamara Hayle's personal life story and to that of the people she knows.[3] The layout of the city reflects and shapes social and racial relationships and is the breeding ground for the crime with which Tamara is confronted. Tamara divides the space available to her into a professional (her office) and a private place (her home/house), spaces that she tries to keep separate. Her knowledge of the city, her office, and her home become empowering agents in her successful work as a private investigator.

THE SPATIALIZATION OF HISTORY: PUBLIC AND PRIVATE

Her first novel, *When Death Comes Stealing*, presents Tamara Hayle's assessment of the historical, social, and racial situation of Newark:

> Newark is a survivor city—an old fighter who won't go down for the count. Johnny [her brother] used to talk about how Broad Street stretched out— grand movie theaters, department stores, big-time musicians playing Newark *first*, and you couldn't make it down the streets on a Saturday night. But everything changed after the '67 riots. (1994, 15)

Tamara personifies the city, emphasizing its toughness and the necessary drive for survival. While the preceding chapter had introduced the case she is asked to investigate as well as her family and life situation as a single mother to her son Jamal, this quotation embeds her private life in that of a tough city. This contextualization associates Tamara Hayle with the city's fight for survival, because she claims: "But I'm a Newark girl at heart, always will be" (1994, 15).[4] Her description marks three important phases of the city. The first one is the glamorous one of the first half of the twentieth century when, similar to the situation in Harlem during the Harlem Renaissance, cultural activities, particularly in the music industry, and financial growth boomed, sometimes even before they reached New York City. In a recent interview, Wesley describes Newark as

> an old industrial town. It was really big in the 1930s and 40s because it is situated on a river, has a big port and heavy industry. Many blacks moved to it during its boom time. Waves of immigrants came to the city, too, Italians, Jews, Portuguese and most recently Latinos. It has always been a working-class city of working men with broad shoulders and big hands. And it has its various ethnic suburbs. (Matter-Seibel 2001, 11–19)

138   CARMEN BIRKLE

A female PI in this city certainly has to have the stamina of a survivor. Tamara's memory of the city's past is intimately connected to her brother Johnny (a policeman who committed suicide by shooting himself) and his tales, because at the time of his death Tamara was not even ten years old.[5]

These times of cultural flowering abruptly ended with the race riots in 1967 when "cops beat up some cabbie right around the corner from where I lived, and word had it that they'd killed him. Newark folk, who don't take no shit, went into the streets" (Wesley 1994, 15). Although neither cops nor cabbie are racialized, the confrontation is clearly that of white racism toward blacks. While Tamara defends and justifies the communal action taken by the black community of Newark, she also mourns its consequences and the beginning of a second phase of cultural and financial decline: "When things cooled, nothing was the same. All the money left, the big bucks and the little. My parents moved to East Orange a year later" (1994, 15). Tamara's story about Newark reads like a parallel to that of Harlem in New York City and thus shifts the readers' focus from the global city—whose history everyone believes he or she knows—to local, suburban history. The consequences of this financial and cultural exodus are spreading poverty, a ghettoization of African Americans and other ethnic groups, and increasing violence and criminal activities.

Yet, in contrast to representations of Harlem in Chester Himes's fiction or of San Francisco in Dashiell Hammett's novels, Newark never becomes the ultimately evil space with a criminal underworld that slowly undermines the city's social foundations. As Wesley's novels show, there are bad characters, people who deserve to be punished, but these people were frequently hurt themselves at some point in their lives and often simply take revenge years later. One example is July in *When Death Comes Stealing,* who kills three sons of Tamara's former husband, DeWayne Curtis, because he accidentally killed his first baby son and put the blame on her. As a consequence, her mother disintegrated mentally and killed herself. Similarly, in *Easier to Kill,* Odell Johnson murders several people close to the radio star Mandy Magic, with whom he had a child when they were both in their late teens. In an act of desperation, Mandy shook her daughter Amanda to death because she simply never stopped crying. Odell Johnson is punished in the end, whereas Mandy Magic's secret of the "Shaken Baby Syndrome" (1998, 268) is never revealed to the public. Although they do not justify the deeds, both Tamara and Jake Richards, her lawyer friend, show sympathy for Odell and Mandy. Their kind of crime is clearly rooted in and motivated by the poor social and racial living conditions in the aftermath of the 1967 riots. Thus, Tamara's cases are always intimately connected to the specifics of life in Newark, and she finds the solutions only because she knows and is part of this life.

INVESTIGATING NEWARK, NEW JERSEY   139

Finally, and again in contrast to Hammett's and Himes's cities, Wesley's Newark develops and takes a positive turn into the third phase of recovery and reconstruction: "Things are coming back now, block by block rising from the ashes—like that Egyptian bird. This city of mine has seen some hard times, but keeps climbing back, just don't know when to leave that ring" (1994, 15–16). In *Easier to Kill*, Tamara explains, "things were beginning to look up . . . thanks to . . . NJPAC, the newly built performing-arts center . . ." (1998, 5). Wesley once more emphasizes the city's instinct for survival, its cultural renaissance, expressed in a comparison with the Egyptian phoenix, who was worshiped as holy by the Egyptians because the bird burned itself but rose out of the ashes and therefore turned into a symbol of eternal life. This bird, commonly known in Egyptian and Greek mythologies, not only symbolizes recovery, but also establishes a parallel with former world empires and thus emphasizes the importance of the city of Newark. However, rise and fall are intimately connected, never permanent, and always part of a fight, as indicated by the boxing reference "leaving the ring."

Despite the hardships in the city, Newark is "[t]his city of mine," as Tamara says, and she moves freely and self-confidently in its streets. In typically American fashion, the reader never sees her walk the streets, but sees her drive in a car that is constantly on the verge of breaking down,[6] as is Tamara's financial situation. But like the city, Tamara manages to always just make it. She used to be a police officer, like her brother Johnny, because she wanted law and order in her city. The disappointment, however, came when she experienced the racism and sexism of her fellow police officers—black and white—who "preferred to see a 'nigger bitch' dead or lying on her back rather than sporting a badge like she deserved to wear it" (1994, 106). She describes her time with the police as a "struggle as the lone female, lone black cop on the force . . ." (1994, 106). In an interview with Wesley, Dorothea Fischer-Hornung comments on Tamara's negative relationship with the police, who "are a part of Newark": "Tamara's difficult relation with the police seems to be connected with the problems between the city's police and the community" (Fischer-Hornung and Mueller 2003, 314). While she, with her survivor instinct, fought racism and sexism in the police force (see Walton and Jones 1999, 109), she finally resigned when her son Jamal became the object of police brutality:

> I quit after three of my brethren in blue picked up my son and beat his babysitter and some of his friends to within an inch of their young lives basically because they were black in Belvington Heights after-hours. They claimed the boys resisted arrest and were disorderly—that old song and dance cops trot out when they're looking for a legal excuse to whip somebody's ass. (1998, 42–43)

140   CARMEN BIRKLE

She makes this decision because her priority in life is her son Jamal and
only then her own well-being and financial security. In contrast to the heroes of classic hard-boiled fiction, she decides as a mother (see Hedderich
2001, 294–95) and thus contributes to the city's human qualities. Wesley
describes this combination of humanity and strength for survival as "medium-boiled" (Matter-Seibel 2001, 115).

When one of Tamara's cases brings her back to the decayed housing
project where she as well as Mandy Magic, her client, once used to live
with their parents, memories of her family and neighbors, who survived
the hardships and became stronger in their aftermath, return: "Many families had survived and thrived, and they had left, their spirits and wills stronger
for the experience. I was stronger for it—I knew that now" (1998, 38). But
this place, the Haye Homes, also brings back the memory of an abusive
and cursing mother. Although Tamara Hayle wonders about the damage
her mother possibly did to her, she refuses to be determined by this hatred
and violence and instead has become a loving and caring mother: "He [her
son] gives me all the things my mother thought I took from her" (1998, 39).

Yet, in spite of all her strength and intimacy with the city, Tamara Hayle
never ignores its current problems and knows that there are parts of the city
that are not on the upswing and have not developed toward the third phase:
"We drove into a part of the city that I'd never seen before, a side street off
a deserted one that looked like it hadn't been repaved since the 1930s.
There was a dreariness to it, a deadness that made me fearful of what I
would find" (1998, 174–75). Intuitively, she connects what she sees to a
man whom she has met earlier and who turns out to be the killer: "The
despair on his [an elderly man's sitting on a broken kitchen chair] face
made me think for a moment about Johns [Odell Johnson], the man from
the parking garage . . ." (1998, 175). Even when cases such as the one she
is hired for by Lincoln E. Storey, a highly successful black businessman,
take her into the vicinity of Newark, namely to Belvington Heights, it is
not turf that she does not know, because it is the town, as Tamara says,
"where I used to be a cop" and that "is separated from the city of my birth
by race, money, and sixteen miles worth on the Garden State Parkway"
(1995, 27). Wesley uses this rich white context to have Tamara think about
the social status of black women:

> It's easy to follow somebody who doesn't know you from nothing, espe-
> cially if you're black and a woman. The world takes you for granted then,
> and you're always somebody's something else—sister-lady ringing up the
> groceries or sweeping up the floor. I do my best work when people are
> limited by their own expectations. . . . A pleasant young Negress. A de-
> pendable, unassuming presence. (1995, 27–28)

INVESTIGATING NEWARK, NEW JERSEY 141

Wesley thematizes black women's social invisibility, which is based on racism as well as an unjustified white superiority complex; as the African American detective fiction writer Barbara Neely rightly claims in an interview: "[W]hat you see is not what you get" (Birkle and Hedderich 2001, 129). This example points to what Stephen Soitos calls "double- [or even triple-] consciousness detection" (1996, 11) and shows how Wesley correlates the genre of detective fiction with particular African American concerns and thus joins other African American writers who "signif[y] on elements of the detective genre to their own ends" (Soitos 1996, 3). Like Komo's Clio Browne and Neely's Blanche White, Tamara Hayle "uses her blackness as part of her detective trade" (Soitos 1996, 229; see also Bailey 1999).[7]

As the examples in this section have shown, Newark is not just a city with geographical dimensions; Wesley purposefully chooses Newark as the setting for her fiction and roots her PI Tamara Hayle in these surroundings. Not only does Wesley's Newark tell its own story of historical, social, and cultural development and offer its own manifestations of race conflicts, but its geographical layout also narrates Tamara Hayle's personal life story. Her cases lead her to places that bring back memories of her childhood and family as well as to places that she connects to the sexism and racism that she has experienced as a policewoman. By following Tamara through the streets of Newark and to Belvington Heights, social criticism is voiced, and personal and private histories unfold that are indispensable for the successful fight against crime.

THE PROFESSIONALIZATION OF SPACE

Because professional and private lives are so inextricably linked for Tamara, she decides to separate them at least physically by working her cases from her own office:

> When I first got my P.I. license, I worked out of my kitchen, but there are just too many folks in this business whom you'd rather not see sitting around your house, and I got tired of meeting clients in diners. People don't take you seriously when you talk business over a cheeseburger and hits from the Seventies at Dinsey's diner. Annie gave me a good deal, and so I've been here for about three years. Even though it's expensive as hell and half the time I just break even, I love this place. It's where I come to take stock of my life, do my serious thinking and remind myself that I really *do* have a job. (1995, 63)

Although this place is barely and poorly furnished because of lack of money, Tamara is satisfied with it.[8] The decision to take an office marks her increasing

142   CARMEN BIRKLE

professionalization and her ownership of Hayle Investigative Services, Inc. Working out of her kitchen entails the stigma of a private as well as of a woman's sphere, a space that is not taken seriously by clients that come to ask for her help. Although she knows most of her clients in some way because of their common past and background (as Stephen Soitos claims, "the blues detective's identity is directly connected to community" [1996, 29]), Tamara wants to protect her son Jamal from these encounters. Similarly, meeting clients in diners does not give her the touch of a successful professional. Additionally, her own office—separate from her home—turns her into an individual and gives breathing space in which she can develop her own ideas. Here she is not a mother but a professional and independent woman. As a former police officer she has to get used to the idea that working independently is as much a job as being employed by the police force, even though as a PI she will never have financial security. The office space reminds her that the work of a detective is not an unsuitable job for a woman, so that she can respond to Lincoln E. Story's question "Do you find this line of work hard for a woman, a black woman?" with "No harder than being a cop" (1995, 5).

Tamara's office not only professionalizes her work, but also emancipates her and turns her into a self-confident woman. What Michel de Certeau claims for postmodern cities also holds true for Tamara in reference to the city of Newark: "They [postmodern cities] become liberated spaces that can be occupied. A rich indetermination gives them, by means of a semantic rarefaction, the function of articulating a second, poetic geography on top of the geography of the literal, forbidden or permitted meaning" (Certeau [1984] 2000, 132). Tamara calls the room that she rents from her friend Annie "her office" and thereby determines the function of a previously empty space. This appropriation can be seen as a parallel to imbuing the city of Newark with her personal life story. The office becomes the first stable point in her life when she moves around the city; her house is the second one.

THE PRIVATIZATION OF SPACE

Although Tamara Hayle is a survivor figure and frequently mingles her work life and her private life, she needs a space where she can be herself, where she can live out her desires and relax without having to be tough. Her house offers her this space despite the fact that there she also fulfills the role of mother and the former wife of DeWayne Curtis. While her office empowers her professionally, her house does so privately: "There are three things in this life I cherish: my independence, my son, Jamal, and my peace of mind" (1994, 6). Her house is "a tiny two-bedroom yellow and green two-story Cape Cod that [she] inherited from [her] parents . . ." (1994, 59). Logically, the house is full of memories of her own past: "I wondered if he [Basil Dupre] could sense the ghosts—Johnny, my parents—that haunted it" (1994, 141), but also full of hope for the future. It literally and physically gives her comfort when she feels down, because it heats up quickly (1994, 59). Waking up early in the morning, particularly on Sundays, and staying in bed gives her the time and space to think about both personal and professional matters. To continue her analytical, professional train of thought, she goes to her office. In her home, she talks to her son Jamal about private concerns, such as his education, her job, their family.

Her house is also the place where she dreams of being sexually involved with Basil Dupre, a businessman born in Kingston, Jamaica: "Desire for him swept through me as I lay in a sensual netherhood between sleep and awake imagining his lips caressing my neck and back, imagining the way he would have felt if I had stayed" (1994, 128). It is also the place where she finally has sex with Basil Dupre and experiences desire and "sexual fever" (1994, 148). Yet, she is constantly haunted by the fear of her son surprising them and the nagging thought that Basil Dupre might be the killer of her ex-husband's sons. While Tamara is sexually attracted to him, the thought of his possible involvement in crime and even murder never leaves her and prevents her from entering into a more regular and permanent relationship with him. In *The Devil Riding*, Basil Dupre's daughter is killed; Delmundo Real, suspected of this as well as other murders and threats to Tamara, is suddenly shot to death by an unknown assailant (2000, 188). Dupre is never identified as the perpetrator, but Tamara leaves with an uneasy feeling; yet, she is also grateful that Delmundo Real is dead, because he would have continued to follow her and others involved in the Desmond case everywhere. While law and order are restored, taking the law into one's own hands—even if the victim is a boss in the gambling and prostitution business—is simultaneously embraced and questioned but ultimately undetected.

Despite the fact that she tries to separate private and professional life, personal and public space, her first case ends in a shoot-out in her own house. Tamara's case in *When Death Comes Stealing* is a family drama triggered by her ex-husband, DeWayne Curtis. July, his stepdaughter from his first marriage in Virginia, systematically kills his sons by various women and consequently finally arrives at Tamara's house in order to kill Jamal. Because of the research she did in Virginia, Tamara knows the truth and arrives at home just in time to prevent the worst, but she herself has to kill July in self-defense: "They never tell you how hard it is to kill another person, how it messes with you, even when it goes down like it did be-

144   CARMEN BIRKLE

tween me and July. It was a blot on my soul, and I knew it. A wound that would have to grow into a scar . . ." (1994, 287). In contrast to a classical PI, she goes to visit July's grave and says "a prayer, asking for salvation and strength to heal my spirit and that of my son" (1994, 288). This is the only case that ends in Tamara's home—a sign that she is still undergoing a transition between private and professional life.

In *The Devil Riding*, her work frequently takes Tamara to Atlantic City, the Las Vegas of the East. Gambling, prostitution, and murders are part of everyday life, and even Tamara is physically threatened when her car is trailed and finally destroyed. Therefore, her final return to Newark, to her house and her son, seems like the return to a safe haven. While Tamara longs for this safety, she has successfully mastered the evils of the big city by employing her emotions, her intellect, her experiences as a mother, and her memory of her brother Johnny.

In contrast to a classical hard-boiled detective's almost nonexistent private life, Tamara's experiences, her knowledge of Newark, and her sympathy with people's suffering are rich and indispensable sources for the criticism of "the social conditions in the black community . . ." (Décuré 1999, 183) and of white racism (see Walton and Jones 1999, 140), for the solution of her cases, the punishment of crime, and for the restoration of law and order. In that sense, Wesley's novels are "crossover texts" (Walton and Jones 1999, 63), simultaneously social criticism and detective fiction.

CONCLUSION

Even by her sixth novel, *The Devil Riding*, Tamara Hayle has not managed to separate her private sphere completely from her work sphere, and she probably never will be able to do so. She is too heavily rooted in her environment; she is too much part of the geographical, social, and racial layout of the city to keep private and business matters separate. Working as a black and female PI in the city of Newark where she was born always also means that every investigation is also an investigation into her own past and her family's history, as well as a confrontation with the city's latent racism and sexism. Tamara concludes in *The Devil Riding:* "My roots run deep. I could never live far from Newark where they are planted, and my history and those I've lost cling to me no matter where I am—shadowing my dreams and walking in my present" (2000, 158). Wesley's detective novels entertain and satisfy their readers with the solution of criminal cases and represent the history of the city of Newark as intertwined with Tamara's struggle for a satisfactory private and professional life.

With Tamara Hayle, Wesley, in continuation of Dolores Komo's Clio

INVESTIGATING NEWARK, NEW JERSEY — 145

Browne, sets the guidelines for black female private investigation by converting the city into familiar territory that, unlike the city as enemy in classical hard-boiled fiction, becomes a character in the investigation. The streets of the city offer clues and are hardly threatening to either Clio Browne or Tamara Hayle, who both cruise the streets in their old cars. Black female private investigation takes back the cities and familiarizes hitherto threatening white male terrain. In this sense, both Newark on the periphery of New York City and Tamara as a black woman are powerful survivors with whom Valerie Wilson Wesley's readers can identify.

NOTES

1. According to Nicole Décuré, the "first black women detectives, in the 1980s, were written by white women, Susan Moody and Dolores Komo" (1999, 158), but Stephen Soitos considers Dolores Komo the first African American woman writing a novel with a black female detective (1996, 226), *Clio Browne, Private Investigator* (1988). Komo's Clio Browne certainly is the first well-known black female detective, whereas Komo's ethnicity seems to remain a mystery. Clio Browne alludes to the scarcity of black detectives by bringing up the idea of writing "the definitive history of black private investigators in this country" (Komo 1988, 69). If she were to begin writing her book now, she would have to include names such as Nikki Baker, Eleanor Tyler Bland, Charlotte Carter, Grace Edwards, Martha McMahon Grimes, and Barbara Neely. For a detailed comparison of Barbara Neely's detective Blanche White and Wesley's Tamara Hayle and their contribution to the debate about gender and genre, see Monika Mueller's "Hard-Boiled Domestic(s)? Die Kriminalromane von Valerie Wilson Wesley und Barbara Neely" (2001).

2. The relationship between Clio Browne and the city of St. Louis is similar to that of Tamara Hayle and Newark. Clio Browne also grew up in St. Louis, knows the city and its people intimately, and continues her father's Browne Bureau of Investigation. She, too, has close connections to the local police, because she was married to a policeman, who died in action, and still works closely with her deceased husband's partner, Felix Frayne, the officer in charge of the murder investigation.

3. Newark is the setting of most of Wesley's fiction, except for two novels. In *Where Evil Sleeps*, Tamara takes a one-week vacation in Kingston, Jamaica, and is confronted with a case primarily because those involved are also from Newark: "Newark? My daddy grew up in Newark. On Waverly Avenue. But he left to go to Jersey City before I was born. Called it bettering himself. That's funny, ain't it?" (1996, 6). In *The Devil Riding*, Tamara is asked to investigate in Atlantic City to find the young daughter of the rich Desmond family from Belvington Heights, a rich white town near Newark.

4. Similarly, Janet Evanovich's bounty hunter, Stephanie Plum, grew up and lives in a small part of Trenton, New Jersey, lovingly called "the burg." Like Tamara Hayle's family, Stephanie's parents and grandparents have lived in the same house for decades; in their case they had immigrated to Trenton from Eastern Europe. Stephanie knows the neighborhood and its criminals and is intimately involved with the police, namely with Joe Morelli, whom she comes close to marrying in *Seven Up* (2001).

5. Since in *Clio Browne* Clio's husband dies, a conclusion could be that women's "medium-boiled" detective fiction seems to emphasize women's survival in contrast to men's tragic failures. Women's survival empowers female agency.

146 CARMEN BIRKLE

6. Like Tamara and Clio, Evanovich's Stephanie Plum constantly has trouble with her car simply because she cannot afford to buy a new one. Like her African American predecessors and contemporaries, Stephanie is on good terms with the police, but like theirs, her relationship with the police is never without confrontations. The police officers are always male, either a father figure (as in Tamara's relationship with white Captain deLorca) or a friend (Clio Browne's husband's partner Felix Frayne) or lover (Stephanie's Joe Morelli). In all cases, the men are slightly patronizing, albeit well-meaning, but the women prove to be right in their investigations.

7. See also Clio Browne's comment in Komo's novel: "It always amazed Clio how invisible the maid became as secrets were openly discussed or classified materials were left carelessly about" (1988, 9).

8. Clio Browne, Tamara's predecessor in the investigation business, is similarly attached to her office and therefore shocked when she gets a note of eviction because the building is going to be sold: "Clio felt a heavy weight descend on her heart. Browne had occupied this space for nearly forty years, fifteen of which were her years" (Komo 1988, 117).

Works Cited

Bailey, Frankie Y. 1999. *"Blanche on the Lam*, or The Invisible Woman Speaks." In Klein 1999, 186–204.

Birkle, Carmen, Sabina Matter-Seibel, and Patricia Plummer, eds. (in collaboration with Barbara Hedderich). 2001. *Frauen auf der Spur: Kriminalautorinnen aus Deutschland, Großbritannien, und den USA*. Tübingen: Stauffenburg.

Birkle, Carmen, and Barbara Hedderich. 2001. "'Blanche Is My Political Heroine': Interview mit Barbara Neely." In Birkle, Matter-Seibel, and Plummer 2001, 125–33.

Certeau, Michel de. [1984] 2000. "Walking in the City." In *The Cultural Studies Reader*, edited by Simon During, 126–33. London: Routledge.

Chandler, Raymond. [1939] 1948. *The Big Sleep*. New York: Penguin.

———. [1944] 1946. "The Art of Simple Murder." In *The Art of the Mystery Story*, edited by Howard Haycraft, 222–37. New York: Grosset and Dunlap, Universal Library .

Décuré, Nicole. 1999. "In Search of Our Sisters' Mean Streets: The Politics of Sex, Race, and Class in Black Women's Crime Fiction." In Klein, 158–85.

Dietze, Gabriele. 1997. *Hardboiled Woman: Geschlechterkrieg im amerikanischen Kriminalroman*. Hamburg: Europäische Verlagsanstalt.

Evanovich, Janet. 2001. *Seven Up*. London: Headline.

Fischer-Hornung, Dorothea, and Monika Mueller. 2003. "An Interview with Valerie Wilson Wesley." In *Sleuthing Ethnicity: The Detective in Multiethnic Crime Fiction*, edited by Dorothea Fischer-Hornung and Monika Mueller. Madison, N.J.: Fairleigh Dickinson University Press.

Hammett, Dashiell. [1930] 1980. *The Maltese Falcon*. In *Five Complete Novels*. New York: Wing.

Hedderich, Barbara. 2001. *"Novel Economics:* Leichter Lernen mit Krimis." In Birkle, Matter-Seibel, and Plummer 2001, 287–303.

Himes, Chester. [1957] 1991. *A Rage in Harlem*. New York: Vintage.

Keitel, Evelyne. 1998. *Kriminalromane von Frauen für Frauen: Unterhaltungsliteratur aus Amerika*. Darmstadt: Wissenschaftliche Buchgesellschaft.

Klein, Kathleen Gregory, ed. 1999. *Diversity and Detective Fiction*. Bowling Green, Ohio: Bowling Green State University Popular Press.

Komo, Dolores. 1988. *Clio Browne, Private Investigator: A Woman Sleuth Mystery*. Freedom, Calif.: Crossing Press.

Matter-Seibel, Sabina. "'A Medium-Boiled P.I.': Interview mit Valerie Wilson Wesley." In Birkle, Matter-Seibel, and Plummer 2001, 115–22.

Mendelsohn, James. "Newark, New Jersey, City in Northeastern New Jersey, Home to a Large African American Population." www.africana.com/articles/tt_950.htm (26 March 2002).

Mosley, Walter. [1990] 1995. *Devil in a Blue Dress*. New York: Pocket.

Mueller, Monika. 2001. *"Hard-Boiled Domestic(s)?* Die Kriminalromane von Valerie Wilson Wesley und Barbara Neely." In Birkle, Matter-Seibel, and Plummer 2001, 163–78.

Soitos, Stephen F. 1996. *The Blues Detective: A Study of African American Detective Fiction*. Amherst: University of Massachusetts Press.

Walton, Priscilla A., and Manina Jones. 1999. *Detective Agency: Women Rewriting the Hard-Boiled Tradition*. Berkeley and Los Angeles: University of California Press.

Wesley, Valerie Wilson. 1994. *When Death Comes Stealing*. New York: Putnam's.

———. 1995. *Devil's Gonna Get Him*. New York: Putnam's.

———. 1996. *Where Evil Sleeps*. New York: Putnam's.

———. 1997. *No Hiding Place*. New York: Putnam's.

———. 1998. *Easier to Kill*. New York: Putnam's.

———. 2000. *The Devil Riding*. New York: Putnam's.

From Roots to Routes:
Sleuthing Identity in Two Juvenile Ethnic Detective Novels

SABINE STEINISCH

In the world in which I travel, I am endlessly creating myself.
—Frantz Fanon, *Black Skin, White Masks*

Rewriting the World for Adolescents

As much as language represents our world, language creates and shapes worlds. Thus, the possibility of decolonizing culture, of moving beyond a culture of domination and marginalization, resides primarily in the activity of writing and reading. Especially for children and young adults, reading experiences play a vital part in the construction of their worldview and in finding their own subject position in relation to a hybrid and complex community. Works by writers of ethnic minorities have an important share in the shaping of hybrid cultures and transnational identities, because they give voice to the experiences of loss and displacement suffered by those who live in between cultures.

Due to its generic conventions, the detective novel provides a fruitful ground for the exploration of the issue of identity. The central question of a detective novel is, after all, one of identity: Whodunit? The detective investigates a crime and, finally, after collecting and evaluating clues and evidence, s/he uncovers the criminal's identity and comes up with the solution to the mysteries that unsettled the world order. It is the detective's power to fix identity, to divide the world into good and bad, and to unambiguously assign the positions of victim and evildoer that restores the prevailing social order. This affirmative ideology is prevalent in traditional, classic detective fiction, which upholds a philosophy of rational individualism, presenting people as fixed components in an immutable social, political, and economic system. According to Peter Freese, the "genre's welcome message that the disturbed order of the world can be restored by means of the eventual discovery and punishment of every criminal" (1992, 8) accounts for the outstanding success of the detective novel in today's literary mass market. In particular, the majority of detective novels written especially for children and young adults adhere to the affirmative ideology of essentialized dichotomies and transport the idea of unified subjectivity, rooted in the rationality of the individual. This is one of the reasons why young readers respond so positively to the conservative endings of, for example, numerous series of juvenile detective novels. The detective's prominent position answers the readers' desire for orientation. The reader, who belongs to the detective's in-group, lives through every step s/he takes, shares success and failure, and finally finds him/herself confirmed in the assumption that science and logic are the keys that render human behavior calculable and controllable. So young readers enjoy the suspense of the mysteries that unsettle their world order all the more because there is absolute certainty that this order, much as in fairy tales, will be restored in the end.

Detective stories by authors of cultural minorities, however, tend to subvert the existing social order and to upset the hierarchical binaries of center/margin, black/white, and native/foreigner. Multicultural detective stories present "murder with a message," as Adrienne Johnson Gosselin puts it, a message reaching far beyond the reassuring security of confirmation that Freese observes. Gosselin points to the pedagogical potential of multiethnic perspectives in detective literature: "[T]heorizing the nature of inadvertent learning in multicultural detective fiction—or even the nature of multicultural detective fiction itself—is something like theorizing 'from the borderlands'" (1999, 4). The process of "inadvertent learning" that Gosselin has in mind is grounded in the power of language and literature to create worlds and to shape and reshape readers' consciousness. Ethnic detective novels do much more than serve as "showcase windows to exotic cultures" (1999, 6) or "fulfill the function of anthropological handbooks and provide their readers with exciting introductions to unknown cultures" (Freese 1992, 10).

Gosselin foregrounds the ethnic detective novel's political and culturally innovative potential, which is also the starting point for Ruth McKoy Lowery's study *Immigrants in Children's Literature*. Lowery explores the ways in which migration, which has always been and still is a formative component of American society, is represented in children's literature. She emphasizes the important role juvenile literature plays in counteracting the widespread discomfort in the United States, emerging from the current controversy surrounding recent immigration, as well as in posing alternatives to the negative image of people of different racial, ethnic or socioeconomic background spread by the media:

> After hearing about immigrants from the media, in their homes, or elsewhere, children do develop an image of what an immigrant is. School is often the main forum where American children may interact with immigrant children. How they perceive their immigrant peers can directly influence the relationships they may or may not develop. Although the need for presenting information about immigrants in literature is great, there is an even greater need to present positive information that can counter stereotypes. . . .
>
> Literature has always been important in people's lives. It is a medium of representation used with children in classroom settings and many times presents views that children would not otherwise experience. Literature is a vital source that helps us to navigate our way through past and present views of who we are and who we might become as members of a diverse society. (2000, 3)

Juvenile literature can thus become a powerful tool for the formation of a hybrid society with a multiplicity of transnational identities. In this paper, I will focus on two juvenile detective novels published in the United States by authors of ethnic minorities, the children's novel *Thief of Hearts* (1995) by the Chinese American Laurence Yep and *The Disappearance* (1979), written for a readership of young adults by Rosa Guy, who immigrated to the United States from Trinidad. Yep and Guy use the genre of the detective novel to heighten the awareness in young readers of the problems arising from living on the borders of culture. I would like to explore how they subvert the notion of ethnic identity as rooted in national or geographic origin and point to the ways in which they offer their young readers a concept of subjectivity based on openness. The crossing of borderlines, the movement between worlds, is the central metaphor of both novels, as the protagonists come to terms with migration and its effects and literally travel between two cultural spaces. Yep and Guy favor a notion of ethnic identity thought along the lines of never-ending routes rather than the fixed stability of roots.

CAUGHT IN BETWEEN: LAURENCE YEP'S *THIEF OF HEARTS*

Laurence Yep's novel *Thief of Hearts* (1995) focuses on the marginalization and experiences of discontinuity of those living on the borderline of cultures. Yep succeeds in presenting the fragmentation and displacement of migrants and their descendants in a way easily comprehensible to a reader-

FROM ROOTS TO ROUTES   151

ship of children aged ten to thirteen years, even if they have no experience of migrancy at all. In adapting Homi K. Bhabha's theories of multicultural hybrid identities as well as Salman Rushdie's concept of an "imaginary homeland," Yep's novel explores the problems children growing up with a migrant background face in finding a subject position somewhere in between conflicting frames of values. In his essay "Imaginary Homelands," Rushdie describes the problematic nature of the concept of home. To those who experienced migrancy, home is a space in the past that can only be remembered in fragments; it can never be perceived as a whole. In establishing a vision of his/her lost home, the migrant is always aware that s/he cannot reclaim precisely the thing that was lost, even if it is possible to visit the geographical place of origin. S/he is "obliged to deal in broken mirrors, some of whose fragments have been irretrievably lost" (1991, 11). The loss of the past and the feeling of discontinuity resulting from it is encountered by migrants in an intensified form. As Homi Bhabha observes, the borderline comes to be a threshold full of ambivalence, as it simultaneously divides and joins together different realms: "The beyond is neither a new horizon, nor a leaving behind of the past. . . . [W]e find ourselves in the moment of transit where space and time cross to produce complex figures of difference and identity, past and present, inside and outside, inclusion and exclusion" (1994, 1). It is these moments of transit and their importance for the construction of ethnic identities that Yep is interested in. He illustrates that, apart from the actual act of migration, these border crossings imply an imaginative movement beyond patterns of thought and behavior, values, beliefs, and traditions. With Bhabha and Rushdie, Yep stresses the positive implications of the migrant's fragmentary vision: the migrant is well aware of the "provisional nature of all truths" (Rushdie 1991, 12) and can offer a "stereoscopic view in place of 'whole sight'" that leaves any process of forming an ethnic/racial identity open for change (see Rushdie 1991, 19). Yep emphasizes the creative forces inherent in the space created by the intertwining of past and present, of inside and outside. He offers an image of ethnic identity grounded in the notion of movement and fluidity, encouraging his young readers to appreciate the borderland with its inherent multiplicity as a space from which to construct their own subject positions.

Yep recounts two days in the life of Stacy, a thirteen-year-old Chinese American girl. He describes how her ideas and attitudes towards the culture she lives in are challenged and how she gains insight into the ways in which her mixed Chinese and American heritage enriches her world. During the process of her development toward a more mature understanding of her own position, Stacy has to solve a case of petty thievery that causes trouble in her school. The incidents around the thefts and the arrival of a new classmate from China trigger Stacy's search for identity, which comes to be the central issue of the novel: "All the time there was just one thought inside my mind—one as hot as a potato that you've just taken from a campfire; so hot you keep tossing it from one hand to the other but can't let go. And that one thought was: Who am I?" (Yep [1995] 1997, 55).

Yep delineates the matrix of Stacy's conflicts on the first pages, where Stacy, who up to this point does not have a particular awareness of herself as being different, "the other" of white American society, learns about marginalization, dislocation, and loss of roots due to the migrancy imposed upon her mother and upon her great-grandmother Tai-Paw. She is surprised to find out about the discrimination her parents suffered because they are "what is politely called a mixed couple" (Yep [1995] 1997, 8); she recognizes that even Tai-Paw, whom she herself perceives as a "friendly but alien presence" (2) in their household, might feel lonely and displaced, and that her mother found it difficult to adjust when she first came to San Francisco's Chinatown as a girl.

Whereas Stacy's mother, Casey, who grew up in Chinatown, still tries to recapture the feeling of her old neighborhood by establishing a network of ex-Chinatowners and newcomers from China in what Stacy calls "Mom's Chinese love fests" (Yep [1995] 1997, 5), she never felt the urge to associate with the diaspora community her mother values so much. Stacy's comfortable life in Almaden, a suburb of San Francisco, radically changes when she is assigned to accompany and help Hong Ch'un, who has newly arrived from China with her mother. The first encounter between the two girls on their way to school renders obvious the clash of cultures. Hong Ch'un, who undergoes the painful implications of actual migrancy, has a strong sense of unbelonging. She suffers from the loss of roots, of customs, traditions, and values. Disoriented and scared by her new surroundings, she does not want to change and to adjust, because she fears losing even more—her identity. In an act of self-defense, she hurtfully expresses her being "out-of-country and out-of-language" (Rushdie 1991, 12) by reproaching Stacy heavily for not speaking Chinese:

> "Chinese is . . . beautiful and noble." She paused as she struggled to put her words into English. I had the same trouble when I tried to speak Chinese. "It's what makes you Chinese."
>
> Our school has a pretty active exchange program with other countries, so I'd met exchange students from Europe and Latin America, and I'd gotten along with them all by trying to see things from their viewpoints. So I attempted to see hers now. And I guess that if I had been born in China, I would have felt that way, but I had been born here. "I'm not Chinese," I tried to explain, "I'm an American. . . ."
>
> "I don't see why you can't be both," Dad suggested.
>
> It was a compromise that satisfied no one. (Yep [1995] 1997, 13)

FROM ROOTS TO ROUTES 153

It comes as a shock to Stacy when she discovers that she is perceived as being Chinese by her mother and by the school's vice principal, who is proud to claim his African heritage. Both want Stacy to take care of Hong Ch'un because of their common roots. The girls themselves, however, draw rigid borderlines between each other; they think in binaries of inside/outside, native/stranger. Hong Ch'un despises Stacy for her mixed heritage. She even insults Stacy by calling her a "t'ung chung," the Chinese word for half-breed, and shocks her into recognizing that she doesn't belong: "All my life I thought I had lived in a safe, warm, secure world where I was just like everyone else, but it had only been my little fantasy. I looked too Chinese. And yet, even if I learned Chinese and the culture, I looked too American" (45).

Yep parallels Stacy's journey toward herself with her investigation into the case of small thefts at school. Hong Ch'un is accused of having stolen several small objects that served as lucky charms and that, although of little monetary value, are precious to their owners for their emotional significance. Stacy readily believes that Hong Ch'un is guilty, because the objects are found in her backpack. In desperation, Hong Ch'un runs away to Chinatown, and Stacy sets out with her mother and Tai-Paw to find her. The two women's and the girl's car trip to San Francisco's Chinatown is the centerpiece of the novel, as it metaphorically makes them relive the crossing of the borders between cultures.

For Tai-Paw and Casey, Chinatown is the place where they spent most of their lives after their immigration from China some thirty years ago and the home where they kept alive their values and traditions. Stacy, however, is immersed in a world entirely new and "strange as a slice of the moon" (Yep [1995] 1997, 93). Although Stacy knew that "the American way isn't the only one" (14), the experience of a world so different from the one she is acquainted with leaves her helpless and confused. Already painfully aware of her otherness in the white American suburban community of Almaden, she realizes that she is a complete outsider in Chinatown. Here, Stacy is "out-of-language"; she is excluded from the world of her Chinese heritage. Stacy feels estranged, fragmented, dispersed. Yet, the two Chinese American immigrant women are outsiders in Chinatown, too. They are shocked to recognize that Chinatown had radically changed since they had last seen it, and they are unable to recognize anything. Yep reveals "home" to be a mythic place of desire, a place of no return. Chinatown comes to be Casey's and Tai-Paw's "imaginary homeland":

> "A lot can happen in all these years," I said.
> "Yes, but I always thought I could come back. I've been away too long," Tai-Paw said sadly. "All these years, I thought it would always stay the same: my friends, the good places. But they're all gone."
> I felt sorry for her. It must be hard to leave your home like Rip van

154 SABINE STEINISCH

Winkle and then find everything changed when you come back. Maybe I wasn't the only one out of place and time. (99–100)

Significantly, it is on the borderline between cultures, during their car trip to Chinatown, that Tai-Paw tells Stacy the old Chinese story "The Thief of Hearts," in answer to Stacy's questioning why someone would steal objects of little worth. "The Thief of Hearts" is the story of a young man who falls in love with an ogre's daughter. In order to gain her love he has to steal the girl's heart, which is not inside but outside of her body. The young man succeeds in stealing the jar with her heart in it, but the girl would still not have him: "'But he's a . . . a human,' the horrified daughter insisted. 'And our children would be half of our world and half of that other'" (82). The young man returns to his village and finds that it has grown into a big city—he had been away for centuries. "I may have stolen her heart, but someone has stolen my world" (84). The young man dies, and all that is left of him is a heart of jade, which sings of lost worlds and kingdoms, lost loves and dreams. The ogre steals the jade heart; his daughter recognizes the voice of her lover and is moved to tears by its sad song of unrequited love: "'He has truly stolen my heart now,' she mourned. 'For all I can think about is what I have lost'" (86).

The tale, woven into Stacy's story at this point, serves several functions. She begins to see that the thief of the lucky charms is a "thief of hearts" because the objects he or she took away from his or her classmates had a bit of their owners' souls tied up in them. Significantly, Stacy discovers through the tale and the ensuing conversation with Tai-Paw that migration "steals bits of hearts" and takes away worlds, and that, like the Thief of Hearts in the tale, her mother and great-grandmother have lost their worlds. She recognizes that this loss is painful and even frightening, because it deprives people of the security offered by familiar values and patterns of thought. Although Stacy did not emigrate herself, she still experiences the repercussions of migrancy in her own problematic position in relation to her home and host country:

> "I think the Thief of Hearts died because he had missed a whole world— not just the ogre's daughter. What she had stolen from him was a lot worse than anything he stole from her. . . ." "There are always new worlds. . . . How do you find them?" Tai-Paw frowned as if she did not understand the question at all. "You look for them." She knew who she was. I envied her confidence, but I was like the Thief of Hearts, wandering alone through the world. (Yep [1995] 1997, 88)

Through the tale, Stacy achieves insight into her great-grandmother's wisdom, which she had failed to notice. Ninety-year-old Tai-paw embodies

FROM ROOTS TO ROUTES 155

the knowledge of traditional Chinese values and the complex nature of human relations. She believes in the necessity of patience and tolerance in understanding difference, in the power of love and friendship and the ability to forgive. In this respect, she does not act as an antagonist but rather as a complement to her daughter, Casey, whose perspective on life and human relations is that of a Western professional psychologist. Stacy discovers that when she was a child, the knowledge conveyed by her great-grandmother's stories seemed much more accessible to her than her mother's psychological terminology, because Tai-Paw's observations and ideas were expressed in simple words. So it is through language in its traditional oral form that Stacy comes into contact with her heritage again and gains new knowledge about her in-between position.

In spite of the initial disappointment with their visit in Chinatown, Tai-Paw's diaspora network of friends there is still functional, and it is with the help of this network that they eventually find Hong Ch'un. Through Stacy, Yep exemplifies that moving beyond borderlines can disrupt established reactions. Crossing the border between cultures has changed her perspective; although puzzled by the multiplicity of viewpoints, she accepts that "things can be true and false at the same time" (Yep [1995] 1997, 160) and understands that what joins people together goes "beyond labels like Chinese and American" (194). The compromise her father opted for—which in the beginning of the novel "satisfied no one" (13)—is now the basis of her view of her relations to others. She views Hong Ch'un in a different light now, as she understands Hong Ch'un's loss of roots and displacement as a part of her own history, too. Stacy accepts Hong Ch'un's apology for her superior behavior and her insult and finally becomes convinced that Hong Ch'un is not guilty of the thefts. In contrast to the traditional detective novel, it is not the detective's individual rationality that leads to the solution ōf the mystery, but Stacy's new capability to think beyond dichotomies that helps her see that Hong Ch'un is innocent. With Tai-Paw's and her father's help, Stacy discovers her best friend, Karen, to be the thief. Stacy uncovers the criminal's identity and restores order in that the offender is named and the stolen goods are returned to their owners. Still, *Thief of Hearts* denies a solution in clear-cut categories of good and evil. Stacy's success in solving the case is a loss at the same time. She is disappointed in Karen and feels deceived. But her borderland experiences enable her to see beneath the surface of Karen's offense; she recognizes low self-esteem as the cause for Karen's desire to steal "little bits of hearts." Karen is the guilty party in the case of petty thievery, but, on the other hand, she is also the victim of her parents' disinterest and neglect.

As Tai-Paw and Casey recollect their past in scraps and pieces and partial memories, "in broken mirrors" (Yep [1995] 1997, 11), Stacy develops an understanding of the richness and struggle of their past lives in Chinatown. In letting Stacy discover the various stages of their routes through life, Yep explicitly shows subjectivity to be multilayered and fluid. Stacy is "restaging the past" by learning to incorporate her Chinese heritage into her life in Almaden. Tai-Paw's values of love and friendship gain a new meaning for Stacy, when in a final gesture of understanding toward Hong Ch'un she asks her to "forgive Karen . . . and try to be her friend" (186). Yep's message to his young readers lies in Tai-Paw's knowledge of the world:

> "What if there isn't a world anymore?" I just stood there, knowing my safe little universe had come apart and feeling my joints and limbs ache in sympathetic pain—and knowing that there was no way to put things back together, either in that universe or in me. . . . Tai-Paw studied me thoughtfully. "I'm sorry you had to grow up so fast. . . . Don't listen to small-minded people. . . . They judge people by looks. They don't understand how big the world really is." (193)

Tai-Paw's advice to Stacy to look for her new world herself encourages and requests readers to take the shaping of their selves into their own hands and to value the knowledge that no truth can ever be whole.

THE DIFFERENCE WITHIN:
ROSA GUY'S *THE DISAPPEARANCE*

In Rosa Guy's novel *The Disappearance*, the movement beyond boundaries does not, as in *Thief of Hearts*, take place between the dominant and the marginalized, but within an ethnic/racial minority at the borders of American society. Guy analyzes the position blacks, as "the other," occupy in relation to white hegemonic culture as well as the differences within the black community. She points to the displacement and discontinuity that migration as a shared experience imposes upon those who left their home country or continent, no matter when the physical act of crossing the border took place. Twentieth-century immigrants share the disruption of their past and the fragmentary vision of the world with descendants of the first slaves taken to the United States in the seventeenth century. Nevertheless, Guy emphasizes the heterogeneity of subject positions that constitute the category "black" as constructed by Western hegemonic discourse. Guy epitomizes in her novel what Stuart Hall theorizes as "new ethnicities." There is no "black experience" as a singular and unifying framework based on the building up of identity across ethnic and cultural differences. "What is at issue here is the recognition of the extraordinary diversity of subject posi-

FROM ROOTS TO ROUTES   157

tions, social experiences and cultural identities which compose the category 'black'" (Hall 1996, 443).

The Disappearance explores the issue of ethnic identity, focusing on differences of socioeconomic background by crossing the borders between worlds; like Laurence Yep, Guy foregrounds moments of transit to create a space for new formations of subjectivities that go beyond static models of rootedness and perceive identities as discursive products: "It is the space of intervention emerging in the cultural interstices that introduces creative invention into existence. . . . [T]here is a return to the performance of identity as iteration, the re-creation of the self in the world of travel, the resettlement of the borderline of migration" (Bhabha 1994, 9). Guy's emphasis is on the individual's creative powers to construct and reconstruct identity on the subject's routes through life in the spaces between cultures. In *The Disappearance*, the characters' imaginative border crossings open up spaces for the formation of new individual subjectivities. Through the disruption of conventional patterns of thought these border crossings also help to incorporate the notion of heterogeneity and multiplicity of ethnic communities into a social order that traditionally perceives ethnic identity as unified and unchanging.

Imamu Jones, the sixteen-year-old protagonist of the novel, is doubly displaced. Unlike Stacy, Imamu, based on his early childhood in Harlem, is well aware of his marginalized position in white American society. Although Imamu did not migrate himself, living at the borders makes him feel the full force of not belonging, of not fitting into the dominant system. Although Guy's critique of white superiority only becomes evident in a few instances, it forms the implicit basis for the message of her novel. Imamu sees the lack of education and resulting high unemployment rates that increase the impoverishment of people of color in Harlem as a constituent trait of American society. Al, one of Imamu's Harlem friends, puts it like this:

> Uncle Sam knows what he's doing. . . . Keep the streets full of poor suckers—in their place. That keeps the jails running; troops at the reach of the army. Put poor dudes to work and screw the economy? All them policemens out a work? All them judges out a work? Them lawyers? And don't even start talking about them half-assed politicians. Baby, the life of the country depends on you being out of work! (Guy [1979] 1992, 157)

Imamu is "a cat from the streets," and he is accustomed to living with aggression, violence, and fear. The story opens with Imamu returning home from the youth house, after being acquitted of murder, to the neglected Harlem apartment he shares with his alcoholic mother. The contrast Guy focuses on is between the worlds of Harlem and Brooklyn, where Imamu

158   SABINE STEINISCH

will stay with the Aimsley family. Mrs. Aimsley, who made it her job to "give our own a chance" (13) by supporting children and teenage offenders in their trials, is appointed his guardian by the family court. Whereas Ann Aimsley never doubted that Imamu is innocent of murder, his mother, who had not been to his trial even once, throws him out of his home because she is afraid of his alleged aggression. Imamu's sense of unbelonging parallels the loss of home experienced due to migrancy:

> "[Mrs. Aimsley] let me come home—to say good-bye." . . .
> "You ain't have to come back for that. You done said what you got to say. Go back where you belong."
> "I figgered I belong here."
> "No, you ain't. You belong nowhere. Ought to be glad that lady even want you . . . 'cause Lord knows nobody else want you." (7–8)

The first encounter between Imamu and his foster family intensifies his awareness of dislocation. Just as Imamu is "the other" in relation to white America, he is "the other" in his new Brooklyn neighborhood: "What was he doing in this strange land, far away from New York? Far from everything he had ever known? A stranger on foreign turf. Brooklyn. He bit his lips to keep down tears" (48–49). The tension between the two worlds, portrayed in the conflict between the responsibility Imamu feels toward his helpless mother as well as his gratitude for Mrs. Aimsley's support and his desire not to disappoint her, leaves Imamu disoriented.

The next turning point in Imamu's life is when Perk, the family's young daughter, does not return home from school on his second day with the Aimsleys. To the police and to the family, Imamu is the first and only suspect. When he is accused of being responsible for Perk's disappearance and when even Mrs. Aimsley turns against him, Imamu's disorientation turns into utter despair; he is on the verge of giving himself up altogether. Only the brutal maltreatment by two police officers who almost beat him to death rouses his will to live: "They'd never know. With him dead they'd believe that everything he knew about her died with him and was buried with him. And thinking that, Imamu's need to live stirred. He didn't want to die. He had to know what happened to Perk" (Guy [1979] 1992, 127). So the investigation into the mystery of Perk's disappearance is essential to Imamu's notion of himself.

Imamu's quest for self in the area of conflicts between life in Harlem and Brooklyn is illuminated from various perspectives. Basically, the difference consists in the contrast of appearance versus reality—in an indirect, intellectual outlook on life and perception of social imbalance on Ann's and her sixteen-year-old daughter Gail's part and the immediate everyday life encounters with discrimination, violence, and injustice on Imamu's

FROM ROOTS TO ROUTES 159

part. Although Imamu had to learn to live with violence and fear in the streets of Harlem, he still received honest empathy and responsibility when he was a child. In the Aimsley family, however, solidarity with those who are underprivileged seems less heartfelt. It is rather seen as a political and moral obligation or even made to serve the purpose of covering lifetime deceptions hidden beneath the surface, much like the plastic furniture covers in the immaculate Aimsley home, where "an everyday sameness prevailed, cloaking the family in a sort of perfection" (Guy [1979] 1992, 15). Guy repeatedly points to the importance of outer appearances in the Aimsley family and thus refers to the secrets hidden beneath the surface. Ann Aimsley and Dora Belle—a close friend of Anne's and godmother to the girls and thus virtually a member of the family—are the characters who most prominently depend on outer appearances. When the police come to the Aimsley's house to investigate Perk's disappearance, Imamu is confused by Mrs. Aimsley's shrinking size and diminishing importance:

> Imamu found himself wishing that she had changed from her house dress back to her skirt and blouse to speak to the policemen. That would have impressed them, made them look up to her. Instead they looked down. Her authority seemed as faded as her cotton dress. (108–9)

The central metaphor that in the end turns out to be the key to the solution of Perk's case is that of hair and hairstyles. Dora Belle is exceptionally proud of her beautiful hair, done in long curls. Perk admires Dora Belle's hair and wants to look the same as her godmother, whereas Ann and Gail prefer their hair short. Ann defends Gail's Afro: "Dora Belle, you live in yesterday's worlds. Haven't you heard? Today we are trying to find a link to our African heritage. . . . We are past that good-hair-nearer-to-white" (25–26). Unlike the search of the three generations for their common past in *Thief of Hearts*, Ann's and Gail's search for African roots is limited to the surface; Ann Aimsley herself is not aware that her lifestyle is an exaggerated, ironic copy of white, middle-class life. Superficial matters of outer appearance, however, have never played a role in Imamu's life so far. Masks and disguises had existential importance as a means to survive in the streets and to escape the police, who "would take a dude apart—particularly if that dude happened to be black or Puerto Rican—for the 'truth'" (107). A striking evidence of Gail's intellectual approach to life is her use of language to understand and order her world: "After all, the best way to get an understanding is through intelligent dialogue. . . . To discuss is the only way to find out about each other" (46–47). At the Aimsley's, Imamu is "on the receiving end of words" (111), because for him, "it is too hard to explain. He didn't have the words. He never had had words" (241).

The novel's key scene is the encounter of Imamu, his mother, and Gail

160 SABINE STEINISCH

at the police station. Both Gail and Imamu's mother, afraid of losing him, come to "claim" him, to collect him and take him "home." Imamu decides to return to Harlem to protect and take care of his mother, but to go back to Brooklyn for as long as it takes him to find out the truth about Perk despite Mrs. Aimsley's "betrayal." With Imamu and Gail's decision to perform this search together, Guy conveys her message that the solution lies in the mingling of multiple perspectives. However, it is Imamu who leads the way in their investigation:

> "Are you sure you want me with you? . . . I guess you call this a part of your street thing. . . ." Pulling her to him in what he intended to be a consoling hug, his body felt suddenly big, broad, at the feel of her slimness against him. He held her tight, making her respond to his heart slapping against his chest. He wanted to tell her how great she was to let him do the thinking when she was nothing but a bunch of brains. (Guy [1979] 1992, 185–86)

It becomes quite clear that intelligent dialogue and discussion are not the only means to gain an understanding of complex relations. Imamu's street-trained instinct, his knowledge and experience of fear and aggression, helps him sense that the explanation for Perk's disappearance must lie somewhere in the field of conflicts between two worlds. His talent for observation and his awareness of people's fears—both indispensable capacities to anticipate dangers and thus survive in Harlem—soon lead Imamu to Dora Belle as the centerpiece in Perk's disappearance.

More clues assemble during Gail and Imamu's search in the neighborhood. Listening to Mrs. Briggs's painful experience of migration is even more revealing to Imamu than the neighbors' observations concerning Perk's way to school. With her story, loss of home and fragmentation gain significance in Imamu's understanding of the causes for the deceptions in the Aimsley household as well as the mystery of Perk's disappearance.

The old lady came to Brooklyn from Jamaica with her husband, only to find herself let down by Mr. Briggs. Mrs. Briggs's way of dealing with her displacement and rootlessness is silence: "Forty years . . . not one word did cross these lips. . . . Not one word so long as he see fit to leave me and go out gallivanting in the night. For I ain't leave me father house and me mother house to come to this cold country to stay by meself alone, lone, lone" (Guy [1979] 1992, 189). Now that her husband is dead, Mrs. Briggs breaks her silence but, as in the past forty years, her thoughts circle only around her loss of home. Mrs. Briggs' permanently felt loss of roots parallels Dora Belle's, who emigrated to the United States from "the Island." Mrs. Briggs's story also points to Imamu's own displacement and Mrs. and

FROM ROOTS TO ROUTES

Mr. Aimsley's, who both came to Brooklyn from Harlem. They all suffer marginalization within their cultural community.

Guy weaves Imamu's search for sexual identity into his investigation of Perk's disappearance. Imamu's awakening sexual desire is roused and fed by Dora Belle, who does not miss a chance to show off her pretty hair, "the symbol for her pride and beauty" (Guy [1979] 1992, 206), and attractive body in a favorable light to impress the men around her. Dora Belle even tries to seduce Imamu, especially when he visits her at home and thus gives "his manhood a real leap forward" (82). Although attracted by Dora Belle's beauty, Imamu is sure that her explicit "offering him herself and three houses" (41) only serves as a cover for a secret. When he visits Dora Bell to search for confirmation of a yet vague suspicion, he finds her in her bedroom, naked in front of her dressing table, a towel around her head. When Dora Belle turns her head, the towel falls down and reveals that she is entirely bald, except for wispy strands of gray hair. With her reaction to Imamu seeing her without her wig, her mask, the bits and pieces of the puzzle fall into place: "'You spying bitch!' she hissed, springing at him. 'I going fix your fronting ass! I going pave the road with your bowels so your foot will find it way'" (206–7). Imamu is convinced that Perk went to Dora Belle's in the morning to have her hair done and caught her by surprise without her wig on. Sure to find Perk's body there, he enters Dora Belle's new, unoccupied house. When he does not find her right away, there is a moment of doubt:

> He had laid everything—his experience, his knowledge, his street thing, his instincts—on this search. Everything that had been sharpened by his short and insightful suspension between two worlds had been into this, and everything had failed. (215)

After all, his "suspension between two worlds" does not fail; he finds Perk's body in a freshly cemented grave in the cellar. Imamu reveals Perk's death to be an accident: Dora Belle confesses that she attacked Perk in fury when she discovered her beauty to be a deception, causing her to fall and hit her head. Yet, as in *Thief of Hearts*, uncovering the guilty person's identity does not reestablish dichotomies. Guy deconstructs the binary of either/or, of inside/outside, in that Imamu arrives at the solution of the case through "the suspension between two worlds" (214). The categories of good and evil are also dissolved. Imamu understands that Dora Belle's violent reaction toward Perk only discloses her to be the victim of an immense pressure to lead a successful life according to the standards of the white dominant order. Her physical attractiveness and most of all her "good-hair-nearer-to-white" serves as a means to compensate for her "ethnic inferiority." The

162   SABINE STEINISCH

same is true for Ann and Peter Aimsley. They tried to negate their Harlem history, a life in dirt, aggression, fear, and unemployment, in their exaggerated efforts to present an immaculately clean "Hansel and Gretel household" and in their "twisting things into right-wrong, pretty-ugly, good-bad" (242). Even Ann's commitment to the cause of giving "our own a chance" can be seen as a way of making up for her own Harlem past. With the solution of the mystery of Perk's disappearance, more secrets and lifetime deceptions are revealed: the tragedy of Mrs. and Mr. Briggs, who were the epitome of success in the neighborhood, and Ann Aimsley's jealousy of Dora Belle. Even the intellectual pride and innocence about what life really is like, which has led Gail to compartmentalize the world in binaries, are revealed to be a disguise to protect her from hurt.

At the novel's end, Imamu is still a stranger to Brooklyn; he returns to Harlem to live with his mother. He has gained an awareness of his new subjectivity dependent upon his suspension between the two worlds. His diverse experiences with emotional closeness and responsibility and with violence and fear enable him to look at life and the people he is related to from various angles: "Sure, it stood to reason, that being out there had given him advantages. But they'd never see that. They were programmed to suffer the pain of his being disadvantaged for their own benefit. . . ." (Guy [1979] 1992, 239) and "Folks like her just didn't see the disadvantages as being a plus" (245). Imamu's search for identity is still not complete. He quite consciously takes another route that will lead to broadening his horizon: "And the way I see it, a dude got to keep moving from where he's at. . . . You ain't losing me, you know. I'm just expanding" (246).

Beyond Boundaries: Departure Toward Hybridity

Both *Thief of Hearts* and *The Disappearance* deny their young readers the affirmative ideology of traditional detective novels, subverting the conventional reader's expectations of finding the world divided into good and bad. In neither one of the two novels does the detective's superior command of the situation grounded in unified subjectivity offer orientation to juvenile readers. Yep's and Guy's message is conveyed especially through the fragmentary, heterogeneous vision of their detectives. In both novels, the key to the solution of the cases does not lie in the logic and rational capacities of the individual, but rather in the protagonists' insight into the fragmentary, provisional, and temporary nature of truth. This insight arises from the displacement that migration imposes upon migrants and their descendants. Yep and Guy propose a notion of ethnic identity liberated from the restrictive concept of rootedness and cultural, racial, or national purity.

FROM ROOTS TO ROUTES

The solution of the criminal case is not the end of the protagonists' quest for self, but a starting point for new routes. In *Thief of Hearts*, the clash of dominant and marginalized cultures provides the framework for the search for identity; *The Disappearance* explores the differences within a single cultural group. Both novels accentuate the creative powers inherent in border crossing and celebrate the interstices as the spaces from where hybrid and fluid subject positions can be constructed. The process of "inadvertent learning" (Gosselin 1999, 4) is not, however, restricted to the novels' function as models for the individual juvenile reader. Language represents and depicts our world, but most of all, language creates and shapes worlds. In articulating the experiences of migrants and their descendants in contemporary America, both Yep and Guy "write back" against oppressive homogenizing discourses of literary canonization and ethnic marginalization within the borders of the United States. Yep's and Guy's novels contribute to the formation of a hybrid society that acknowledges the multifarious voices of ethnic minorities "as an indigenous or native narrative internal to its national identity" (Bhabha 1994, 6). With their writing, Yep and Guy open routes toward a common attitude of mind in which movement and border crossing are paramount.

Works Cited

Bhabha, Homi K. 1994. *The Location of Culture.* London: Routledge.

Fanon, Frantz. [1952] 1986. *Black Skin, White Masks.* London: Pluto.

Freese, Peter. 1992. *The Ethnic Detective: Chester Himes, Harry Kemelman, Tony Hillerman.* Essen: Die Blaue Eule.

Gosselin, Adrienne Johnson. 1999. "Multicultural Detective Fiction: Murder with a Message." In *Multicultural Detective Fiction: Murder from the "Other" Side,* edited by Adrienne Johnson Gosselin, 3–14. New York: Garland.

Guy, Rosa. [1979] 1992. *The Disappearance.* New York: Bantam.

Hall, Stuart, 1996. "New Ethnicities." In *Stuart Hall: Critical Dialogues in Cultural Studies,* edited by David Morley and Kuan-Hsing Chen, 441–49. London: Routledge.

Lowery, Ruth McKoy. 2000. *Immigrants in Children's Literature.* New York: Lang.

Rushdie, Salman. 1991. *Imaginary Homelands: Essays and Criticism, 1981–1991.* London: Granta.

Yep, Lawrence. [1995] 1997. *Thief of Hearts.* New York: HarperCollins.

"A Great Space Where Sex Should Be," or "Who's the Black Private Dick Who's Not a Sex Machine to All the Chicks?": *Shaft* (2000)

STEPHANIE BROWN

THE JUNE 2000 U.S. RELEASE OF THE FILM *SHAFT* MIGHT HAVE BEEN HAILED AS marking the birth of a new genre in black film, the "postblaxploitation movie." A sequel that is also a remake of sorts, the new film alleges to take up where the old one left off, introducing Samuel L. Jackson, arguably best known to the world for his roles in Quentin Tarantino's *Pulp Fiction* and *Jackie Brown*, as the nephew of and successor to the private detective character created in 1971 by Richard Roundtree, then best known as a model for Afro-Sheen. *Shaft* (2000) is no parody, like the Wayans brothers' 1986 comedy *I'm Gonna Git You Sucka*; rather, it wants to be a slyly postmodern pastiche of the original blaxploitation movie[1] as well as a compendium of much recent African American cinema, one whose mixture of retro and contemporary clichés can entertain without offending because of their ostensible lack of relevance to an America that in the past decade has increasingly sought to conceive itself as "postethnic."[2] The new *Shaft* partakes of the hunger for retro-chic and the urge to recycle cultural artifacts from recent decades that have characterized a distinct strain of popular American filmmaking of the past decade. Like *The Brady Bunch Movie* (1995), *The Avengers* (1998), or even *Charlie's Angels* (2000), *Shaft* (2000) seeks to capitalize on the potential for kitsch in any cultural icon more than twenty years old.

But the new *Shaft* offers a substantial revision of the original character of John Shaft, "the black private dick who's a sex machine to all the chicks." It finds itself in the awkward position of attempting to provide an earnest "political corrective" to its predecessor's unself-conscious playfulness, relentlessly highlighting its own political affiliations. I do not mean to suggest that play and politics cannot coexist; obviously they can and do. Nor do I mean to imply that the original *Shaft*, released in the immediate wake of the landmark events of the civil rights movement and directed by Gordon Parks, who only two years before had become the first African American to direct a major Hollywood motion picture (*The Learning Tree* [1969]), does not have a political agenda. However, I would argue that the original *Shaft* articulates its politics in more complex and subtle ways than its successor. Furthermore, the new film does not see itself as having the option of combining the political with the playful, perhaps because it believes it must articulate race difference more forcefully in an era in which both academic theorists and popular pundits are willing to argue that race no longer exists, except as an outmoded idea based on biological suppositions viewers are too sophisticated to believe in any longer.

The new *Shaft* has no room for ambiguity in its heroes or its bad guys—Samuel L. Jackson's Shaft is ultraviolent and self-righteously vengeful, while his enemy Walter Wade Jr. (played by Christian Bale, fresh from his starring role as another cold-blooded killer in *American Psycho*) is so supremely evil as to be a caricature. The conflict underlying the plot itself is literally black and white: an audience can only feel revulsion when an ultraracist white villain first provokes, then brutally murders an innocent black man for being "uppity" in front of his white female companion; afterward the white man boasts that his rich father will help him to evade the consequences. By contrast, although the original *Shaft* has its share of unsubtle moments, the plot is far more nuanced, in that Shaft is forced to negotiate complex conflicts between the black Mafia, the white Mafia, black revolutionaries, and a largely white police force of which he is from the beginning emphatically not a part. Asked to investigate the disappearance of a black mob boss's daughter at the hands of unknown kidnappers, Shaft finds himself at odds with nearly everyone, black and white.

Partially as a result of the absence of complexity in the plot of *Shaft* (2000), the second film insists far more dramatically on Shaft's credentials as a race man whose primary allegiance is to his community. The connection of the ethnic detective to his or her community, in opposition to the lone-wolf classical or hard-boiled detective whose personal life and social attachments are unknown or poorly described, is one of the key markers of his or her difference identified by critics of the genre.[3] Stephen Soitos writes of what he calls the "blues detective":

> His identity is directly connected to community. The detectives studied [in *The Blues Detective*] range from servants to intellectuals, but all of them are aware, and make the reader aware, of their place within the fabric of their black society. (1996, 29)

The original John Shaft, despite a constant stream of remarks about the oppression of blacks, seems ultimately unwilling to commit himself to a politics beyond the immediately personal. Although he objects to Bumpy Jonas's drug dealing in Harlem, he agrees to track down Bumpy's daughter for pay: "I get $50 a day," he says abruptly, after a lengthy tirade against Bumpy's heroin business and the damage to the community for which drug use is responsible, "and expenses." Furthermore, he is also unwilling to identify himself with the radical politics of his friend Ben Buford. "When the revolution comes, you better hope whitey's standing still," he tells Ben. "'Cause you ain't running too fast."

By contrast, the new Shaft cannot emphasize enough his enormous commitment to the community; in direct contrast to his predecessor, Jackson's Shaft not only will not do business with drug dealers, he devotes a thoroughly gratuitous scene to the brutal beating of a local teenage dealer who is corrupting the young son of one of his informants. It is clear throughout the film that this new Shaft is less concerned with solving mysteries than with social justice; his pursuit of Wade is a personal crusade against white hegemony and courtroom bias, rather than a job undertaken for cash. *Shaft* (2000) ends, in fact, with Shaft beginning his official career as a private eye (he begins the film still a member of the police department) by volunteering, as part of his quest to "straighten out" his community, to beat up the abusive boyfriend who has blackened the eye of a young black woman who then comes to the police station seeking help. Shaft's excessive performance of his devotion to community can be read as a response to the reception of blaxploitation films following the release of *Superfly* in 1972. In his comprehensive history of the American exploitation film *At a Theater or Drive-In Near You*, Randall Clark states:

> *Superfly* and other "lawbreaker" blaxploitation films were met with much criticism from the African American community. Vernon F. Jordan, the executive director of the National Urban League, stated "Hollywood is back at its old game of creating vicious stereotypes of Black people for popular consumption. . . . [W]hen the Black hero of one of these films is not tossing around in bed with a variety of women, he's pushing dope. . . ." (1995, 156)[4]

However, it is in the almost complete erasure of the sexuality that was perhaps the defining feature of the original *Shaft* that *Shaft* (2000) makes its real break with its forebear. The new film's curious sexlessness struck more than one reviewer as strange. Elvis Mitchell feels that "[t]hough an outrageous flirt, the nouveau Shaft has more affection for his wardrobe than anything else. . . . [I]t would be nice if he at least had a steady girlfriend" (2000).

The new *Shaft* reverts to an earlier formula for black fiction, one that precedes not just postmodernist play but also the civil rights movement. Jackson's John Shaft, like Roundtree's, is a "bad nigger" in the sense of being a righteously motivated Stagolee whose lawlessness elicits admiration from his community, grudging respect from his enemies, and applause from the audience. However, his hypermasculinity, performed again and again in a shower of bullets, does not include the performance of his sexuality, especially (and this is the crucial issue) with white women. Indeed, his inability to express his sexuality, combined with his theatrical gunplay and overwrought fisticuffs, calls to mind James Baldwin's observation, in his postmortem analysis of the career of Richard Wright, that

> in books written by Negroes there is usually a great space where sex should be, and what usually fills that space is violence. . . . The violence is gratuitous and compulsive because the root of the violence is never examined. The root is rage. It is the rage, almost literally the howl of a man who is being castrated. (1961, 188)

There are no sex scenes in *Shaft* (2000), unless one counts the blurry and stylized montage of unidentifiable and weirdly truncated entwined bodies that opens the film and has no diegetic relation to anything that happens afterward. Jackson's John Shaft, stripped of his ability to parade his sexual prowess on screen and barely allowed to flirt, finds himself instead forced to redouble his efforts to prove his masculine superiority through acts of violence.

By contrast, Roundtree's John Shaft expends as much energy on his lady-killing as on any other kind; seducing white and black women with the same ease and perfect success rate, Shaft considers sex both a thoroughly equal opportunity enterprise and an integral part of his workaday life. The film emphasizes the importance of sex as a key element of Shaft's milieu during the long tracking shot accompanying the opening credits. Before allowing the viewer to see John Shaft's face, the camera pans over a series of cinema marquee titles, beginning with the 1968 Burt Lancaster film *The Scalphunters*, and including *He and She* (1969), a Finnish soft-porn film; *School For Sex* (1968); and *The Wild Females* (1971). The juxtaposition of the two genres of film, the western and the porn flick, establishes Shaft as both an urban version of the traditional American frontier hero[5] and as a sexual adventurer. As Shaft saunters down 42nd Street, the theme song puns on his being "the black private dick that's a sex machine to all the chicks"; Isaac Hayes's use of a nonspecific relative pronoun allows the interpretation of which "dick" is the subject of his question to remain ambiguous.

It is tempting to argue that Shaft's extreme sexuality merely partakes

168   STEPHANIE BROWN

of the discourses constitutive of what Kobena Mercer has termed "the hegemonic repertoire of images of black masculinity . . . [including] 'Superspade' figures like Shaft" (1994, 137), in which black men are exoticized as sexual supermen, sometimes with the result that these images influence the self-conception of black male viewers themselves. As sociologist Robert Staples writes,

> When [black men] have been unable to achieve status in the workplace, they have exercised the privilege of their manliness and attempted to achieve it in the bedroom. Feeling a constant need to affirm their masculinity, tenderness and compassion are eschewed as signs of weakness. . . . (1982, 85)

In this formulation (which Mercer ultimately dismisses as limited and "evad[ing] the complexities of personal experience" [151]), Shaft's much-vaunted sex appeal, as well as his dismissive treatment of the women he beds, becomes a means of compensating for his lack of power in the white world.

Yet John Shaft uses his sexuality not ultimately as a compensatory mechanism the victims of which are the women he seduces, but rather as a means of negotiating his position vis-à-vis the white men around him. Black sexuality is contrasted forcefully with the resounding lack of heterosexual potency in the whites Shaft has contact with.[6] Reminding them of his sexual prowess enables him to assert his dominance, as in the first scene between Shaft, Vic Androzzi, the white police lieutenant who badgers Shaft from the beginning for information about his involvement with Bumpy Jonas, and his sidekick, the uptight Sergeant Tom Hannon. Androzzi sends Hannon on an errand while he questions Shaft, who puts him off with a series of nonsensical, but pointed, responses: "How come a couple of cats from Harlem came downtown this morning looking for John Shaft?" "Well, they're soul brothers; they came downtown so I could teach them the handshake." Returning, Hannon finds Shaft making a hasty departure and asks "Where the hell are you going, Shaft?" "To get laid," he announces, laughing loudly. "Where the hell are *you* going?"[7]

Shaft also uses his sexuality without humor, however, as a weapon in his seemingly endless arsenal of insults that he directs at white policemen. After a man dies mysteriously in a fatal fall through a plate glass window, Androzzi asks Shaft to find out all he can about the situation and report back. Shaft meets the lieutenant in a coffee shop the next day, after a night spent with an unnamed woman. "Well, what'd you get?" Androzzi asks eagerly. "I got laid," replies Shaft, and abruptly departs, divulging no further information.

Androzzi turns the tables on Shaft briefly when he witnesses the denouement of one of Shaft's one-night stands, this one with a white woman he has picked up in a bar. Shaft kicks the woman out of bed and out of his apartment when he receives a call from an informant; the woman remarks that, although he is a great lover, he is 'pretty shitty the morning after." He ignores her critique, saying only, "Close the door after you, baby," to which she responds, "Close it yourself, shitty." Androzzi walks into Shaft's apartment unexpectedly through the open door, and informs Shaft that he has been sent to bring him to the station, which he will in fact not do. The two men reach a new level of understanding, with Shaft agreeing for the first time to cooperate with Androzzi; as Androzzi leaves, Shaft asks *him* to close the door, and he responds in a falsetto, "Close it yourself, shitty." Shaft's face registers first antagonism, then relaxes into a laugh, as if to dissipate the tension of Androzzi's unexpected use of the discursive practices, previously his own exclusive province. The joke recurs in the final scene of the film; after Shaft locates Bumpy's daughter and decimates the white Mafia that is attempting to take over Harlem, he goes immediately to a phone booth, calls Androzzi, and tells him that he has more or less wrapped up the case, and all that remains is for him to "Close it yourself, shitty." By reintroducing the discourse of his own sexuality, Shaft regains the upper hand.

By contrast, Samuel L. Jackson as Shaft maintains a celibacy seemingly designed to undermine the stereotype of the hypersexed black man who is irresistible to white women. The earlier film in no way emphasizes the fact that some of Shaft's sexual encounters, including the one shown most explicitly, are apparently interracial, while the new film suggests, by opening with a scene in which a young black man's death follows his appearance on screen in the company of his white girlfriend, that interracial relationships are dangerous for black men. However, not only does the new Shaft stay away from white women entirely, he only flirts with black women in ways that are not situationally compromised. Meeting an ex-girlfriend at the bar in the Lenox Lounge, Shaft asks her where she straps her piece when she's dressed in such a skimpy outfit. But Shaft is clearly loitering without intent; it becomes immediately clear not only that she is not single, but that she is part of a setup to lure Shaft into a surprise party in his honor. Later that evening he again seems poised to score, responding to the open invitation of the bartender, whose advances are apparently propelled by the spectacle of his uncle (Richard Roundtree's reprise of the original Shaft) departing in the company of not one but two women, one apparently black and the other (perhaps) white, both considerably younger than he. But at no point do we actually see the younger Shaft take anyone home, and in fact, as the action of the film gets underway, women are relegated to one of two roles, neither of which is as a sex partner. *Shaft* (2000) portrays women in one of two ways, either as harmless buddies, such as a dowdied-down Vanessa Williams as Lieutenant Carmen Vasquez; or as unwitting abettors of crime, like the victimized and vilified Diane Palmieri (Toni Collette).

Diane Palmieri, the white waitress who witnesses the murder, is the object of Shaft's pursuit throughout the first three-quarters of the film. Diane flees the scene of the crime and tries to disappear, aided by her fearful mother and hulking brothers, who attack Shaft when he comes looking for their sister. Though ultimately Shaft tracks her down and convinces her to testify against Walter Wade, Diane is hardly a sympathetic character. She is never anything but reluctant to play her part, despite being surrounded by women of color who work together to ensure that Wade is punished for his crime (Vasquez, a black fellow waitress who gives Shaft Diane's address, and the victim's mother who ultimately decides that white justice can only fail her and shoots Wade on the courthouse steps, in a plot device lifted from 1991's *New Jack City*); when she finally confesses to Shaft that she not only refused to testify out of fear but also because she had taken bribe money to keep quiet, she loses any lingering claim to sympathy.

Carmen Vasquez is a somewhat more complex character. Her relationship with Shaft, characterized by violent bonding in lieu of physical attraction, illustrates his inability to articulate sexuality except as violent action. Violence is an obvious substitute for sexuality, as the felicitous overlap in terminology makes clear from the outset: "They like fucking people, huh?" he asks Carmen Vasquez after a meeting with Latino drug dealer Peoples Hernandez (Jeffrey Wright), in which Hernandez (who has previously joined forces with Walter Wade) refuses to cooperate with Shaft. "Well, I guess I'm going to have to show them what fucking people's all about." His vendetta with Hernandez escalates into a bloodbath of epic proportions, as Shaft "fucks" his way through legions of Hernandez's henchmen, Vasquez often at his side. At the apex of this shoot-out, Shaft and Vasquez discover that they have been betrayed by a traitorous cop who has secretly gone to work for Hernandez; Shaft holds the man hostage at gunpoint until Vasquez arrives on the scene; then, in a tender moment, he allows her to shoot him in the head. Shaft's and Vasquez's relationship remains emphatically sparkless; leaving the police station for the last time, Shaft kisses Vasquez good-bye—on the cheek.

This asexual new Shaft looks on the surface like a return to the hardboiled detective of the 1930s and 1940s, whose successful negotiation of his role as detective could only be accomplished by keeping a close rein on sexual desire.[8] Yet because *Shaft* (2000) is not merely a detective film, but also an example of black cinema, this refusal of sexuality must be interpreted differently—open sexuality for black men, especially in an interracial context, is more problematic and ideologically loaded than for whites.

Reworking the conventions of the blaxploitation film in a political climate radically unlike that which gave rise to the original, the latter-day *Shaft* decides that it cannot afford to take the risk of allowing its protagonist to fulfill stereotypes. Despite the fact that race in 1990s America has allegedly been reconceptualized as largely performative, a collocation of signifiers unconnected to any essential, let alone biological, identity, *Shaft* (2000) seeks to reify blackness by opposing it to a version of whiteness seemingly constructed exclusively to convey a sense of separation rather than of overlap, difference rather than continuity. Although *Shaft* (2000) pays lip service to what has been called a "postracist" aesthetic by offering one character whose insensitive remarks and apparently racist attitudes are revealed ultimately to hide an egalitarian heart of gold,[9] this lone attempt to demonstrate the recuperability of racist language into a discourse that recognizes the damage it does while neutralizing its threat is too isolated and too much at variance with Shaft's own lament that he is "too black for the uniform, too blue for the brothers" to undercut the film's dominant reading.

Despite its stridency, the depiction of racism in the new *Shaft* is ultimately less powerful because it is so unlikely, crystallizing racism into a single two-dimensional character whose hatred of blacks is as unmotivated as it is unrealistically great.[10] By removing any of the factors that might animate a genuine understanding of race hatred in the late twentieth century, the film makes the villain even less plausible and so less powerful. Furthermore, by reinscribing interracial sex as taboo, the film sets up the dynamics Baldwin identifies in Wright's *Native Son*. The problem here is that John Shaft is not, and is not supposed to be, Bigger Thomas; the era of the protest novel, of the starkly delineated racial conflict designed to serve as an object lesson to a society in denial of the realities of racism, is supposed to be over.

It is without doubt true that the desire to label millennial American society somehow "postracist" springs in part from a misguided wish to see American society as having moved beyond ugly recent history, and black film, whatever we take that term to mean, must grapple with that fact. "As a primarily oppositional practice engaged in resistance and affirmation," writes African American critic Tommy L. Lott, "black cinema need not be presently defined apart from its political function" (1999, 151). *Shaft* (2000)'s very explicitness suggests that audiences must be reminded, in a decade in which Dinesh D'Souza can blithely announce in a book entitled *The End of Racism* (1996) that race is nothing more than a "neurotic obsession" in America, that the fight against racism has not been won; while the original film, created in the wake of a decade encompassing nationwide race riots and the assassination of Martin Luther King Jr., could take for

172 STEPHANIE BROWN

granted that its viewers knew the battle for equality was still going on outside the cinema walls. Shaft is no postmodern ethnic detective performing
his raced identity; rather, beneath his sleek Armani jacket, he is a return of
the repressed rage of the protest novel, dressed (literally) to kill.

NOTES

1. It goes without saying that "blaxploitation" is a broad term, designed to encompass multiple generic affiliations; however, the conventions of the blaxploitation movie, no
matter what its premise, are fairly constant, including, according to film historian Randall
Clark, "sexual encounters with both African American and white women . . . a superficial
acknowledgement of the problems faced by the African American lower class, and a throbbing musical score . . ." (1995, 152).

2. I borrow this term from David A. Hollinger's *Postethnic America: Beyond
Multiculturalism*. Hollinger prefers to dispense with even the term "race," for he argues
that it has less intellectual currency and fewer practical applications than ever in a contemporary America whose "extraordinary increase in marriage and reproduction across the
lines of the ethno-racial pentagon presents a fundamental challenge to the authority of de-
scent-defined categories" (1995, 165).

3. This theory has been interestingly challenged in recent essays by John Cullen
Gruesser (1999) and Liam Kennedy (1999), both of whom choose to reexamine this issue
of the black detective's relationship to his community through the fiction of Walter Mosley.
Gruesser's argument is that Easy Rawlins's decision to become a detective makes problematic his relationship with other blacks, while Kennedy maintains that blackness is appropriated in classic white hard-boiled detective fiction not as a signifier of community but as a
mark of difference, emphasizing the detective's position as societal outcast (see Gruesser
1999 and Kennedy 1999).

4. *Shaft* (2000)'s aggressively antidrug stance is perhaps not unsavvy, given the box
office catastrophe of the *Superfly* sequel, *The Return of Superfly*, whose 1990 release followed a decade ravaged by the introduction of crack cocaine into inner-city communities.

5. The city as urban frontier is a trope well established in criticism of the hard-boiled
detective novel and the film noir.

6. In fact, the one white man Shaft meets who is shown to be sexually aware at all is
a flamboyantly gay bartender. Telling Shaft of the overt interest manifested by one of the
bar's (white, female) patrons, he remarks that the woman's companion evinced interest in
him, despite the fact that "I told her I was gay. You know what she said? That she'd straighten
me out."

7. The original John Shaft's cocky sense of humor was a considerable breakthrough
in African American film at the time. Though the character was modeled on Sidney Poitier's
Virgil Tibbs of *In the Heat of the Night* (1967), *Shaft*, like many of its successors in the
blaxploitation genre, owes a debt as well to the popularity of the 1970 film adaptation of
Chester Himes's 1965 *Cotton Comes to Harlem*. Himes's novel, part of a series of detective
novels originally published and widely read in France, mingled grim humor and graphic
violence in a tale of two black Harlem police officers, Coffin Ed and Gravedigger Jones,
whose beat forces them to confront racism in the ghetto and at the station on a daily basis;
the comedic film, however, opts to emphasize the humorous aspects of Himes's work rather
than dwell on its extreme brutality. Elements of combined political commitment and humor

were nothing new to detective fiction; however, both the book and the movie of *Cotton Comes to Harlem* managed to be funny and to indict racism simultaneously, a thing films that sought to address African American themes and subject matter had seemed unable to do previously. Film scholar Jesse Algeron Rhines notes in *Black Film/White Money* that "Negro cycle" films "emerged with the sit-ins. These were films produced and directed by whites . . . [whose subject was often] the deplorable way whites treated blacks much more than the life lived by African Americans" (1996, 40). The late 1960s brought revolutionary changes to the genre, but few laughs. Gordon Parks's first Hollywood feature film, *The Learning Tree* (1969), is an autobiographical drama about growing up black in the pre–World War United States, while Melvin Van Peebles's seminal 1970 film *Sweet Sweetback's Baadasssss Song* is an angry denunciation of The Man in which the title character's many sexual conquests seem less pleasurable than politically motivated.

8. Christopher Metress, in "Living Degree Zero," broadens the definition of dangerous desire: "[The detective's] quest for justice is repeatedly threatened by the temptations of power, money, and sex. The detective succeeds as the hard-boiled and masculine hero of his narrative because he is able to control his passion for these first three temptations and keep them subordinate to his more noble desire for justice" (1994, 156).

9. In an early scene, Shaft is shown in all his glorious liminality when a white fellow officer calls a black suspect "cornbread" and Shaft objects, offering to "[ethnic sensitivity] workshop my foot up your ass." The suspect thanks Shaft for his interference, and Shaft snaps, "Shut the fuck up!" In a much later scene, the two officers work together successfully to intercept Wade's attempt to put a hit on the only witness to his crime; in a moment of buddy solidarity afterward, Shaft says, "Hey, you still my fucking cracker, you know that, don't you?" His colleague smiles and replies, "Hey, fuck you too, cornbread," and the two high-five each other, laughing.

10. Why would the superprivileged, Harvard-educated Wade object so vehemently to a black man sitting in a predominantly white bar? We know so little about the character that any speculation is worthless. Our only glimpse into Wade's personal life reveals that he is angry with his father for having replaced his mother with a younger partner (whether second wife or mistress is never made clear). If there is a connection between his rejection of his father and his own violent behavior, it is never spelled out, and the origin of Wade's enormous rage remains mysterious.

WORKS CITED

Baldwin, James. 1961. *Nobody Knows My Name.* New York: Dial Press.

Clark, Randall. 1995. *At a Theater or Drive-In Near You: The History, Culture, and Politics of the American Exploitation Film.* New York: Garland.

Cripps, Thomas. 1993. *Making Movies Black: The Hollywood Message Movie from World War II to the Civil Rights Movement.* Oxford: Oxford University Press.

D'Souza, Dinesh. 1996. *The End of Racism: Principles for a Multiracial Society.* New York: Free Press.

Gruesser, John Cullen. 1999. "An Un-Easy Relationship: Walter Mosley's Signifyin(g) Detective and the Black Community." In *Multicultural Detective Fiction: Murder from the "Other" Side*, edited by Adrienne Johnson Gosselin, 235–55. New York: Garland.

Hollinger, David. 1995. *Post-Ethnic America: Beyond Multiculturalism.* New York: Harper Collins.

174 STEPHANIE BROWN

Kennedy, Liam. 1999. "Black Noir: Race and Urban Space in Walter Mosley's Detective Fiction." In *Diversity and Detective Fiction*, edited by Kathleen Gregory Klein, 224–239. Bowling Green, Ohio: Bowling Green State University Popular Press.

Lott, Tommy L. 1999. *The Invention of Race: Black Culture and the Politics of Representation*. Oxford: Blackwell.

Mercer, Kobena. 1994. *Welcome to the Jungle: New Positions in Black Cultural Studies*. London: Routledge.

Metress, Christopher. 1994. "Living Degree Zero: Masculinity and the Threat of Desire in the *Roman Noir*." In *Fictions of Masculinity: Crossing Cultures, Crossing Sexualities*, edited by Peter F. Murray, 155–84. New York: New York University Press.

Mitchell, Elvis. 2000. "*Shaft:* A Black Gumshoe Who Built a Genre Is Back on the Job." *The New York Times,* 30 April, late edition, sec. 2A, 28.

Rhines, Jesse Algeron. 1996. *Black Movies/White Money.* New Brunswick, N.J.: Rutgers University Press.

Shaft. 1971. Directed by Gordon Parks. Performed by Richard Roundtree, Moses Gunn, Charles Cioffi, and Christopher St. John. MGM.

Shaft. 2000. Directed by John Singleton. Performed by Samuel L. Jackson, Christian Bale, Jeffrey Wright, and Vanessa Williams. New Deal Productions.

Soitos, Stephen F. 1996. *The Blues Detective: A Study of African American Detective Fiction.* Amherst: University of Massachusetts Press.

Staples, Robert. 1982. *Black Masculinity: The Black Man's Role in American Society.* San Francisco, Calif.: Black Scholar Press.

The Mystery of Identity:
The Private Eye (I) in the Detective Fiction
of Walter Mosley and Tony Hillerman

ALISON D. GOELLER

THE INCREASING POPULARITY AND COMMERCIAL SUCCESS OF THE ETHNIC DETECTIVE novel over the past several decades point to the inroads that ethnic literature has made into mainstream popular fiction. A reader need only browse through the shelves of nearly any bookstore these days to discover a crime section amply stocked with novels by "ethnic writers." But, of course, most of these novels, dealing as they do with marginalized, colonized figures, go beyond mere entertainment, which is primarily why they have now been championed by academics. Like their predecessors, the hard-boiled novels of the thirties, which, as David Madden suggests in his introduction to *Tough Guy Writers of the Thirties*, deal with an "indifferent, violent, deceptive world" that treats the tough guy "like an object" (1968, xviii), much ethnic detective fiction has imbedded in it strategies for exposing the social and economic disparities that ethnic Americans face. Crime becomes a metaphor for all that is wrong in America, a strategy for critiquing injustices resulting in racial discrimination. Wayne Templeton, in an article on Tony Hillerman, furthers this idea when he says that ethnic detective fiction often deals with two sorts of crimes: the immediate, obvious crimes—murder, usually, which is always solved at the end of the novel—and the "larger, more pervasive, injustices" (1999, 38), which are, of course, not resolved. Thus, the detective's main purpose, though not always deliberate, is "not solving the lesser crimes but constantly pointing out the larger ones and revealing how they continue to victimize" (39). Taken even more globally, murder can come to represent "a postcolonial metaphor for cultural genocide" (44).

Certainly, the detective novels of Tony Hillerman and Walter Mosley

176   ALISON D. GOELLER

employ such a strategy. Hillerman's best-sellers about crime in the Navajo communities of the Four Corners region in the Southwest repeatedly expose the precariousness of the Navajo culture as it comes into contact with the white community and the injustices that exist because of that contact.[1] Jim Chee—the Navajo policeman who appears in most of Hillerman's books—is a paradigm of this struggle, constantly in conflict with the FBI, who represent the white world and who never solve the crimes on the reservation because they do not understand the Navajo culture and thus do not know what clues to look for. Although he shares with his supervisor, Joe Leaphorn (Hillerman's original Navajo detective), a knowledge of the culture, Chee demonstrates a much more rebellious nature when it comes to cracking cases on the reservation.

Walter Mosley's series of detective novels also critique American society's treatment of minorities. Covering a period of American history from 1939 until 1963, the novels follow Easy Rawlins's life as an African American "favors man" as he migrates from Texas to Los Angeles after fighting in World War II, becomes briefly involved in communism in the fifties, begins to accumulate property in his attempt at becoming part of the middle class, marries and has a child, adopts two other minority children, and finally, in the last novel in the series, faces the death of his best friend, Mouse, on the day of John F. Kennedy's assassination in 1963. Mosley has indicated in interviews that one of his goals in writing the Easy Rawlins books was to educate his audience about the history of black Americans in the twentieth century (Woertche 1994, 117). Influenced by the Marxist literary theorist and critic George Lukács and having studied political theory at the University of Massachusetts, Mosley is also clearly interested in exposing the "voracious maw of capitalism" (see his essay *Workin' on the Chain Gang: Shaking Off the Dead Hand of History* [2000, 16]), a theme that shows up in most of his novels in one form or another. In *Devil in a Blue Dress* (1990), the first novel in the series, for instance, Easy, a recent veteran of World War II who is eager to build a new life for himself in Los Angeles, a potential paradise, is fired for refusing to kowtow to his white boss at Champion Aircraft. Easy recognizes what is at stake financially in his refusal, but his integrity and his insistence on being treated like a man and not a boy overpower his desire for economic (middle-class) stability. "A job in a factory is an awful lot like working on a plantation in the South" (1990, 62), Easy tells his readers.

Both Easy's and Jim Chee's predicament—a result of their dealings with the white world—brings to mind yet another metaphor. I would like to suggest that in detecting the "lesser crimes," Easy and Chee are more importantly trying to solve their own personal mysteries, which is who and

THE MYSTERY OF IDENTITY   177

where they want to be in a society that does not value them, in a society where they are invisible, or at the very least treated as second-class citizens. Their personal identity, which is constantly being negotiated, constantly being challenged, is, then, the biggest mystery of all, and cracking that mystery becomes the most intriguing aspect of the novels.

Let's look at Walter Mosley's sleuth first. Easy's name belies his situation since his life is anything but easy. Living in Los Angeles, the favorite stomping grounds of the hard-boiled detective, Easy becomes a "favors man" who takes on sleuthing jobs because he needs the money to hold on to the property he has been accumulating, a necessary commodity in a capitalist society for his entrance into the middle class: "I felt that I was as good as any white man, but if I didn't even own my front door then people would look at me like just another poor beggar" (1990, 9). Ironically, it is Easy's desire for a conventional life that plunges him into the work of a hard-boiled detective, complicating things because of the tension between his middle class aspirations and his attraction to the "mean streets." Easy is also seduced by his tricksterlike capacity to dart in and out of cheap bars and juke joints, making small talk to gather clues. "Nobody knew what I was up to and that made me sort of invisible; people thought that they saw me but what they really saw was an illusion of me, something that wasn't real" (128), he tells us in *Devil in a Blue Dress*. According to Theodore O. Mason Jr., Easy is also a good sleuth because, as the white cops and crooked businessmen tell him, he can go places they cannot because he's a black man; he knows the territory. In fact, Easy becomes "Mr. Rawlins," a shift in identity, when his white clientele want a favor from him. And, finally, Easy is forced into sleuthing in order to prove he is not the criminal, an accusation that repeatedly occurs because he is black: "I had been seduced, hoodwinked, and blamed for a thief; I'd been bullied and looked at like a crook instead of an honest man. I could have gone home but I knew I wouldn't be able to sleep" (Mosley 1996, 45).

His smooth shifts from street dialect to standard English to suit the situation and the ease with which he can supply phony names, for himself and for others, further indicate his negotiating identities, a strategy which in this case produces positive results because it helps him solve the crimes. But according to John Cullen Gruesser, in his analysis of Easy as a signifying detective, Easy's trickster self often alienates him from his own black community: "juggling linguistic and social codes to deceive both white and black characters" (1999, 235), intensifying his deceptive personality. Daphne Monet, the "devil in a blue dress" whom Easy has been hired to find, is his perfect trickster double in this respect, which is one reason they are attracted to each other:

178   ALISON D. GOELLER

> Daphne was like the chameleon lizard. She changed for her man. If he was
> a mild white man who was afraid to complain to the waiter she'd pull his
> head to her bosom and pat him. If he was a poor black man who had soaked
> up pain and rage for a lifetime she washed his wounds with a rough rag and
> licked the blood till it staunched. (Mosley 1990, 183)

Even more dramatic, her hair color, her eye color, and her language change
throughout the novel, and eventually Easy discovers she's not French at all
but a light-skinned black woman named Ruby. Although Easy's physical
appearance does not change as dramatically, his language and manners do:
he readily admits to shifting from standard English to street dialect when it
helps him uncover crucial information to crack a case and "exploits his
Southern roots and manners to gain information" (Gruesser 1999, 243). So
just as Daphne tries to "pass" as a white woman, Easy does his share of
passing in order to carry out the job of sleuth.

   Unfortunately, although his finesse at changing identities helps him
solve crimes and find missing people, it alienates him from his own community. In other words, Easy is invisible in both the black and white worlds.
As Mouse, Easy's evil best friend, says to Easy, "You just like Ruby. . . .
She look like she white and you think like you white. But brother you don't
know that you both poor niggers" (Mosley 1990, 205).

   In *A Red Death* Easy's identity is further complicated when, after being caught for tax evasion, he makes a deal with the FBI to spy on an
alleged communist union organizer, Chaim Wenzler, a Polish American
Jew who is working at the First African Baptist Church. Like his fictional
cousins, Richard Wright's Bigger Thomas and Ralph Ellison's Invisible
Man, Easy finds himself seduced by communism's appeal to the working
class and by the parallels Wenzler draws between Jews and American blacks,
both economically and socially, particularly when Wenzler reveals to Easy
that his own brother had been hanged by the Nazis. This, of course, reminds Easy of his own people's bloody history:

> I'd seen lynchings and burnings, shootings and stonings. I'd seen a man,
> Jessup Howard, hung for looking at a white woman. And I'd seen two
> brothers who were lynched from two nooses on the same rope because
> they complained about the higher prices they were charged at the county
> store. (Mosley 1991, 136)

Easy makes a further connection when he discovers the body of Poinsettia
Jackson "hanging from the light fixture in the middle of the ceiling. She
was naked and her skin sagged so that it seemed as if it would come right
off the bone any second" (63–64). When he eventually figures out that
Poinsettia was murdered for not paying her rent, he realizes just how right

THE MYSTERY OF IDENTITY 179

Wenzler has been in connecting capitalism with oppression. He also realizes, towards the end of the novel, when someone takes a shot at him, that all he has suffered personally is perhaps because he "wasn't, and hadn't been, my own man" (203).

Easy's shifting of identities becomes especially problematic when it spills over into his personal life. This is most apparent in Mosley's third novel, *White Butterfly*. Now married and the biological father of Edna and the foster father of Jesus, a Mexican American boy whom he had rescued in *A Red Death* from child prostitution, Easy appears to want to settle down and be a family man. But his shifting identity and attraction to invisibility seem to preclude this desire. Never a clear hero, Easy drinks too much, cheats on his wife with his best friends' partners, including Mouse's ex-wife, Etta, and finds it nearly impossible to be honest with his wife about his finances. After he has become a legitimate property owner by working as a sleuth and saving money from various jobs, he still refuses to tell Regina where his money is coming from, and this, unfortunately, leads to the dissolution of his marriage and the loss of his biological daughter, Edna, in *White Butterfly*. Regina, understandably, simply cannot tolerate his unwillingness to be open and honest with her. Easy knows he is wrong to hide the source of his income from Regina because it prevents them from having an intimate relationship and makes him feel lonely. Just after Regina hangs up on him, he thinks: "When I cradled the phone I felt very lonely. All of what I had and all I had done was had and done in secret. Nobody knew the real me" (Mosley 1992, 179). Some critics have suggested that perhaps the reason Easy is so secretive is that Mosley is caught in the hard-boiled tradition where the sleuth must necessarily be a loner, be secretive. Later, in *A Little Yellow Dog*, Easy offers us an explanation for his secrecy when he blames his cultural background: "Where I came from you kept everything a secret—survival depended on keeping the people around you in the dark" (Mosley 1996, 200).

The most mysterious and troubling aspect of Easy's multiple identities, however, both for the reader and for Easy, is his capacity for violence; although living in Watts as an African American male is reason enough to explain this, there is still within him a potential for evil that cannot be blamed on outside sources. As Mosley himself has said in an interview about Easy, "It's not only outside oppression from the world but inside he is really held back" (Silet 1993, 13). Mosley has also said that he didn't want Easy to be a hero: "I hate setting up heroes that we can't really live by. You know, real people make mistakes, have flaws, do the wrong thing . . ." (14), but, in fact, there often is not much dividing Easy from the criminals he is investigating. It is no mistake that his best friend is Mouse, whom Easy describes as "the darkness on the other side of the moon"

180   ALISON D. GOELLER

(Mosley 1994, 77), a man who shoots first and doesn't bother to ask questions, a man who kills his stepfather over money and probably has killed his real father as well (see Mosley 1997). He is Easy's shadow side, someone Easy could easily turn into and nearly does in the last novel.

There are numerous examples of Easy's capacity for violence. The most troubling one is the scene in *White Butterfly* when Easy and his wife, Regina, have sex just after she has confronted him about where all his money is coming from. Although the description of their lovemaking is admittedly ambiguous—"She gave in to my caresses but she wouldn't kiss me. I rolled up on top of her and held her head between my hands. She let my leg slip between hers but when I put my lips to hers she wouldn't open her mouth or her eyes. My tongue pushed at her teeth but that was as far as I got" (Mosley 1992, 32)—both Regina's labeling of it later as rape and Easy's own association of it through a dream with one of the rape/murders he is investigating point to a violent and dark element in Easy (32–33) that is, to say the least, unsettling:

> Regina was leaning up against the tree with both hands. Her skirt was hiked up above her buttocks and a large naked man was taking her from behind. Her head whipped from side to side and she had a powerful orgasm but making the same kind of strange noises that Bonita Edwards made. (34)

Easy's violent side is temporarily put on a shelf in the fourth novel, *Black Betty,* when he is seriously wounded and finally forced to get off the streets and come to terms with his messy life. Having moved out of Watts into a better neighborhood with Jesus and Feather, the mulatto daughter of Cyndi Starr, the White Butterfly whose death he had been investigating in the previous novel (her mother had been killed by her own grandfather for bearing a black child), Easy appears to have settled into a more stable life. This is echoed in the parallel historical event mentioned in the novel: the election of Kennedy as president and the references to Martin Luther King. Thus, Easy's situation, like the nation's, seems to be on the upswing. Furthermore, as the foster parent of multiracial children, Easy also points to the possibility that racial lines are breaking down. Moreover, his reading of *Huckleberry Finn* suggests a kind of negotiating yet comfortable status, for he finds no difficulty in identifying with both Huck and Jim: "I could have been either one of them" (Mosley 1994, 13), he tells the reader. Easy even attempts to build a black shopping mall, Freedom's Plaza, thus hoping to break through the color line in commercialism, though his plans are thwarted by the white city bureaucrats who want his property for a sewage plant (71).

In the next novel and the last of the Easy Rawlins novels so far,[2] *A Little Yellow Dog*, Easy loses his taste for real estate deals; we find him,

THE MYSTERY OF IDENTITY 181

instead, the head custodian at the Sojourner Truth Junior High School, working with an Italian Chinese secretary and a blonde Negro from Iowa, and giving orders to whites. However, his tenuous self-identity once more manifests itself in violence and secrecy as he comes dangerously close to exchanging roles with Mouse, who is now out of jail and trying to lead a crime-free life. "Somewhere on the lineup I had become invisible again. I'd taken on the shadows that kept me camouflaged, and dangerous" (Mosley 1996, 156). As William Nash has pointed out in his article, "'Maybe I Killed My Own Blood': Doppelgängers and the Death of Double Consciousness in Walter Mosley's *A Little Yellow Dog*," "Easy begins his movement back towards the streets as Mouse self-domesticates by taking a job as a night watchman at the school where Easy has been working as head janitor and by giving up the street life" (1999, 304). In a passage that strongly suggests that Easy and Mouse have exchanged roles, Mouse tells Easy: "but right now I just wanna see what it's like to live wit' your family an' work at a job. . . . I'm lookin' for a new way—that's all" (Mosley 1996, 257).

Ironically, it's Mouse who recognizes Easy's existential problem: "[A] nigger ain't never gonna be happy 'less he accept what he is" (Mosley 1990, 205). But, of course, the question for Easy, the same question Ellison's famous narrator faced, is "Who am I?" Or, more importantly, "Who do I want to be: the tough, hard-boiled, streetwise, invisible undercover sleuth or a loving, responsible, and hard-working father?" As he is coming out of one of the clubs he has so loved haunting, Easy thinks: "I wondered if there was a place for me that could be like this and still allow me to hear the children's laughter in the morning" (Mosley 1996, 186). Trying hard to be like his namesake, Ezekiel, the Hebrew prophet who called for the Jews exiled in Babylon to return to godliness and faith, Easy's quest for a place in the world has, nonetheless, been arduous and uncertain. The little yellow dog reminds him of his capacity to slip over the edge: "As the days passed I began to accept him as part of my life; the dark, dangerous part that always threatened. As long as Pharaoh was around snarling and cursing I'd remember the kind of trouble that a man like me could find" (307).

Critics have suggested that with the presumed death of Mouse at the end of *A Little Yellow Dog*, Easy could well be on his way to a new life and a solution to his personal mystery. Perhaps with Mosley's more recent books, *Always Outnumbered, Always Outgunned* (1998), and *Walkin' the Dog* (1999), which feature Socrates Fortlow, an ex-convict trying to build a life for himself by doing "good if the chance came before him" (Mosley 1998, 60), Mosley has been able to work out some of the problems of identity Easy faces.

Tony Hillerman's Navajo policeman Jim Chee, "a complicated mixture of intelligence, romanticism, logic, and idealism" (1993, 273), is also

182 ALISON D. GOELLER

looking for a place where he can find contentment, professionally, socially, culturally, and spiritually. Like Easy, who uses his cultural knowledge of the street to solve crimes, Chee cracks the cases on the reservation because he is immersed in the Navajo culture. Hillerman's novels are saturated with examples of this. Chee also cannot resist solving puzzles. Secretly taking on cases, much to the annoyance of the ubiquitous white FBI who almost always have jurisdiction on the reservation, particularly in felony cases, and to the annoyance of his kind but less adventurous supervisor, Joe Leaphorn, Chee is also an expert sleuth because his Navajo upbringing has taught him that everything in the universe is connected:

> Sooner or later he would understand this business. He'd find the cause. Senseless as it seemed, there'd be a reason behind it. The wind did not move, the leaf did not fall, the bird did not cry, nor did the windmill provoke such violent anger without a reason. All was part of the universal pattern, as Changing Woman had taught them when she formed the first four Navajo clans. Jim Chee had ingested that fact with his mother's milk, and from the endless lessons his uncle had taught him. "All is order," Hosteen Nakai taught him. "Look for the pattern." (Hillerman 1982, 57)

However, Chee, like Easy, has a hard time reconciling his native culture with other aspects of his life. The legal question of jurisdiction, of border rights, is mirrored in Chee's living between cultures. For one thing, he is studying to be a Navajo shaman, or healer, an identity he readily admits is totally "incongruous" with his job as policeman, because the Navajo ethical code, unlike the American legal system, does not believe in punishment:

> Someone who violated basic rules of behavior and harmed you was, by Navajo definition, "out of control." The "dark wind" had entered him and destroyed his judgment. One avoided such persons, and worried about them, and was pleased if they were cured of this temporary insanity and returned again to *hozro*. But to Chee's Navajo mind, the idea of punishing them would be as insane as the original act. (147–48)

His adherence to the Navajo codes of conduct, then, causes Chee to break the very laws he is supposedly trying to enforce as a reservation policeman: like Easy Rawlins, he constantly goes outside his jurisdiction, which is very limited on the reservation, thus getting himself into trouble with the FBI and occasionally with his supervisors. In this respect, Chee is also a trickster, shifting identities between two worlds and both literally and figuratively crossing borders. Chee also withholds and sometimes destroys evidence or doesn't turn in a criminal after he's solved the crime because

THE MYSTERY OF IDENTITY   183

"there are higher laws than the white man's" (196). In *Sacred Clowns*, for instance, Chee refuses to turn in Clement Hoski, after he discovers Hoski is the hit-and-run driver the FBI have been looking for, because he realizes that Hoski's fetal alcohol syndrome grandson, Ernie, needs him in order to survive. Likewise, at the end of *The Dark Wind* Chee dumps the long sought-after cocaine into the river, a clear instance of disposing of evidence, because all the puzzles have been solved and there is no need for the FBI to have it.

The imperative for Chee to straddle cultural borders, both literally and figuratively, although problematic, also allows him a tolerance for contradictions and ambiguity, a near necessity in a postmodern world. More importantly, it has developed in him a flexibility that every good detective needs. Gloria Anzaldúa, in *Borderlands/La Frontera: The New Mestiza*, writing of her experience as a Mexican American, underlines this point:

> The borders and walls that are supposed to keep the undesirable ideas out are entrenched habits and patterns of behavior; these habits and patterns are the enemy within. Rigidity means death. Only by remaining flexible is she able to stretch the psyche horizontally and vertically. *"La mestiza"* constantly has to shift out of habitual formations, from convergent thinking, analytical reasoning that tends to use rationality to move toward a single goal (a Western mode), to divergent thinking, characterized by movement away from set patterns and goals and toward a more whole perspective, one that includes rather than excludes. (1987, 79)

And it is precisely this ability to include and to think "outside the box" that allows Chee to solve cases others cannot.

Another dilemma Chee faces in most of Hillerman's novels, directly connected to his multiple identities as both Navajo and policeman, is with whom and if he wants to be romantically involved. Although he does exhibit many of the qualities of the hard-boiled detective, in particular his attraction to living alone—"He had placed the trailer here under this lonely cottonwood for privacy and isolation" (Hillerman 1982, 237)—his mind is often occupied with thoughts of romance. In the early novels, his girlfriend is blonde-haired, blue-eyed Mary Langdon, a white schoolteacher, who wants him to quit the Navajo police force, move off the reservation, and become an FBI agent, which, of course, in light of how Chee views the FBI, would be tantamount to treason. But Chee actually considers this a possibility because he is deeply in love with Mary and is, at this point, not quite sure where he wants to be. When Mary finally gives up on Chee and moves to Wisconsin, Chee becomes interested in Janet Pete, a half-Navajo lawyer; this shift seems to suggest that he is moving toward a more integrated life in his Navajo community. However, Janet also poses problems.

184   ALISON D. GOELLER

For one thing, she wasn't raised as a Navajo and so has trouble fully understanding Chee's Navajo ways, and, for another, she is not quite sure whether she wants to settle on the reservation and work for the Navajos or live in Washington, D.C., and become a high-powered lawyer. From time to time Janet is involved with an ambitious white lawyer, John McDermott, whom Chee suspects is using Janet as the token Indian lawyer. Just as it looks as if Chee and Janet will finally marry, however, another problem connected to cultural identity arises. Since Janet never knew her father, she doesn't know the name of her clan; consequently, Chee is not sure they can go through with the marriage, because marrying within one's clan is taboo, an act of incest, and this uncertainty finally leads to their breakup. In the latest novel, *Hunting Badger,* Chee shows interest in Bernadette Manuelito, a young Navajo policewoman who could possibly be a satisfying solution to Chee's romantic problems, because she seems much more suited to Chee's life as a Navajo. But we will have to wait for another Tony Hillerman novel to find out.

A final mystery for Chee is whether or not he has met the standards for becoming a full-fledged medicine man. In *Coyote Waits* Joe Leaphorn registers doubts about Chee's ability to mix police work with spiritual healing:

> This business of trying to be a *hataalii* and a policeman at the same time, for example. It wasn't just impractical. How the hell could a cop get time off at the drop of a hat for a nine-day sing? It was incongruous. It was like being an investment banker and a Catholic priest at the same time. Or a rabbi and a clown. (Hillerman 1991, 247)

Throughout *Hunting Badger*, so far the last of the Chee novels, he has been waiting for his Uncle Nakai to tell him the last secret that will guarantee this. Unfortunately, Uncle Nakai rules against Chee, telling him that he is too modern. Although Chee is disappointed, he is not as devastated as he had thought he would be: "Freeing him to be the sort of modern man he was becoming. . . . [T]here was a sense of relief in that, mixed with a dreary sense of loss" (Hillerman 1999, 115). Thus, Chee is released from an essentialist notion of himself, free to negotiate his place in the world, which, of course, is constantly shifting, anyway. Ironically, this, in some ways, makes him even more Navajo, since adaptability, not to be confused with assimilation, has always been characteristic of Navajo culture. It is the Navajo belief in *xojo* or harmony that allows him this. And like Tayo, in Leslie Marmon Silko's novel *Ceremony*, who learns that "things that don't shift and grow are dead things" (1977, 126) and that "ceremonies have always been changing" (126), Chee is perhaps better equipped to survive and even thrive in a multicultural society such as America because he can adapt and change, while retaining his sacred Navajo beliefs and ways.

THE MYSTERY OF IDENTITY   185

Identity, then, for both Chee and Easy remains a continuous process, not a fixed site, contingent on all the elements that both include them and exclude them. It is a complex entity, if, in fact, it can ever be called an entity. Writing about identity in a postmodern world, Stuart Hall, in his introduction to *Questions of Cultural Identity*, says this:

> The concept of identity . . . is not an essentialist, but a strategic and positional one. That is to say, directly contrary to what appears to be its settled semantic career, this concept of identity does not signal that stable core of the self, unfolding from beginning to end through all the vicissitudes of history without change, the bit of the self which remains always-already "the same," identical to itself across time. Nor—if we translate this essentializing conception to the stage of cultural identity—is it that "collective or true self hiding inside the many other, more superficial or artificially imposed 'selves' which a people with a shared history and ancestry hold in common" . . . and which can stabilize, fix or guarantee an unchanging "oneness" or cultural belongingness underlying all the other superficial differences. (Hall and Du Gay, 1996, 3–4)

Such a position, however, can only be advantageous, because, as Hall has said in another context, the tension resulting from the negotiation of multiple identities enriches debate since "it holds theoretical and political questions in an ever irresolvable but permanent tension. It constantly allows the one to irritate, bother, and disturb the other, without insisting on some final theoretical closure" (Hall 2001, 1907). So although the overt mysteries in Mosley and Hillerman's novels are always solved, their protagonists' personal mysteries, their identities, remain elusive, shifting, and tenuous. This, after all, is why they engage us as they do.

NOTES

1. Hillerman, though not a Navajo himself, grew up in Oklahoma among the Seminoles and Potawatomi and has dedicated much of his life to anthropological and social research of the Navajo, Zuni, and Hopi cultures (see his acknowledgments in, for instance, *The Blessing Way*), earning for himself the unique status of "Special Friend of the Navajos"; and his novels are read in Navajo classrooms because, according to the librarian at St. Catherine Indian School, they "make us feel good about being Navajos" (quoted in Templeton 1999, 45). Hillerman shares many similarities with the Australian crime fiction writer Arthur Upfield, who wrote about Aboriginals, though he himself was not one, and whose detective, Inspector Napoleon Bonaparte, uses his knowledge of native ways and outback geography to solve cases.

2. Although *Bad Boy Bobby Brown*, another Easy Rawlins book that takes place in the sixties, was due for publication in 1996, it has yet to be published.

186   ALISON D. GOELLER

Works Cited

Anzaldúa, Gloria. 1987. *Borderlands/La Frontera: The New Mestiza.* San Francisco, Calif.: Aunt Lute.

Gosselin, Adrienne Johnson, ed. 1999. *Multicultural Detective Fiction: Murder from the "Other" Side.* New York: Garland.

Gruesser, John Cullen. 1999. "An Un-Easy Relationship: Walter Mosley's Signifyin(g) Detective and the Black Community." In Gosselin 1999, 235–55.

Hall, Stuart. 2001. "Cultural Studies and Its Theoretical Legacies." Reprinted in *The Norton Anthology of Theory and Criticism*, edited by Vincent B. Leitch, 1898–1910. New York: W. W. Norton.

Hall, Stuart, and Paul Du Gay, eds. 1996. *Questions of Cultural Identity.* London: Sage.

Hillerman, Tony. 1970. *Blessing Way.* New York: HarperPaperbacks.

———. 1982. *The Dark Wind.* New York: Harper.

———. 1988. *A Thief of Time.* New York: HarperPaperbacks.

———. 1989. *Talking God.* New York: Harper and Row.

———. 1991. *Coyote Waits.* New York: HarperPaperbacks.

———. 1993. *Sacred Clowns.* New York: HarperPaperbacks.

———. 1999. *Hunting Badger.* New York: HarperCollins.

Madden, David, ed. 1968. *Tough Guy Writers of the Thirties.* Carbondale: Southern Illinois University Press.

Mason, Theodore O., Jr. 1992. "Walter Mosley's Easy Rawlins: The Detective and Afro-American Fiction." *Kenyon Review* 14, no. 4:173–83.

Mosley, Walter. 1990. *Devil in a Blue Dress.* New York: Pocket Books.

———. 1991. *A Red Death.* New York: Pocket Books.

———. 1992. *White Butterfly.* New York: Pocket Books.

———. 1994. *Black Betty.* New York: Pocket Books.

———. 1996. *A Little Yellow Dog.* New York: Pocket Books.

———. 1997. *Gone Fishin'.* New York: Pocket Books.

———. 1998. *Always Outnumbered, Always Outgunned.* New York: Pocket Books.

———. 1999. *Walkin' the Dog.* Boston: Little, Brown and Company.

———. 2000. *Workin' on the Chain Gang: Shaking Off the Dead Hand of History.* New York: Ballantine.

Nash, William. 1999. "'Maybe I killed my own blood': Doppelgängers and the Death of Double Consciousness in Walter Mosley's *A Little Yellow Dog*." In Gosselin 1999, 303–24.

Silet, Charles L. P. 1993. "On the Other Side of Those Mean Streets: An Interview with Walter Mosley." *The Armchair Detective* 26, no. 4:8–19.

Silko, Leslie Marmon. 1977. *Ceremony.* New York: Penguin Books.

Templeton, Wayne. 1999. "Xojo and Homicide: The Postcolonial Murder Mysteries of Tony Hillerman." In Gosselin 1999, 37–59.

Woertche, Thomas. 1994. "Interview mit Walter Mosley." *Sirene* 12/13:115–23.

Detecting from the Borderlands:
Aimée and David Thurlo's Ella Clah Novels

KATRIN FISCHER

> One is not a detective *and* a Navajo, not a puzzle solver *and* a loving
> human being. . . . [O]ne is everything at once.
> —John M. Reilly

"THE MEETING OF CULTURES IS THE GREATEST OF THE WORLD'S STORIES," JUNE NAMIAS states in *White Captives,* her compelling study of gender and ethnicity on the American frontier (1993, xiv). Encounters across cultural borders have in fact always been a source of both spine-chilling fear and intense fascination. The overwhelming popularity of captivity narratives from the colonial period onward, for example, testifies to the white readers' unbroken curiosity about the Native American. Stories of captives' lives among the indigenous peoples present the reading audience with an intersection of cultures and reveal how European Americans thought about issues of race and gender when confronted by the continent's native inhabitants.

Ever since Columbus set foot on the American continent, the picture of the Native American produced by white culture has been in a constant state of flux. Depending on the specific historical circumstances, the Native American has most often been stereotyped as either a noble savage or a bloodthirsty, brutal beast. However, whether portrayed as noble or depraved, "the Indian as an image was always alien to the White" (Berghofer 1979, xv). In fact as well as fiction, America's native peoples have served as "the quintessential Other, whose role is to be the object of the White, colonialist gaze" (Bird 1998, 4).

Not only has Western culture's perception of Native Americans changed over time, but the means of transmission of cultural knowledge about them have changed as well. Although some of the earlier stereotypes are still perpetuated, visual mass media and popular literature increasingly contribute to a more thorough and realistic understanding of Native Americans. In movies, they are no longer portrayed as "vicious, horse-riding Plains nomads menacing unwary settlers," while in fiction, "a whole new genre of pulp literature has emerged . . . written by authors with allegedly expert inside understanding of particular groups of Indians" (Clifton 1989, 2).

Crime and detective fiction is a case in point. As a Western cultural product, detective fiction had long been considered inadequate for the discussion of cross-cultural themes. John G. Cawelti, in a discussion of Arthur William Upfield's detective serial about the half-Aboriginal Napoleon Bonaparte (called Bony), claims that the "angle of vision enforced by the classical detective story is inevitably a limited one, because its basic assumptions are bound to the social and ideological patterns of Western bourgeois democracies of the nineteenth and twentieth centuries" (1977, 39). The standard detective formula, the writer argues, "seems to require the importation of certain presuppositions about society, law and morality from the Anglo-American tradition" (39) and thus to prohibit "the expression of deeper and more complex cultural perspectives" (39). While Cawelti's statement holds true for the vast majority of novels written during the Golden Age of detective fiction,[1] it can no longer be applied to the current state of affairs. Today's mystery writers prove Cawelti wrong. In an attempt to do more than to simply delight their readership with the puzzling aspects of a crime, they include substantial social and cultural information in their detective plots. Contemporary crime fiction combines entertainment with information. Increasingly, it gives visibility and voice to authors and protagonists who are not necessarily male[2] and/or of Anglo-American descent. If the criminal investigator is removed from his or her conventional European American environment, detective fiction—traditionally supposed to be apolitical and restricted to its basic formula—assumes the function of a social document. In these cases, the detective's quest for restoring order "inadvertently turns into an illustration of ethnic friction and cultural confrontation and thus into a comment on the challenges of everyday life in a 'multicultural' society" (Freese 1992, 9–10).

Due to its great popularity, detective fiction can serve to illuminate minority cultures and groups that have long been neglected in American literature. One of these ignored peoples are the Native Americans, regarded as "the oldest and only native element of the ethnic crucible known as the mythic American 'melting pot'" and "the one which the European and even the average American knows the least about" (Freese 1992, 169). Keeping in mind that the "images produced by popular culture play a real role in shaping people's perceptions" (Bird 1998, 11), I will examine how Native Americans are represented in contemporary crime fiction. While the inclusion of other ethnic minorities in the detective genre has been widely discussed,[3] American Indians have only recently been given more extensive critical attention.[4]

For a long time, literary criticism has been preoccupied with the works of Tony Hillerman, one of the most acclaimed contemporary detective writers. Hillerman's first novel, *The Blessing Way* (1970), broke new ground in that it was set in Dinetah, the heartland of the Navajos, and introduced a Native American sleuth, Lieutenant Joe (Joseph) Leaphorn. Although Navajo by birth, Leaphorn has replaced much of his faith in traditional Navajo ways with a much stronger belief in Western rationality and logic. Unlike Leaphorn, Officer Jim Chee, who made his debut in *People of Darkness* (1980), retains his faith in the spiritual beliefs of his people. He follows a more traditional way of life than Leaphorn and devotes his spare time to preparing himself to become a shaman in the Navajo culture.[5] Hillerman's exciting stories illustrate the perpetual conflict between a traditional way of life and the Anglo-American society's materialist values. Hillerman, who is himself an Anglo, manages to portray Navajo culture with insight and wisdom. His mysteries teach the readers about an alternative way of conceptualizing the world. They are received very well, not only by white readers, but also by the Navajo community.[6]

However, the still evolving subgenre of detective fiction by and/or about Native Americans is not restricted to Hillerman's Navajo mysteries. By now it includes well-known and appealing series by Margaret Coel, James D. Doss, Micah S. Hackler, Jean Hager, J. F. Trainor[7] and many other writers.

One striking example of the combination of Native American concerns and the detective formula is the mystery series by Aimée and David Thurlo,[8] themselves a couple of mixed ethnicity. Aimée—who is much better known for her romance series about the Brothers of Rock Ridge, two sexy Navajos steeped in the traditions of their tribal heritage—is a native of Havana, Cuba. David, on the other hand, grew up on the Navajo Reservation near Shiprock, New Mexico. With their mystery series, the Thurlos successfully venture into Hillerman's domain. Their novels bring the Navajo reservation to life, and they can be enjoyed at least as much as those of the "grand master." In taking a closer look at their series, I will explore how the mystery genre can be a brilliant device for discussing cross-cultural themes and for exploring the interface between white and Native American culture.

The central character in Aimée and David Thurlo's detective series is Ella Clah. Although she is a Navajo, she no longer lives with her tribe. After the premature death of her husband in a traffic accident, she has decided to pursue a career as an FBI agent off the reservation.[9] Her job as criminal investigator keeps her on the move and far away from her home in northwestern New Mexico. Ella knew about and welcomed the job-required

190   KATRIN FISCHER

rootlessness, which "was meant to protect agents and their integrity" and to keep them "far from investigations that might involve friends and family" (Thurlo and Thurlo 1995a, 12). In leaving the reservation for a career with the FBI, Ella attempts to get away from her past and to start a new and different life. Moving frequently from one city to another is well-suited to this goal. Applying for a job with the FBI marks a turning point in Ella's life. While married, she had taken on the traditional woman's role and defined herself mainly through her part as Eugene's wife. Now she stands completely on her own and realizes that she is capable of accomplishing almost anything she sets her mind to. Working through loss and mourning, "she'd found a new direction for her life, and strength she'd never thought she had. Something good had sprung from the bitter ashes" (68).

Ella is a highly professional career woman, who—at the beginning of the series—professes to have found self-fulfillment in her work. Soon, however, it becomes apparent that though she derives satisfaction from her job, "something was missing from the center of her life" (Thurlo and Thurlo 1995a, 91). The series focuses on Ella's rediscovering this something—her identity. Each sequel describes a further step in the long and often painful process by which Ella comes to terms with her past. It is the story of a Navajo woman who struggles to find a "true self" in a world of conflicting demands, beliefs, and value systems. Ella oscillates between the Navajo world and the white world, fully accepted by neither but needed by both. She is an ethnic detective who, according to Peter Freese's definition, "not only solves a murder mystery, be it by means of superior ratiocinative powers or daringly active interference, but who also introduces the reader to an unknown ethnic culture and thus assumes the function of a cultural mediator" (1992, 9). Going through the process of alienation and return, a common theme in Native American fiction, Ella takes on the role of a cross-cultural detective and finally manages to position herself in both the white world and the Indian world. Ella Clah's personal story demonstrates how detective fiction can be used for discussing the intermingling of different cultures.

In *Blackening Song*—the debut novel of the series—Ella lives and works as an FBI agent in Los Angeles. From the very beginning, she is characterized as an outsider among her white, male peers. As an American Indian and female investigator, she is marginalized twice. Being a successful woman in a male-dominated profession alone causes many problems. Ella knows from experience that

> guys, no matter what P. D. [Police Department] they serve in, tend to resent the presence of women. . . . They put on their badges, and that becomes their trademark. They want the world to believe they are the biggest, baddest guys around, and the crooks should all be shaking in their

DETECTING FROM THE BORDERLANDS

boots. Then they see someone else wearing a badge, only she's prettier to look at, and undoubtedly smells nicer. It sorta smashes the tough-guy image they cherish in their little hearts. (Thurlo and Thurlo 1995a, 15–16)

Ella detects from the borderlands of gender as well as of race. The series tightly knits together these two discourses. Being a female Native American investigator gives her "the right to cross borders previously closed, [and] to unfix definitions, [and] to ramble through society with a mobility long considered exclusively masculine" (Rich 1989, 24). This enviable ability to cross borders, however, is not achieved without pitfalls. Frequently, Ella encounters resentment and distrust. More than once, she is discriminated against on grounds of her race and sex. Ella is an interloper, not only in the white, male-dominated universe of the FBI, but also—as will be shown in detail later on—in her own family and tribe.

With her FBI colleagues, Ella has a reputation for being a loner. Instead of celebrating a successfully solved case with her fellow agents, she prefers to sit alone in her favorite Los Angeles coffee shop. Her idiosyncratic behavior calls for explanations, one of which is already offered in the introductory scene. The reader is subtly informed that it is not the company Ella is afraid of, but "all the drinking" (Thurlo and Thurlo 1995a, 11). Seeing people drink triggers memories of her past life on the reservation where alcoholism is one of the most pressing social problems. "Poverty and harsh living conditions . . . had led to a high rate of alcoholism" (1998, 55), and Ella had "seen too much of it on the reservation she grew up on" (1995a, 12). Early in the series, very real problems that face Native Americans are woven into the fictional story. The inclusion of social predicaments fits the authors' intention "to portray life on the reservation with . . . realism" (1995b, 382). The books' authenticity derives largely from David's having been raised on the Navajo reservation himself. In their note at the end of *Blackening Song* the authors reveal that the idea for the series was born during a trip back to Shiprock to attend David's high school reunion. While strolling around the campus, they noticed a dead horse in the grass near the thirty yard line of a football field. The fact that "[n]o one, including the curious children, looked at it or were tempted to approach . . . served as a powerful reminder of how old beliefs and modern education could exist side by side" (381–82). Accepting that, the Thurlos reached the conclusion that their detective "would have to have her feet firmly planted in two very different worlds" (382). Hence, Ella and the other characters are confronted with a series of tough issues, among which unemployment, drugs and alcoholism feature prominently. Back on the Navajo reservation, where she investigates later in the series, Ella frequently has to deal with cases of excessive drinking, drunk driving, and people "dying of exposure after passing out drunk" (1998, 103). In *Enemy Way*, the fourth sequel, Ella is

192   KATRIN FISCHER

personally affected when her mother is seriously hurt in a car accident and the offending driver turns out to be a heavy drinker. "Alcoholism is"—as Ella's brother asserts in *Enemy Way*—"an imported illness and one of the many signs that the traditions and beliefs she [their mother] holds dear are slowly fading away" (1998, 95). Rose's accident—as well as crime, murder, and gang violence—can be interpreted as a direct result of the Anglo world's negative influence on the Navajo people.

As an FBI agent, Ella performs her work excellently, but the fact that she remains an outsider among her colleagues points to a severe identity crisis. Ella is torn between two cultural poles. Although her life on the Navajo reservation "seemed like a century ago" (Thurlo and Thurlo 1995a, 12), she has not really become part of the white world she opted for. Her Native American identity is frequently probed and at times even overshadows her accomplishments as FBI agent. Her physical appearance, which clearly marks her as different,[10] not only arouses curiosity but also triggers racial prejudices. As the story opens, Ella is sitting in her favorite Los Angeles diner when a heavily armed man starts taking hostages. In order to calm him down and to win time, she tries to engage him in conversation. Soon the topic switches to Ella's racial identity:

> "What the hell are you?"
> The question threw her [Ella]. "Huh?"
> "You're not a spick or mulatto. What are you?"
> She forced her voice to stay even. "Indian."
> "You don't look Indian. There's no dot on your forehead. What part of India are you from?"
> "New Mexico, U.S.A. I'm an American Indian." (17)

After being told that Ella is a Native American, the kidnapper states: "Then you must hate whites. Probably as much as I hate the stinking minorities. They come here and take our jobs, like that nigger. . . . They make us grovel for work, forgetting that we were here first" (17). Viewing different cultures or races through binary oppositions of "us" versus "them" is—as Edward Said and other critics point out—a decidedly Western habit of thought. Implicit in the abductor's ignorant remarks is the belief that the white race is superior to the African or American Indian one, and his verbal attack culminates in the overt racist statement that "the cavalry should have killed all you [American Indians] off a hundred years ago" (18). Moreover, the fact that Ella has a job with the FBI is not attributed to her professional qualities but to the results of affirmative action: "Probably had some quota to take ten Indians that day" (19–20). Asked by the abductor why she did not stay on the reservation and try to improve the living conditions there, Ella answers that "people belong wherever they can make a place for themselves" (20). It is Ella's search for this place that the series is about. This kidnapping scene at the beginning of *Blackening Song* establishes her as a self-confident, well-trained FBI agent and sets the basic conflict between the white worldview and the Indian one—the problem of how to live with and reconcile differences of race and culture. Unlike the abductor, whom Ella finally shoots dead at point-blank range, Ella in the end proves able to successfully bridge the gap between the white man's and the Navajo's way of life.

Readers soon notice that Ella—as well as most of the other characters in the books—can be described in terms of her connection to her cultural roots. Living in Los Angeles and hard work have not brought the intended and longed-for break with her past. While trying to calm down the kidnapper, Ella refers to the Navajos as "my people" (Thurlo and Thurlo 1995a, 18), which suggests that she still has strong feelings toward her Native American ancestry. However, the fact that she does not "share the Navajo belief in the *chindi*, the evil in a man that remained earthbound after death" (22), marks her as removed from Navajo traditions. Another strong indication of her still active emotional connection to her regional as well as cultural roots are her frequent visits to the Southwestern Museum. Ella subconsciously yearns for the place and culture she comes from. Though working in the midst of white culture, Ella is not fully assimilated into the Anglo-American mainstream. The fact that she prefers to sit alone in her favorite café underlines her reluctance to embrace white civilization.

In starting their series by tracing an American Indian's life in Los Angeles, the authors unfold the background for tensions between Navajo and Anglo-American value systems. Robbery, murder, assault, and other violent crimes are an everyday occurrence in the city. Accordingly, Ella's "instincts never slowed, even at home" (Thurlo and Thurlo 1995a, 26). In the urban metropolis, Ella does not experience the safety and security of the tribal community, but rather individual isolation, which—as Yi-Fu Tuan points out—is a "widely noted feature of modern life, which distinguishes it from earlier times" (1992, 36). It not only differentiates past from present, but also the Western from the Navajo way of life. Looking back at her time as an FBI agent in Los Angeles, Ella characterizes herself as "busy, but too alone" (1996, 234). She suffers from the metropolis's emotionally cold atmosphere, which is set off against the Navajos' strong emphasis on community.

Modern life in the city signifies danger in many respects, not only regarding anonymity and a high crime rate. Los Angeles becomes a metaphor for an inherently dangerous world, in which the possibility of losing one's identity is a constant threat, especially for members of small ethnic groups. Ella's reputation of being a loner indicates an underlying lack of

194 KATRIN FISCHER

identity—of not being at home in both a literal and a figurative sense. Outward signs of this condition are her sparse living arrangements. What she calls home in Los Angeles is a highly secure, tiny apartment, described as a place she uses mostly to sleep and shower and whose furniture she does not even own. FBI agent Ella Clah's apparent isolation and rootlessness provide a counterpoint to the Navajo's insistence on family ties, tradition, and identity. For Native Americans like Ella, city life is associated with displacement and loss. At the same time, Aimée and David Thurlo's portrait of Los Angeles reminds the reader of Raymond Chandler's "mean streets." Amidst the urban jungle, Ella appears to be an updated, ethnically defined version of the self-confident but alienated "tough guy" of the American hard-boiled school. Like Philip Marlowe, Chandler's detective/narrator, Ella lives alone in a rented, comfortless flat and works alone on her cases; like Marlowe, she does not have much of a private life. Her isolation in Los Angeles as well as back on the reservation is described as a source of both vulnerability and strength.

Ella's investigative efforts as FBI agent—and later as special investigator of the Navajo Tribal Police—run parallel to a search for home in its wider sense. As a representative of an ethnic minority, she experiences firsthand the "unhomeliness" that, according to Homi K. Bhabha, is "the condition of extra-territorial and cross-cultural initiations" (1994, 9). The encounters across borders of culture and gender that she has as an FBI agent in Los Angeles and other cities significantly contribute to and accelerate the process that finally leads her back to her roots. In *Death Walker*, the second novel of the series, she vividly remembers life in the cities where she had worked with the Federal Bureau of Investigation and concludes that "she'd never felt more lonely than she had during those days. She'd drowned herself in her work as a way to avoid the loneliness. Even if she'd lived out there by herself, with only the mesas as neighbors, she'd never suffer from the isolation she'd felt back then. The Colorado Plateau, as inhospitable as it seemed at times, was home" (Thurlo and Thurlo 1996, 178).

Ella's process of redefining herself and gaining identity is set off by the shockingly brutal murder of her father in *Blackening Song*. Raymond Destea, a Navajo preacher, "had been speared and stabbed to death with edged weapons, then scalped. His ears had been cut off and were missing. All the tendons from his legs, arms, and neck had also been taken" (Thurlo and Thurlo 1995a, 72). In order to find the murderer, Ella follows her mother's desperate call to come home. After more than six years, Ella returns to the reservation where she was born and grew up. Her journey back to the Navajo reservation is the first step in a complicated soul-journey toward her true self. In order to cope with this extremely difficult situation, she has to come to terms with the world she is now forced to reenter and has to face everything she previously pushed away.

According to the strict rules of the FBI, Ella is not allowed to investigate Raymond Destea's murder. Soon, however, it turns out that she is "the only hope of catching her father's killer" (Thurlo and Thurlo 1995a, 31). In traditional crime fiction, the investigator is an emotionally uninvolved outsider. Here, however, being an outsider would not constitute an advantage. Since the murder occurred on reservation land and carries ritualistic overtones, a detective is needed who is not only a professional but also deeply familiar with Navajo customs and beliefs.[11] The tribe's traditions provide the insight necessary to comprehend the significance of the crime and its consequences for the tribe. Ella knows that "traditionally, a mutilation like this was done to a slain enemy warrior who'd fought bravely. A medicine man could use the stolen items for his medicine bundle. This was supposed to be a powerful ward against the medicine man's enemies" (73). The details of the murder make it quite plain that Skinwalkers are involved, evil witches who subvert traditional rituals in order to hurt people and gain power. Ella's task is to fight them and to restore harmony on the reservation.

In her quest for order she learns that if she wants to solve her father's murder and expose the Skinwalkers, she must respect Navajo traditions. In the process, she recognizes that she has not completely forsaken her Native American roots. Again, she is forced to define herself in relation to both the Navajo and the Anglo-American world. In order to be able to restore balance among the Navajos, she first has to turn her gaze inward and find her own personal balance. Matters of religion feature prominently in this process.

The series is written with a sharp eye for the perpetual conflict between traditionalist and modernist ways of life. The authors maintain that their aim has been to show readers "how old beliefs and modern education could exist side by side" (Thurlo and Thurlo 1995b, 382). This self-proclaimed goal is achieved on the character level through contrasting different life concepts. Ella's family, which is religiously split, is a mirror of the situation on the reservation. While her mother, Rose, had kept her traditional Navajo beliefs, her father had adopted Christianity; their marriage illustrates that both religions can peacefully exist side by side and complement each other. In retrospect, Ella muses that her "mother and father had been like counterweights that balanced each other" (Thurlo and Thurlo 1995a, 177)—an equilibrium destroyed by Raymond Destea's senseless death.

Even within her family, Ella is trapped in between. Contrary to her brother, who chose to follow the old ways, Ella had refused to make a decision and does not share either of her parents' religious beliefs. When asked by her close friend Wilson Joe which side she supports, she answers "I'd be starting a third group, and insisting that all parties involved reach a compromise. . . . I *really* don't favor one over the other. What I do favor is the right to free choice" (Thurlo and Thurlo 1995a, 200). Her careful answer reveals that she has not yet found her individual balance. She still has to figure out a way to fit in and to combine the old and the new. Like Ella, Wilson has lived in both worlds for a long time. His heart, as he says, is still with the old ways, but he also knows that "we need the new to survive as a people" (200). Ella envies his ability to position himself in both the progressive and the traditional world. What surprises her is his ability to be comfortable anywhere. Wilson and Clifford and Rose all present role models for Ella and function as guiding spirits on her journey back to her roots.

On the reservation, Ella recognizes at once that the Dineh—as the Navajos call themselves—treat her like a stranger. Although she was born and raised among the Navajos, people are suspicious of her. She is considered an outsider because of her long absence from the reservation. People do not forget that she favored the Anglo-American way of life, left the reservation, and turned her back on Navajo customs and traditions. With her father on the progressive side and her mother on the traditional one, there is much speculation as to where Ella stands. As an FBI agent, Ella is bound to uphold the rulings of Anglo law, which often conflict with the Navajos' claims and interests. Not surprisingly, reservation people wonder where Ella's loyalties lie—with the old ways or the new, with the progressives or the traditionalists, with her tribe or with the FBI. Many consider her using the grants and scholarships the tribe offers for pursuing a law enforcement career off the reservation an act of treason:

> "Are your loyalties to the bureau greater than those you feel for the Dineh?" . . .
> "The two don't conflict," she [Ella] answered. "The bureau is an investigative service, which serves the people as well as others."
> "How does your being a federal agent help the tribe? Isn't it a form of disloyalty to use tribal scholarships to get an education that will benefit those outside the Rez more than us?"
> "Our ways teach that everything is interrelated; one event always affects another. What I do outside the Rez isn't separate from what happens here; it's all part of the balance," Ella said. (Thurlo and Thurlo 1995a, 203)

No matter how strong her arguments are, Ella has a hard time proving her trustworthiness and winning back social acceptance in her tribe. Navajo society appears to her as a labyrinth of traditions, customs, and rules to which the tribal community denies her access. Having been away for a

DETECTING FROM THE BORDERLANDS

long time, she lacks knowledge—not of how to combat criminals, but of the intricacies of Navajo customs, traditions, beliefs, and secrets. Ella's duty is not only to bring murderers to justice, but also to reestablish the connection to her people. Ella is set apart from the other characters in the series by the difficult task of soul-searching and the need to define herself.

Ella's strong belief in logical patterns and rational explanations—acquired as an FBI agent in the white world—is threatened by what happens on the reservation, where "things moved at their own pace and in their own way" (Thurlo and Thurlo 1995a, 38). Here she is forced to accept a different reality, which more than once conflicts with the law enforcement career she works hard to attain. She is caught between two opposing worlds, the rational one of modern law enforcement and the spiritual, harder to grasp Navajo one. For the first time in her life, Ella feels caught by something she cannot control by reason: "Throughout your career," Clifford reminds her, "you've found a way to avoid the things you feared the most. . . . Intangibles have always frightened you far more than anything you could visualize and define" (119). Encountering her worst fears is one of the most serious challenges Ella faces. Consequently, all her beliefs about herself and about life undergo a transformation.

Rose and Clifford, her mother and brother, are crucial to Ella's growing awareness of Navajo traditions, without which no headway can be made in the case of her father's murder. They both provide help and guidance in understanding the dangers the tribe is facing. Rose is introduced into the series at the end of the first chapter of *Blackening Song*. Asked by Rose to come home, Ella realizes that it "was the first time her mother had ever asked her for anything" (Thurlo and Thurlo 1995a, 27). It becomes obvious that the relationship between Rose and Ella is unusual in many respects. Whereas Rose embodies traditional Navajo values, Ella stands for the modern Anglo-American way of life. The contrast between Ella and Rose is manifested visibly in their style of clothing:

> Ella was dressed for work in the city, complete with coordinating jacket to hide the pistol at her waistband. Her mother wore a traditional blouse and skirt, concha belt, and many turquoise strands, or *heishi*, as a necklace. Rose's hair was in a tight bun while Ella allowed hers to fall loosely around her shoulders. (79)

However, their differences go far beyond outward appearances. Although Rose loves her daughter, she does not trust her. Ella's refusal to accept the old ways stands as an insurmountable barrier between them. To carry out her investigations, Ella needs information from Rose, "but her mother's facts were often rooted in beliefs that Rose didn't want to expose to Ella's coldly logical viewpoint" (55). Like Wilson, Rose successfully manages to

198   KATRIN FISCHER

bridge the gap between the old and the new. Contrary to Ella, she is accepted by both traditionalists and progressives: "The traditionalists admired her because she's held on to her beliefs despite the path her husband had chosen. The progressives respected the way she'd learned to live in both worlds, a goal they often professed to hold" (95). While Ella claims that "what counts is knowing," not "believing," her mother accuses her of being ignorant of "our people's beliefs" and speaking "like a *bilagáana*" (53).[12] Although Ella is aware of the fact that ancient beliefs and Skinwalker rituals are involved in the case, she refuses to admit that there are things that cannot be explained logically. With her insistence on the omnipotence of rationality, Ella reminds the reader of the classical detective. She relies "on logic and common sense to find firm ground" (287) and simply denies the existence of the supernatural. She is convinced that she "can use logic to explain the insights you [Rose] call magic" (286). On the reservation, however, "rules shaped by logic and nature sometimes twisted, forming a different reality" (103). Slowly, she begins to think about alternative concepts of reality. Although she continues to emphasize the need for rigorous scientific methods, she wants to learn more about the Dineh. She starts to remember her people's ways and becomes more sensitive to Navajo beliefs. She grows to accept "beliefs that were as old as the Dineh," reconnects to her roots, and becomes a "part of what she'd left behind" (107).

Her brother Clifford plays an important role in this process. Unlike Ella, he had not refused to make a decision, but turned against his father's adopted religion and decided to follow the old ways. As a *hataalii*, a medicine man, he spends his time and energy "bringing the old ways back, and teaching others our beliefs, before what makes us Navajo is lost forever" (Thurlo and Thurlo 1995a, 44). Each in their own way, Ella and her brother are committed to restoring harmony. They are like the "Twin Sons of Talking God" (254): "Together, she and Clifford would support and help each other, like the children of Talking God, until they found a cure to the terrifying threat they faced" (256). They need each other, for neither of them can succeed on his own in the fight against the Skinwalkers. They both possess special talents, which set them apart from the rest of the Navajo community. Ella contributes her training and intuition, Clifford his extraordinary abilities as *hataalii*. Whereas Ella denies the existence of the supernatural, it is Clifford's area of strength. Together, Ella and Clifford are constant reminders that old traditions and modern ways can coexist successfully side by side.

The clash between Western rationality and Native American beliefs is further intensified through Ella's forced interaction with Dwayne Blalock, the white FBI agent in charge of Raymond Destea's murder. Immediately, Ella realizes that Blalock is the wrong person to solve crimes on Navajo land. Looking "as if he arrived by limo from a Washington, D.C., board-room" (Thurlo and Thurlo 1995a, 36), he simply does not fit in. Not only is his appearance inappropriate, but his behavior is inappropriate as well. Blalock rigidly adheres to the principles he learned and shows absolutely no sympathy for Navajo culture: "He wants to conform us [the Navajos] to his ways and doesn't understand that he has to do the adapting" (55). With his arrogant behavior towards the locals, he "sticks out like a sore thumb" (39) and encounters strong resistance from the Navajos, who regard him as an unwelcome intruder. Being white and unwilling to adapt, he does not "have a prayer of solving the case. No one would talk to him about the things he needed to know, and even if they did, she [Ella] doubted he'd understand any of it" (73). Soon it becomes clear that to get anywhere, he is going to need cooperation from "someone like me [Ella] who is part of this world and yours" (37).

To some extent, all the main characters of the series—Clifford, Rose, Wilson, and even Blalock—find their equivalent in Ella's nature. Blalock, who is as well-trained as Ella, marks the starting point of her journey back to her roots. Throughout the series, she distances herself from him and comes closer to Wilson's, Clifford's, and Rose's way of seeing the world. When she had first returned to the reservation in *Blackening Song*, she had encountered distrust instead of acceptance. Many Navajos had called her "L.A. Woman" (Thurlo and Thurlo 1995a, 194), and had done whatever they could to avoid her. Two years later, in *Enemy Way*, she has already made a place for herself and enjoys "the peace that came from finally coming home" (Thurlo and Thurlo 1998, 292). Her training and expertise is needed by the Dineh; she is "an asset to the tribe, one that would be hard to replace" (268). Throughout the series, Ella matures and gradually discovers the manifold reasons for her isolation and loneliness:

> *Alone.* That word suddenly had many meanings to her. As a girl, the feeling she had attempted to describe with that word had really been the desire to find someone who could understand her needs and fears. Denied that, she'd eventually tried to become another person entirely, hoping to ease the chill inside her. But she'd never quite fit in anywhere.
>
> Now, as she gazed at the empty stretches of desert, she knew that she was truly home. Here, others could love her as she was. For the first time, Ella realized, that her brother and her mother had each known the solitary walk between the ordinary and the borders of darkness. What bonded them was infinitely stronger than whatever separated them, and that was their greatest strength. (Thurlo and Thurlo 1995a, 290–91)

The process of coming home, however, is not finished yet. Instinctively Ella knows that she is destined to follow in her mother's footsteps: "Her heart often whispered that what her mother was she would someday be, when the wheel of fate completed one full turn" (Thurlo and Thurlo 1997, 53).

With their Ella Clah series, Aimée and David Thurlo have made a significant contribution to the subgenre of detective fiction about Native Americans. Setting the story on reservation land and choosing a Navajo female detective enables the authors to explore themes of cultural difference within the confines of the mystery genre. It also gives them the opportunity to dramatize the opposing pulls of modern life in the urban city and traditional Navajo life on the reservation. Native Americans are no longer depicted as the colonized Other; they are subjects in their own right. In their ongoing series, the Thurlos explore the high price paid for progress and illustrate the drastic consequences of the loss of the old ways for the Navajo people. In narrating Ella's personal story of alienation and return, they reflect on the importance of identity and of finding one's home in both the old world and the new.

Ella must retain her spiritual and psychological balance as she oscillates between modern industrialized society and the indigenous traditions of the Dineh. Paramount in the series is Ella's process of rediscovering and accepting her Navajo heritage, which results in an intriguing synthesis of two conflicting worlds and value systems. Ella learns to live with the differences without compromising her own views. At the end of *Blackening Song*, she resigns as criminal investigator from the FBI and applies for a job with the Navajo Tribal Police: "I belong here. I've never been as certain of anything else before in my life" (Thurlo and Thurlo 1995a, 378). Managing to reconnect to her people while working as tribal policewoman, Ella becomes a healthy, integrated person, with self and profession almost indivisible: "[T]his police work is what you [Ella] were meant to do," Rose observes, "we need you to stand and fight for us" (Thurlo and Thurlo 1998, 324).

Ella Clah is a complex, well-crafted character with both strengths and weaknesses that make her appealing to readers. Aimée and David Thurlo satisfactorily combine a modern woman sleuth with an age-old culture. Thus, they probe the eternal clash between good and evil, which is at the very heart of all mystery fiction, and provide the readers with valuable glimpses into an ancient culture. The series demonstrates that the detective genre can successfully be used to impart knowledge about the dichotomy between Native American and Anglo worldviews. As a "'binocular eye,' the insightful [wo]man with 'double vision'" (King 1980, 260), Ella demonstrates "two-world, or two-interpretive-community, competence" (Schöler 1987, 27). She is well versed in two rather different cultures and manages to bridge the gap between both. Her intricate story serves as an impressive example of how the mystery formula can be a powerful instrument for discussing "the greatest of the world's stories" (Namias 1993, xiv), the meeting of different cultures.

NOTES

Thanks are due to Jennifer Hohensteiner, who discussed this article with me and proofread it.

1. The Golden Age of detective fiction signifies the heyday of the genre in Britain between World War I and World War II. It is closely connected to the writings of the four "queens of crime": Agatha Christie, Ngaio Marsh, Margery Allingham, and Dorothy Leigh Sayers. Along with the publication of Freeman Willis Croft's *The Cask* (1920), the publication of Christie's *The Mysterious Affair at Styles* (1920), which introduced her famous Belgian detective Hercule Poirot, is commonly said to mark the beginning of the Golden Age (see DeAndrea 1994, 402).

2. Until the 1970s, the prototypical detective was white and male. In 1977 Marcia Muller broke new ground with the introduction of Sharon McCone in *Edwin of the Iron Shoes*. McCone, whose heritage is Scots-Irish and Shoshone Indian, is considered the first female hard-boiled private eye of detective fiction (see DeAndrea 1994, 251).

3. For the depiction of African Americans in crime and detective fiction, see Bailey 1991, Lock 1994, and Soitos 1996.

4. See Gosselin 1999 and Klein 1999.

5. Leaphorn investigates solo in *The Blessing Way* (1970), *Dance Hall of the Dead* (1973), and *Listening Woman* (1978); Chee appears solo in *People of Darkness* (1980), *The Dark Wind* (1982), and *The Ghostway* (1984). *Skinwalkers* (1986), the seventh sequel, introduced Chee and Leaphorn working together on cases.

6. For an exhaustive discussion of Tony Hillerman's series, see Freese 1992, 168–245.

7. Margaret Coel's serial takes place among the Arapaho tribe on Wyoming's Wind River Reservation. It features Father John O'Malley, head pastor of St. Francis Mission, and the Arapaho attorney Vicky Holden. James D. Doss's novels center on the investigative efforts of the Ute tribal policeman Charlie Moon in the land of the Southern Colorado Utes. Sheriff Cliff Lansing, Micah S. Hackler's detective protagonist, is plunged into Native American magic as he tries to unravel mysteries in New Mexico's mountain country. Set in Oklahoma, Jean Hager's mysteries about Mitch Bushyhead and Molly Bearpaw are played out against a background of Cherokee tradition. J. F. Trainor created Angela Biwaban, an Anishinabe (Chippewa) sleuth.

8. Five books have been published so far: *Blackening Song* (1995), *Death Walker* (1996), *Bad Medicine* (1997), *Enemy Way* (1998), and *Shooting Chant* (2000).

9. In Tony Hillerman's series, Jim Chee is faced with the difficult decision whether or not to become an FBI agent, leave the reservation, and assimilate deeper into Anglo-American culture. When he makes his debut in *People of Darkness*, Chee has been accepted as a student at the FBI Academy in Virginia, where he is due in about five weeks. Contrary to Ella, Chee finally decides against a career with the FBI. A full explanation as to why he turns down the career prospect is given in *A Thief of Time*, the eighth sequel: "He [Chee] could still be a Navajo in the sense of blood, but not in the sense of belief. He would be away from family and the Slow Talking Dineh, the brothers and sisters of his maternal clan. He would be outside of Dineh Bike'yah—that territory fenced in by the four sacred

202 KATRIN FISCHER

mountains within which the magic of the curing ceremonials had its compulsory effect. He would be an alien living in exile" (1988, 205).

10. Ella is described as a "well-proportioned woman of slightly more than medium height, copper skin deeply tanned from her daily cross-country run, black hair and black eyes" (1995a, 17).

11. The same applies to Tony Hillerman's Joe Leaphorn and Jim Chee. In *Dance Hall of the Dead* the reader gets to know that Leaphorn, who belongs to the Slow-Talking People Clan, "had been raised at the knee of Hosteen Nashibitti, a great singer of the Beautyway and the Mountainway and other curing rites" (1973, 75). Frank Sam Nakai, a famous shaman, was mentor to Chee and taught him to be a ritual singer.

12. *Bilagáana* is a term used by Navajos to mean white people.

WORKS CITED

Bailey, Frankie Y. 1991. *Out of the Woodpile: Black Characters in Crime and Detective Fiction.* New York: Greenwood Press.

Berghofer, Robert F., Jr. 1979. *The White Man's Indian: Images of the American Indian from Columbus to the Present.* New York: Vintage Books.

Bhabha, Homi K. 1994. *The Location of Culture.* London: Routledge.

Bird, S. Elizabeth, ed. 1998. *Dressing in Feathers.* Boulder, Colo.: Westview Press.

Cawelti, John G. 1977. "Murder in the Outback." *The New Republic,* 30 July, 39–41.

Clifton, James A. 1989. "Alternate Identities and Cultural Frontiers." In *Being and Becoming Indian: Biographical Studies of North American Frontiers*, edited by James A. Clifton, 1–37. Chicago: Dorsey Press.

DeAndrea, William L. 1994. *Encyclopedia Mysteriosa: A Comprehensive Guide to the Art of Detection in Print, Film, Radio, and Television.* New York: Prentice-Hall.

Freese, Peter. 1992. *The Ethnic Detective: Chester Himes, Harry Kemelman, Tony Hillerman.* Essen: Die Blaue Eule.

Gosselin, Adrienne Johnson, ed. 1999. *Multicultural Detective Fiction: Murder from the "Other" Side.* New York: Garland.

Hillerman, Tony. 1973. *Dance Hall of the Dead.* New York: HarperCollins.

———. 1980. *People of Darkness.* New York: HarperCollins.

———. 1988. *A Thief of Time.* New York: HarperCollins.

King, Margaret J. 1980. "Binocular Eyes: Cross-Cultural Detectives." *Armchair Detective* 13:253–60.

Klein, Kathleen Gregory, ed. 1999. *Diversity and Detective Fiction.* Bowling Green, Ohio: Bowling Green State University Press.

Lock, Helen. 1994. *A Case of Mis-Taken Identity: Detective Undercurrents in Recent African-American Fiction.* New York: Peter Lang.

Namias, June. 1993. *White Captives: Gender and Ethnicity on the American Frontier.* Chapel Hill: University of North Carolina Press.

Reilly, John M. 1996. *Tony Hillerman: A Critical Companion.* Westport, Conn.: Greenwood Press.

Rich, Ruby B. 1989. "The Lady Dicks: Genre Benders Take the Case." *Village Voice Literary Supplement,* June, 24–26.

Thurlo, Aimée, and David Thurlo. 1995a. *Blackening Song*. New York: Tom Doherty.

———. 1995b. "A Note from the Authors, Aimée and David Thurlo." In *Blackening Song*, 381–82. New York: Forge.

———. 1996. *Death Walker*. New York: Tom Doherty.

———. 1997. *Bad Medicine*. New York: Tom Doherty.

———. 1998. *Enemy Way*. New York: Tom Doherty.

———. 2000. *Shooting Chant*. New York: Tom Doherty.

Schöler, Bo. 1987. "Interpretive Communities and the Representation of Contemporary Native American Life in Literature." *Native American Studies* 1, no. 2:27–30.

Soitos, Stephen. 1996. *The Blues Detective: A Study of African American Detective Fiction*. Amherst: University of Massachusetts Press.

Tuan, Yi-Fu. 1992. "Place and Culture: Analeptic for Individuality and the World's Indifference." In *Mapping American Culture*, edited by Wayne Franklin and Michael Steiner, 27–49. Iowa City: University of Iowa Press.

"Crime Spirit":
The Significance of Dreams and Ghosts in Three Contemporary Native American Crime Novels

ESTHER FRITSCH and MARION GYMNICH

THE INCORPORATION OF FEATURES THAT REFLECT A SPECIFIC ETHNIC BACKGROUND may take on various guises in ethnic detective fiction. In the crime novels written by Native American authors Sherman Alexie (*Indian Killer,* 1996) and Louis Owens (*The Sharpest Sight*, 1992, and its sequel *Bone Game*, 1994) the ethnic background manifests itself in particular in the signifi- cance attributed to dreams and ghosts. The high status conferred on dreams and dreaming is often considered a hallmark feature of Native American cultures. In contrast to the Western psychoanalytic tradition, which regards dreams as manifestations of the dreamer's subconscious, Native American cultures tend to view dreams as basically identical to conscious sensory perceptions and at the same time as potentially visionary experiences.[1] This concept of dreams plays a crucial role in the novels by Owens and Alexie. In these three novels dreams not only affect the dreamer's process of iden- tity formation, but are also closely tied to a number of genre-specific ques- tions such as: Who committed the crime(s)? What is the motivation for actions related to the crime(s)? How does the detective figure gain access to information? In addition, dreams are one of the ways of establishing contact with ghosts, which often turns out to be essential to solving the crimes presented in the novels. Ghosts and the supernatural have tradition- ally been regarded as inimical to the genre of detective novel. Prescriptive accounts of this genre have actively discouraged the use of such elements. In the novels written by Owens and Alexie, ghosts fulfill a variety of func- tions. They appear as potential danger, but also as helpers and even as benign mentors for the various detective figures. They may establish a con- nection between the present and the past, in particular by relating the crimes

INSIDER KNOWLEDGE VERSUS OUTSIDER PERSPECTIVE

that are being investigated to violent acts in the past. The ghosts are, however, not only mediative agents but also actively shape the course of events. Although in many cases it remains unclear whether the ghosts themselves are to be seen as evil or not, their appearance is always indicative of the presence of evil in the protagonists' lives. By assigning both dreams and ghosts a key role in their novels, Owens and Alexie modify the genre of crime fiction in a way that validates Native American cultures and alternative concepts of reality.

Louis Owens's *The Sharpest Sight* deals primarily with the events following the violent death of Attis McCurtain, a Choctaw mixed-blood Vietnam veteran and inmate of a psychiatric ward. Attis was found guilty of the rape and murder of his ex-girlfriend, Jenna Nemi. This crime is explained as a consequence of Attis's experiences in Vietnam, as a manifestation of "post-Vietnam-syndrome and post-traumatic-shock" (1992, 32). One night Attis disappears from the psychiatric institution. His younger brother Cole and Mundo Morales, who is Attis's best friend, served with him in Vietnam, and is the small town's deputy sheriff, try to find out what happened to Attis and engage in a search for him or his body. These two characters function as detective figures without, however, fulfilling this role in a prototypical way, as they are to a certain extent guided by dreams, visions, and encounters with ghosts. Cole, a nineteen-year-old trying to avoid being drafted into the Vietnam War, is convinced that his brother has been killed. Deeply affected by his brother's death, Cole is instructed by Luther, the family patriarch, to find Attis's bones for a proper burial. The search for his brother becomes a quest for his own mixed-blood Choctaw identity. Mundo Morales is also firmly convinced his friend has been murdered and, consequently, is looking for a culprit, motivations, and the body, in spite of being discouraged by his superiors from conducting an official investigation. Similar to Cole, Mundo gains new insights into his ancestry in the course of the investigation, which makes it necessary for him to reassess his identity.

Mundo exhibits some traits of the typical hard-boiled detective, while at the same time deviating from this paradigm in several ways. That his investigation is unauthorized, that he is even considered a suspect by an FBI investigator, and that he has a criminal record himself are traits that are reminiscent of the tough-guy detective in the hard-boiled tradition. But both his ready acceptance of spiritual matters, which verges on an inability to distinguish between the material and the spiritual world, and the way he cares for his friends and his family—as opposed to the stereotypical figure of the hard-boiled investigator, who is a loner with troubled relationships to women—set this character apart from the traditional hard-boiled detective. Mundo's reluctance to distinguish precisely between dreams and sensory perceptions is revealed, for example, when he sees Attis's body floating in the river. Right to the end it remains unclear whether what he sees in this instance is a fact or a vision. But the experience prompts him to start his search for Attis, since for Mundo this vision is sufficient evidence of his best friend's death.

Despite the impact visions have on the way he approaches the investigation, Mundo acts like a professional investigator to a certain extent. He looks for tangible evidence and questions suspects and people who may provide relevant information. The way Cole proceeds, however, is purely intuitive and spiritual. Before he can set out on the search for his brother's body, he has to undergo what seems to be a spiritual apprenticeship with his great-uncle Luther and Onatima, a wise old woman. In this apprenticeship, Cole learns to acknowledge his Choctaw heritage and to conceptualize reality differently. His uncle teaches him, among other things, to become aware of the significance of dreams: "Most people think dreams is only for the time we're asleep, they don't know that dreams is how we see in the dark, when we're most awake" (Owens 1992, 112). After having completed this formative period Cole is able to rely exclusively on his intuition, which draws him to the place where Attis's body was carried by the river. It is indicative of the importance assigned to an intuitive rather than to a predominantly rational approach in *The Sharpest Sight* that Cole is successful while Mundo, systematically searching the riverbanks, fails. The difference in the outcomes of Cole's and Mundo's searches for Attis's body suggests that Cole is destined to find his brother.

In spite of differences in their methods as "investigators," both Mundo and Cole vividly experience the presence of ghosts in the course of their quests. The most striking example of how the dividing line between the spiritual and the material world becomes blurred for Mundo are his conversations with his late grandfather Antonio and the dead Mondragon sisters, whose status as ghosts is, however, only revealed in retrospect. These obviously benign ghosts support him in his quest for the truth, making him aware of dangers and uncovering family secrets. Mundo is frequently accompanied by his grandfather Antonio's ghost, who likes to give his grandson advice from the backseat of the police car. Mundo's reactions indicate that he is neither disturbed nor particularly surprised by Antonio's appearances. He engages in everyday discussions with the ghost and—more or less willingly—accepts the old man's advice. Antonio, for example, warns Mundo of Jenna Nemi's younger sister Diana, whom he refers to as a *bruja* (witch) and who—according to generic conventions—plays the role of the femme fatale, seducing Cole and strongly tempting Mundo.[2] The old man urges his grandson to confront Diana, which ultimately contributes to the disclosure that it was Diana who killed Attis, presumably in revenge for her sister's death. The culprit is thus identified as a direct result of supernatural interference.

Another aim pursued by Antonio's ghost is the unearthing of a secret branch of the family tree. One of their ancestors was a Native American female slave, whom the racist Morales family, which prided itself on its Castilian blood, considered an outcast and a disgrace to be hidden from future generations. For Mundo, this revision of the family history brings about a recognition of his mixed ethnic identity, which would not have been possible without supernatural interference. In the course of his conversations with ghosts, Mundo learns more and more about the nature of good and evil as well as about himself. Antonio summarizes his grandson's development: "My grandson has become more comfortable with the dead. . . . He knows at last who he is." (262).

Cole's experiences with ghosts differ significantly from Mundo's. Not only are the ghosts he encounters more closely connected to Attis's death, but they reflect Choctaw beliefs and traditions with respect to the dead and their relationship to the living. According to Choctaw religion, Choctaws unite two "shadows," distinct constituents of the self, during their lifetime. This duality inherent in the living person also manifests itself when a person dies. As Onatima explains to Cole:

> Every person has two shadows, grandson, an inside shadow and an outside one. When a person dies, the inside shadow, the *shilombish*—that's kind of like what white people call the soul—goes to wherever it's supposed to go. . . . Now the outside shadow, the *shilup*, is different. It stays around the dead person's body and scares people. It's similar to what white people call a ghost. (Owens 1992, 110–11)

This concept of the duality of shadows explains the presence of ghosts, which makes itself felt in various ways. Several times in the novel characters are alerted to the presence of a ghost by the cry of an owl that is not answered by another call.[3] In addition, ghosts are visually perceived as an indistinct dark shadow. This is the way Attis's ghost is seen by Luther, Onatima, and Cole, but also by two FBI agents, who are trying to find both Attis and Cole (125–26). Unlike the ghosts encountered by Mundo, which reveal themselves only to particular individuals, Attis's ghost can be seen by everyone present, irrespective of whether they are cultural insiders or not. Moreover, the "Catholic ghosts" (Antonio and the Mondragon sisters) play an active role in the course of events, whereas Attis's *shilup* is entirely passive and has to wait for his brother to recover his bones. As Luther puts it: "You have to find the bones. . . . And bring them back here. Your brother cannot go on until you do this thing" (98). The *shilup*, although it is not evil

208 ESTHER FRITSCH AND MARION GYMNICH

in and of itself, constitutes a potential danger to the living, because it "is very lonely and always wants to take a loved one, or anyone, with it" (114). For this reason, speaking a deceased person's name is taboo, since uttering the name reinforces the link between the living and the dead and attracts the *shilup*. Luther deliberately broke this taboo out of pity for Attis, which has brought Attis's *shilup* to Luther's cabin.

Attis's *shilup* does not dare to leave Luther's cabin, and thus the old man's sphere of power, for fear of falling prey to the *nalusachito*, the so-called soul-eater that prowls the surrounding forest in the form of a mountain lion. This soul-eater is one of the possible incarnations of evil in traditional Choctaw stories; it can be kept at bay with the help of totem or medicine bags. The traditional stories about evil do not explain its presence in the world or its nature, but they do provide ways of protecting oneself against evil. They are an attempt to capture the abstract principle of evil in a shape that can be imagined: "Us Choctaws made up stories that told us about these things, stories like soul-eater, so we could have words for such things and watch them carefully. If we didn't have the stories we couldn't live in this world" (Owens 1992, 97). The stories provide a way of ordering human experience and imposing control on one's way of reacting to the world.

That the essence of evil is ultimately beyond human imagination is attested to by its omnipresence. Evil manifests itself in manifold acts of violence: the murders of Jenna and Attis, the rape of Diana, the deadly fight between Dan Nemi and Jessard and the subsequent shoot-out between Jessard, Mundo, and Hoey, and the horrors of the war in Vietnam. These individual instances of evil are not independent of each other, but they are seen as being connected, even if the exact nature of the connection escapes human knowledge. Luther tells Cole:

> There's something loose in the world now, something bigger than soul-eater even. Soul-eater is just a little thing now. What your brother was doing in that war, that was part of it. They're doing it everywhere in the world now. And what he did to that girl, that was part of it, and she was part of it, too. (Owens 1992, 97)

Evil can neither be defined nor explained in terms of its origins; it is perpetuated by fear and hate, which drive people to commit further acts of violence. In an epiphanic vision Attis had in Vietnam, he saw a giant cobra that appeared to him as "a reminder of what awaited all of them" and as "something they created, a simple distillation of all their fear and hate conjured out of the land to destroy them" (93). The recognition that individual violent acts are just a facet of something much more extensive does not absolve the individual from his/her responsibility. It does, however, rule

INSIDER KNOWLEDGE VERSUS OUTSIDER PERSPECTIVE 209

out revenge as a way of achieving justice, since this would simply amount to a continuation of violence by way of giving vent to and generating more fear and hate. Hoey, Mundo and Cole act on this insight insofar as they do not insist on Diana being brought to trial for the murder she committed. The ending of *The Sharpest Sight* thus deviates from traditional crime fiction, where law and order are reestablished in the end. Moreover, the concept of evil expressed by various characters clearly defeats all attempts at a definitive resolution. The story reaches only partial closure, since there remain "many things no one would ever know" (262), and it questions notions of justice prevalent in the dominant culture. The action culminates in a dramatic fight and shoot-out between Jenna Nemi's father and the rapist Jessard Deal, Mundo, and Hoey, Cole's father. Both Jessard and Nemi are killed. This outbreak of violence seems to offer at least a partial and temporary solution: "It's all over, Mundo, for now," as Hoey puts it (258). As a result of these deaths a precarious balance seems to be achieved. This balance cannot be reduced to a reestablishment of law and order—a rejection of the binary opposition of justice versus injustice that traditional crime fiction is based on.

Owens's *Bone Game* is set some twenty years after the murder of Attis McCurtain, which constitutes the central mystery of *The Sharpest Sight*. The later novel once more prominently features Cole McCurtain, now a professor of English at the University of California at Santa Cruz; he is recently divorced, drowning in self-pity, and well on his way to becoming an alcoholic. He is visited by his nineteen-year-old daughter, Abby, whose presence becomes an important catalyst in the development of events. The narrative deals with several murders and leads up to their resolution. Both ghosts and dreams are again crucial in the process of discovering what happened and who did what.

In the epigraph to *Bone Game,* events that took place at the mission of Santa Cruz in 1812 and a crime that happened in contemporary Santa Cruz in 1993 are juxtaposed.[4] In this way a link is established between the torture and murder of the Spanish missionary priest Padre Andrés Quintana at the beginning of the nineteenth century and the murder and mutilation of a young woman at the end of the twentieth. A connection between the two time periods also manifests itself in Cole McCurtain's dreams. Several nights in a row Cole is visited by dreams in which he finds himself involved in the events at the mission of Santa Cruz in 1812: in the cruel rule of Padre Quintana, his exploitation of the natives, his rape of a young woman, and the torture and violent death of the padre at the hands of Venancio Asisara, a spiritual leader of the Ohlone who was one of the victims of the padre's cruelties. Cole describes the state of mind in which he finds himself like this:

> I am losing my mind, he thought, watching his teaching assistant. Owls attack me and ghosts taint my dreams. I am guilty of sins I cannot fathom, and my life has tumbled like a scree slope. Nightmares paint themselves and seek me out. I teach amidst madness. (Owens 1994, 17)

What is particularly disturbing for him is the fact that in his dreams he experiences events from opposed points of view simultaneously, which can be seen as an expression of his identification with two antagonistic cultures:

> It's as if I'm everything and everyone at the same time. I'm the priest whipping the Indian's back to a bloody pulp, and I feel every second of it. And love it. I want to kill them all and spread their guts out to dry, hate them because their souls are somewhere I can't reach. . . . And it's me tied to the tree and getting my back cut to shreds. . . . And it's me standing above it all, seeing it like somebody watching a goddamned movie. (95)

These dreams are extremely intense and persistent, and his curiosity is awakened by the fact that they seem to give him access to knowledge about historical events previously unknown to him. The nature of Cole's dreams prompts him to find out more about the past of the place where he lives.

His attempts to elucidate the meaning of his dreams and their relationship to historical events turn Cole once more into a willy-nilly investigator. Just as it was in *The Sharpest Sight*, Cole's search is largely a spiritual one, and he relies to a great extent on the guidance of others to solve the mystery. The tribal elders Onatima, Luther, and Hoey, who already guided his quest for his brother twenty years before, again come to his help. His friend and colleague Alex Yazzie, a Navajo anthropologist, also supplies Cole with valuable information and moral support. All of those helpers encourage him to overcome his apathy and get to the bottom of the mystery posed by the dreams.[5] Thus, Cole sets out on a primarily spiritual and personal quest and does not even consider undertaking a deliberate investigation of the serial murders that occur around the Santa Cruz campus and that started with the dismembered body of a woman being washed ashore at the Santa Cruz beach. The investigation again, as in *The Sharpest Sight*, departs from what one expects to find in crime fiction. Nevertheless, Cole's way of proceeding contributes to the discovery of the killers and thus to a solution of the mystery.

In Cole's quest the figure of the painted gambler plays a key role. The gambler is a human figure painted in black and white who gambles with bones—the activity that the title *Bone Game* refers to. Cole sees this mysterious figure in his dreams, but also when he is awake. Moreover, he is not the only one who sees the gambler, which demonstrates that this figure cannot simply be explained as a figment of Cole's imagination. Onatima mentions that she also saw the gambler in her dreams: "I dreamt of a painted man in a clearing between tall trees, his body half black and half white" (Owens 1994, 70). That Cole's daughter, Abby, encounters the gambler emphasizes that the painted figure is more than just an apparition that haunts various characters' dreams and suggests that he possesses a power to be reckoned with. Moreover, Abby's encounter with the gambler points to the crucial part that she will play in bringing about the resolution, since it shows that she is deeply involved in the mystery surrounding the gambler. When Cole takes part in a Native American Church ceremony and is under the influence of the hallucinogenic drug peyote,[6] it is once more his turn to confront the gambler:

> Hopelessly, he [Cole] went to the gambler and sat upon the ground. The gambler looked directly into Cole's eyes, and Cole looked back into the brown eyes of Attis, his brother, half a lifetime before. Attis sang and shook his fists and wove patterns in the air, his head bobbing in time to the gambling song. Cole reached to touch the left hand. Movement stopped. Attis opened both fists, palm upward, and smiled. The painted bone lay in the right hand. (200)

The gambler, who is identified here as Cole's long-dead brother Attis, is shown to make movements that obviously constitute an invitation to join in the bone game. Cole accepts this offer and gambles, choosing one of the closed hands.[7] Since he survives the bone game unharmed, Cole apparently has made the right choice in what is presumably a game of life and death.

The danger involved in entering the bone game played by the gambler is shown most clearly in another encounter between the gambler, Cole, and Abby, which occurs near the end of the story. It is in this final bone game that Cole finds the solution to at least part of the mystery. He does this by saying aloud the name of the gambler when the latter is in the midst of gambling with Abby. The name Cole pronounces is that of Venancio Asisara. It is made quite clear that the act of pronouncing the gambler's name, which is a violation of the taboo against saying a dead person's name, saves Abby's life. Cole later comments on his decision to pronounce the gambler's name, whom he apparently recognizes as the figure he encountered in his dreams: "It was what he wanted all the time" (Owens 1994, 243). This statement explains both Cole's recurring dreams and the previous apparitions of the gambler as an appeal to recover the memory of events and persons that have been forgotten. The gambler can thus be seen as an expression of an imperative to remember a people who had been wiped out. Uncle Luther explicitly explains the gambler's apparitions when he says:

> It happened so quick with these Indians here, not like with us where it took three hundred years. It's very sad: One minute these people was living like they always did, and the next minute everything was gone. They seen their children die. They seen their whole world die. And they remembered. When I go to bed in this house, I hear all that out there. Now they woke this gambler up, and he wants his world back. (224)

When Cole finally pronounces the name of Venancio, who was a leader of the Native Americans who were victims of the missionaries' cruel deeds, this amounts to an acknowledgment of all that he has learned about the events that took place in Santa Cruz almost two centuries ago. Cole's spiritual quest leads him to recover memories that had long been lost. The fact that long-lost memories have been recovered is once more emphasized in the last words of the novel: "*Eran muy crueles*" (243). These are the words that Cole heard repeatedly in his dreams and that were also spoken to him by the gambler in their final encounter; the last words of the novel, thus, once more refer to the deeds of the Spanish missionaries and implicitly repeat the appeal to remember.[8]

The serial murders, however, are solved in a different way—albeit one that also centers on the figure of the gambler, whose shifting identities remain mysterious right to the end. The gambler who was seen by Cole in his dreams is identified as Venancio Asisara, but in one instance Cole clearly identifies the gambler as his long-dead brother Attis. There is yet another painted gambler as well, who has started a game of life and death of his own: Robert Malin, Cole's teaching assistant, who turns out to be a pathological killer. Robert is responsible for some of the murders committed in the environment of the Santa Cruz campus. He paints himself black and white to commit the murders, which he sees as ritual sacrifices that will help reestablish a natural balance that has been generally lost in modern society. He is convinced that his killings will prevent natural disasters:

> Native Americans know that the world is precariously balanced between good and evil, light and dark, black and white. It is up to us to maintain that balance. Mother Earth gives us life and asks that we give something in return. One man consenting to be murdered can protect the millions of other human beings living in the cataclysmic earthquake/tidal area. (Owens 1994, 238)

It is unclear whether this explanation of the killings, in which Robert mingles traditional Native American views and New Age beliefs, is nothing but the product of a sick mind or the result of spiritual possession. There are certain hints that suggest that Robert has been possessed by a ghost, presumably by Venancio Asisara; Robert claims that he was driven by dreams to do what he did:

INSIDER KNOWLEDGE VERSUS OUTSIDER PERSPECTIVE   213

> I'd have dreams, and I'd get so angry. It was like there was a voice telling
> me what I had to do, but it wasn't really a voice because there weren't any
> words. . . . It was like I knew all these things that I had to do, and I'd paint
> myself and do them. I can't explain it. It's like dreams when I'm awake.
> (235)

The fact that several characters appear in the guise of the gambler alludes
to a view of the presence of evil and of death that echoes the views expressed in *The Sharpest Sight*. Just as in Owens's previous novel, Onatima
once more situates the evil that occurs and specifically the bone gambler in
a much larger context: "He's part of something too big. It's everywhere
now. We all have to live with this thing" (209).

That violence cannot simply be explained as the result of the doings of
an individual is also emphasized by the fact that there are two serial killers
in Santa Cruz. In two different showdowns, in which Abby and Alex play
key roles and manage to incapacitate the killers, the serial murders are
solved. It turns out that Paul Kantner, a student of Cole's, is responsible for
several murders, which he committed as a result of his pathological hatred
of women. He is first trapped by Alex and Abby and then killed by Robert
Malin, the second killer. The final showdown culminates in Abby killing
Robert in self-defense, when he appears once more in the guise of the gambler. She and the tricksterlike figure of Alex manage to put an end to the
series of crimes and thus take on a more active part than Cole in bringing
about the resolution, since the latter has not followed his hunch that the
murders follow two patterns rather than one. This outcome shows that in
Bone Game evil can be contained only by communal effort rather than by
the activities of a single detective figure. This emphasis on the social network is one of the recurring features of ethnic as well as women's crime
fiction. Moreover, dreams and visions, as well as physical action and powers of deduction, are necessary to solve the crimes. The way the resolution
is brought about subverts the conventions of traditional crime fiction, thus
lending authority to alternative conceptualizations of the world.

Sherman Alexie's *Indian Killer* deals with serial killings in Seattle in
the mid-1990s that are ascribed to a Native American. A number of white
people are killed, mutilated, and scalped; in addition, a white boy is kidnapped, but later released. Both the scalping and the "signature"—two owl
feathers—left behind by the killer in all of these cases are seen as a clear
indication that the culprit is a Native American, and, thus, the murderer is
soon referred to as the "Indian Killer." Unlike most people, Marie Polatkin,
a Spokane Indian student at the University of Seattle and committed political and social activist, questions this conclusion when she asks: "What if
the Indian Killer isn't an Indian guy? What if this Indian Killer is just trying

to make people think an Indian guy did it?" (1996, 333). For Truck Schultz, a white racist radio talk-show host, however, there can be no doubt about the killer's ethnic origin. The serial killings provide him with an opportunity for fueling racial hatred among his listeners and even for inviting them openly to seek retribution.

The most obvious suspect among the characters is presumably the high-rise construction worker John Smith, a Native American who was adopted by white parents immediately after his birth and who suffers from intense feelings of personal and cultural deracination.[9] He has been unable to find out which tribe he belongs to, since even his adoptive parents were not given any information about John's origin. Trying to cope with his identity problems, John often visualizes himself in an alternative life on a reservation, surrounded by an imaginary Native American family and friends. He is seriously disturbed psychologically; he is haunted by visual and acoustic hallucinations as well as a paranoid fear of being poisoned, but refuses to seek help. As a result of his cultural deracination, he has, however, always suffered from frequent and violent bouts of aggressive behavior, which he has, for the most part, successfully suppressed. Since readers are granted insight into John's fantasies of violence, which are directed specifically against white men, they are likely to see the young man as the prime suspect. John's desire "to see fear in every pair of blue eyes" (Alexie 1996, 30) and what sounds like a plan to kill a white man ("John knew exactly what to do with his life. John needed to kill a white man" [25]) at first seem to make it fairly obvious that he is responsible for the crimes. John's reflections on the choice of a suitable victim suggest that his desire to kill a white man is not just a matter of personal revenge, of trying to punish someone for the deracination he has suffered from all his life. He aims at something more than personal revenge by attempting to single out and kill the white man who is "responsible for everything":

> John knew he could kill a white man, but he was not sure which white man was responsible for everything that had gone wrong. . . . Which white man had done the most harm to the world? Was it the richest white man? Was it the poorest white man? (27)

Here John sets himself an impossible task: to reduce the sum total of historical injustice to such an extent that one individual can be held responsible. His attempt to personalize evil and to assign guilt unambiguously by identifying one culprit is an expression of his need for clarity in the face of his precarious ethnic and cultural position, which leaves him stranded between what he perceives as antagonistic cultures.

But John is not the only Native American character to experience bouts

INSIDER KNOWLEDGE VERSUS OUTSIDER PERSPECTIVE 215

of aggression directed against white people and to feel the need for retribution. In the course of the novel, readers gain insight into the minds of various characters, revealing that there are a number of characters who might have both the aggressive potential and the motivation to commit the murders. The readers even see the crimes happening through the eyes of the murderer without, however, being given any clues as to the killer's identity. Marie, one of the characters who shows considerable aggressive potential, is repelled by the appropriation and distortion of Native American culture and literature by her university teacher Dr. Mather and expresses her fury by attacking him verbally. On a wider scale, Marie feels anger because of the violence Native Americans had to suffer: "She . . . knew that Indian blood had often spilled on American soil. She knew there were people to blame for that bloodshed. She felt a beautiful kind of anger" (Alexie 1996, 360). Marie's cousin Reggie Polatkin also displays a strong potential for violent actions, and he is even suspected of being the killer—at least by Mather, who reports to the police that his former student Reggie is very aggressive and even "said he dreamed about killing people" (394).

Similar to many of the characters in Owens's novels, the main characters in *Indian Killer* are haunted by dreams. In John's case, these dreams are comparatively loosely related to the crimes. In a recurring dream he sees Father Duncan, a Spokane Indian and Jesuit priest, who was John's mentor for several years and who later went to Arizona, where he at some point disappeared into the desert without a trace. Compared to the specific relevance to the crimes that dreams usually have in Owens's novels, John's dreams are of a relatively unspecific nature ("Duncan never spoke. He just brought the smell, sounds, and images of the desert into John's head" [Alexie 1996, 16]), but they are still highly relevant to John's sense of identity. Father Duncan, the only Native American who was involved in John's socialization, constitutes the central figure of identification for the young man, who perpetually feels out of place. What Father Duncan signifies for John is mainly deracination and being a part of a culture that is or at least was extremely hostile to one's culture by birth. The colorful stained-glass windows in Father Duncan's church, which depict Jesuits being slain by Indians, are a reminder of the dilemma both Father Duncan and John find themselves in, the dilemma of being part of the culture of the perpetrators and of the victims at the same time:

As a Jesuit, he [Father Duncan] knew those priests were martyred just like Jesus. As a Spokane Indian, he knew those Jesuits deserved to die for their crimes against Indians. "John," Duncan said after a long silence. "You see those windows? You see all of this? It's what is happening inside me right now." (15)

In their schizophrenic identification with antagonistic cultures, they resemble Cole McCurtain, who also feels himself to be in the position of both opponents and who expresses this mixed identification, when he introduces himself to Alex Yazzie as "Choctaw-Cherokee-Irish-Cajun" (26). Throughout the novels, mixed ethnic identity is shown to be a potential source of strength, but more often an obstacle to achieving a coherent sense of self.

Another character in this novel who is haunted by disturbing dreams is Jack Wilson, an ex-cop and crime writer whose novels feature a Native American sleuth called Aristotle Little Hawk. Wilson has this character often solve crimes with the help of dreams, thus projecting onto his fictional alter ego his idea of how Native Americans approach reality ("[H]e knew that Indians were supposed to listen carefully to their dreams" [Alexie 1996, 338]). Wilson's dreams are much more obviously related to the crimes committed by the serial killer than John's dreams are: "He dreamed constantly about the murders. He saw the face of that man in Fremont when the knife slid across his throat, and felt the weight of that little boy's body" (337). In one of his dreams Wilson at first sees John as the killer, but then all of a sudden he himself slips into the role of the murderer:

> Wilson was thinking about John Smith, then fell so quickly to sleep that he effortlessly slipped into a dream about Smith. He dreamed about Smith pushing that knife into the white man in the University District. He saw Smith slit the throat of the businessman. Then Smith was smiling as he lifted the young boy from his bed. Then Wilson saw himself with that knife. Wilson saw himself pushing the knife into one white body, then another, and another, until there were multitudes. Isn't that how it happened? (390–91)

This dream seems to suggest that Wilson shares the feelings of aggression against white people that are expressed by John as well as by other Native Americans in the novel (in particular by Reggie and Marie Polatkin), and the dream might even be read as a clue that Wilson is the killer. What one learns about his biography and his psychological disposition would result in a reasonably plausible profile of the "Indian Killer," and there are even striking parallels between his psychological profile and John Smith's. Both Jack Wilson and John Smith were brought up by adoptive parents, and both suffer from serious identity problems as a result. In fact, John was slightly more fortunate than Wilson, since the latter was passed on from one family to the next. His biography certainly predisposes Wilson to develop a personality disorder, perhaps a split identity. Wilson has, in fact, created an imaginary identity based on his ill-founded claim to be a descendant of Native Americans. This claim turns him into an object of ridicule in the eyes of his former colleagues and of the Native Americans at the

INSIDER KNOWLEDGE VERSUS OUTSIDER PERSPECTIVE   217

Indian bar he frequents, where he finally is exposed as a fraud and publicly humiliated. If Wilson were the Indian Killer, his pathological overidentification with his imaginary Native American heritage, no matter how ill-founded this feeling may be, would explain the supposedly Indian features of the serial killings as an emulation of what he considers to be typically Indian.[10]

Wilson, however, is not only one of the suspects, but also the only character that at least partly fulfills the role of an investigator. Several of his personality traits are reminiscent of the hard-boiled tradition, while others rather disqualify him from that role. He is described as a loner who has been a social outcast from his unhappy childhood on. The fact that he drinks milk in the bar he attends regularly strongly suggests that he is a recovering alcoholic. Being an ex-cop, he still uses his contacts with former colleagues, and his methods are roughly those of a police investigator—seeking out or observing people and places connected to the crime—although he sometimes operates beyond the limits of the law. Thus, he fraudulently poses as a policeman to gain information on his prime suspect, John Smith, and suppresses evidence obtained in this manner in order to go on his own manhunt. An important difference between Wilson and the prototypical hard-boiled detective figure is his becoming an object of ridicule in his environment. His motivation for the investigation is the gathering of material for his book in progress, which has as its subject the serial killings in Seattle. Moreover, John Smith is seen by Wilson as his brainchild Aristotle Little Hawk come to life; consequently, Wilson transfers his identification with his fictional hero to Smith. Ultimately, Wilson manages to complete his book on the "Indian Killer," but does not solve the crimes. Instead, he becomes a helpless victim reduced to tears and whimpering when John Smith confronts him.

In a climactic encounter between Wilson and John, which takes place on a skyscraper being erected in Seattle, the latter at first intends to kill the white crime writer, since he believes that he has at last found the man who is responsible for everything bad: "John finally understood that Wilson was responsible for all that had gone wrong" (Alexie 1996, 404). But John refrains from killing Wilson and instead slashes his face, explaining to the seriously injured man: "No matter where you go . . . people will know you by that mark. They'll know what you did" (411). Whether this act of mutilation, which leaves Wilson with a kind of mark of Cain on his face, can be seen as the result of a delusion on the part of John or whether it can indeed be regarded as a punishment for a crime committed by Wilson remains an open question. Perhaps Wilson is the Indian Killer after all, or perhaps John picks him out as a scapegoat for crimes committed by white people in the past. When John refrains from killing Wilson and subsequently commits suicide by stepping off the skyscraper,[11] this behavior also raises a number of questions: Is John the Indian Killer, who, considering his self-imposed task of finding the white man "responsible for everything," kills himself? Or does the fact that John does *not* kill Wilson after all rather indicate that he is not the Indian Killer? The showdown between two suspects thus does not provide the reader with a solution, but toys with genre expectations.

Jack Wilson's solution to the crime is to identify John Smith as the killer—a solution accepted by the police as well, which makes it possible to close the case. This view is also shared by a number of characters for a short period of time, but many of them quickly dismiss the thought. Among the characters who intermittently consider John Smith's potential to be the Indian Killer are the two clerks of the doughnut shop where John is a regular customer, his mother, Olivia, and a police officer who—drawing on the many lessons of "practical psychology" on the streets of Seattle—ultimately judges John as a danger to himself rather than to others. That the identification of John as the serial killer is far from being a conclusive one is reinforced when John's death leaves Marie convinced of his innocence; she declares: "I know that John Smith didn't kill anybody except himself" (Alexie 1996, 418). Marie herself is suspected of being the killer by Boo, a paraplegic white war veteran who admires her. The anthropology professor, Dr. Mather, still believes that Reggie Polatkin is to blame for the crimes and publishes his version of the story in a quasi-documentary.

Marie Polatkin is not interested in pinning down one individual as "the killer," but redirects the issue toward the possible motivation she senses behind the serial killings:

> And if some Indian is killing white guys, then it's a credit to us that it took over five hundred years for it to happen. And there's more. . . . Indians are dancing now, and I don't think they're going to stop. (418)

What Marie suggests in this speech is that the serial killings are just the beginning of a major collective bid for retribution on the part of Native Americans. The dance Marie refers to in the passage quoted above is the Ghost Dance,[12] which was part of a largely religious movement that spread among the Plains tribes in the late nineteenth century. For the tribes that had suffered territorial loss, mass killings, and epidemics, which had devastating effects on their social structures, this religious movement provided a way out of their crisis. The Ghost Dance was the most prominent among several revival movements, promising the return of dead ancestors, the disappearance of the whites and restitution of tribal lands, and a return to the old ways of living. This was to be brought about by cataclysmic events such as whirlwinds, earthquakes, and floods; songs and a circular dance

INSIDER KNOWLEDGE VERSUS OUTSIDER PERSPECTIVE   219

were supposed to hasten this apocalypse. The movement's prophets, such as the Paiute "Messiah" Wovoka, preached a return to old values and non-acceptance of white ways of life.[13] Drawing on this historical pantribal movement, Marie even wonders whether the Indian Killer might not have been created by the Ghost Dance:

> Wovoka said if all Indians Ghost Danced, then all the Europeans would disappear, right? . . . So maybe this Indian Killer is a product of the Ghost Dance. Maybe ten Indians are Ghost Dancing. Maybe a hundred. It's just a theory. How many Indians would have to dance to create the Indian Killer? A thousand? Ten thousand? (313)

According to this explanation of the crimes, which has clear metaphysical overtones, the killer is the product of an aggressive spirit of resistance and revival among Native Americans.[14] The view of the killer as a supernatural being correlates with impressions created by some of the earlier descriptions of the killer's actions that suggest a ghostlike quality of the perpetrator ("[T]he killer descended from the tree and floated away from the Jones's [*sic*] home" [300]). Moreover, after his release, the little boy who was kidnapped identifies the kidnapper as a birdlike figure. The last chapter, which is titled "A Creation Story" and which is stylistically reminiscent of oral storytelling, seems to support Marie's vision of the Ghost Dance spreading once more among Native Americans, since it depicts the killer performing a ritual dance in which he is joined by birds of prey and by more and more Indians: "The killer sings and dances for hours, days. Other Indians arrive and quickly learn the song. A dozen Indians, then hundreds, and more, all learning the same song, the exact dance" (420). Whether this scene is a vision, a prophecy, or a dream remains open to interpretation. This refusal of a neat solution, which even has metaphysical overtones, subverts genre conventions, while simultaneously asserting the validity of specifically Native American cultural forms—storytelling and the Ghost Dance.

In the crime novels by Owens and Alexie both the crimes and their resolution are interwoven with ethnographic detail. In this point they resemble the crime fiction written by Tony Hillerman, whose novels are often seen as paradigmatic of the subgenre of Native American crime fiction. The novels by Hillerman, who is not himself a Native American, feature the detectives Jim Chee and Joe Leaphorn, who work for the Navajo Tribal Police. Both Louis Owens and Sherman Alexie explicitly acknowledge this legacy by making use of intertextual references to Hillerman—albeit with an ironic twist. In *Bone Game* Alex Yazzie jokingly refers to himself as a graduate of the "Jim Chee tribal investigator correspondence school" (Owens 1994, 223). In *Indian Killer* a police officer is so engrossed in one of Hillerman's novels that he fails to see the killer walking past the police car: "Silently singing an invisibility song, the killer walked past the police car parked outside the Jones's house. The officer was reading a Tony Hillerman novel and never looked up as the killer passed within two feet of him" (Alexie 1996, 299). Furthermore, the character of Jack Wilson, a "wannabe" Native American who writes "Indian" crime fiction and who invented the Native American private investigator Aristotle Little Hawk, may be thought of as a—not very flattering—allusion to Hillerman.

A crucial difference between Hillerman's novels and the crime fiction written by Owens and Alexie is the degree to which the investigation, the outcome, the motivation, and the crimes themselves are dependent on dreams, visions, ghosts, and similar features that reflect a specific ethnic background and have supernatural overtones. Owens and Alexie subvert genre conventions, for example, by denying the reader the satisfaction of a neat solution and by foregrounding the supposedly supernatural. In general, Hillerman's novels correspond much more closely to established formulas of detective fiction, although the police work depicted "is blended with a strong element of Navajo customs" (Fredriksson and Fredriksson 1991, 537). Early descriptions or rather prescriptions for the genre of the detective story ruled out supernatural elements, such as ghosts. This is reflected in "Ten Commandments of Detection" by Monsignor Ronald Knox (1928), which also recommend that the detective not "ever have an unaccountable intuition which proves to be right" (Symons 1972, 9–10). Similarly, the oath sworn by the members of the "Detection Club," an association of British writers of detective fiction founded in 1928, explicitly restricts the use of ghosts (Holquist 1971, 142). These supernatural elements were seen as incongruous to the world of the detection story with its prime focus on rationality, although, as Symons points out, a lot of stories do not actually adhere to these prescriptions.

Alexie's and Owens's Native American crime novels deviate from some of the basic rules of traditional detective fiction in significant ways, but they also make use of the formulas of the genre. The basic elements of detective fiction—the figure of the detective, the process of detecting, and a solution to the mystery—are modified. In *The Sharpest Sight*, *Bone Game*, and *Indian Killer* the role of the investigator is split between several characters, detective figures are often unwitting investigators, and the investigation is intuitive and coincidental rather than rational and goal-oriented. The solution to the puzzle is only partial, remains highly ambiguous, or is denied altogether. In all three novels the focus is not exclusively on the crimes at hand; both the crimes and their solutions are placed in a larger context of evil and specifically historical injustice against Native Americans. The disavowal of a neat ending, in which all questions are answered, can

INSIDER KNOWLEDGE VERSUS OUTSIDER PERSPECTIVE   221

be seen as a consequence of this larger focus, since it defies all attempts to provide complete and unambiguous solutions. What the novels have in common is that they more or less directly imply an appeal to acknowledge and remember the past and its lasting impact on the present. This appeal emphasizes the need for storytelling and for individual and communal continuity—be it in the form of family and tribal history or of a continuation of a pantribal movement such as the Ghost Dance. Thus, the three novels exemplify "the new ghost dance literature" (1994, 106) that Vizenor envisions.

NOTES

1. For the significance of dreams in Native American cultures, see the *Handbook of American Indians North of Mexico:* "Most revelations of what was regarded by the Indians as coming from the supernatural powers were believed to be received in dreams or visions. Through them were bestowed on man magical abilities and the capacity to foresee future events, to control disease, and to become able to fill the office of priest or of leader" (Webb Hodge 1959, 400).

2. For an interesting analysis of the character of Diana Nemi, see Dwyer (1998), who sees this character as modeled upon the ancient Roman goddess Diana of Nemi.

3. In *The Sharpest Sight*, examples of owls evoking death are to be found on pages 26, 93–94, and 217. Both in *Bone Game* and in *Indian Killer,* owls are also shown to be connected with death and the dead. According to the *Handbook of American Indians North of Mexico*, "the identification of the soul of the dead with the owl . . . is of almost universal occurrence" (Webb Hodge 1959, 618).

4. The events that are referred to in the epigraphs are based on historical incidents. The events in 1812 constitute one of the many Native American acts of resistance to the exploitation through the mission system, and in the 1970s Santa Cruz was shaken by serial murders. For a short account of this historical background and its use in *Bone Game,* see Venuto 1998.

5. This reliance on a social network—as opposed to an emphasis on individualism—is a feature that sets Cole apart from the loner in the hard-boiled tradition.

6. The Native American Church is a syncretic religion combining pantribal and Christian traditions. *The Native North American Almanac* defines peyote as "[a] bitter stimulant obtained from the button-like structures of the mescal cactus plant, which some Indian groups use as part of their religious practices. The peyote buttons are taken during ceremonies of the Native American Church, which was officially established in 1918, but began on the Plains as early as the 1860s" (Champagne 1994, 1214).

7. According to the *Handbook of American Indians North of Mexico*, the hand game is "[t]he commonest and most widely distributed of Indian guessing games. Two (or four) bones or wooden cylinders, one plain and one marked, are held in the hands by one player, the other side guessing in which hand the unmarked cylinder is concealed. The game is commonly counted with sticks and is played to the accompaniment of songs or incantations" (Webb Hodge 1959, 485).

8. In an interview with John Purdy, Louis Owens described the appeal to remember as one of the things he wants to achieve with his writing: "I guess one thing I'm working on in most of my writing is the way America has tried, and continues to try, to bury the past,

pretending that once it's over we no longer need to think about it. We live in a world full of buried things, many of them very painful and often horrific, like passing out smallpox-infested blankets to Indians or worse, and until we acknowledge and come to terms with the past we'll keep believing in a dangerous and deadly kind of innocence, and we'll keep thinking we can just move on and leave it all behind" (Purdy 1998, 11–12).

9. It is somewhat ironic that the protagonist in *Indian Killer* is named after the English explorer John Smith (1580–1631), one of the founders of Jamestown, the first permanent settlement in North America. On one of his expeditions Smith was captured by Native Americans and, according to his own account, rescued from being executed by the daughter of the chief Powhatan, the thirteen-year-old Pocahontas. This story gave rise to one of the principal myths about relations between whites and Native Americans.

10. For a discussion of appropriations of "Indian" identities by white American males, see Deloria 1998.

11. At this point in the novel the idea of dead persons becoming ghosts, which plays such a prominent role in Owens's two novels, is brought up: John's spirit is shown as separating from his body after his death, which turns him into a ghost.

12. The Ghost Dance has been the subject of many ethnological, religious and historical studies. See Mooney [1896] 1975, Spicer 1969, and LaBarre 1970.

13. Wovoka's Christian name was Jack Wilson. That the "wannabe" Indian crime writer in *Indian Killer* is also called Jack Wilson gives his overidentification with Native Americans a further ironic twist.

14. The historical movement of the Ghost Dance was, however, primarily a nonviolent movement: "The Ghost Dancers were remarkably pacific, putting their trust in supernatural deliverance. In only one tribe—the Sioux—did the Ghost Dancers take up violence, with results which dealt a mortal blow to the movement" (Hertzberg 1971, 11). In *Bone Game* the Ghost Dance is only mentioned in passing, but the way it is characterized, as "the necessary violence that would inflame the stars" (Owens 1994, 100), seems to be echoed in the way the Ghost Dance is depicted in *Indian Killer*.

WORKS CITED

Alexie, Sherman. 1996. *Indian Killer*. New York: Warner Books.

Champagne, Duane, ed. 1994. *The Native North American Almanac*. Detroit, Mich.: Gale.

Deloria, Philip J. 1998. *Playing Indian*. New Haven: Yale University Press.

Dwyer, Margaret. 1998. "The Syncretic Impulse: Louis Owens' Use of Autobiography, Ethnology, and Blended Mythologies in *The Sharpest Sight*." *Studies in American Indian Literatures* 10, no. 2:43–60.

Frederiksson, Karl G., and Lilian Frederiksson. 1991. "Hillerman, Tony." In *Twentieth-Century Crime and Mystery Writers*, edited by Lesley Henderson, 535–37. 3d ed. Chicago: St. James Press.

Hertzberg, Hazel W. 1971. *The Search for an American Indian Identity: Modern Pan-American Movements*. Syracuse, N.Y.: Syracuse University Press.

Holquist, Michael. 1971. "Whodunit and Other Questions: Metaphysical Detective Stories in Post-War Fiction." *New Literary History* 3, no. 1:135–56.

LaBarre, Weston. 1970. *The Ghost Dance: Origins of Religion*. New York: Doubleday.

Mooney, James. [1896] 1975. *The Ghost Dance Religion and Wounded Knee*. New York: Dover.

INSIDER KNOWLEDGE VERSUS OUTSIDER PERSPECTIVE 223

Owens, Louis. 1992. *The Sharpest Sight*. Norman: University of Oklahoma Press.

———. 1994. *Bone Game*. Norman: University of Oklahoma Press.

Purdy, John. 1998. "Clear Waters: A Conversation with Louis Owens." *Studies in American Indian Literatures* 10, no. 2:6–22.

Spicer, Edward. 1969. *A Short History of the Indians of the United States*. New York: Van Nostrand Reinhold.

Symons, Julian. 1972. *Bloody Murder: From the Detective Story to the Crime Novel: A History*. London: Faber and Faber.

Venuto, Rochelle. 1998. "*Bone Game*'s Terminal Plots and Healing Stories." *Studies in American Indian Literature* 10, no. 2:23–41.

Vizenor, Gerald. 1994. *Manifest Manners: Postindian Warriors of Survivance*. Hanover, N.H.: Wesleyan University Press.

Webb Hodge, Frederick, ed. 1959. *Handbook of American Indians North of Mexico*. 2 vols. New York: Pageant Books.

Part III:
Globalizing Ethnicity

"Here's tae Us, Wha's Like Us":
Val McDermid's Lindsay Gordon Mysteries

SAMANTHA HUME

Norway, too, has noble wild prospects; and Lapland is remarkable for prodigious noble wild prospects. But, Sir, let me tell you, the noblest prospect which a Scotchman ever sees, is the high road that leads him to England!

> —Samuel Johnson, 1709–84
> English poet, critic, and lexicographer

Minds like ours, my dear James, must always be above national prejudices, and in all companies it gives me true pleasure to declare, that, as a people, the English are very little indeed inferior to the Scotch.

> —Christopher North (Professor John Wilson), 1785–1854
> Scottish literary critic

THESE QUOTATIONS MAKE IT ABUNDANTLY CLEAR THAT THERE IS AND ALWAYS HAS been a definite distinction made between the English and the Scots. The statements themselves reflect a rivalry that has existed for centuries, and as anyone who has recently attended a Scotland versus England football match would testify, it is still very much the status quo.[1] The rivalry has taken on a playful aspect, on the whole, in social interaction, but where the question of identity is concerned, the distinctions between Scots and English are earnest indeed. Having a Scottish sleuth in an English environment serves to act as a site in which some of these distinctions can be highlighted.

Val McDermid's Lindsay Gordon series comprises five novels: *Report for Murder* (1987), *Common Murder* (1989), *Final Edition* (1991), *Union Jack* (1993), and *Booked for Murder* (1996), in which the young reporter Lindsay Gordon inadvertently becomes involved in solving five murders. Gordon is a Scot; she also describes herself as a "cynical socialist lesbian feminist journalist" (1987, 3). In the course of the five novels she uses her investigative reporting skills to solve murders in which either she herself *(Union Jack)* or one of her friends has been implicated. The novels work on various levels, incorporating socialist, lesbian, and feminist issues intertwined with many, often clichéd, Scottish attitudes. They describe how she implements her investigative journalistic know-how to reveal the real culprits behind the murders she becomes embroiled in, although the police have come to different conclusions in accordance with genre expectations. The narratives are caustic in their wit, sarcastic, but at times also profoundly touching. Because of the recurring characters in the community in which she lives, they resemble five chapters in a family saga. Many of the characters reappear at different points in the series, and this, combined with the integration of political and social issues of the late eighties to the late nineties, serves to add to the sense of consistency and reality, thereby constructing a fictional world around Gordon that is completely believable. Furthermore, they offer the author a space in which to create a sense of normality specifically with respect to a lesbian lifestyle and to criticize the often random rejection of individuals simply on the basis of sexual orientation.

IDENTITY

In 1707 Scotland and England were "unified" under the new name "Great Britain." Before and ever since, the Scots and the English have maintained countless prejudices toward one another. These can be seen in language as well as in expectations of behavior and beliefs about their respective cultures. Many foreigners use the term "England" to mean the whole of Great Britain, implying Scotland has no greater importance than a region of England. While this is a thorn in the side of every Scot, an unfortunate side effect is that there are even some English people who use the term England to mean Great Britain. This only serves to fuel the impression among Scots that the English are arrogant and imperialist by nature, considering Scotland inferior with no more than a type of colonial status, thereby denying the Scots their distinct national and ethnic identity. Therefore, due to these past injustices, it cannot be surprising that the Scots not only have a strong sense of justice for and protection of the underdog, but also an unwillingness to remain silent about injustice. The Scots are not renowned for their skills in diplomacy, but rather for barging into situations, acting first and asking questions later, often "making a fuss" or "causing a scene"—the utmost faux pas in polite English society. These conflicting characteristics are acted out in detail throughout McDermid's Lindsay Gordon crime thrillers by both Gordon and other Scottish characters, underpinning Scottish

"HERE'S TAE US, WHA'S LIKE US" 229

identities and cultural attitudes. The contrast of Scottish versus English as a distinct feature of the novels can also be seen in the fact that although only *Final Edition* is set in Scotland, many of the recurring characters are Scots, and there are extensive dialogue passages that depict "typical" Scottish directness and in-your-face brashness. Further, there are references to Gordon's homesickness for the Scottish landscape and comparisons made with England and the English, as well as the use of cultural contrasts in events such as the *ceilidh* in *Union Jack*.

As a Scot and daughter of a fisherman, Lindsay "learned about socialism as soon as she could grasp the concepts" (McDermid 1993, 9) and has a keen sense of what is and what is not just, irrespective of what the law dictates. She often portrays a somewhat puritanical and often extremist value system, but one which simultaneously harbors the implicit contradictions in the reality of a fallible and human modern world. Her socialist convictions are made immediately clear in the first pages of the first novel, *Report For Murder*, when describing her distaste at having anything at all to do with a public school.[2] She argues throughout that private education for the privileged is repugnant to her, also not an uncommon view in Scotland. Lindsay, however, has to bypass her principles in order to pay her tax bill and goes to the school to write an article on their attempt to save their playing fields. But she is not above making it known that she thinks the situation of such a privileged environment is contemptible:

> "I gathered it was serious from your letter. But I can't help feeling it wouldn't be such a bad thing if the public schools felt the pinch like everyone else. It seems somewhat unreal to be worrying about playing fields when a lot of state schools can't even afford enough books to go around."
> "Even if it means the school closing down?"
> "Even if it means that, yes."
> "And put another sixty or seventy people on the dole queue? Not just teachers, but cleaning staff, groundsmen, cooks, the shopkeepers we patronise? Not to mention the fact that for quite a lot of the girls, Derbyshire House is the only stable thing in their lives. Quite a few come from broken homes. Some of their parents are living abroad where the local education isn't suitable for one reason or another. And others need the extra attention we can give them so they can realise their full potential."
> "Oh, Paddy, can't you hear yourself?" Lindsay retorted plaintively, and was rewarded by scowls and whispered "shushes" from around the room. She dropped her voice. "What about all the kids in exactly the same boat who don't have the benefit of Mummies and Daddies with enough spare cash to use Derbyshire House as a social services department? Maybe their lives would be a little better if the middle classes had to opt back into real life and use their influence to improve things. I can't be anything but totally opposed to this system you so cheerfully shore up. And don't give me

230   SAMANTHA HUME

those spurious arguments about equal opportunities. In the context of this
society, what you're talking about isn't an extension of equality; it's an
extension of inequality. Don't try to quiet my conscience like that."
(McDermid 1987, 8)

This contempt of privilege and class criticism is brought out further at a
later stage in *Report for Murder* when Lindsay visits her potential new
lover Cordelia's luxurious London flat, full of Chesterfields and fancy
kitchen gadgetry, which Gordon finds obscene. As a socialist and somewhat puritanical Scot, influenced by a Protestant value system and a working-class background, Lindsay interprets this luxury as a selling out of principles for material wealth. In this first novel she recognizes this as a chasm
between herself and Cordelia, whom she has just met, but is falling in love
with. She realizes almost immediately that the relationship with her may
ultimately be doomed to failure because of their inequality. It also introduces the issue of identity politics in the lesbian community and problems
with equality and inequality, which were discussed extensively in the 1980s.
This is expanded upon in *Common Murder*, where Lindsay has moved to
London to live with Cordelia, despite her reservations, and where she is in
the process of reevaluating their relationship. The comfort and security of
Cordelia's prosperous surroundings are set in harsh contrast to the makeshift plastic sheets formed into shelters (called benders) in the peace camp
at Brownlow Common, the central focus of action in the novel.[3] In addition, Gordon's use of the peace camp as a "bolthole" (McDermid 1989, 5)
in which she feels at home illustrates how she expresses her political alle-
giances by actual presence as opposed to Cordelia's more tempered letters
to the *Guardian* or her M.P. The relationship with Cordelia ends when
Gordon has to flee security services at the end of this novel. On her return
from this self-imposed exile in novel number three, *Final Edition*, she discovers that Cordelia has a new partner in the lawyer Claire. Although old
bonds and loyalties are still palpable, Cordelia's new partner is someone
from a similar class and with a similar taste for luxury, and she seems much
happier. It is not without irony, then, that the ending of *Final Edition* sees
Cordelia discredited and herself forced into exile. She has coolly murdered
the journalist Alison Maxwell in order to hide the fact that she has stolen a
manuscript from a South African dissident and sold it as her own work.
Nevertheless, Lindsay, although she knows that Cordelia has committed
murder, allows her to escape, another sign of her own human weaknesses
and contradictions.

The themes of class, wealth, and economic prosperity are features of
all five thrillers, and on the whole, the lack of modesty with regard to the
characters' sometimes immoral accumulation of wealth is frowned upon in

Gordon's Scottish puritanical manner. This is especially true for wealth come to by dishonest or less than noble means: Cordelia's antifeminist television chat-show in *Report for Murder,* which is used to fund her luxurious lifestyle and her misappropriation of another writer's work to further both her fame and economic success in *Final Edition;* the young computer genius Simon Crabtree's sale of military secrets to the "enemy" in *Common Murder* to fund his own business; the power-hungry and corrupt union boss Tom Jack in *Union Jack,* using his position to bankrupt Gordon's close friend Dick McAndrew and close down his paper, *Socialist Today;* and, of course, the Mafia-style money laundering carried out by the ruthless Danny King in *Booked for Murder.* This criticism also panders to the prejudice about the immorality of the (prosperous) English who are willing to exploit others for their own profit. There are also, of course, other English characters who represent socialist values, as for example the women in the peace camp, and, similarly, there are Scots characters who are exploitative, as for example the politician in *Final Edition* who uses very young rent boys for homosexual sex and yet boasts antigay opinions in public. Nevertheless, the binary, essentialist oppositions are maintained between the Scottish detective and the English criminals: Gordon and James Cartwright, the builder and developer who will stop at nothing, not even murder, to get his hands on the school's playing fields in *Report for Murder;* Gordon and Simon Crabtree; Gordon and Cordelia; Gordon and Tom Jack; and finally Gordon and Danny King.

The Lindsay Gordon character is herself not left unscathed by this critical eye in that she faces a mass of contradictions in her own profession. She unhesitatingly sells information or photographs of friends, often given in confidence, to fulfill her need to make a living. As a journalist on a tabloid often looking for sensationalist stories, she frequently finds herself in conflict with her own values, her only defense being that "if people with brains and compassion opted out the press would only sink further into the gutter" (McDermid 1987, 3). Further, she uses her position as a journalist with an ability to publicize embarrassing and damaging information about people's lives to pressure them into giving her information they would not otherwise reveal. She seems to justify this to herself and the others by saying she is the better of the evils, made up of the other tabloid journalists, because she has a conscience and will use the information with discretion. In the last two novels she returns to Britain, having lived in California for the interim and having stopped working as a journalist to teach journalism; she becomes a great deal more critical of the profession and the invasive and "hard-boiled" behavior of her former colleagues.

In promoting egalitarian values and integrity of character, Lindsay Gordon is a representative of relatively traditional values in our modern

232   SAMANTHA HUME

world of high finance and the quest to make the proverbial "quick buck." Nowadays, anonymity makes it much easier not to care about whom one is exploiting and where exactly the wealth is coming from. The Lindsay Gordon character, while on the one hand conforming to some of the conventions of the detective fiction genre with its implicit search for truth, on the other hand subverts the anonymity, because she solves the murders and thus finds the "true" culprits, but also does this out of a sense of loyalty, friendship and emotional attachment. Her socialist identity functions almost like a moral conscience, and the use of Scottish friends like Dick McAndrew (*Common Murder* and *Union Jack*), who display similar attitudes toward justice and socialist ideology, underpins that identity as being "typically" Scottish.

CRIMES, POLICE, AND (IN)JUSTICE

Interestingly enough, the crimes in all five novels are directly related to greed and the desire to increase the perpetrators' own wealth. In *Report for Murder,* famous cellist Lorna Smith-Couper is murdered because of a developer's wish to buy land leased to her former school to make money by building homes on it. Smith-Couper will not be bribed and refuses to discredit the fund-raiser at the school by withdrawing from a concert, and so the developer and father of one of the girls murders her. In *Common Murder*, a young computer expert, Simon Crabtree, turns spy in order to acquire the economic financing he needs to buy equipment for his computer business, which his father has refused him; when the former finds out about the spying, Simon kills him in a panicked confrontation. In *Final Edition*, Gordon finds out that her former lover, Cordelia, has murdered a journalist because she had threatened to reveal that she had stolen the manuscript of an African dissident writer and sold it as her own to enhance her own reputation and, of course, wealth; and in *Union Jack*, Gordon uncovers the corruption within the union executive and the siphoning off of excess pension funds when investigating the death of the unpopular and tyrannical union leader Tom Jack, who has fallen out of *her* tenth-floor hotel room window. Both this and the fact that she has had numerous public rows with him make her a suspect. In *Booked for Murder*, there is a critical view of the publishing business as Gordon uncovers a Mafia money-laundering scheme after thugs have killed her friend, the writer Penny Varnavides, because she had found out how they were laundering the money and wanted to expose them in her forthcoming novel.

The abilities of the police to solve the crimes in detective fiction entails, of course, a large collection of bumbling police officers. The Gordon mysteries have a slightly different perspective. In *Report for Murder*, the police do not have any insight into the other possible motives for the murder except the obvious ones. They are unaware of the closet lesbian teacher Margaret MacDonald, who could be a possible suspect, having had an affair with the murdered cellist Lorna Smith-Couper when she was a pupil at the school. This is a world they are not privy to, and since they already think they have their murderer locked up, they are not committed to looking any further. Similarly, in *Final Edition*, there is no apparent need for any investigation, because the murderer has been found guilty, sentenced, and already imprisoned, and in *Booked for Murder* the death is considered accidental, or again the police believe their suspect, Varnavides's ex-lover, is the only one possible. For them, the motivation of the lesbian lover's jealousy is a straightforward and plausible explanation. In *Union Jack*, the police are very much in the background, thinking that the death may in fact have been an accident, and in *Common Murder* there is an added element to the relationship between the police and the sleuth when Lindsay and Rigano, the detective in charge of the investigation, agree to work together. All of the mistakes made by the police are necessary elements of the plot as they pave the way for the suspects to ask for Gordon's help and thus also supply the arena in which she can then act. As she is independent of the police and has access to knowledge of interpersonal relationships they are not privy to, she is at an advantage and, therefore, also has a greater chance of finding out the truth.

The texts all deal with murder and offer an opportunity to look closely at police behavior toward their suspects. As the suspects are all women, this gives insight into police treatment of women murder suspects and also the effects of imprisonment on women. Ultimately, it is Gordon who finds out the truth the police have been unable to uncover, not only because of incompetence, typical of their role in the genre, but also because of their failure to acknowledge the rights of the women professing their innocence, a commitment that Gordon feels keenly. Jill Radford, in her essay "Lindsay Gordon Meets Kate Brannigan," calls this outcome the superiority of the "big purple cells" over the "little grey ones," that is, "women's superior use of logic and also 'feminine intuition,' or actually hearing what is said" (1998, 84). The attitude of the police toward women is not portrayed favorably, as can be seen in the reluctance of the women at the peace camp to turn to them for assistance when they have been threatened and harassed by a group of bikers from the local community:

> "We must call the police!" Lindsay exclaimed.
> "It's a waste of time calling the police, Lindsay. They just don't want to know. The first time they threw blood over our benders, we managed to get

234 SAMANTHA HUME

the police to come out. But they said there was no evidence of our allegations. Tyre tracks in the mud don't count, you see. Nor do statements of over forty women. It doesn't really matter what crimes are perpetrated against us, because we're sub-human, you see."

"That's monstrous," Lindsay protested.

"But inevitable," Jane retorted. "What's going on here is so radical that they can't afford to treat it seriously on any level. Start accepting that we've got any rights and you end up by giving validity to the nightmares that have brought us here. Do that and you're half-way to accepting that our views on disarmament are a logical position. Much easier to treat us with total contempt." (McDermid 1989, 16–17)

This view of the police and their attitudes towards women who challenge their place in the patriarchal order by refusing to accept what they consider unacceptable policy is, unfortunately, reflected in much of the real-life experience of women as rape victims, as victims of domestic violence, and as political activists. In *Report for Murder* and *Final Edition* the reader is given a clear impression of the devastating effects that imprisonment has on the women characters, destroying their dignity and self-confidence and making them merely shadows of their former selves:

After a few minutes, a door at the opposite end of the room opened, and the officer returned with Paddy. Already life behind bars had left its mark on her. Her skin had an unhealthy sallowness. There were dark bags beneath her eyes. But what was most striking was that she seemed to have lost all her self-confidence. Fewer than three days of living behind bars had cut her down to less than life-size. (1987, 98)

The power of the police is illustrated in an episode in *Common Murder* when the secret service bug the local police officer's office. They kidnap Gordon at knifepoint in the middle of the night, threatening her life if she does not sign the Official Secrets Act and back off from her investigations into Simon Crabtree. She nevertheless uncovers the truth, and the article she writes reveals the willingness of the security forces to sacrifice an innocent citizen to protect a useful spy, although they are aware that he is a known murderer and potentially dangerous. The fact that Gordon outwits these forces by having the article uncover the spying activities and the tactics of the secret service published abroad, thereby circumventing the Official Secrets Act, is another aspect many women readers might find appealing. As Jill Radford also points out in her discussion of Lindsay Gordon, this is a satisfying outcome for women who are often subjected to a system of (in)justice that is institutionally sexist and patriarchal, and it is

"HERE'S TAE US, WHA'S LIKE US"   235

especially rewarding because it happens so quickly—unfortunately, this does not mirror real-life campaigns.

LESBIAN FEMINIST

Much lesbian detective fiction incorporates the "coming out" story; however, the Gordon mysteries present a lesbian sleuth who is quite secure and open about her lesbian identity as opposed to embarking on discovering it. Her relationships are not simply relegated to paradise or hell, but presented as "normal" relationships that may or may not succeed and that have faults, inconsistencies, and political tensions, just as any heterosexual relationship might have. This serves to offer a sense of reality and normality in a text where sexuality is not a pivotal element of the plot, but simply another part of the human identity of the characters. The attempt to mainstream lesbian identity as simply another element of culture is successful in the depiction of Gordon's networks and friends. In addition to this, however, there is realistic political and feminist criticism voiced in the social attitudes towards lesbianism that are integrated into other, less prominent characters. In *Report for Murder*, the school's music teacher and mentor to the murdered cellist is revealed to be a closet lesbian, who had an affair with the cellist while the latter was still a pupil at the school. It is clear that if she makes it known that she is gay, it will mean the end of her teaching career. In *Common Murder*, Rupert Crabtree withdraws the financial assistance he gave to his daughter for her business when he inadvertently finds out that she is a lesbian. Both of these characters reflect the true social stigma that is still attached to homosexuality in British culture, and it is a theme that appears throughout the series.[4]

The feminist aspects of the novels and the lesbian identity of their main character illustrate a subversion of the traditions of detective fiction. Although she is not a professional private detective, Gordon has the necessary investigative skills of a journalist to help her solve the murders, and as a woman she is in the detective's empowered subject position (traditionally male) in the pursuit of truth. As a lesbian, she has the added ability of being able to present an alternative lifestyle and sexuality outside the conventional binary opposition of patriarchy and can thus threaten its very basis.[5] With respect to sexuality, it is most probably a case of overcompensation for anticipated prejudices in her audience when McDermid presents Gordon's lesbian sexuality as almost a mirror image of the enforced coupledom of heterosexuality. While couples can be said to constitute one possible scenario of lesbian sexuality, it is unfortunate that this is the only image portrayed in this (and other) series, because it conforms to patriarchal social structures and does not explore the other options that "alternative" sexual identity may offer.

It is not only Lindsay Gordon's attitudes and dialogue that convince the reader of the feminist perspective being presented, but also the feminist issues highlighted within the plots that often affect the characters' behavior and the outcomes of the novels. This is especially true of the endings in *Final Edition* and *Union Jack*, in which criticism is levied at two of the strongest institutions of patriarchy: the law and the police. In *Final Edition*, Lindsay Gordon collects her suspects together for dinner to reveal who the culprit is in a Poirot-like climax, only to be humiliated when her witness, a rent boy, points to her former lover, Cordelia, instead of the suspect Gordon has chosen. This seems to be such a ludicrous idea that the witness is apparently immediately discredited. Gordon, however, believes him and has to come to terms with the fact that her former lover is a murderer. Instead of going to the police, however, and having her arrested, Gordon confronts her, but lets her flee and waits until she has had plenty of time to leave the country before informing the authorities. This interesting twist is significant for two reasons. First of all, Gordon prefers to allow Cordelia to escape rather than hand her over to be subjected to patriarchal (in)justice, a consistent reaction for a lesbian feminist, and, secondly, Cordelia is a lesbian and a murderer, constituting a negative lesbian character. However, Cordelia is only one lesbian among a community in the fictional world surrounding Lindsay Gordon, and as the novels were originally published by the Women's Press, the readership would have most likely been predominantly feminist anyway and capable of accepting the character without making generalizations. McDermid has also pointed out that she hopes her subsequent success will encourage all kinds of readers to go back to the Gordon mysteries: "What I'm saying now is that people who read Kate Brannigan[6] are going back to the Lindsay Gordon books and that's great because it's bringing lesbianism into the mainstream and people will hopefully see it as part of the normal spectrum of life" (quoted in Brooks 1993, 13).

In *Union Jack*, the woman assumed to have committed the murder, on Gordon's eyewitness statement, is revealed to be the wrong person. The real culprit is the black secretary, Pauline, who, having been previously sexually harassed and assaulted by Tom Jack, defends herself against him when he tries to rape her based on his sexist and racist assumption that since she is a black woman, provocatively dressed, she must therefore be a whore.[7] He forces her to enter Gordon's room, and when she defends herself by pushing him away, he trips and falls over a chair and through the window to his death. Here, Gordon knows that a predominantly white male police force is not going to be sympathetic toward a provocatively dressed black woman who may have caused the death of a respectable white male, a high-profile, married union boss. She does not tell the police that she was mistaken when she identified Laura Craig, a participant at the conference she is attending, thus protecting a black sister who would certainly have been the victim of injustice. Therefore, Craig, who had in fact murdered Gordon's friend ten years previously, will now face charges for a murder she did not commit, while having escaped from one she did. The irony is voiced in the fact that Gordon does not believe that Craig will be convicted at all, because she has contacts in the police force and has been working for them undercover. In traditional terms, these endings could be interpreted as miscarriages of justice; however, it is not unusual to find that women authors of detective fiction often have a different sense of justice than that which the law dictates. There are numerous studies showing how men and women are treated differently, usually in murder cases to the detriment of women.[8] It is understandable, therefore, that a feminist perspective will dictate a different attitude and different outcomes. This not only reinforces women readers' own sense of (in)justice, but also acknowledges that the "authorities that be" treat women in a biased and unequal way.

Val McDermid considers her audience to consist of angry women: "I think that's one of the reasons why a lot of women both write and read crime fiction—it's a place to put our anger" (1993, 12). This anger can stem from a whole range of experiences in real women's real lives and their frustrations about social, sexual, racial, and ethnic (in)justice, whether it be in education, in the family, in politics, or in law. They all appear as themes in the Gordon mysteries. These themes and the numerous subplots highlighting feminist issues are all packaged in witty, humorous prose. Ultimately, Gordon finds the truth and beats the system, offering women a strong, independent character whose Scottish cynical socialist lesbian feminism affirms the strength of womanhood to succeed even in the most adverse circumstances.

Contrasting issues of ethnicity and gender in an English cultural setting has been extremely successful in the Gordon series. Scotland's clan system treated individuals equally whether they were rich, poor, head of a clan or a tenant farmer. This means that egalitarianism is, based on its particular history and social order, an intrinsic part of the Scottish psyche, and it contrasts with the superiority versus inferiority class system in England. As a Scot, Gordon also embodies this identity, but it does not mean she is uncritical of the more negative aspects of her culture.[9] In addition, both English and Scottish cultures are patriarchal, and any cultural discussion necessitates the inclusion of a gender perspective. As a feminist Scot, therefore, Gordon highlights issues of social inequality, injustice, and gender as elements of her Scottish socialist lesbian identity.

238   SAMANTHA HUME

NOTES

1. A more detailed discussion of the history of the Scottish/English animosity and Scottish identity can be found in Dickson and Tremble (1992, 261–81) and Cooke et al. (1998, 183–91), respectively.

2. It is highly unusual that a Scot would say "public" school. In general in Scotland this is considered to be English arrogance; in Scotland fee-paying schools are referred to as private schools. This may be a concession to a wider reading audience but is striking coming from a Scottish author and a Scottish heroine.

3. Brownlow Common is clearly based on Greenham Common: "A group of women had marched from the West Country to the American airbase at Brownlow Common to protest at the siting of US cruise missiles there. They had been so fired by anger and enthusiasm at the end of their three-week march that they decided to set up a peace camp as a permanent protest against the nuclear colonisation of their *green unpleasant land*" [my italics] McDermid 1989, 4).

4. In 1988 Thatcherite intolerance introduced Section 28 (a law that prohibits the *promotion* [*sic*] of homosexuality in schools), and a recent ruling in England by the House of Lords (July 2000) has decided not to repeal this law. However, in Scotland it has already been repealed, an indication that while mainstream Scottish identity and culture may not always approve of lesbianism, it has a tradition of tolerance. The debate surrounding Section 28 is extensive and beyond the scope of this article; however, it is said to be an expression of the cultural conservatism in England, which on the whole still considers homosexuality to be wrong (*Independent on Sunday*, 30 July 2000, 14–15).

5. Kathleen Gregory Klein's article "Habeas Corpus: Feminism and Detective Fiction" discusses the oppositions in patriarchal discourse in detail and demonstrates how the lesbian position as detective can be a risky one. Not only is the detective as woman a descendent of Eve and therefore a wrongdoer, but as a lesbian, religious views deem her sinful. If she is closeted, "she risks exposure and punishment; if out, she faces homophobic discrimination. In her essence and merely by her existence, the detective who is lesbian approaches the positionality of a criminal to an extent which a heterosexual male detective can reach only if his actions are truly beyond the law" (1995, 177).

6. Kate Brannigan is McDermid's next serial heroine, a Manchester-based, Thai kickboxing PI whose heterosexuality promises a broader readership and mainstream publisher.

7. Social attitudes towards black female sexuality are discussed extensively in Sally Munt's *Murder by the Book* (1997). Interesting here is also the reminder McDermid gives of the white feminist majority arrogance:

> "He started smacking me about the head, giving me all the stuff about how I was just a black slag, a whore . . ." she trailed off and sighed deeply.
> "I'm sure we can fill in the blanks," Sophie said reassuringly.
> "Don't be so sure of that," Pauline snapped back. "Believe me, being working class and black gives you access to a whole new range of insults." (1993, 257)

8. There are extensive case studies of murder inquiries and sentencing practices in England in Radford and Russell 1992 and of police attitudes toward women in Hanmer, Radford, and Stanko 1989.

9. On the contrary, in *Union Jack* McDermid presents the perfect image of a group of sexist Scottish men, drunk and belligerent at the Celts' *ceilidh:* "The Celts are a thirsty people. Historically, we've got a lot of sorrows to drown" (1993, 96). This excessive drink-

"HERE'S TAE US, WHA'S LIKE US"   239

ing is an intrinsic part of Scottish social interaction, whereby there can be no social gathering without the consumption of alcohol.

WORKS CITED

Brooks, Libby. 1993. "A Place to Put Our Anger." *Harpies and Quines* 9:12–13.

Cooke, Anthony, et al., eds. 1998. *Modern Scottish History, 1707 to the Present.* East Lothian, Scotland: Tuckwell Press.

Dickson, Tony, and James H. Tremble. 1992. *People and Society in Scotland, 1919–1990.* Vol. 3. Edinburgh: John Donald Publishers.

Hanmer, Yalna, Jill Radford, and Elizabeth A. Stanko, eds. 1989. *Women, Policing, and Male Violence.* London: Routledge.

Hutton, Elaine, ed. 1998. *Beyond Sex and Romance? The Politics of Contemporary Lesbian Fiction.* London: Women's Press.

Irons, Glenwood, ed. 1995. *Feminism in Women's Detective Fiction.* Toronto: University of Toronto Press.

Klein, Kathleen Gregory. 1995. "Habeas Corpus: Feminism and Detective Fiction." In *Feminism in Women's Detective Fiction*, edited by Glenwood Irons, 171–89. Toronto: University of Toronto Press.

McDermid, Val. 1987. *Report for Murder.* London: Women's Press.

———. 1989. *Common Murder.* London: Women's Press.

———. 1991. *Final Edition.* London: Women's Press.

———. 1993. *Union Jack.* London: Women's Press.

———. 1996. *Booked For Murder.* London: Women's Press.

Munt, Sally. 1997. *Murder by the Book: Feminism and the Crime Novel.* London: Routledge.

Radford, Jill. 1998. "Lindsay Gordon Meets Kate Brannigan." In Hutton 1998, 81–105.

Radford, Jill, and Diana E. H. Russell, eds. 1992. *Femicide: The Politics of Woman Killing.* Buckingham, U.K.: Open University Press.

The Hard-Boiled Pattern as Discursive Practice
of Ethnic Subalternity in Jakob Arjouni's
Happy Birthday, Turk! and Irene Dische's *Ein Job*

KONSTANZE KUTZBACH

Both Jakob Arjouni's *Happy birthday, turk!* (1985) and Irene Dische's *Ein Job*[1] (*A Job*, 2000) are embedded in the tradition of the hard-boiled detective novel. The novels' protagonists—a detective and a hired assassin, respectively—act more or less according to the traditional pattern of the detective as a "man of the wilderness" (Grella 1950, 112) who swears, smokes, drinks, and has casual sex. George Grella has summed up the characteristics of the hard-boiled detective and his universe in the following statement: "All hard-boiled novels depict a tawdry world which conceals a shabby and depressing reality beneath its painted façade. . . . [T]he detective has no other place to go. A man of the wilderness, he finds the wilderness destroyed, replaced by the urban jungle" (1950, 112). In both novels discussed here, the hard-boiled pattern serves as an ideological foil that is frequently—but also rather ironically—referred to in order to foreground a discourse of alterity that is explored from the perspective of the protagonist's particular ethnic background.

This recent focus on ethnicity in detective literature reflects a paradigm shift that registers a "new found attention to difference" (Hall, quoted in Wells 1999, 209) and a growing awareness of subalternity, which is stereotyped less frequently than before. As Cohen points out, this shift in emphasis has added a new level of sophistication to the (ethnic) detective novel: "More subtle works . . . displace the otherness of the villain by emphasizing that of the detective, or displace it entirely onto the victim" (1999, 156). This displacement of the subaltern from margin to center coincides with an increasingly complex and differentiated representation of subalternity as a potentially subversive force:

THE HARD-BOILED PATTERN IN ARJOUNI AND DISCHE 241

> Paradoxically in our world, marginality has become a powerful space. It is
> a space of weak power but it is a space of power nonetheless. The emer-
> gence of new subjects, new genders, new ethnicities, new regions, new
> communities, hitherto excluded from the major forms of cultural represen-
> tation, unable to locate themselves except as decentered or subaltern, have
> acquired through struggle, sometimes in very marginalised ways, the means
> to speak for themselves for the first time. And the discourses of power in
> our society, the discourses of the dominant regimes, have been certainly
> threatened by this decentered cultural empowerment of the marginal and
> the local. (Hall, quoted in Wells 1999, 209)

Arjouni's and Dische's novels accomplish a displacement of the subaltern
from a marginal to a central perspective; as representatives of ethnic
subalternity the protagonists—along with the victims in the detective plot—
are granted a voice of "decentered cultural empowerment."

Both the protagonist of Dische's *A Job*, a Kurd named Alan, who is
sent to New York as a contract killer, and Kemal Kayankaya, the Frank-
furt-based ethnic detective from *Happy Birthday, Turk!*, are permanently
aware of their otherness. Thus, they constantly have to face what Pepper
refers to as an "appropriately fractured sense of self":

> [B]ecause [the detective] has traditionally been forced to live in *at least*
> two worlds (that of his or her culture, which itself needs to be seen in
> fragmented terms, and that of the so-called "dominant" culture, be it white,
> Western, or Anglo in orientation), he or she will automatically possess an
> appropriately fractured sense of self; appropriately because it necessarily
> problematizes a straightforward model of identity formation. Moreover,
> such a detective . . . is arguably better able to view the polyethnic environ-
> ment in suitably ambiguous terms. (1999, 242)

Pepper's analysis ties in with W. E. B. Du Bois's model of a "double consciousness,"[2] which likewise stresses "[t]he idea of the detective as double
sided . . . as a result of this ambiguous racialized context" (Wells 1999,
214).

Since ethnic alterity apparently causes alienation that is both cultural
and psychological, I would like to investigate the similarities and differences between the detective's or assassin's sense of alienation from simultaneously his "familiar/foreign" surroundings and himself. I will analyze
the different strategies employed by the "hard-boiled" protagonists in their
struggles to come to terms with the ambivalence of their locatedness in a
fractured ethnic and cultural environment. There is a correlation between
the protagonists' lack of orientation regarding their ambivalent cultural
location and their need to have recourse to typical hard-boiled behavior
due to a subliminal discrepancy based on the arbitrary nature of the signifier-

signified relationship.[3] This inconsistency basically derives from conflicting notions of meaning attached to different languages and linguistic universes.

My analysis is based on a poststructuralist approach that views (ethnic) identity as unstable and constructed. According to Pepper, "Terms like race and ethnicity no longer refer to categories that are fixed and stable but to ones that are best seen as fluid and relational, reflecting a growing awareness of the temporary and socially constructed nature of all identities" (1999, 243). Since identity is discursively constructed, it is necessarily dependent on power as it is exerted and reflected by language.[4] A definition of identity as constructed and fluid ties in with a Foucauldian approach, which likewise emphasizes the interdependence of identity, discursive practice, and power:

> [Discourses are not to be treated] as groups of signs (signifying elements referring to contents or representations) but as practices that systematically form the objects of which they speak. Of course, discourses are composed of signs; but what they do is more than use these signs to designate things. It is this *more* that renders them irreducible to the language *(langue)* and to speech. (Foucault 1972, 49)

These basic assumptions about the nature of identity-formation provide a tool for explaining and analyzing the ambivalence in Arjouni's and Dische's protagonists' awareness of ethnic difference. The "fractured sense of self" that the protagonists of both novels experience corresponds to a similar ambivalence of ethnic location. Yet, in order to cope with their sense of fragmentation and unbelonging, Alan and Kemal pursue different strategies and relate differently to the "hard-boiled" behavior pattern that they at times adopt. Whereas Kemal, who remains within the dual frame of his ethnic background, consistently reverts to the hard-boiled pattern, Alan eventually abandons it. Originating from a rather chaotic multiethnic background, Alan starts out as a hard-boiled contract killer, who in early childhood vowed to pursue a career as a political assassin and, accordingly, discarded any traces of emotional weakness. But as the novel progresses, he becomes less and less hard-boiled and eventually settles down in the United States, living the idyllic soft-boiled life of an "American" husband and father who is glad to have reclaimed his fear at last.

Before turning to the different discursive practices that exert conflicting forces on Alan and Kemal, I will look at the differences and similarities of their ambivalent cultural location. In both cases their (early) childhood experiences have set the stage for the development of the protagonists' "appropriately fractured sense of self" and account for their adult hard-boiled behavior. But despite these similarities, there are also differences in

THE HARD-BOILED PATTERN IN ARJOUNI AND DISCHE   243

terms of quality, especially concerning the complexity of the conflicting forces and the protagonists' respective reactions to them.

Kemal Kayankaya was born in Ankara as the son of Turkish parents. His mother, Ülkü, died at his birth, and a year later his father, Tarik, left for Germany with his son: "He went to Frankfurt and worked for three years for the municipal garbage disposal service, until he was run over by a mail truck" (Arjouni 1996, 10). After only a few weeks Kemal was adopted by a German family, which made him a German citizen. Thus, from the very beginning, Kemal is ambivalently located between (two) disparate cultures that do not provide him with any certainty about his family roots or any sense of authentic ethnic belonging. His main cultural identification, however, is formed within a German frame of reference: "Thus I grew up in a thoroughly German milieu, and it was a long time before I began to look for my true parents. At the age of seventeen I traveled to Turkey, but wasn't able to find out any more about my family than I already knew from the orphanage records" (11). From early childhood, Kemal has learned to conform to the norms of German culture. This, however, fosters anxiety, since he feels pressured into conforming to the signifying system of a culture from which he is alienated. When he investigates the murder of a Turkish worker who was stabbed to death in the red-light district of Frankfurt, his cultural background gains a strong impact on his work as a PI. On the one hand, he seems the right person for the job because he is located at the interstices of two cultures; on the other hand, the ambivalent nature of his ethnic location causes new problems for Kemal and, ultimately, makes him a hard-boiled detective.

The difficulties he faces when pursuing his investigations of the murder case in *Happy Birthday, Turk!* also result from being torn between two different signifying systems that he has to negotiate according to the differing expectations of his surroundings. This maneuvering is and remains binary. He is stereotyped and marginalized according to a German frame of reference, which ostracizes him on the basis of both his physical appearance and his biological heritage. But since he lacks Turkish acculturation altogether, he seems to feel even more excluded from the signifying system applied to him by his fellow Turks. Thus, pressure is exerted on Kemal by two signifying systems, neither of which accommodates his ethnic specificity. Throughout the novel, Kemal pursues more or less successful self-help strategies designed to enable him to reconcile conflicting outer expectations. Thus, he sometimes makes clumsy efforts to empathize, especially with Turks, but, more frequently, he conceals his insecurity behind his hard-boiled behavior. This becomes evident right at the beginning of the novel, when Ilter Hamul, his client in the murder case, enters his office and tries to talk to him in their mother tongue, which he does not understand:

244   KONSTANZE KUTZBACH

> The black thing was a small Turkish woman in a mourning veil and thick
> gold earrings. . . . She mumbled something in Turkish, a language I don't
> understand even when it is spoken loudly and clearly. I explained to her
> that I was indeed an ethnic compatriot, but that due to special circum-
> stances I neither spoke nor comprehended the Turkish tongue. (1996, 12)

Ilter Hamul immediately becomes suspicious and wants to leave his office,
but Kemal tries—as nicely as possible—to assure her that they will find a
way to communicate. After a while she decides to confide her story to him:
a few days before, her husband, Ahmed Hamul, had been stabbed to death
in the red-light district close to the Frankfurt train station. Kemal agrees to
take the case but is upset by the fact that his investigations will lead him
into a rather unpleasant neighborhood known for its ethnic unrest.

On his way to his client's family, he is confronted with anti-Turkish
prejudice when he accidentally kicks an empty beer can against "a flannel-
clad leg right in front of [him]" (Arjouni 1996, 18). The owner of the leg,
not having seen Kemal right away, at first chides him in a rather indifferent, neutral tone. Kemal smiles at him, but upon seeing Kemal's face, the
stranger reacts in "typically" German fashion: "'Oh, I see! No speaka da
lingo, eh?' He turned to establish eye contact with his three companions.
They stood there with big grins on their porcine mugs. 'This Germany!
This no Turkey! Here beer cans go in garbage! And Turk fellow drive garbage truck'" (18).

Since Kemal "[can't] think of anything to say suitable to the occasion"
(Arjouni 1996, 18–19), he leaves the three people and walks to a nearby
restaurant, where he orders a coffee and a Scotch in a very cool manner,
trying to set himself apart from the suddenly loathed German surroundings. His increased awareness of ethnic unbelonging becomes evident in
his immediate reaction. Thus, he describes the German patrons, who unap-
petizingly devour "typically" German dishes, in terms of animal imagery:

> The neighbouring tabletops were filling up with platters of sauerkraut,
> bratwurst, and schnitzels. In the muggy air, jaws were tearing into breaded
> meat, lips smacking, vocal chords groaning and interspersing those noises
> with occasional speech. Tongues emerged to lick greasy chops. (20)

But this attempt to compensate for his own exclusion by excluding representatives of the dominant culture as "other" must necessarily fail, since
Germanness is an integral part of Kemal's fractured identity. Thus, his reaction can be viewed as part of an autoaggressive mechanism that causes
self-alienation. The sudden split in his personality brought on by his encounter with ethnic prejudice is represented by the revolting act of his
burping up a piece of *Sachertorte* as if it were the German part of his iden-

THE HARD-BOILED PATTERN IN ARJOUNI AND DISCHE 245

tity: "I had to burp, and a slightly sour-tasting crumb of *Sachertorte* landed on my tongue. When I began to feel really nauseated, I paid my tab and left" (20).

Right after this rather frustrating experience, Kemal succeeds—at least on a small scale—in counteracting his unease with some rather blunt and offensive thoughts that make dark-skinned women the target of a sexist and racist fantasy. Thus marginalized, Kemal seeks emotional relief from being excluded by likewise excluding others, as the following thoughts on "smooth brown Bacardi girls" betray:

> I trotted through the downtown area, stopping in front of the window displays of several travel agencies to enjoy their pictorial representations of turquoise seas, endless white beaches, . . . and smooth brown Bacardi girls. . . . I considered how many Ahmed Hamuls would have to bite the dust before I could spend seven days building sandcastles, imbibing rum, and having my feet washed by ladies the colour of instant chocolate. (Arjouni 1996, 20)

In this case, his strategy of compensating for his sense of ethnic unbelonging through recourse to the offensive attitude and language of the hard-boiled detective proves successful. Oscillating between the two cultural poles that demarcate his fractured ethnic identity, he again gravitates more toward his German side. But this brings about new problems when he visits his Turkish client's family at their home, where Kemal suddenly feels like an intruder. In the following passage describing the visit, the intercultural tension deriving from seemingly incompatible cultural backgrounds is palpable:

> All of them stared at me in silence. . . . Ilter's brother was sitting to my right, on a dark blue sofa. He cast a quick angry glance at her, but she kept staring at her shoes. . . . The atmosphere was about as relaxed as the final minutes of a world soccer championship. All right, stop pussyfooting, I told myself. Let's get this over with as quickly as possible. (22–23)

This lack of communication which causes a highly charged atmosphere of mutual suspicion due to reciprocal cultural attributions in this scene is still rather subliminal. It surfaces more intensely in the course of the novel, where, during his investigations, other aspects of the hard-boiled behavior pattern emerge as a consequence of Kemal's cultural helplessness. Driven by anger over his cultural unbelonging, he goes about insulting other outsiders, such as prostitutes. Every now and then he celebrates his solitude with the help of a bottle of whiskey. Kemal moves back and forth between mustering the toughness required of the hard-boiled detective and showing

246 KONSTANZE KUTZBACH

rare bursts of self-doubt; his ambivalent behavior throughout the novel betrays this pattern of unstable identity.

But the novel's ending is rather predictable and traditional. Kemal eventually manages to convict the murderer, but he can even sympathize with him to a certain extent. Although Kemal knows that it was Yilmaz Ergün, Ilter's brother, who killed her husband, Ahmed, he does not divulge this piece of information to the police, because his Turkish side feels solidarity and empathy with the "ethnic" motivations of the murderer:

> Because it was what happened to your sister Ayse that finally drove you to kill Ahmed. You couldn't forgive him for getting Ayse hooked on heroin. . . . It must have seemed like a solution to all your problems. You would have your revenge for the jealousy[5] of all those years, and your family could live in peace, at long last. Ayse's addiction gave moral justification to the deed. And so, what had been only an idea became a plan, a task. For the salvation of the family. (Arjouni 1996, 188–89)

All's well that ends well: Kemal reveals the criminal involvement of Superintendent Futt, who resembles the "picture of a jumping German shepherd on his office wall" (33) and who was a heroine dealer, and of his sidekick, Eiler, who had killed Vasif Ergün, Ilter's drug-dealing father.

After the case is resolved, Kemal remains safely located between the Turkish and German value systems. He has reestablished justice according to German law and also in accordance with the ethnic values of his fellow Turkish countrymen. Thus, he has indeed managed to do justice according to the requirements of his dual cultural location.

Alan, Dische's protagonist, presents yet another aspect of conflicted ethnic alterity and identity. His cultural and familial origins are more complex than Kemal's, and his ethnic affiliation becomes increasingly convoluted—especially after he travels to New York as an adult and has to find his niche in the American way of life. As a Kurd, Alan had to get used to a subordinated but rebellious position in his "home country." When he was still in school, he felt an urge to assert his Kurdish ethnicity against the dominant Turkish culture:

> Seine Raserei setzte am Abend ein wie ein plötzliches Fieber nach Tagen kühler Gefügigkeit in der Schule, wo er Türkisch lernte, türkische Gedichte, die Geschichte türkischer Heldentaten und türkischer Vorstöße und Eroberungen in Europa. Seinen Lehrern gelang es, den kurdischen Akzent spurlos aus ihm herauszuprügeln. (Dische 2000, 7)

> [His ravings started in the evening like a sudden bout of fever after days of quiet obedience in the school where he was learning Turkish—Turkish

poems, the deeds of Turkish heroes, their challenges and conquests. His teachers succeeded in beating every trace of his Kurdish accent out of him.]

Orphaned like Kemal, Alan lived with his grandmother after his mother's early death. From childhood on, he had to cope with the influence of arbitrary mechanisms of social hierarchies of power on his subaltern ethnic position. When Alan was a first-grader, his father suffered from random acts of violence inflicted on him by Turkish soldiers. He eventually died of injuries sustained during a street fight between two Kurdish clans, the Bruki and the Cumki.

His father's death coincided with a key experience in Alan's life, after which he decided to become an assassin. Having plotted to throw some snowballs at his designated enemies—as a sign of his rebellion against the Turks—he accidentally slipped and was trapped, upside down, in a pile of snow. Just after he had resigned himself to the fact that his life was over, he was saved and taken home by a Turkish soldier. This humiliation inflicted on him by the enemy influenced his decision to leave his emotions behind in the pile of snow and to concentrate on his calling with an increased and focused impact: "Am nächsten Tag war der Attentäter wieder auf seinem Posten. Diesmal steckte er einen Stein in jeden Schneeball, spuckte drauf und presste die Masse fest. Er hatte seine Berufung gefunden" (Dische 2000, 9) [On the next day the assassin was back at his post. This time he put a stone in each snowball, spat on it and formed a hard ball. He'd found his calling]. Thus, Alan's decision to become a contract killer and Kemal's calling as a PI seem to have been influenced by rather similar circumstances. Alan is also faced with an ethnic "double consciousness" that distances him from the signifying system he is required to use. As a consequence, like Kemal, he is also alienated from himself; this is illustrated by his attempt to discard an integral (that is, the emotional) part of his self in the snow-pile scene.

Despite the similarities between the protagonists' ethnic locations, there are also some fundamental differences: while Kemal keeps oscillating between clearly defined positions within a dichotomous frame of ethnic reference, Alan is exposed to a more complex grid of conflicting cultural discourses. This dissimilarity accounts for differences in Kemal's and Alan's "appropriately fractured sense of self." Kemal has to face smaller crises, but is—on the whole—always able to reconcile his dual internal discourses of identity; throughout the novel this enables him to compensate by means of hard-boiled behavior patterns for what he perceives as shortcomings occasioned by his conflicted ethnicity. Alan's development, on the other hand, can be characterized as a downward trend, betraying an increasing disintegration of his fragile identity as he finds it very difficult to handle the impact of the conflicting discourses exerted on him. He has a long way to go before—at the end of the novel—he finds emotional rest as an "American" husband and father, the owner of a gas station who is proud of having been awarded a prize for productivity and cleanliness.

While he is still in his "home country," Alan's ethnic identification, like Kemal's, is of a rather ambivalent, yet still only dual, nature. It does, however, become more complex when Alan is sent to the United States to pay back his fellow Kurdish countrymen for helping him flee from prison in Istanbul. In New York he finds out that his former (dual) system of ethnic identification does not seem to apply anymore. And he has a difficult task ahead of him. He not only has to cope with the cultural difference of a place whose way of life (let alone language) are totally unfamiliar to him, but he also faces the problem of having to accomplish a very difficult job after an orientation period of only six days: he is supposed to kill the wife and children of the former Turkish governor of a Kurdish province. The insignificance of his "real" cultural identity in his new surroundings is illustrated by the "brand new German passport" (Dische 2000, 12) that he has received as part of his cover. Moreover, he has to adopt the name Alan Korkunç, along with a fabricated biography.[6]

Although these and other circumstances contribute to the slow disintegration of his original ethnic identity, he does, at least for some time, succeed in defying the inevitable identity crisis by displacing his anxieties by means of hard-boiled behavior. When he is finally able to reduce the conflicting discourses that constitute his (ethnic) identity, he actually learns to come to terms with them. This process of acculturation, ultimately, sets the stage for an unexpectedly happy ending that indicates that the protagonist has learned to resolve the arbitrariness of a formerly chaotic and disturbing choice of ethnic identifications.

Before the hard-boiled protagonist "self-deconstructs" at the end of the novel by having a nervous breakdown and failing to accomplish the assassination, he often experiences exclusion and a lack of orientation. Having provided Alan with the new passport, Mr. Ballinger, his client, shows him his "official car," a taxi. When Alan, who has never driven any cars other than Mercedes Benzes, immediately becomes indignant about this insult, Mr. Ballinger, who is not a Kurd but speaks all four Kurdish languages, tells him, "Aber Leute, die kein Englisch sprechen, fahren in New York nun mal Taxi" (15) [In New York, a taxi is the only appropriate car to drive for people who don't speak English]. After that he says something in English to his buddies, whereupon there was "Großes Gelächter. Unsagbare Isolation, wenn andere lachen, und du verstehst nicht, warum" (16) [Loud laughter. Unspeakable isolation when others laugh and you don't know why]. Alan's inability to speak and understand English is a crucial aspect that excludes him from the powerful and threatening discourse, renders him helpless, and accounts for his increasing disintegration. His unstable system of ethnic identification has dissolved even more, and thus, for Alan, discourse functions, as "[a system] of exclusion, [which] concern[s] that part of discourse which deals with power and desire" (Foucault 1972, 220).

Having no access to the English language, Alan is thus faced with a much more difficult situation than Kemal, as far as the availability of language itself (as a particular form of discourse) is concerned. This feeling of unbelonging is intensified when Alan, in the fashion of a solitary wanderer, drives through New York for the first time. Assuming a traditionally male-connoted sun, the following scene evokes an autoaggressive self-image in the protagonist, which gives the reader insight into the assassin's quite morbid psychological disposition, as Alan inappropriately employs his familiar Kurdish-Turkish system of reference to the topography of New York:

> Das Taxi bog in eine Seitenstraße ein, die auch auf einen Fluss zuführte, einen Fluss so breit wie der Bosporus. Die Sonne schien auf der Wasserober-fläche aufgeschlagen und dort in zwei Teile zerbrochen zu sein. Blutrot färbte sich die Unglücksstelle. Aber der Trick war in Istanbul jeden Tag zu besichtigen. (Dische 2000, 17)

> [The taxi turned into a side street that also went towards a river, a river as wide as the Bosporus. The sun seemed to have hit the surface of the water and been split into two parts. The scene of the accident became bloodred. But this was something you could see in Istanbul any day of the week.]

Alan tries to counteract this process of alienation and disintegration by means of suppressing conflicting cultural discourses (especially those he is excluded from), thus reducing their complexity as well as the arbitrary nature of the signifier-signified relationship. He repeatedly has recourse to a familiar system of reference—rather than an unfamiliar one—in order to express himself "authentically":

> Alan steckte sich in aller Ruhe eine Zigarette an, . . . [z]wischen einzelnen Zügen sang er, um sich zu beruhigen, ein kurdisches Lied, die Ballade von der reichen Jungfrau, die sich in einen armen Schäfer verliebte, aber der arme Schäfer hatte keine Lust. (40)

> [Alan calmly lit up a cigarette; between drags he sang a Kurdish song to calm his nerves—the ballad of the rich virgin who fell in love with a poor shepherd who didn't happen to want her.]

This strategy of using a familiar Kurdish pastoral ballad for stress management is certainly comic in its effect, since it so obviously interferes with the behavior we have come to expect of a hard-boiled assassin.

250   KONSTANZE KUTZBACH

Like Kemal, Alan also employs hard-boiled behavior whenever he feels threatened by cultural difference. Thus, he represses his own feelings of being excluded by othering others. The following scene indicates that he boosts his self-esteem by engaging in sexist and xenophobic thoughts, but it also betrays his sexual attraction:

> [Alan] versetzte dem Hund einen kurzen, gemeinen Tritt in die Rippen, und kein Blitz schoss vom Himmel herab, um ihn für diesen Frevel zu strafen. . . . Endlich war der Weg frei, und Alan betrat den Donut-Shop. . . . Eine Kellnerin in Weiß lehnte hinter dem Tresen. . . . Der eintretende Gast bemerkte mit Vergnügen, dass sie nicht zu dünn war. . . . Das Namensschild an ihrem Revers besagte "Pat." Alan schlenderte hinüber zum Tresen, starrte auf ihre *memik*, was als Kompliment gemeint war. Pat richtete sich auf, legte das Buch weg. Alan war plötzlich verwirrt. So nah hatte er noch nie vor einem solchen Gesicht gestanden. Sie kam aus Afrika. *Kanibal. Yam-yam.* . . . Über Afrika hatte er Horrorgeschichten gehört. Andererseits hatte er aber auch schon Bilder von nackten schwarzen Frauen gesehen. Sie hatten die schönsten Früchte. Die Riesenfeigen hier zum Beispiel steckten mit Sicherheit in Spitzenkörbchen. Er fragte sich, wie wohl die *serimemekin* in der Mitte aussahen. Vermutlich wie harte, dunkle Stiele. Die hätte er gerne gesehen. . . . Auch den duftenden Busch unter ihren Achseln. (Dische 2000, 25–26)

> [{Alan} gave the dog a short, mean kick in the ribs and he was not struck by lightening as punishment for his wrongdoing. . . . Finally there was nothing in the way and Alan went into the donut shop. . . . A waitress in a white uniform was leaning against the counter. . . . Alan noticed with pleasure that she was a bit on the round side. . . . The name tag on her collar read "Pat." He casually walked over staring at her *memik*—which was meant as a compliment. Pat straightened up and put her book away. Alan suddenly felt confused. He had never been so close to such a face before. She was from Africa. *Cannibal. Yum, yum* . . . He'd heard horror stories about Africa. On the other hand, he had seen pictures of naked black women. They had the most luscious fruit. These giant figs must be stashed in lace cups. He wondered what the *serimemekin* at the center looked like. Probably like hard dark stems. He would just love to see them. . . . And the fragrant bush in her armpits.]

Alan's recourse to these pejorative stereotypes—as well as his hard-boiled posturing—can be viewed as a necessary but unsuccessful strategy of trying to maintain his identity and orient himself in an unfamiliar environment.

According to Julia Kristeva's theorization of alterity in *Strangers to Ourselves*, Alan has almost but not quite recognized the "foreigner" in himself:

THE HARD-BOILED PATTERN IN ARJOUNI AND DISCHE   251

Strangely, the foreigner lives within us: he is the hidden face of our identity, the space that wrecks our abode, the time in which understanding and affinity founder. By recognizing him within ourselves, we are spared detesting him in himself. A symptom that precisely turns "we" into a problem, perhaps makes it impossible, [*sic*] The foreigner comes in when the consciousness of my difference arises, and he disappears when we all acknowledge ourselves as foreigners, unamenable to bonds and communities. (qtd. in Oliver 1997, 264)

This process of self-discovery, which goes hand in hand with the increasing disintegration of his hard-boiled identity, is the result of two important developments: he finds a sidekick—simultaneously figuring as alter ego and surrogate mother—in the elderly Mrs. Allen. And he also undergoes a change in his psychosexual disposition that initiates a process of feminization, causing him to discard masculine behavior patterns.

The disintegration of his hard-boiled identity begins when he meets Mrs. Allen, whose last name is a homophone of his first name. Since he (mostly subconsciously) starts to claim the old lady as his alter ego, he necessarily has to get back in touch with discarded feelings and behavior patterns that counteract his hard-boiled "masculine" attitude.

When he first meets Mrs. Allen, who lives next door to him, invites him in, and offers him something to eat, he is astounded by her name. He reluctantly accepts her offer and finds out some major and minor biographical details about her: she is an atheist and speaks Turkish (but she does not speak Alan's home dialect, Kurmanci). Her son, whom she will probably never see again in her life, is about the same age as Alan. Upon his next encounter with Mrs. Allen, he is shocked to find himself acting very unlike the hard-boiled assassin that he is supposed to be:

Aber dann hörte er sie stolpern. . . . Er lief los. . . . Eine braune Einkaufstasche drohte ihr aus der Hand zu rutschen. Alan bekam die Tüte gerade noch zu fassen. Kopfschüttelnd und tief gerührt sah sie ihm zu. Er bot ihr seinen Arm, sie nahm das Angebot an, hielt sich an ihm fest. Alan war über sich selbst empört. Er war nicht nach Amerika gekommen, um anderen Leuten die Einkaufstüten hinterherzutragen, anschließend in deren Wohnung gebeten zu werden und sich dann als unfähig zu erweisen, die Einladung abzulehnen. (Dische 2000, 67–68)

[Then he could hear her stumble. . . . He started running. . . . A brown shopping bag was about to slip out of her hands. Alan caught it just in time. Shaking her head, she looked at him deeply moved. He offered her his arm; she accepted and held on to him. He was mad at himself. He had not come to America to carry other people's shopping bags, to be invited in and to be unable to refuse.]

252   KONSTANZE KUTZBACH

It becomes obvious here that Alan is losing control of his actions and that this is because of his friendship with Mrs. Allen. He shows a fractured sense of self that is psychologically much more complex than it is in Kemal Kayankaya's case. Alan feels his exclusion not only in terms of ethnic but also in terms of emotional belonging. Meeting Mrs. Allen is the starting point for a total disintegration of his old identity and the acquisition of a new one.

Mrs. Allen fascinates Alan mainly because she is tolerant, open-minded, and sophisticated. For Alan she figures as a paradigm that he—although he does not know it at this point—is in search of. Well-versed in the ways of the world, she is a very caring person who does not seem to think in terms of absolutes and therefore appears rather content and authentic. Alan, in contrast, having just arrived in New York, still has a rather limited perspective that is, however, gradually widened by Mrs. Allen. Since language is a central aspect in the protagonist's quest for locating his identity, it is very important for Alan to discover that Mrs. Allen speaks a number of different languages:

> Als Alan, gedankenverloren, nicht sofort darauf antwortete, meinte sie: "Entschuldigen Sie, ich hatte ganz vergessen, dass Sie Kurde sind. Und ich spreche Türkisch mit Ihnen! Vielleicht ist Ihnen ja Persisch lieber?," fragte sie auf Farsi. Wiederum wusste Alan nicht, was er darauf sagen sollte. "Auf jeden Fall freue ich mich, dass wir Nachbarn sind," fügte sie auf Arabisch hinzu. "Nein, Türkisch ist gut," antwortete er, begeistert über ihre magischen Sprachfähigkeiten. (Dische 2000, 70)

> [When Alan, lost in thought, didn't answer right away, she said, "Excuse me, I completely forgot that you are a Kurd. And I'm speaking Turkish with you! Maybe you'd prefer Persian?" she asked in Farsi. Again, Alan didn't know what to say. "In any case I am glad that we are neighbors," she added in Arabic. "No, Turkish is fine," he answered, amazed at her magic command of different languages.]

Alan is, literally, speechless as she presents herself as fluent and comfortable in so many different languages. This, as well as Alan's listening to the stories of her past that she confides to him, fosters his ability to reconcile different value systems and thus help him accept different discourses and their implications. She further tells him, "Mein Mann war Orientalist. Er hatte eine Professur in Wien. Als die Nazis kamen, sind wir nach Istanbul gezogen. . . . Unser Sohn ist in Istanbul geboren" (73) [My husband was a specialist in Oriental studies. He was a professor in Vienna. When the Nazis came, we went to Istanbul. . . . Our son was born there"].

As they develop closer ties to each other, Alan recognizes in Mrs. Allen

THE HARD-BOILED PATTERN IN ARJOUNI AND DISCHE   253

his alter ego and a complementary part of himself—the emotions he has suppressed since his childhood. He defies a hard-boiled convention by choosing her as a rather odd sidekick who will later accompany him as he observes the Turkish family he is supposed to kill. Mrs. Allen teaches him to discard one-way thinking (concerning others and himself), because she represents many different areas of possible alterity (religion, ethnicity, age, sex), within which different interpretations are equally valid. But since Alan had always lived in a world in which good and evil were defined in very dichotomous (ethnic) terms and since he has just been exposed to a severe culture shock in New York, her good example is more than he can put up with for the time being. By exposing him to the idea that absolute truths do not exist—especially in terms of ethnicity—Mrs. Allen causes vast confusion in Alan, who is not used to being confronted with such seemingly arbitrary and conflicting discourses. These divergent discourses force him to redefine the different aspects of his personality—as a Kurd, as an assassin, as a caring being. Therefore, his confusion will eventually culminate in a nervous breakdown.

A second area in which his increasing disintegration is revealed is Alan's psychosexual disposition. As a hard-boiled character, Alan is represented as someone who more often than not opts for the gratification of his sexual urges. This representation is, however, ironically counteracted every now and then. In the following quotation sexual imagery suggesting castration is used to point out Alan's feminization and fear of castration:

> Seit seiner Verhaftung eine Woche zuvor hatte Alan keine Waffe mehr in der Hand gehabt, und dieses unerfüllte Grundbedürfnis ließ ihn sich unvollständig fühlen, als hätte er ein Gliedmaß verloren. Außerdem war er eine Diva und daran gewöhnt, dass die Handlangerdienste von niederen Chargen getan wurden. (Dische 2000, 48–49)

> [Since his arrest a week ago Alan had not held a gun in his hand. Since this basic need had been unfulfilled, he felt incomplete as if he had lost a limb. Besides, he was a diva used to having menial jobs done for him by lowly servants.]

Several scenes indicate how strongly this psychosexual focus influences his thoughts and behavior. The reader learns this through a flashback about the protagonist's rite of (sexual) initiation:

> Aber da [der Körper der Schwester] für ihn tabu war, hielt er sich an das schlechter gesicherte *qunek* der örtlichen Damen—der Esel, Hühner und Schafe. Tatsächlich wurde er an einer schönen braunen Ziege zum Mann. (80)

[But since it {his sister's body} was taboo, he stuck with the more accessible *qunek* of the local ladies—the donkeys, the chickens, and the sheep. In fact, he became a man thanks to a beautiful brown goat.]

Immediately after these reminiscences, his thoughts—as so often—turn to masturbation. To alleviate his sexual guilt and to express discontent with his present way of life, he cuts off his goatee. Alan continues to reflect on his masturbation—this development parallels his increasing psychological disintegration, which is the result of the disparity of the conflicting cultural discourses he is confronted with. But Mrs. Allen's sad story of her missing son introduces him to an expanded meaning of sexuality as linked to love and altruistic motifs, such as the love between mother and son. Mutual (nonsexual) affection becomes evident in their reciprocal relationship, in which they function as surrogate mother and surrogate son. By the end of the novel, Alan has actually learned to sublimate his egocentric libidinal drives and also to use them for procreation, manifest in the birth of his daughter, Eliza.

This discussion of Alan's changing sexual attitudes provides another instance of how his "appropriately fractured sense of self" increasingly disintegrates because he suffers from a double—or rather, multiple—consciousness that goes beyond the initially central focus of ethnicity. Ethnicity is still an important issue, but other aspects of his identity formation have acquired a similar importance. Unlike Kemal, Alan is eventually unable to cope with the impact of his confusion and alienation based on a complex symbolic order that overwhelms him. The hard-boiled pattern does not allow him to locate himself successfully. He eventually has a mental breakdown when he and Mrs. Allen are having dinner in Alan's apartment. This breakdown is triggered by Mrs. Allen's sudden fainting after he has cut himself while trying to open a can. And it indicates that he has almost completely discarded the hard-boiled aspect of his personality—his suppressed agony forcing open his façade of coolness as the highly charged imagery of the following scene (reminiscent of *Harold and Maude*) suggests:

> Dieses nagende Gefühle, das ihn schon den ganzen Tag nicht losgelassen hatte, verstärkte sich, und immer noch konnte er es nicht benennen. Ihm war nur schlecht. Mrs. Allen war tot, von nun an war er wirklich ganz allein. Und er musste ihre Leiche auch noch irgendwo verschwinden lassen. Er trug die Tote in sein Wohnzimmer, legte sie aufs Bett und zog ihr die Turnschuhe aus. Er küsste sie auf die Stirn und auf ihr flaumiges weißes Haar, legte dann seinen Kopf auf ihre Brust. Sein Kummer wuchs. Seine Gelassenheit zeigte Risse, und aus dem Leck begann sein Elend zu tröpfeln. Es wurde zu einer Sturzflut. Die Verzweiflung ist ein tückischer Strom.

Alan rang nach Luft und klammerte sich an sie. Er fing an zu weinen. Nach einer Weile schlug sie die blauen Augen auf und sah ihn an. (Dische 2000, 123)

[This uncomfortable feeling, which he had not been able to shake all day, only got worse and he still couldn't put his finger on it. He was simply sick. Mrs. Allen was dead and from now on he really was totally alone. And he had to get rid of the corpse somewhere, too. He carried her body into the living room, put her on the bed and took off her sneakers. He kissed her forehead and her white hair, rested his head on her breasts. He felt worse and worse. His carefree demeanor was crumbling and his misery was beginning to seep out. The leak became a flood. Despair is a dangerous stream. Alan fought for breath and clutched her body desperately. He started to cry. After a while she opened her blue eyes and looked at him.]

Once Alan has happily regained his alter ego, he and Mrs. Allen eventually fall peacefully asleep in front of the television set. He has reconnected with the dreaded emotions that he had buried in the pile of snow when he was a child. Additional proof of his anxiety is provided later in the novel when Alan finds himself crouching on the kitchen floor after Mr. Ballinger has paid a final threatening visit to him. Mr. Ballinger puts a gun to Alan's head to remind him to actually go through with the assassination. Alan, who has developed an increasingly sane and pragmatic attitude in New York, is now almost ready to reintegrate his fractured sense of self by means of refocusing his multiple consciousness and—in a Foucauldian sense—discarding unnecessary and threatening discourses. In doing so, he eventually manages to feel comfortable in a symbolic order with a clear relation between signifier and signified. The transformation of his identity also affects his outer appearance: "Schließlich rasierte er sich gründlich. Zum ersten Mal seit Jahrzehnten trug er weder Bart noch Koteletten. Er sah aus wie ein Bubi. Wie ein typischer Amerikaner" (153) [Finally he had a good shave. For the first time in years he had neither a beard nor sideburns. He looked like a nice, clean-cut boy—like a typical American].

For fear of being sent back to prison, he still tries to do his job and go through with the assassination, but his contemplations at that point begin to reveal his doubts. He actually goes to the former governor's house but fails to kill the Turkish family: "Aber der Killer hatte schon längst keinen Plan mehr. Er wollte nur, dass dieses Drama ein Ende nahm" (Dische 2000, 159) [But the killer had abandoned his plan a long time ago. He just wanted this to end]. Moreover, the patriotic Kurd is metamorphosing into a very unpolitical and pragmatic person: "Alan zog ein gutes Auto allemal einem eigenen Staat vor" (136) [Alan simply preferred a good car to Kurdish nationhood].

Together with Mrs. Allen, he flees from New York and settles in Nevada in the middle of nowhere, where he finally ends up living the idyllic life of a husband and father of a little daughter. Here the reader witnesses an ironic reversal of his earlier statement. He had once thought, "Alan braucht nicht zu Englisch zu gehen, Englisch geht zu Alan" (Dische 2000, 32) [Alan doesn't need to go to English; English will come to Alan]. But he then discovered that "Nach einer Weile kam auch das Englisch zu Alan. Er hieß es willkommen" (164) [After a while English actually did come to Alan and he welcomed it]. This increasing coherence within the protagonist's symbolic order, however, is reflected not only in his acquisition of the English language, but also in his identification with the American notion of "rags-to riches."

Alan has now successfully managed to reconcile the contradictions he had been exposed to and has created the best of all possible worlds, a moderate yet authentic one, in which he owns a gas station and is awarded, "die Jim-Smith-Medaille für Produktivität und den Joel-Elliot-Preis für die saubersten Toiletten. . . . An einen hervorragenden Menschen. Mr. Douglas Allen" (Dische 2000, 168) [the Jim Smith Medal for productivity and the Joel Elliot Prize for the cleanest toilets. . . . To an outstanding person. Mr. Douglas Allen]. This passage, written in a style exaggerated to the point of caricature, represents Alan as totally assimilated to the U.S. system of values—even to the point of, in true immigrant style, changing his name. This value system provides a reduced, yet appropriately coherent, interpretation of the formerly arbitrary relationship between signifier and signified.

The protagonists of *Happy Birthday, Turk!* and *Ein Job* clearly represent different degrees of hard-boiled behavior. Kemal conforms to the behavior patterns of the hard-boiled detective, but there are occasional overtones of irony regarding his actions. The protagonist's fractured sense of self caused by his ethnic unbelonging leads to a lack of orientation that is expressed in hard-boiled behavior. He suffers from a double consciousness because he oscillates between the signifying systems of two different ethnicities. But, unlike Alan's, Kemal's ethnic locatedness remains binary and therefore comparatively stable and reliable. Since he always manages to reconcile dichotomous discourses within himself, he is able to avoid severe mental pain.

In *Ein Job*, however, there is much more emphasis on the personality makeup of the protagonist; this renders Alan's psychological development more complex and sophisticated. Alan's sense of ethnic unbelonging is much more acute, since his symbolic order is constituted of a more disparate grid of identity-forming discourses. Struggling to redefine himself in the foreign surroundings of New York, he moves away from the hard-boiled behavior pattern and eventually totally discards it. His hard-boiled attitude initially serves to protect him from threatening ethnic discourses, but it eventually becomes inadequate because he finds a new "authenticity" in and through his alter ego, Mrs. Allen. Unlike Kemal, Alan is afflicted not only with a double consciousness, but with a multiple one that renders the signifier-signified relationship of his symbolic order even more arbitrary and confuses him completely. His situation culminates in a nervous break-down that, ultimately, allows him to relocate himself by means of reducing the conflicting discourses exerted on him. The psychological development that enables his idyllic life in Nevada is again conveyed in snow imagery, but with changed implications. The near-death experience that he had as a child trapped in the pile of snow is fundamentally life-threatening, but in this scene "the snow," as Meyer-Gosau points out in her review of *Ein Job*, is entirely harmless, because it comes out of the freezer (2001, 115): "[Alan] blieb kurz an der Eismaschine stehen und nahm sich eine Hand voll Kunst-schnee heraus" (Dische 2000, 167) [{Alan} stopped for a moment at the ice-maker and took out a handful of crushed ice]. Ultimately, the novel effects an ironic reversal of the traditional hard-boiled formula, which, ac-cording to Grella, ends in disaster: "[The hard-boiled detective] does not find the Edenic land of his dreams, the Great Good Place of the American imagination, but the Great Bad Place. . . . He finds the American Dream metamorphosed into the American Nightmare" (1950, 112–13).

Both novels contribute to the generic modification of the detective novel because they alter its traditional characteristics. In *Happy Birthday, Turk!* the hard-boiled pattern is to some extent counteracted through irony. This becomes apparent especially in the way in which the solution of the murders is handled. Kemal sympathizes with his fellow Turks and applies his own moral standards, finally letting one of his Turkish countrymen get away with murder. But the novel, nevertheless, conforms to the traditional pattern by foregrounding the detective plot rather than the psychological conception of the protagonist. *Happy Birthday, Turk!* maintains the hard-boiled pattern, but utilizes irony and comic effects derived from its ethnic component.

Ein Job, however, provides a much more significant modification of the hard-boiled detective genre. The author focuses on the psychological etiology of the failure of a hard-boiled assassin rather than on a conven-tional detective plot. The novel consistently mocks and counteracts the protagonist's hard-boiled behavior as well as his ethnopolitical bias. Ethnicity is an important issue in the protagonist's life and for the novel, but it is not put on the pedestal of political correctness, which, at least to my mind, renders the novel more convincing in terms of the fictional rep-resentation of alterity. Moreover, *Ein Job* does not suggest value judgments regarding the workings of power in view of different aspects of subalternity, since the protagonist often finds himself in the position of the subject as well as the object, the excluder as well as the excluded, the assassin as well as the victim—in short, neither the protagonist nor the author suggests a moral solution. This is something Alan has finally accepted when he settles in the best of all possible—though also ironicized—American worlds.

NOTES

1. *Ein Job* was originally written in English but has been published exclusively in German translation. All translations in brackets have been provided by the editors of this volume.

2. Although Du Bois's model refers to blacks, it applies to other "visible" ethnicities as well.

3. This is in keeping with de Saussure's assumption of the arbitrary nature of linguistic reference: "Saussure proposed that reference is not a necessary relationship between a word and a thing, but an arbitrary relationship between a word and a concept; the signifier and the signified have an arbitrary relationship. Meaning is the result of a system of differences without any positive terms" (Oliver 1997, xii–xiii).

4. Oliver relates Heidegger's assumption that "language is not a mere instrument for the communication of information. Rather, language is the unfolding of meaning itself, including the meaning of human experience. We do not speak language; rather, language speaks us" (1997, xii).

5. Yilmaz despised Ahmed because Yilmaz's father, Vasif, always preferred his son-in-law to him.

6. The name Alan has implications in both American and Kurdish culture: "Wie immer. Alan. Mem Alan, König der Kurden! Aber Alan ist auch ein guter amerikanischer Name" (Dische 2000, 15) [As usual. Alan. Mem Alan, King of the Kurds! But it is also a good old American name].

WORKS CITED

Arjouni, Jakob. [1985] 1996. *Happy Birthday, Turk!* Trans. Anselm Hollo. Harpenden, U.K.: No Exit Press.

Cohen, Michael. 1999. "The Detective as the Other: The Detective versus the Other." In Klein 1999, 145–57.

Dische, Irene. 2000. *Ein Job.* Hamburg: Hoffmann und Campe.

Du Bois, W. E. B. [1903] 1996. *The Souls of Black Folk.* New York: Penguin.

Foucault, Michel. 1972. *The Archaeology of Knowledge and the Discourse on Language.* New York: Pantheon Books.

Grella, George. 1950. "The Hard-Boiled Detective Novel." In *Detective Fiction: A Collection of Critical Essays*, edited by Robin W. Winks, 103–20. Englewood Cliffs, N.J.: Prentice-Hall.

Klein, Kathleen Gregory, ed. 1999. *Diversity and Detective Fiction.* Bowling Green, Ohio: Bowling Green State University Popular Press.

Kristeva, Julia. 1991. *Strangers to Ourselves*. Translated by Leon S. Roudiez. New York: Harvester Wheatsheaf.

Meyer-Gosau, Frauke. 2001. "Der Schnee fällt aus der Kühltruhe." *Literaturen* 3–4 (March–April): 115–16.

Oliver, Kelly. 1997. Introduction to *The Portable Kristeva*, edited by Oliver Kelly, xi–xxix. New York: Columbia University Press.

Pepper, Andrew. 1999. "Bridges and Boundaries: Race, Ethnicity, and the Contemporary American Crime Novel." In Klein 1999, 240–59.

Wells, Claire. 1999. "Writing Black: Crime Fiction's Other." In Klein 1999, 205–23.

Frenchness and Arab Alterity in Jean-Christophe Grangé's *Blood-Red Rivers*

DOROTHEA FISCHER-HORNUNG

A cop is always a headache. And an Arab cop is a fucking migraine.
—Jean-Christophe Grangé, *Blood-Red Rivers*

Come on, Susie, border cities always bring out the worst in a country!
—*Touch of Evil*, directed by Orson Welles

No one today is purely *one* thing.
—Edward Said, *Culture and Imperialism*

A FRENCH CRIME NOVEL OPENS WITH CROWDS CHANTING IN SPANISH: *GANAMOS* ("We won"). The Paris police are using military maneuvers in their attempt to keep apart two non-French teams, Saragossa and Arsenal, a "marching army" with "absolute lack of accountability" (Grangé [1998] 2000, 2) that is "attacking with their fists, iron bars and steel toecaps" (4). It is in the midst of this pitched multinational battle with fans, whose uncontrolled violence characterizes many European soccer matches,[1] that the reader is introduced to Superintendent Pierre Niémans—at the very moment he loses control:

> He struck with his fist, with his truncheon. He knocked down a big lad, then laid straight into him, hitting his ribs, his belly and face. He was suddenly kicked from the right. Screaming, he got to his feet. His baton wrapped itself around his aggressor's throat. His blood boiled in his head, a metallic taste numbed his mouth. His mind was empty. He felt nothing. He was at war and he knew it. (5)

When a rival hooligan uses his machete to attack, "relentlessly slicing into the man on his knees" (5), and subsequently throws the body over the rail-

FRENCHNESS AND ARAB ALTERITY IN GRANGÉ   261

ing of a bridge, Niémans follows the perpetrator into a horse stable. When the rampaging fan slashes at Niémans, he misses and hits the horse, which then kicks the hooligan:

> The officer grabbed his chance, threw himself onto the man, turned round his gun and used it as a hammer. Again and again he hit him, then suddenly stopped and looked down at the hooligan's bloodied features. His bones were sticking up through the shreds of his skin. An eyeball dangled down on a mess of fibres. . . . The murderer was now motionless. Niémans grabbed back hold of his gun, took its blood-stained grip in both hands and rammed the barrel into the man's split mouth. He took off the latch and closed his eyes. He was about to fire when a shrill noise interrupted him. In his pocket, his cell phone was ringing. (7–8)

This is certainly crime fiction in the super-hard-boiled category. Yet, much like the uncontrolled violence of the soccer hooligans, this is not an isolated incident of out-of-control violence on the part of the police officer: "For the thousandth time, he thought how Rheim's phone call had certainly stopped him from killing someone. He thought about his uncontrollable fits of violence, which blinded his conscience, ripping apart time and space, causing him to commit outrageous acts" (10–11).

Niémans attempts to come to grips with the violence that so closely ties the police officer as a law enforcer with those who break the law, but he remains a lonely street warrior who operates on the fine line that separates legality from illegality. After killing his first man, he decides that "[n]o, he would never be a proud warrior, a valiant army officer. But he would be a restless, obstinate street fighter, who would drown his own fears in the violence and the fury of the concrete jungle" (Grangé [1998] 2000, 27). -

Six chapters and one atrocious fetishized murder later, two seemingly insignificant crimes are committed in Sarzac, a small French village several hundred kilometers to the west. Grangé introduces a second police officer, Karim Abdouf, who, like Niémans, operates on the borderlines and who will investigate a seemingly unrelated case of apparent grave desecration and a robbery in a local school. Abdouf is an orphaned, "young, second generation Arab" (Grangé [1998] 2000, 44) raised in a French home run by Catholic nuns in Nanterre, one of the desolate contemporary ghettos on the fringes of Paris, a "colorless, graceless neighborhood . . . a world peopled by ultra-violent beings, inaccessible estates, blood-stained cellars" (45–46). The mean streets of classic noir are now the drab, underclass high-rise suburbs of Paris populated by the French who often originate in the former colonies—the colonial margins that now haunt the center, the metropole.

262   DOROTHEA FISCHER-HORNUNG

Two plots, two locations, and two detectives alternately vie for the reader's attention throughout much of the novel, a structural complexity that heightens the suspense for the reader who knows that the two plots must inevitably come together. Two very French detectives, exiled respectively to two very French villages, are played off one against the other. One of those French officers happens to be an Arab:

> Karim was a lost child. Or a foundling. It all depended on which way round you looked at it. Whichever, he had never known his parents and nothing in the education that he subsequently received had served to remind him of his origins. He could not speak Arabic very well and he had only the vaguest knowledge of Islam. The adolescent had rapidly rejected his guardians—the carers in the home, whose simplicity and general niceness made him want to puke—and he had given himself over to the streets. (Grangé [1998] 2000, 45)

Grangé leaves no doubt that for his environment Karim Abdouf is reduced to his physical appearance—a second-generation Arab from the Maghreb[2]— yet culturally he is undeniably French.[3] Nevertheless, Grangé undercuts this seemingly easy ethnic divide by styling Abdouf as a six-foot-tall Arab in Rastafarian garb, "[a] devil sprung out of the Caribbean" (55), complete with his woolly cap in the colors of the Jamaican African diaspora, dreadlocks, and multiple earrings—a man certainly not easy to place: "At twenty-one, Karim passed his law degree. What now? Lawyers would not take on a six feet six tall Arab, as slim as a rake, with a goatee, dreadlocks and his ears full of rings, even as a messenger boy" (48).

Karim Abdouf's appearance is certainly based on his biological roots in the Maghreb, but his getup is decidedly performative. He chooses to emphasize neither of the two most obvious potential garbs—that of a Frenchman or an Arab. Rather, he chooses to mimic a Rastafarian, whose religion of peace and love in the Jamaican diaspora is, like his "Arabness," an affront in its unsettling mimicry.[4]

Citing Lacan, Homi Bhabha points out that mimicry reveals something that is similar yet decidedly distinct and refracted from what is being mimicked, entailing elements of aggression as well: "The effect of mimicry is camouflage. . . . It is not a question of harmonizing with the background, but against a mottled background, of becoming mottled—exactly like the technique of camouflage practiced in human warfare" (1994, 85). The better the colonized other knows the colonizer the more likely mimicry is to become mockery.

Much like Niémans, who had been rejected by the French army and therefore joined the Paris police force, Abdouf decides to become a cop because his chances of being a lawyer in bourgeois French society are essentially nonexistent. His desire to leave the "mean streets" is made impossible by society's inability to accept his challenge to bourgeois Frenchness:

> He would then live in that same arcane universe, but sheltered from the laws he despised, and hidden from the country he wanted to spit on. One thing he had never forgotten from his childhood was this: he had no origins, no homeland, no family. He was a land unto himself, and his country was limited to his own breathing space. (Grangé [1998] 2000, 48)

Not only are the doors to the French middle class closed to Abdouf, but the French police subject him to racial profiling, limiting his choice of possible professional activities. They suggest he join

> the anti-terror brigade—so that he could infiltrate the Islamic fundamentalists in suburban hotspots. Immigrant cops were too rare a commodity to miss out on this chance. He refused. . . . Karim wanted to roam through the kingdoms of the night, go after killers and face them on their own turf, wander off into that parallel world which was also his own. (53)

One of his first acts as a police officer is to revenge the death of Marcel, a friend from the streets, an AIDS-infected "peroxide skinhead" who listened to Liszt's *Hungarian Rhapsodies* (47). Abdouf hunts down the drug addicts who had killed and tortured Marcel. In prose that certainly measures up to the mega-hard-boiled description of Niémans's violence, Grangé describes Abdouf's motivation:

> The little fuckers would never have imagined that one of Marcel's mates was a cop. Nor would they have imagined that this cop would have no bones about killing them, both for old times' sake, and from a personal conviction that life just should not be that fucking awful. (50)

> Karim shot him twice in the face. He got the bullets back out of the burnt fibres of the mattress, stuffed the burning-hot cases into his pocket then left without looking back. (52)

Much like in the Western, the combination in a single figure of the outlaw and the detective is often a defining feature of the modern, hard-boiled detective story:

> The inner life of the figure is that of the outlaw, whose perspective is that of a victim of social justice. He has seen the underside of American democracy and capitalism and can tell the difference between law and justice. Yet he also embodies the politics of the police detective, the belief that we need order, some kind of code to live by if we are to keep from degenerating into

264   DOROTHEA FISCHER-HORNUNG

a government of pure muscle and money. (Slotkin, quoted in Walton and
Jones 1999, 191)

In addition to the loner and outlaw motif, the doppelgänger and mirror are
undoubtedly central tropes in a genre where appearances—both false and
true—are the core of the construction of suspense and mystery. Grangé
pulls all stops on the doppelgänger theme: a set of twins who were separated at birth in a diabolical eugenic plot, but who also function as femmes
fatales; two outsider, loner cops, both of whom have trouble controlling
their isolated fits of violent anger and retribution and have even killed under extremely questionable circumstances.

The novel is populated by a seemingly unending array of loners. Cro-
zier, Karim's boss, an ex-soldier with no wife or children, is described as
follows:

> The solitude attracted Karim, but it was their only point in common. Apart
> from that, the Chief was every inch a narrow-minded, chauvinistic police-
> man. The sort of bloodhound who would like to be reincarnated as a pit-
> bull.
> Karim knocked and entered his office. An iron filing cabinet. The smell
> of scented tobacco. Posters of the glory of the French police force contain-
> ing stiff, badly photographed figures. The Arab felt vaguely sick once more.
> (Grangé [1998] 2000, 66)

The juxtaposition of two protagonists, one representing the more socially
restricted, conventional personality and the other embodying the often less
restricted, sometimes even criminal self, is characteristic of many crime
novels. But this may be much less applicable in ethnic crime fiction that
focuses on the particular situation of a frequently double or triple outsider
detective. In Grangé, much like in Walter Mosley through his doubling of
Easy Rawlins and his almost pathologically outlawed doppelgänger Mouse,[5]
neither cop is by any standards free or unrestricted in his twinned alienation from Frenchness and Arab alterity. Precisely the opposite holds true.
These cops may be unattached loners, but they are caught in the collective,
existential alienation of modern society—victims of their estrangement
while guilty of violent transgression. In contrast, the murder victims seem
to be innocent, but they are, we are soon to learn, guilty of a much greater,
unseen, structural, societal brutality. Niémans sees the overall process of
detection as one great mirrored reflection and refraction:

> Look this is the way I see things. When a murder has been committed, you
> have to look at every surrounding detail as though it was a mirror. The
> body of the victim, the people who knew him, the scene of the crime. . . .

FRENCHNESS AND ARAB ALTERITY IN GRANGÉ   265

> Everything reflects the truth, some particular aspect of the murder, see what I mean? . . . We're in a hall of mirrors, Joisneau, a labyrinth of reflected images. So take a good look. At everything. Because somewhere inside one of those mirrors, in a dead angle, the murderer is hiding. (25)

The doppelgänger motif is constantly underscored by references throughout the novel to the refracted broken images of globalization. Refracted doubleness is emphasized in the theme of French national borderlands and postcolonial alterity. Guernon, located near Grenoble, marks the border between France, with its colonial history, and Switzerland, with its banking and financial network connected to profits based both on the war industries and exterminated Jews. Germany, the Holocaust, and the ideology of racial superiority is not far away. Like the used-to-be police officers Sam Spade or Chester Himes's detective pair, Grave Digger Jones and the scarred and violent Coffin Ed Johnson, Pierre Niémans and Karim Abdouf are put out to graze in the liminal borderlands after they have overstepped the boundaries set to the use of force and violence by the police, borders which are implicit in an officer's duty to enforce the laws of civil society.[6] For Niémans it was a life sentence to die of boredom, "For any other cop, a post in a central office was a promotion. For him, it was being put out to grass—plush grass, admittedly, but the move had still mortified him" (12). For Abdouf, transferred to Sarzac,[7] in the "*département* of the Lot . . . a region where the trains did not stop any more," (53) the effect is very much the same:

> the lousiest prison of all: a small provincial town, as boring as shit, in the midst of a rocky plain. A prison with neither walls nor bars. A psychological prison which was gnawing away at his soul. (44)

> [T]his region was an insult to Karim's personality. He was second-generation Arab, off the street, nothing could be stranger to him than this two-bit provincial town. (53)

It is the inability of both cops to control their alienated personality, a reflection of the late-twentieth-century *condition humaine,* that makes them at one and the same time both the outlaw and the enforcer of social value. But it is the alienated, isolated outlaw who remains most clearly in the reader's mind—a fundamental tension that is characteristic of hard-boiled fiction:

> The internal structure of the police, while altered to fit its particular needs, retains strong ties to the dominant social framework. Such mirroring guarantees the continuity of the contractual relationship. . . . Becoming a police officer, then, requires an expected, deep-seated adherence to society's dominant ideals and practices, as well as demands an intense, all-encompassing

266   DOROTHEA FISCHER-HORNUNG

> allegiance to the specific communal values of law enforcement. (Betz 1999, 87)

Grangé clearly situates his officers beyond the public pale, beyond communal values. Yet it is this very potential to test the limits that makes Niémans a living legend, albeit an ambiguous one, for younger police officers. When he reaches the scene of the crime in Guernon, he is immediately recognized by the young officer guarding the scene of the crime. This junior officer cheekily reminds Niémans of his legendary status, even if he is now a has-been: "The ex-star of the anti-terrorist squad. The ex-head of the vice squad. The ex-hunter of killers and dealers. The ex of a lot of things, in fact. . . . You know you are an idol, don't you? The 'supercop'" ([1998] 2000, 14).

If the detectives in Grangé's novel seem far from ordinary—a violent French police legend who can barely control his own violent tendencies and a six-foot Rastafarian Arab-French cop—the murder victims initially seem to be totally unremarkable Frenchmen: a university librarian and an orderly in the local hospital. Yet it is these invisible, totally unobtrusive citizens, the seeming victims, who are the perpetrators of a far greater violence than anything the reader has witnessed by way of violent excess on the part of cops or soccer hooligans.

Each corpse is first seen indirectly, mirrored symbolically and placed in ritualized positions with fetishized mutilations inflicted on them: the first is found mirrored in a lake that lies below where the corpse had been wedged in the fetal position in the mountains overlooking the university; the second is found when it is mirrored in the ice of a crevasse through which Niémans is later guided by Fanny, who is subsequently revealed to be one of the doppelgänger twins and the murderer:

> In the transparent wall, a veritable mirror of white water, the shape of a body imprisoned in the ice suddenly surged out. In the foetal position. Its mouth was voicing a silent scream. The incessant shallow torrent that passed over the image distorted that vision of a bruised and battered corpse. (Grangé [1998] 2000, 143)

The similar appearance of the victims leads the police to believe that either a sexual motive or an American-style serial killer[8] is at work: "Same age. Same pointed features. Same hair cut. Two slim, handsome young men whose expression seemed to conceal some hidden anxieties" (145).

But not only have the bodies all been positioned symbolically, as well as tortured; their eyes have been excised from their sockets and their hands either lack fingerprints or have been cut off, robbing them of their identity. In a tour de force on the theme of reflection and refraction, Chernecé, a

FRENCHNESS AND ARAB ALTERITY IN GRANGÉ 267

famous ophthalmologist, a murderer himself, and subsequently also the third murder victim, explains to Niémans:

> Our eyes and our hands are the only two unique parts of our anatomy. . . . They are the only parts of our bodies to have a biological, or biometric signature, as the specialists put it. Deprive a body of its eyes and hands, and you take away its external markers. Now, what is a man who dies without such markers? Nobody. An anonymous corpse, which has lost its personal identity. Even its soul, perhaps. Who knows? In some ways, it is the worst possible end. An unmarked, common grave of dead flesh. (Grangé [1998] 2000, 209)

In addition, the eye sockets have been filled with water or glass. In the first case, the victim's eye sockets have been filled with water containing pollutants that could not have come from Guernon or are characteristic of a time thirty-five years earlier when acid rain was caused by Central or Eastern European industries. This peculiarity leads to the discovery of the second corpse, in whose eye sockets particles of glass are found. Later in the novel, the third crucified body, the body of Dr. Chernecé, is found by Niémans reflected in the conservatory rotunda. "'[E]vil,' 'violence,' 'torture' and 'ritual' . . . 'water', 'eyes' and 'purity'" (83) become the key words Niémans asks his investigators to pursue in the university library. This also provides the reader with clues to work with in trying to solve the mystery as well—one of the primary pleasures for readers of crime fiction.

Undoubtedly, the fundamental question in the detective novel as a genre is one of identity. Yet the fundamental question "Who done it?" can turn, especially in ethnic crime fiction, into a more profound question about society. And, again as in many other ethnic crime novels, it is not the immediate crime that is at the center of Grangé's plot, but rather a greater societal or historical crime. Implicitly, this is already inherent in the tension caused by societal corruption in classic hard-boiled fiction, but it acquires a specific focus in ethnic crime fiction. In discussing the novels of Tony Hillerman, Wayne Templeton notes:

> So, like Dashiell Hammett, whose existential protagonists realize that they are solving lesser crimes such as murder in a corrupt society in which there exist unsolved far more effective crimes involving crooked politicians, cops, and business people, Hillerman uses crimes as a metaphor for crime— small for large—and has created detectives whose main purpose is not solving the lesser crimes but constantly pointing out the larger ones and revealing how they continue to victimize. (1999, 39)

From the onset Grangé creates a racially charged atmosphere that points to a far more diabolical, invisible, societal, and racially motivated eugenic

268   DOROTHEA FISCHER-HORNUNG

crime—the attempt to create a "super race." The architecture of the university in Guernon is reminiscent of monumental Nazi architecture of the 1930s and has "Stalinist dimensions" ([1998] 2000, 38); the gym is described as a bunker (37). Niémans notices photos in the entrance hall of the first victim's university residence:

> The black and white photographs apparently dating from the 1930s or 1940s. Olympic athletes in full flight spiraled into the sky, or dug their heels into the grounds, in postures of religious pride. Their faces, figures and positions gave off a sort of worrying perfection, the inhuman purity of statues. (38)

The reference is, of course, to Leni Riefenstahl's 1938 film *Fest der Völker* (also released as *Götter des Stadions*)[9] about the 1936 Berlin Olympic games. The stills from this film, which still exude much of their original atavistic power today, mesh with the topic of Rémy Caillois's thesis on the history of the Olympic games. Sophie Caillois, his wife, explains:

> His thesis was about the relationship between the sporting event and the sacred. Between the body and the mind. He was studying the myth of the *athlon,* the first man who made the earth fertile by his own strength, by transcending the limits of his own body. . . . Rémy said that those Games had revived the profound nature of the Games of Olympus, which are based on the marriage of mind and body, of physical effort and philosophical expression. (41)

In tune with his generalized suspicion of intellectuals[10] and their neat solutions, Niémans inquires if this is not Nazi ideology. Sophie Caillois explains Rémy Callois's clear separation not of mind and body, but of philosophy separated from its real-life ideological implications and political applications: "'The nature of the thought being expressed didn't matter to my husband. All he was interested in was that fusion of an idea and a force, of thought and action.' This sort of clap-trap meant nothing to Niémans" (41).

It is also the *athlon* that establishes an indirect connection to the violence portrayed in the opening scene of the novel—not the Olympic perfection of the pure unity of mind and body but rather the reality of football rowdyism: "For example, the *athlon,* the ideal athlete, could unleash the hidden powers of the earth by surpassing his own physical limitations. Mind you, when you see the hysteria at some football matches, it really does seem as though sport sets off strange forces . . ." (Grangé [1998] 2000, 200–201).

Much later in the investigation it is not only the nightmare of the rampaging, murdering sports fans and the result of his own uncontrolled violence that haunt Niémans—these photos become Niémans's nightmare:

The German photographer's pictures had taken on flesh. Athletes with shaven heads were running in the pre-war Berlin stadium. Nimble. Powerful. The race had fallen into the rhythm of an old flickering movie, with grainy images, coloured like the covering of a tomb. He watched the men run. He heard their heels on the track. He sensed their hoarse breathing, beating in counter-point to their strides. But soon other confusing details appeared. Their faces were too somber, too rigid. Their brows were too strong, too prominent. What lay behind their staring eyes? As a deep, hysterical cheering started up among the spectators, the athlete's eyes suddenly seemed to have been ripped out, their sockets were empty, but this does not stop them from seeing or from running on. Instead, within those gaping wounds, things were apparently swarming around . . . tongues clicked . . . scales gleamed. . . . (Grangé [1998] 2000, 195)

Much later in his investigation, Niémans encounters Dr. Champelaz, an ophthalmologist who runs a local eye hospital and who studied the degenerative eye diseases prominent among his patients. Champelaz had observed that over the years the exclusive isolation of the university elite, who married within their own exclusive circles, had led to genetic degeneration based on inbreeding. This degeneration had been suddenly, inexplicably, reversed in the last generation: "The children of the university families have magically become extremely strong, while the offspring of the country folk have become corrupted. . . . It is as if the children of the university were robbing their little neighbors of their life force" (260).

Although Dr. Champelaz suspected strongly that something inexplicable was occurring, he never pursued his suspicions—an example of the "silent majority" who go along and therefore make infamy possible: "Chernecé belonged to the university elite, you understand? He was one of the region's most eminent ophthalmologists. A prestigious professor. As for me, I-just look after this little place . . ." (263). In face of the power wielded by the university elite, he chose not to see the obvious, not to pursue his horrific suspicions about these "genetic vampires" (311).

He failed in his human and civic duty as so many Germans did when they closed their eyes to what was going on around them under the Nazis. Such silent complicity made the Holocaust possible and lends particular weight to the inscription found in the notebook of Philippe Sertys, the second victim:

WE ARE THE MASTERS, WE ARE THE SLAVES.
WE ARE EVERYWHERE, WE ARE NOWHERE.
WE ARE THE SURVEYORS.
WE CONTROL THE BLOOD-RED RIVERS. (Grangé [1998] 2000, 161)

The most unobtrusive of good citizens "brought together the grey matter of Guernon and the bodily vigour of the outlying villages, to fuse together the academics' brain power and the natives' physical prowess" (307). In a diabolical plot, they not only set up marriages between selected students and programmed the births, they went even further in that they switched babies and smothered the degenerate progeny of the academics. In their lowly jobs they could control the destinies of the entire region, making of the slaves masters and masters of the slaves. The eugenic crimes become the bloodred rivers of the title.

Grangé picks up the theme of the vital genetic code physically inherent in these mountain folk by attributing to their genes the ability to vitalize and strengthen the degenerate gene pool of the university's academic elite clique. They supply the strong "body" required to meld with the degenerated, weakened genes of the "mind."[11] The diabolical plot of the bloodred rivers is modeled closely on the *Lebensborn*, centers where young women who were "racially pure" according to Nazi criteria could meet and bear children with SS officers. These children were then raised in nurseries to further the creation of the *Herrenrasse*.[12]

It is through the racialized nature of the crimes investigated by Niémans and Abdouf that their two cases are eventually joined. Abdouf sums up what the reader has known from the outset:

> "And as far as mirrors are concerned, our two investigations go together like this."
> He put out his two palms and pointed them slowly towards each other.
> "They're mirror reflections, get me? And in one of the dead angles, Jesus I'll bet on it, the murderer is lurking." (Grangé [1998] 2000, 216)

Karim Abdouf is investigating the mysterious burglary in a school, where seemingly nothing much is stolen but for a few records. On the same day a sepulcher is broken into in the town's cemetery. Abdouf's discussion with Sélier, a fellow officer, concerning Jude Ithero, the name on the grave, is strongly gendered and racialized:

> "That's a girl's name, isn't it?"
> "No, it's a boy's name."
> "But it's English, no?"
> "No, Jewish."
> Sélier wiped his forehead.
> "Jesus Christ, is this a desecration like the one in Carpentras?[13] Some extreme right-wing loonies?" (60)

In German, of course, "Jude" translates into "Jew." After the child's photo had been stolen from the sepulcher, Jude Ithero, the would-be boy and Jew, is "faceless," and it is this lack of identity that deeply ties this dead child to

Karim Abdouf, the orphaned Arab other. Abdouf eventually deciphers the child's real name and sex as Judith Hérault, daughter of Fabienne Hérault, a teacher in this provincial French village.

The French skinhead scene has also made its nest in provincial France. Karim Abdouf is forced by his superior to pursue the lead connecting a group of local skins to the sepulcher desecration. He enters their hideout and finds that "[t]he walls were tagged with red swastikas. Nazi symbols were daubed alongside pictures of concentration camps and blow-ups of tortured Algerian POWS" (Grangé [1998] 2000, 70). This is one of the few overt references to France's colonial history in relation to Algeria, and it is linked here directly to symbols of fascism. To overcome his own fear of confronting this racist pack as an Arab Rastafarian cop, Karim Abdouf—in a gesture that reminds one of absurdist scenes in the late Chester Himes's novels—literally glues the skinheads' hands to the floor before he interrogates them (73). After finding out that they, the most likely suspects for a racially motivated desecration, actually did not have anything to do with the crime, he reminds them, "A cop is always a headache. And an Arab cop is a fucking migraine. Go out beating up darkies again and your head will be splitting . . ." (75), adding one last kick to the ribs of the downed skinhead leader to underline his seriousness.

It is Grangé's pairing and mirroring of the violent outsider French cop and the violent outsider French-Arab cop that challenges the essentialism of "Frenchness" and "Arabness" as ethnic and racial categories. And it is in this sense that Grangé's novel can be read as an oppositional, postcolonial narrative. According to Homi Bhabha, "fixity" is an important part of colonial discourse—always a discourse of difference to overcome the ambivalence of unfixity through the repetition of the stereotype. Foreignness, difference, mixing, miscegenation, and impurity become part of a fetishized system of control and oppression for the colonizer (see 1994, 66–75). Grangé's approach, therefore, "unfixes" Frenchness, substantiating Sally Munt's observation that "[c]rime fiction is a site for the expression of anxieties about society, and the appeasement of that fear is structurally inscribed in the narrative" (quoted in Gosselin 1999, 124). This casts a particular light on the idea of miscegenation in an ethnic/racialized context and explains the need of most of the French characters in the novel to reduce Karim Abdouf to his biological origins in the Maghreb, denying him his French identity.

There are numerous examples of Karim's French compatriot's essentializing attitude toward Abdouf's appearance—despite both his profession as a cop and the performativity of his appearance as a Rastafarian. For the skins, for example, "Cop or not, Karim was first and foremost an Arab. And an Arab's hide was not worth shit in a warehouse full of these bastards"

272 DOROTHEA FISCHER-HORNUNG

(Grangé [1998] 2000, 71).[14] The caretaker of the cemetery who catches Abdouf in the sepulcher simply refuses to believe that, because of his physical appearance, Abdouf is a police officer, "Course you are, you fucking A-rab. And I'm the Queen of bloody England. Don't move!" (228). But the most extreme example of such essentialist exclusion is that of his colleagues, who, although they work with him on a day-to-day basis and should know him as an individual, mark him as a total outsider—sexually, religiously, and culturally:

> He lived alone, slept alone, worked alone. At the police station which must have been one of the smallest in France, he was simultaneously feared and hated. His fellow cops called him "Cleopatra" because of his locks. Since he did not drink, they thought he was a fundamentalist. And, because he always declined the obligatory stopover chez Sylvie during their nightly rounds, they imagined he was gay. (54)

A notable exception to this fixed reaction to Abdouf is provided by the French nuns whom Abdouf visits in his search for the key to the identity of the mysterious girl and her mother. They seem to encounter him without a hint of animosity; they are simply curious about how he actually goes about "doing" his dreadlocks:

> "How do you do about making those plaits."
> "They're natural," he replied. "Frizzy hair naturally goes into plaits like this. In Jamaica they're called dreadlocks. The men never cut their hair and never shave. It's against their religion, just like with rabbis. When the locks are long enough, they fill them up with earth to make them heavier and . . . " (167)

Abdouf's description of his choice of hairstyle underlines the performative nature of his appearance. He is not a Rastafarian and does not share their religious convictions but has appropriated their appearance. Despite the alienating statement made by his exterior, he is far closer to the religious world of the nuns, and his encounter with them evokes old, warm memories of his upbringing—pleasant memories he basically rejects. As Bhabha points out, "The very concepts of homogenous national traditions, or 'organic' ethnic communities—as the grounds of cultural comparativism—are in a profound process of redefinition" (1994, 5). And in *Culture and Imperialism*, Edward Said elucidates the inability of putting any individual in a postcolonial, globalized culture in any one specific slot:

> No one today is purely *one* thing. Labels like Indian, or woman, or Muslim, or American are no more than starting-points, which if followed into

FRENCHNESS AND ARAB ALTERITY IN GRANGÉ   273

actual experience for only a moment are quickly left behind. Imperialism consolidated the mixture of cultures and identities on a global scale. But its worst and most paradoxical gift was to allow people to believe they were only, mainly, exclusively white, or black, or Western, or Oriental. Yet just as human beings make their own history, they also make their cultures and ethnic identities. . . . [T]here seems no reason except fear and prejudice to keep insisting on their separation and distinctiveness. . . . (1993, 408)

In Grangé, the nuns, women who have cloistered themselves and lead a life of prayer as far away from the "mean streets" as possible, are truly "catholic" in their response, encountering Abdouf with an open mind and not immediately racializing him. Grangé, to make his point about French society (or, equally, European or Western society), in his characterizations quite logically does the opposite and racializes much of what the reader learns about his detectives through the eyes of the French.

We are first introduced to Karim Abdouf after a night he has spent reading a six-hundred-page paper on genetic sampling: "He evaluated his chances of being able to conduct a genetic enquiry in the one-horse town to which he had been transferred. They were zero" ([1998] 2000, 44). But that is exactly what his case, which initially seems so insignificant, will enable him to do. In the same vein, the first meeting of the two cops is equally racialized. It is from his perspective as the French "supercop" that Niémans first sizes up Abdouf:

He drank in the young Arab's extraordinary appearance. He could now make out the glinting of assorted ear-rings amid the dreadlocks. . . . Nor was he sure whether or not to trust an Arab who measured six foot two, had dreadlocks, carried an unauthorized automatic/weapon, and was driving what was clearly a stolen car. . . . But this take was no crazier than his own hypothesis: the guilt of the victims. And the gutsy enthusiasm of this young Arab was highly contagious. (212, 214–15)

The twinned doppelgänger cops encounter a pair of mirrored doppelgänger twin femmes fatales.[15] Fanny, the mountain-climbing and white-water-rafting professor who discovers the first body, exerts an erotic, spellbinding attraction on Niémans from the beginning: "Fanny threw her sheet of sandpaper into a plastic cup, wiped her hands and lit a cigarette. These simple gestures provoked a feeling of violent desire in Niémans" (30). From the onset, she is associated in their initial encounter with many of the symbolic "keywords" in the case: "She stared at him with her eyes of crystal. Niémans felt decidedly uneasy. Her irises were too light.[16] They were made of glass, white water, as chilling frost" (35).

In a reduction to a physical "dark" type characteristic of the genre, a second femme fatale, Sophie Caillois, the wife of the first victim, also exerts a mysterious attraction on the loner cop. The two form the light and the dark sirens, the desired yet unattainable doppelgänger femmes fatales:

> Fanny Ferreira, the brunette. And Sophie Caillois, the blonde. Two strong, intelligent, aggressive women. The sort of women this policeman would probably never hold in his arms. (Grangé [1998] 2000, 43)

> One of them was as tough as tree-bark. Her muscles must be full, her skin dark and velvety. A taste of resin and rubbed herbs. The other was frail and bitter. She oozed uneasiness, an aggressiveness mixed with fear, which Niémans found equally fascinating. What was the strange beauty and the bony face hiding? (94)

Niémans's brain seems to shut down and his raging hormones take over completely while under Fanny's spell. Much later, after it has become clear to the reader that Fanny is, as femmes fatales inevitably are, a source of danger, he fails to recognize her evil potential. Grangé's novel, like the genre of hard-boiled detective fiction in general, is a testament to the binary reduction of the female under patriarchy, a world that fears female urpower, her destructive and palliative potential. The diabolic temptress is Niémans's downfall, but it is the healing power of the nuns and the young female child that saves Abdouf. Both men react inadequately to this vortex of "body" crime—literally of bloodied, murdered corpses and sullied eugenicized blood.

Having been forced off a bridge by a mysterious car and with a resulting serious head wound, Niémans is blinded to the incongruity of Fanny's noir greeting and his reaction to her presence—simultaneously the Madonna and the whore:

> The door opened to reveal a smile. Pierre Niémans lowered his eyes. He saw the woman's powerful, muscular wrists. Just above them, he noticed the close stitch of her heavy pullover, then he followed it up to the collar and her neck, where her hair was so fine that it formed a sort of misty halo. He thought of her marvelous skin, so beautiful and so immaculate that it magically transformed each material, each garment that it touched. Fanny yawned.
> "You're late, superintendent." (Grangé [1998] 2000, 273)

Her seduction of Niémans is shrewdly calculated to prevent him from going to check on the files that would reveal both the eugenic blood crimes and the motives for her crimes of revenge as well. Niémans is attracted to her like a moth to a deadly flame.

Not unsurprisingly, Karim Abdouf meets his own femme fatale, now the third in the series of doppelgängers, but this femme fatale is one of a very different ilk:

A little girl was staring out at him [from the photograph], her dark face was oval, ringed with brown short-cropped curls. Bright blue eyes shone from beneath the shadows of her brows, emphasized by her long lashes, which were almost too luxuriant. The slightly masculine touch went with her slightly over-aggressive gaze. (Grangé [1998] 2000, 290)

Karim Abdouf learns of the single life that had been led by the twins after the ghastly staged accident that utilized the stolen corpse of a young boy who had been kept on ice for three days in their bathtub. This enables Judith's feigned death and the future life of the twins together in a single identity. Fingerprints were conveniently swapped in the police files, thereby seemingly documenting Judith's death. The twins subsequently took up their single life, overcoming the eugenic brain and body division based on the eugenic crimes of the bloodred rivers:

Fanny was the bright one, so she taught me everything about books, science and geology. And I taught her to climb mountains and navigate streams. The two of us made one incredible being . . . A sort of two-headed dragon. (324–25)

At the end of the novel, when Niémans as well as Fanny are dead—Fanny having ripped out Niémans's guts with a carpet knife and Niémans simultaneously "having finished off his prey" (320) with his gun—Karim Abdouf is left standing at the edge of the cliff over which Niémans as well as Fanny had plunged. He encounters the other half of the twinned sisters

He suddenly screamed and leapt up over the rocks to look for Judith's body, the little girl whom he had loved—he knew that now—more than anything else in the world for the past twenty-four hours. (327)

All of those responsible for the horrific, fetishized murders are female, but they have been the victims of the far more infamous eugenic blood crimes perpetrated by men who are the apparent victims. Yet this gender dichotomy is complicated by the ethnic and racial dimensions of the far greater social crime that goes beyond the murder of three individuals. If the ethnic detective is often a cultural mediator who guides the reader to an understanding of an unfamiliar ethnic culture, as Peter Freese maintains (see 1992, 231–35), what would this cultural understanding be in this instance? Much like

Chester Himes's inability or refusal to "mediate" African American and U.S. culture, what, in the end, could Grangé mediate other than French culture? And if in prototypical detective fiction the mystery surrounds a crime at the beginning, and the detective's answer to the question "who done it" provides closure (Linton 1999, 17), what kind of closure could be provided in this case? What is the reader left with at the end of the novel— a "biological" Arab who is "ethnically" French and an alienated outlaw French police officer and, ultimately, the living "products" of the heinous eugenic blood crimes? This is hardly closure in the traditional sense. The novel closes with the trope of the coming of a new dawn, but it a questionable coming of light into darkness:

> In the distance, a brilliant dawn was rising, searing through the darkness of the mountains.
> Karim took no notice.
> He wondered how much sunlight would be needed to chase away the shadows that were folding around his heart. (328)

The reader is left with the dark vision and only a little hope of the noir shadows being chased away in Grangé's deconstruction and radical rejection of a necessary and binding opposition between "Frenchness" and "Arab alterity."

NOTES

1. A horrific example of such uncontrolled soccer hooliganism occurred at the World Cup in 1998 when Daniel Nivel, a French police officer, was attacked by a German soccer fan, Marcus Warnecke. According to the BBC, "Mr. Nivel, 46, suffered irreversible brain damage. He spent several weeks in a coma, and still has difficulty moving and speaking. . . . Warnecke was in charge of this commando gang, this horde of hooligans," which attacked Nivel after the Germany-Yugoslavia match in Lens. "He [Nivel] suffered appalling head injuries as he was kicked and beaten whilst lying on the ground, having lost his protective helmet. The attack sparked widespread outrage in France and Germany." news6.thdo.bbc.co. uk/hi/english/world/europe/newsid_1344000/1344821.stm (28 September 2001).

2. In the original French, Karim Abdouf is referred to as either "l'Arabe" or "le Beur," French slang used to refer to a second-generation migrant from the Maghreb. Maghreb is the Arabic term referring to all of the northwestern part of Africa, generally including Morocco, Algeria, Tunisia, and sometimes Libya (*Random House Dictionary of the English Language,* s.v. "Mahgreb").

In the devastating war fought by the Algerians for independence from France between 1954 and 1962, the Front de Libération Nationale (FLN) estimated that "nearly eight years of revolution had cost 300,000 dead from war-related causes. Algerian sources later put the figure at approximately 1.5 million dead, while French officials estimated it at 350,000. French military authorities listed their losses at nearly 18,000 dead (6,000 from noncombat-related causes) and 65,000 wounded. European civilian casualties exceeded 10,000 (including 3,000 dead) in 42,000 recorded terrorist incidents. According to French figures, security forces killed 141,000 rebel combatants, and more than 12,000 Algerians died in internal FLN purges during the war. . . . French sources also estimated that 70,000 Muslim civilians were killed, or abducted and presumed killed, by the FLN." memory.loc.gov/cgi-bin/query2/r?frd/cstdy:@field(DOCID+dz0042 (24 October 2001).

I would like to express my thanks to Céline Moreau, a French graduate student in Heidelberg, who, with great dedication and insight, helped me to interpret the original French terminology used in reference to immigrants from the Maghreb in France.

3. The question of just what an ethnic detective is depends, of course, on one's own standpoint: "An initial problem when studying the multicultural detective is deciding exactly what 'ethnic' means. As one's dialect, one usually perceives ethnic difference in others while tacitly assuming one's own way as the norm" (Macdonald and Macdonald 1999, 68).

According to Ed Christian's definition, Grangé's novel would certainly qualify as not only ethnic but postcolonial: *"[P]ost-colonial detectives are always indigenous to or settlers in the countries where they work; they are usually marginalized in some way, and sympathetic characters; and their creators' interest usually lies in an exploration of how these detectives' approaches to criminal investigations are influenced by their cultural attitudes"* (2001, 2; italics in the original).

4. The film based on the novel, starring Jean Reno as Pierre Niémans and Vincent Cassel as Max Kerkerian (the name has been changed from Karim Abdouf), totally de-ethnicizes the plot, reducing it to the astoundingly fascinating visual impression of fetishized frozen corpses and glacial crevasses, the eugenic fascistoid crimes, and the action entailed in the double plotting. The "happy" open ending with Niémans and Judith transported off the mountain after an amazingly bestialized twin slashes across the screen is confusing at best and borders on melodramatic trash. There is a German website devoted to the questions of the confused viewing audience, which points out that the film in simplifying the contents made it very murky. Many of the answers to questions about unclear points in the film start with, "Im Buch wird das klarer verständlich . . ." [In the book this is easier to understand . . .]. www.schreibfabrik.de/txt/fluesse.htm (5 November 2001).

5. See William R. Nash's (1999) excellent discussion of this difficult relationship.

6. Orson Welles explored the potential of border situations in his late film noir *A Touch of Evil* (1958). Welles, in contrast to Whit Masterson's novel upon which the film's script was based, locates the crime on both sides of the border between Mexico and the United States, between the first and the third world. Welles's Mexican detective, Ramon Miguel "Mike" Vargas (Charlton Heston), localizes the problem in the border situation between the two unequal countries, and explains to his newlywed platinum blonde American wife, Susie Vargas (Janet Leigh): "Come on, Susie, border cities always bring out the worst in a country!" Which city on which side of the border is not, of course, made explicit.

7. Guernon and Sarzac are both fictive names.

8. The theme of the Americanization of France crops up throughout the novel: it is emphasized repeatedly that serial killers are not a French phenomenon, but rather an American one: "While serial killers had been imported from America and now peopled the world's books and films, that terrible trend had never really taken off in France. . . . It was not a French specialty" (154). And, as if to underline Niémans's depravity and alienation from alimentary Frenchness, before he leaves for Guernon, Niémans partakes of a final meal in Paris at an all-night McDonald's on Boulevard de Clichy where he "rapidly swallowed two quarter pounders with cheese" (11). And finally, as if all of France had turned into cheap American pulp fiction, Abdouf notes: "Nowadays, in France, you don't say 'inspector' any more, you say 'lieutenant.' Just like in America" (65).

278 DOROTHEA FISCHER-HORNUNG

9. The alternate title of *Götter des Stadions* (Gods of the Stadium) captures Leni Riefenstahl's attempt to portray the ideal of the *athlon* in film. The film was released in 1938 as *Festival of the Nations* in the United States and *Olympic Games Berlin 1936* in the United Kingdom. Aside from directing the film, Riefenstahl appears at the beginning of the film as an uncredited nude dancer. www.us.imdb.com/Name?Riefenstahl,+Leni (9 October 2001).

10. Later in the novel Grangé makes his point quite directly: "Niémans suddenly realized that he not so much distrusted intellectuals as detested them. He hated them to his very marrow. He loathed their distant, pretentious ways, their ability to describe, to analyze and gauge reality, in whatever form it presented itself" ([1998] 2000, 299).

11. This glorification of mountain folk and their physical "purity" also ties this section of the novel to the earlier photos of the *athlon* taken at the 1936 Berlin Olympics by Riefenstahl. She appeared in and/or produced/directed several now classic films about mountain folk: *Der Heilige Berg* (1926); *Die Weiße Hölle vom Piz Palü* (1929); *Stürme über dem Mont Blanc* (1930); *Das Blaue Licht* (1932).

12. From 1939 on, one of the most horrible sides of the *Lebensborn* policy was the kidnapping of children, "racial goods," in the eastern occupied countries. These kidnappings were organized by the SS in order to take by force children who matched the Nazi's racial criteria (blond hair, blue eyes, etc.). Thousands of children were transferred to the *Lebensborn* centers in order to be "Germanized." www.us-israel.org/jsource/Holocaust/ Lebensborn.html (2 November 2001).

13. The grave desecration at Carpentras occurred in May 1990. The grave of Félix Guermon, a Jew who had died two weeks earlier, was opened and his body impaled. About thirty gravestones were moved, smashed, or defaced. In 1996 Yannick Garnier, an unobtrusive security agent from Nîmes, turned himself in to "take the weight off his conscience." Three of his accomplices were then arrested (a fourth had died in 1993). They were skinheads associated with a small group of Nazis (the French European National Party—PNFE); their activities were designed to mark the anniversary of Hitler's death.

I would like to thank Christiane Imbert at the Bibliothèque Inguimbertine Archives et Museés de Carpentras, who provided me with the sources on this historical incident: *Le Monde*, no. 246 (September 1996); *Valeurs Actuelles*, 30 September 1995.

14. Grangé ties Abdouf's alterity to that of the skinheads through the music he hears them listening to, which he immediately recognizes as rap performed by A Tribe Called Quest—rap, of course, is now a major expression of global feelings of existential alterity far beyond the Bronx and African American/Latino culture. Their listening to and his immediate recognition of politicized rap mirrors the alterity of the racist skins with the target of their racism, the French migrant cop from the Maghreb.

15. The plot is further complicated in that there are not two but actually three deadly women: Sophie Caillois, the wife of the first victim; Fanny, the athletic lecturer at the university; and the latter's twin, the presumed dead, presumed male, and faceless child, Jude Ithero, later revealed to be the beautiful Judith Hérault, whose childhood photo becomes Abdouf's fixation.

16. As Dr. Chernecé, the third murder victim, explains to Niémans, the human iris is believed by iridologists to be the gate to the analysis of human health and disease and is also one of the few truly distinguishing and defining details of human individuality: "Some scientists believe that it is possible to read in the irises not only a person's state of health, but also his entire history. Those little circles which glimmer around our pupils carry our very genesis . . ." ([1998] 2000, 210).

Works Cited

Bhabha, Homi K. 1994. *The Location of Culture.* London: Routledge.

Christian, Ed. 2001. "Introducing the Post-Colonial Detective: Putting Marginality to Work." In *The Post-Colonial Detective,* 1–16. Houndmills, U.K.: Palgrave.

The Crimson Rovers. 2000. *(Les Rivières pourpres,* Gaumont et al.) Directed by Mathieu Kassovitz. Performed by Jean Reno, Vincent Cassel, Nadia Farès (U.S.A. 2001).

Freese, Peter, 1992. *The Ethnic Detective: Chester Himes, Harry Kemelman, Tony Hillerman.* Essen: Die Blaue Eule.

Gosselin, Adrienne Johnson, ed. 1999. *Multicultural Detective Fiction: Murder from the "Other" Side.* New York: Garland.

Grangé, Jean-Christophe. [1998] 2000. *Blood-Red Rivers.* Translated by Ian Monk. London: Harvill Press.

Linton, Patricia. 1999. "The Detective Novel as a Resistant Text: Alter-Ideology in Linda Hogan's Mean Spirit." In Gosselin 1999, 17–35.

Macdonald, Gina, and Andrew Macdonald. 1999. "Ethnic Detectives in Popular Fiction: New Directions for an American Genre." In *Diversity and Detective Fiction,* edited by Kathleen Gregory Klein, 60–113. Bowling Green, Ohio: Bowling Green State University Popular Press.

Nash, William R. 1999. "'Maybe I Killed My Own Blood': Doppelgängers and the Death of Double Consciousness in Walter Mosley's *A Little Yellow Dog.*" In Gosselin 1999, 303–24.

Said, Edward. 1993. *Culture and Imperialism.* London: Chatto and Windus.

Templeton, Wayne. 1999. "'Xojo' and Homicide: The Postcolonial Murder Mysteries of Tony Hillerman." In Gosselin 1999, 37–59.

A Touch of Evil. 1958. Directed by Orson Welles. Performed by Orson Welles, Charlton Heston, Janet Leigh. Universal Pictures.

Walton, Priscilla, and Manina Jones. 1999. *Detective Agency: Women Rewriting the Hard-Boiled Tradition.* Berkeley and Los Angeles: University of California Press.

Uncovering Collective Crimes:
Sally Morgan's *My Place* as Australian
Indigenous Detective Narrative

RUSSELL WEST

TWO MEN ARE DISCOVERED DEAD, THE BODIES EIGHTEEN MILES APART, ON A REMOTE sheep station in drought-stricken outback Australia. The murders have no obvious motivation, and no trace is to be found of their perpetrator. Unable to make any headway with their investigations, the police lay the case to rest until, six months later, the part-Aboriginal detective inspector Napoleon Bonaparte, the protagonist of Arthur Upfield's novel *Bony and the Black Virgin*, is called in to reopen the proceedings. Inspector Bony, of course, successfully solves the mystery of the double murder. It is the hero's skill in "reading the Book of the Bush," a motif frequently mentioned in the story, that marks him out from other investigators and makes him the supersleuth that he is. The indigenous people's traditional ability to read the minute details of the land, the marks left by weather, animals, and human beings, constitutes Bony's uncanny powers of detection: "A small problem unworthy of a white man's attention! . . . Meticulous attention to detail, unlimited patience, and unbounded curiosity received their reward from the ancient Spirit of the Land who had tested him. . . . History was written on this page of the Book of the Bush" ([1959] 1984, 76).

But we should note that this is a white writer speaking—the English-born detective novelist Upfield drew upon his experience of working on remote cattle stations in Australia to craft his tales. It is instructive to contrast Upfield's ventriloquism of the black speaker with the chiding tones of a contemporary Aboriginal storyteller in a volume significantly entitled *Reading the Country*: "You people try and dig little bit more deep—you bin digging only white soil—try and find the black soil inside . . ." (Paddy Roe, in Benterrak et al. 1984, 168). If Upfield's tale purports to describe a

UNCOVERING COLLECTIVE CRIMES

detective who brushes away the layers of outback dust to reveal the traces of a crime, the indigenous storyteller of today would appear to be implying that the white man is not genuinely interested in, nor indeed capable of, uncovering the past and its secrets.

In this essay I would like to examine two antipodean variations of the detective narrative, first taking a brief look at this novel by the white Australian writer Upfield, and then moving on to a more sustained reading of an autobiography by the black Australian Sally Morgan, *My Place*. Common to the two texts is the capacity of the indigenous investigator to read Australian history for traces of crimes hidden by the passage of time. The order in which I will examine these two texts does not indicate an implicit cultural hierarchy, but follows a historical development: for the best part of the two centuries after the white occupation of Australia in 1788, white writers described the indigenous peoples whose land they had seized; in the 1970s, however, Aboriginal literary voices became more strident and replaced those which had previously determined their representation in white Australia (see Healy 1989, xx–xxi). Upfield's text figures here as a foil to highlight the full radicalism, but also the limitations, of Morgan's investigative project.

The West Australian writer and artist Sally Morgan published her family autobiography, *My Place*, in 1987. Since then her text has been hugely successful, selling over half a million copies in Australia, as well as abroad under the London Virago imprint, with seven reprints to date. For a small country with a population of nineteen million, a traditional antipathy toward high cultural forms, and an ongoing tradition of racism, sales of this quantity are quite remarkable, all the more so in that indigenous literature does not usually belong on the best-seller lists. Part of the reason for this success is perhaps that *My Place* speaks about a currently much debated aspect of recent Australian history: that of the "Stolen Generation," a term coined to refer to the Aboriginal children forcibly removed from their parents under white government policy until the mid-1970s.

In 1997, "Bringing Them Home," the Australian government report of a national inquiry into the separation of Aboriginal and Torres Strait Islander children from their families, concluded that between one in three and one in ten indigenous children were forcibly removed from their parents and communities in the period from approximately 1910 until 1970. The children were raised in institutions or given to adoptive families, were often subjected to sexual abuse and racial discrimination, and frequently lost contact with their biological parents. Most indigenous families have been affected, in one or more generations, by the forcible removal of one or more children. The long-term psychic trauma and social as well as familial disintegration caused by these government policies are immeasurable, but

282   RUSSELL WEST

the report provides hundreds of individual testimonies to the pain and discrimination experienced by indigenous children and their families in the name of "enlightened" state intervention. The aim of this policy was ostensibly to provide better living conditions for children than in a shattered indigenous society, but it effectively drove a wedge, on the one hand, between "full-blood" Aboriginals, segregated out of sight in conditions of poverty on reserves and marginal settlements, and "half-castes" who were to be assimilated into white society; and, on the other hand, between older and younger generations, so that the linguistic heritage and traditional knowledge of the indigenous peoples was rapidly lost. The policy also aimed to break up a potential block of collective Aboriginal protest by vitiating the cohesion of Aboriginal society. The policy of forced removal needs to be seen in the larger context of the European invasion of Australia and the expulsion of the indigenous people from their lands: the later policy effectively perpetuated the process of cultural destruction initiated by the expropriation of land (the land was the basis for—indeed, the embodiment of—the economic, social, cultural, and religious structures of traditional Aboriginal society, and its reappropriation remains central in Aboriginal activism against all forms of white discrimination). I shall refer consistently to these practices as a form of collective crime, for though child removal was ratified by government legislation, this very legislation deprived indigenous Australians of their most basic human rights on the basis of skin color until into the late 1960s—from the right of free movement, to the right of a minimum standard of living; from the right to sexual and marital self-determination and the exercise of parental responsibility, to the right to legal appeal against such legislation (see Rowley 1972, 183–84). The crime mystery scrutinized in this essay is that of the darker side of white Australia's history and could be placed under the sign of the storyteller Paddy Roe's injunction: "You people try and dig little bit more deep—you bin digging only white soil—try and find the black soil inside. . ." (Roe in Benterrak et al. 1984, 168).

Upfield draws upon such commonplaces of Aboriginal culture to create a new sort of detective. By appropriating this aspect of the indigenous people's intimate knowledge of their country, he secured a lucrative place on the detective fiction market, of which the frequent reprints and worldwide translations of the Bony novels are a clear indicator. But it is important that Bony is not merely one of the Aboriginal trackers—blacks co-opted by the white police in colonial Australia for their superior bush knowledge and their skill at finding the traces of criminals on the run, of which the novel makes mention during the preliminary episodes (see [1959] 1984, 41). Bony is a "half-caste" Aboriginal and thus differentiated from the "real" Aboriginal whose skills are used by the white police without them being of any interest to the narrative. Rather, it is Bony's partly white identity (accentuated by a markedly English touch betraying the author's compensatory need to justify the choice of his protagonist [see Langer 1991, 41 n. 15]) that allows him also to belong to the upper echelons of the white Australian police force. He thereby takes on a mediatory role of discoverer in the narrative process that the text is at pains to underline: "History was written on this page of the Book of the Bush. . . . It was not unlike trying to read a serial story backwards from the installment one picks up by chance" (Upfield [1959] 1984, 176). This, of course, as Tzvetan Todorov points out, is the narrative role of the detective or the concomitant narrator in the crime narrative. In his work on the detective narrative, Todorov adapts the Russian formalist concepts of "story line" *(fabula),* meaning the chronological sequence of events forming the basis of the narrative, and the "plot" *(sujet),* signifying the reconfiguration of the story line within and through the event of narration (see Shklovsky 1990, 170). In Todorov's formulation, the initially obscure series of events resulting in the crime corresponds to the "story line" *(fabula),* and the narrative process of their elucidation is coeval with the "plot" *(sujet)* (see Todorov 1980, 12–13). The detective mediates between the reader and the original course of events, working back from the crime as a culminating point in what can be compared to the *fabula*-function, so as to reconstruct the prehistory of the crime in *sujet*-process in which the reader is called to participate. Bony as a reader of the bush partakes both in indigenous knowledge of the land and, at the same time, in the fragmentary, accumulating knowledge of the perplexed white reader. He is a mediator between two cultures of reading—one black, one white.

Where Upfield himself stands, as a white with considerable knowledge of black culture, is difficult to say. He makes some gestures toward advocacy for the indigenous people, commenting that "much money is spent on [the Aborigines'] education—and barriers erected to prevent them benefiting from it" ([1959] 1984, 107), or deftly reveals the psychological mechanisms of racism: "So many people fail to see the Aborigines for what they are. To regard them as uncouth savages is such a boost for the ego, and yet, search as you might, you won't find a moron among them" (124). Yet at the same time, the reader is confronted with repeated comments that indicate some sort of deeply ingrained and unreflected prejudice, when, for example, we are repeatedly told that "for an Aborigine, she [Lottee, the main indigenous character] was good-looking" (122)—as if Caucasian criteria of physiognomic beauty are held to be a universally valid norm shared by writer and readers, to the exclusion of the indigenous people. The ambiguities of Upfield's position are perhaps understandable. *Bony and the Black Virgin* was published in 1959, less than a decade before the white Australian people voted in a referendum to grant the indigenous population Australian citizenship in 1967. Yet it is worthwhile also bearing in mind that in 1958, the West Australian commissioner of police could publicly justify the use of neck-chains to restrain indigenous prisoners, and that less than two decades had passed since the last paramilitary punitive expeditions were sent out against Aboriginals (see Rowley 1972, 199 and 204).

I would argue that Upfield's detective novel is very much a product of its time, partly expressing outrage at the condition of the indigenous people in an era that would see the first moves toward granting them basic civil rights, and partly a bearer of ongoing attitudes denigrating the original inhabitants of the fifth continent. It is particularly with regard to Bony's own cultural status that the novel operates with a strange sort of double vision made up of insight and willful blindness combined. Bony says he was found as a child beside his dead mother, who had ostensibly been killed for giving birth to him. The boy was raised on a mission, thus excluding him from full knowledge of traditional Aboriginal culture (see [1959] 1984, 66). Here the novel gestures toward a broader practice of removal of "half-caste" children maintained by the Australian government for three-quarters of the twentieth century. This practice was facilitated by the frequent refusal of the white fathers to acknowledge paternity (together with the absence of black mothers' legal rights to half-caste children). Such paternal disavowal is projected by Bony onto the main suspect for the double murder, Eric Downer: Bony hypothesizes that Eric killed the two victims in order to prevent them from publicizing his surreptitious Aboriginal marriage with Lottee, a marriage that his white man's shame does not allow him to admit to friends and family (149–50).

Yet it is the spirit of the Aboriginal mother, we are told, who endows Bony with an acute sense of the limits of his intuitive capacity to read the land and unravel the most difficult of conundrums (see Upfield [1954] 1984, 150). And it is Bony's nostalgic attentiveness to Lottee's voice, an avatar of "the mother voice he had never known and always longed to hear" (154), as the embodiment of a lost narrative of black-white sexual liaison, which leads him to give epistemological weight to Lottee's alternative account of the murders, thus modifying his original supposition. In the final denouement, we learn that Lottee was raped by a white man after her secret marriage to Eric and killed her rapist and a second white man who subsequently threatened her with rape; Eric was merely instrumental in disposing of the bodies (153–54). Moreover, as the title of the novel indicates, the secret marriage does not culminate in sexual union, thus foreclosing the question of "half-caste" children.

In this way, an ostensibly more complex reason than mere racist shame at the sexual entanglement of white man and black woman is given as the motivation for the murders. Both of these issues had literary predecessors, for instance in Xavier Herbert's *Capricornia* (1937) (see Hodge and Mishra 1991, 56–58). And the massive exploitation of Aboriginal women by white men has a long history, which is hinted at by Lottee's (secondary, reactive) violence. Ironically, however, it is Bony's own origins in a crime associated with a black-white sexual union, and his own removal to an orphanage—the shadowy fictional trace of real state practices illegal by international human rights standards—that works to operate the textual shift away from the domain of state policy regarding half-blood children, and towards individual indigenous criminality. Thus a structural, collective crime against the indigenous people is elided in the very act of the solving of the fictional riddle. Upfield may condone Lottee's crime, but he nonetheless places black violence in the foreground of the narrative, not unlike more recent white novelists such as Keneally and Ireland (see Healy 1989, 241–62) and in parallel with practices of stereotyping in other European cultures (see Gilroy 1993, chap. 3). At the close of the story, Upfield has Lottee commit suicide, thus confirming the criminalization that Upfield's enlightened liberalism does not permit him to utter explicitly, and effectively diverting attention from less visible crimes perpetrated by white society against the indigenous population. It is difficult to know whether this elision, on the part of a well-informed observer, was conscious or not. By way of comparison, Rowley's groundbreaking and devastatingly detailed classic of 1970, *The Destruction of Aboriginal Society*, refers to child removal practices but, significantly, gives no indication of their endurance over the century, nor of the extent of their implementation (see Rowley 1972, 232, 236, 302, 380).

Through its privileging of black over white crimes, Upfield's narrative itself figures an enduring pattern of Australian "cultural amnesia" (see Anderson 1991, 204, and Hodge and Mishra 1991, 14), a cultural amnesia that is addressed in a subsequent text also structured by the detective story narrative, Sally Morgan's *My Place*. In what follows, I wish to read Morgan's autobiographical account against Upfield, as a text that also places an assimilated Aboriginal "detective" at the center of the narrative activity, but that is written by an Aboriginal author rather than a white one. Furthermore, in place of a detective fiction, this text relates the detection of nonfictional crimes, though no less shocking for that. And the perpetrators of the crimes are not black, but rather white, the very suspects initially targeted but then exonerated in Upfield's narrative. In many respects, Morgan's text reverses the structures of Upfield's detective fiction, signifying a momentous return-of-the-repressed in contemporary Australian society, accompanied by all the difficulties and pitfalls that such a process entails.

Morgan's immensely successful autobiography contains the narratives of the author herself, as well as those of her mother, her grandmother and her great-uncle. In the opening lines of her grandmother's narrative, Nan, as she is known to her family, introduces herself with the words

> My name is Daisy Corunna. . . . My Aboriginal name is Talahue. I can't tell you when I was born, but I feel old. My mother had me on Corunna Downs Station, just out of Marble Bar. . . . Now, some people say my father wasn't Howden Drake-Brockman [the owner of the cattle station], they say he was this man from Malta. What can I say? . . . Aah, you see, that's the trouble with us blackfellas, we don't know who we belong to, no one'll own up. (1987, 325)

Here the question of white fathers' denial of paternity and the consequences for "half-caste" offspring opens an elderly Aboriginal woman's account of her life, taking up the very same complex of sexual, social, and interracial relationships that Bony initially surmises to be at the center of the double murders in *Bony and the Black Virgin*. Essentially, the same tragic historical entanglements of black and white society are at stake, both on an individual and a collective level, and there is the same attempt to deny that entanglement, whether by the replacement of one murder narrative by another or through the policies of removal and assimilation. It is the former technique of narrative repression and elision that is decisively reversed in Sally Morgan's *My Place* through its historiographical project so as to reveal the full extent of the removal policy and its cultural bankruptcy.

Sally's mother, exasperated by her daughter's constant interrogations regarding arcane details of family history, accuses her of behaving "like a bloody detective" (238). This epithet is more than a mere passing quip, for it points to the very principles upon which the narrative is constructed. Morgan's text is organized as a type of detective story. As mentioned above, Todorov has suggested that the detective story is made up of two narratives: first, an absent story line culminating in the crime; and second, a process of narration that follows the elucidation of that crime or the narrative (re)construction of the earlier chain of events making up the crime (see 1980, 12–13). The opening section of *My Place*, Morgan's narrative of her own childhood and youth, constitutes this second strand of the detective story structure (put more accurately, it is a *fabula* that recounts the preconditions of its own unfolding *sujet*-process). We are told of her growing up in suburban Perth in the belief that she has some sort of Indian ancestry, but the text is strewn with clues that point to a submerged Aboriginal heritage. These clues are clearly planted by the author, but are ostensibly invisible to the protagonist herself and to the uninitiated reader. Thus Sally feels a strange fascination for dark-skinned visiting relatives of her own age from the country, whose language she cannot understand (Morgan 1987, 47), a deep sense

UNCOVERING COLLECTIVE CRIMES

287

of symbiosis with the natural life of the wild swamp biotope behind the
South Perth housing estate (59), or, as an artistically gifted youngster, has
recourse, when paper and pencils run out, to "small pieces of charcoal from
the fire, and . . . strips off the paperbark tree in our yard" (45), thus alluding
to Aboriginal traditions of bark painting. These clues to Sally Morgan's
rootedness in an Aboriginal cultural heritage are inserted in the text without comment and provide the textual dynamic that makes the discovery of
Aboriginal identity an inevitable part of the narrative strategy. This process is accelerated as Sally grows older and little by little explicitly re-
claims her submerged Aboriginal heritage, a journey that culminates in a
visit to the traditional tribal lands, and finally in the project of recording
and transcribing the reminiscences of her mother, grandmother, and great-
uncle as representative of three generations of indigenous experience, material that formed the basis of the later sections of *My Place* (at this point,
the *fabula* of *sujet*-construction arrives at the moment of its own narration,
thus fading into pure *sujet*, foregrounding the process by which indigenous
history comes to light and is narrated by an older generation to the listening younger generation).

However, other clues planted in the text are commented on explicitly
by the narrator but cannot be explained at their points of occurrence in the
narrative. The very fact that these clues cannot be decoded is signaled as a
disturbing hermeneutic problem for the child: "I was often puzzled by the
way Mum and Nan approached anyone in authority; it was as if they were
frightened. I knew that couldn't be the reason, why on earth would anyone
be frightened of the government?" (Morgan 1987, 96). And when one summer the State Housing Commission painted all the houses in the Morgans'
street, the renovation "really panicked Nan . . . I tried to reason with her,
but to no avail. . . . For her, they were here to check on us, and the possibility of eviction was always there, hanging in the air" (103–4). Likewise,
Sally cannot understand Nan's excessive pandering to the rent collector
who comes from the State Housing Commission once a month (104). These
explicitly problematized puzzles within the text do not underpin the affirmation of an Aboriginal identity. On the contrary, they are indices of the
destruction of Aboriginal identity, of a deeply internalized insecurity. As
clues or indices in the etymological sense of the word, they point toward a
concrete causal connection. They are mute, as clues inevitably are, for reasons that are intimately linked to the policies maintained by the white government of Australia.

The causal motivation for these textual puzzles is condensed in a clue
of the first variety mentioned above, a fear experienced on the part of Sally
herself about the time her father died, in 1961: "I felt very strongly about
families sticking together. So strongly, in fact, that I had a secret meeting

with my brothers and sisters; for some reason, I was frightened we would be put in an orphanage" (Morgan 1987, 50). Here the adults' strange silences are elucidated, implicitly, by the small girl's own instinctive fear—for during this period, the policy of forcible removal was still being carried out on a large scale all over Australia. It is precisely this threat which the narrator claims to have instinctively sensed. At this stage in the narrative, however, there has been no explicit mention of these governmental policies, and this childish reaction functions as yet another mute clue buried in the text that neither the reader nor the narrator are yet in a position to interpret.

It is only in the later sections of *My Place*, when Sally's mother, grandmother, and the latter's brother take over the narration, that the *fabula*, or chain of historical events taken up and reorganized by Sally's *sujet*-construction, is revealed. The three later narratives represent Sally Morgan's family history, but also furnish the details of a crime committed collectively over generations against the indigenous peoples. What constantly recurs in the narratives of the two preceding generations are accounts of being taken away from parents by the officials of the Native Welfare Department. Sally's grandmother and her brother Arthur record being taken away from their mother (see Morgan 1987, 332 and 207). In turn, Gladys, Sally's mother, recounts her removal, saying at one point in her account: "Even when I was sick, I belonged to the Native Health Department. I wasn't even allowed to have the comfort of my own mother" (250). Two generations of Aboriginal experience of forcible removal in turn determine the silence that hangs over the third generation, that of the narrator herself. Sally's mother recounts:

> Bill [her white husband] had only been dead a short while when a Welfare lady came out to visit us. I was really frightened because I thought, if she realized we were Aboriginal, she might have taken the children away. . . . It was after the visit from the Welfare lady that Mum and I decided we would definitely never tell the children they were Aboriginal. (304–5)

Even Morgan's disturbed and violent father appears at times to have wielded the threat of forcible removal against his wife, despite his own ostensibly irrational fear that his children might be "stolen" when he is absent at the pub (301).

The historical fact that thus determines the structure of the narrative from the outset is on occasions also inscribed in the margins of Morgan's text, in the clear register of an objective historical discourse. A footnote draws attention to the "active policy of miscegenation in Western Australia through the 1930s," which entailed "the legal removal of 'half-caste' Aboriginal children from their mothers" (Morgan 1987, 211). The text also mentions curfews and pass laws for black people (250 and 334), the sexual exploitation of black girls and women (266 and 336–37), brutal beatings of children in homes (186), and the chaining of Aboriginal laborers or shooting of Aboriginals for sport (181). However, the central structure of the text is determined by the policy of forcible removal of Aboriginal children from their families and the concomitant suppression of the narrator's Aboriginal identity for fear of the family being broken up. It is the pressure exerted upon Aboriginal people over a century by government policy that motivates the hidden core of a detective story whose mystery is, on the one hand, a hidden indigenous identity, and, on the other, a silenced history of cultural and social sabotage systematically undertaken by white government, to a great extent out of sight of the public.

One role of these autobiographical writings is therefore to address a fundamental blind spot in Australian national consciousness. Another Aboriginal woman autobiographer, Ruby Langford (Ginibi), has described her undertaking thus:

> My story is about twentieth century Aboriginal Life. About the way we live today. And it's probably the only information a lot of students get that puts the Aboriginal point of view. Because Koori [Aboriginal] history and culture is almost never taught in schools, and if it is, it is usually as it is seen by whites, and not from an Aboriginal perspective. (1991, 129)

This point is reinforced by the prominent Aboriginal activist Marcia Langton: "Australians do not know and relate to Aboriginal people. They relate to stories told by former colonists" (quoted in O'Regan 1996, 277). Morgan's narrative fulfills this educative role, negotiating between two Australias and two versions of Australian history (see Brewster 1996, 125). Morgan recounts being sent as a child to negotiate between her war-traumatized and deranged father and her terrified mother: "'He'll listen to you,' they said. I don't think he ever did. . . . One night, I told Nan I didn't want to go, but she said, 'You must, there's no one else'" (Morgan 1987, 41–42). This relationship of mediation between violent white father and Aboriginal mother prefigures the later role of *My Place*, that of constituting an appellative form that bridges the gap between indigenous experience and a white audience. Todorov suggests that the narrator in the detective story is a mediator whose *sujet*-construction work makes the buried crime-*fabula* available not only for himself, but also for the reader (1980, 13). In this respect, Morgan performs the role of detective-as-mediator in a manner similar to that of Upfield's Bony. The go-between status of the part-Aboriginal sleuth, bridging the gap between black and white cultures, is crucial to this mediator role. The salient function of *My Place* is to make Aboriginal history, in particular the history of forcible removal, available for Australians. As Muecke pertinently suggests, the text also occupies a synecdochic position, standing for countless other untold stories of indigenous deprivation (1992, 133). Thus *My Place* prefigured by a decade the massive accumulation of bare facts and figures in the "Bringing Them Home" report and quite possibly paved the way for the public reception of the information transmitted in a more detailed fashion in the later report. The detective story structure underlying Morgan's narrative is thus crucial to *My Place*'s status as "a significant act of intercultural brokerage" (Donaldson 1991, 350).

The work of mediation undertaken by the book can also be seen in its appropriation of the recent history of Aboriginal politics. Sally's own rediscovery of her past goes hand in hand with the discrete marking of notable political events in the emergent activism of indigenous people in Australia. Thus, the narrative of Morgan's personal discovery of her Aboriginal identity runs parallel to white Australia's progressive awakening to the presence of an indigenous people demanding public and political recognition. Many of the dates Morgan inserts in her text as chronological markers correspond to political milestones outside the narrator's private world, but whose significance is crucial for the public fulfillment of a private quest.

In this regard, Morgan's text is a hybrid form, straddling personal discovery and public emergence. Her text is an example of what Todorov has called a gnoseological or epistemological narrative: a narrative that emphasizes less the question, "What will happen next?" than the question, "How do perceptions change in the course of the story?" (1987, 53–54). Morgan's story, like all detective narratives, is a narration of epistemological transformation both on the individual and the collective planes. The mediating role of the narrator connects these two functions so as to make indigenous history available in a personalized form for the white Australian reader: "Morgan offers . . . a knowing and ultimately triumphal relationship with history" (Rowse 1993, 102).

However, if Sally as "detective" fulfills the role of mediator that Todorov ascribes to the sleuth, she as an Aboriginal person also constitutes one of the victims of the crimes—and the public with whom she communicates must find itself on the side of the perpetrators. The task of mediation is thus complicated by the fact that the text's principal readers, white Australians, including myself, inevitably read their own indictment in the revelation of a history of injustice (see Rowse 1993, chap. 1). Thus, inherent to Morgan's project are conflicting components which at once enlighten and alienate. Both aspects are acknowledged in Nan's assessment: "There's been a lot of coverin' up," "Time to tell what it's been like in this country," and "The government and the white man must own up to their mistakes" (1987, 349).

This tension between enlightenment and alienation is most clearly evident in Morgan's style. Language is a crucial facet of her undertaking, as is indicated by the narrator's repeated allusions to indigenous languages that remain inaccessible to her as a nontribal Aborigine (see Morgan 1987, 30, 47, 148–49), which in turn is an implicit judgment on the value of the English language. Something that cannot fail to draw the reader's attention in *My Place* is the resolutely colloquial tone of the narrative, its apparent refusal of sophisticated narrative technique, its artless, indeed naive, register. Stated bluntly, the book is exceptionally easy to read, which, incidentally, makes it a favorite choice of students. The tone of Morgan's autobiographical account is typically suburban and lower middle class, ostentatiously Australian with its references to "chip-heaters" and "kero," to the ubiquitous vegemite sandwich or to goannas in the backyard, and characteristically antipodean in its bland unawareness of, or indifference to, the utter banality of such details. However, it is the contrast with the occasional footnotes that makes one realize that this style is not (only) the narrator's natural "tone of writing," but a careful transposition of a particular Australian social register—all the more so in that the transcribed autobiographical texts of her mother and grandmother assume yet other registers (Nan's narrative is strongly marked as nonstandard English). The everyday Australian register is the central vehicle of the autobiography's communicative function. It allows Morgan to perform two otherwise mutually exclusive functions: on the one hand, to speak explicitly as an indigenous person with the moral authority conveyed by that status, and, on the other hand, to speak implicitly as an average Australian, with another sort of moral authority typical of antipodean working-class reverse snobbery.

The use of conversational Aussie-English is the key to the mediating function served by *My Place*. Morgan's text makes the indigenous tradition, and perspectives upon the historical forces responsible for the destruction of that tradition, available to the white Australian readers in a form that can be readily received. As David Napier comments, a given culture can only perceive foreignness, be it ethnic or historical, two pertinent forms of alterity made visible in Morgan's autobiography, if it is encoded in a form "enough like us, and only enough unlike us, to be heuristically useful" (Napier 1992, 140). In their *Dark Side of the Dream*, Hodge and Mishra propound the thesis of a schizophrenic/hebephrenic split in Australian culture, according to which Australian culture oscillates between a paranoid alertness to threatening double meanings in public discourse and a philistine refusal to heed anything but the literal meanings of words. Hodge and Mishra argue that these phenomena are two sides of white Australia's ongoing repression of its colonial past, motivated by a profound but repressed collective guilt regarding the expropriation of Aboriginal land. Thus, a hostile sensitivity to perceived double meanings and the radical rejection of deeper meanings can be seen as two (only apparently) contra-dictory symptoms of national repression of a history of illegitimate confiscation of Aboriginal territory (see Hodge and Mishra 1991, chap. 10). Both these functions can be identified in Morgan's text, and it is not implausible that the acclaim granted to the book is connected to the fact that her style allows these functions to be reconciled. Australian paranoia is given a safe epistemological space in a language that appeals to the featurelessness of Australian discourse; the mystery story allows the admission of a second level of meaning, while couching this discovery in an absolutely flat linguistic code. This dialectic is, of course, central to the detective novel, which alternates between bland surface (whether of persons, events, or things) and a murderous depth. This double function mirrors Morgan's double identity as ordinary Australian and indigenous representative.

In this way, *My Place* can achieve what could only be gestured at by Upfield: the full revelation of a history of white crimes against the original population of the continent. To this extent, Morgan's text touches upon the seldom-asked question of the reader to whom the detective novel is addressed, and of the ways in which the reader is interpellated, manipulated, and guided through the process of discovery of the crime (see Dunker 1991). The principal difference between Morgan's "detective story" and more conventional examples of the genre is that this reader is a collective reader—white Australia as a whole. Thereby, the reader is in some way also identified, albeit never explicitly, and via only one aspect of diverse and complex modes of address in indigenous autobiographies (see Rowse 1993, chap. 4), as carrying some sort of responsibility for the crimes revealed. It is also for this reason that the text is so preoccupied with the establishment of a discursive community: in order not to alienate a public that it inevitably places in the dock. The question is, then, to what extent are the conflicting tasks of Morgan's detective narrative, which combines revelation with accusation, at loggerheads?

The very factors making communication with a white reader possible may well militate against the aim of such communication. The construction of a common discursive ground with white readers has drawn deeply hostile responses from indigenous critics. Sally Morgan has been attacked for reaching some sort of "accommodation" with white Australian society (see Narogin 1990, 14–15). In particular, Morgan's diction would appear to be complicit in this process, as it inevitably panders to the white assumption that a text written by a member of a marginalized ethnic group will lack the sophistication of literary technique and will use an "effortless stream of natural expression from a 'speaking' rather than a 'writing' subject" (Gilbert 1988, 190; see also Muecke 1992, 130). It has been suggested that the individualized narrative voice of *My Place* speaks directly to a comfortable Australian middle-class sensibility and mode of subjectivity and thereby renounces its own potential for cultural subversion (see Jaireth 1995). In comparison, for instance, to Ruby Langford (Ginibi)'s *Don't Take Your Love to Town* (1988), Morgan's text offers a "comfortable positioning of the reader"; it is careful not to unduly disturb the complacency of the reader (see Rowse 1993, 103, and Muecke 1992, 135). In other contemporary indigenous narratives, such as those of the storyteller Paddy Roe, Aboriginal English is used as a cultural bridge between black and white cultures, albeit as one that involves considerably more work for white readers (see Muecke in Roe 1983, vi, and Chambers 1991, 19–20).

Morgan's diction is particularly problematic, because the confessional voice is the primary vehicle of the revelatory function of the detective narrative. This employment of an expressive, individual voice in Morgan's narrative may well be at odds with the defense of indigenous culture to which the text aspires. It is significant that against Sally's coercive drive to revelation and confession, which earns her the epithet of "bloody detective," Nan is less ready to reveal her experience, in keeping with traditional indigenous customs of secrecy and more recent habits of judicious silence in the face of police repression and anthropological probing (see Muecke 1992, 119–30). Sally's triumphant "She's agreed to talk," when Nan finally gives way to the granddaughter's demands for information, acquires chilling associations in this context (Morgan 1987, 320). Moreover, the major accusatory force of the text resides in Nan's sections of the narrative, and not in those of her granddaughter. This suggests that the detective narrative is not the only strategy apt to lay bare a history of oppression. More disturbingly, it also raises the possibility that the detective metanarrative may not always work in the service of indigenous interests; that on the contrary, it may infringe upon or curtail them.

Thus Morgan's narrative style appears to offer itself to recuperation within white society. The deflection of the message implemented by the text, both in its generic (detective) affiliation and its populist diction, runs the risk of having its accusatory force flattened and blunted. In other words, the discursive strategy employed by the text to enable its unpalatable message to be conveyed to white Australia, a collective subject adept at forgetting the racial crimes of the past, may risk vitiating its own objectives. The detective structure of the text reveals a crime, but in the mode of its revelation to a reading public (a public inevitably compromised by that revelation) it implicitly diverts the force of its indictment.

In this context of textual containment it is worth recalling the stalling of the long-awaited reparation of wrongs done to the indigenous peoples of Australia in the 1990s and early 2000s (for regular updates on current issues, see the ATSIC Web address in the Works Cited). Significant in this respect was the Australian government's attempt before the High Court to challenge the historical existence of the Stolen Generation, a revisionist coup that was rejected in decisive terms by the court; the same judge, however, also ruled in 2000 against the first two cases for compensation filed by members of the Stolen Generation. Moreover, as the "Bringing Them Home" report claims, Aboriginal children are still being removed from their families at an unacceptable rate, whether by the child welfare or the juvenile justice systems, or both. This means that a high proportion of the people affected by the past laws, practices, and policies of forcible removal continue to have their own children taken from them in turn. A process of second (or subsequent) generation removal has been found to have occurred in more than one in three cases (see part 12). This larger context in which Morgan's project of detection/accusation is to be situated inevitably modifies the ostensibly optimistic stance of the story, giving its enlightenment values of historiographical education, informed dialogue, and discursive community a decidedly ironic edge. The text celebrates the restoration of indigenous community after generations of deliberate dislocation on the part of white policy; and yet, as the text attains canonical status, the crimes it reveals and "overcomes" by laying them bare continue to be perpetrated by a white Australia reluctant to embrace profound structural change in its relationship to its indigenous peoples.

If *My Place* is to be read as an ethnic detective story, it may need to be categorized as a postmodern antidetective narrative, in which the traditional meting out of justice as a result of the detection of the crime can no longer be taken for granted, in keeping with other postmodern narratives that eschew narrative closure and axiological resolution (see Tani 1984, 39–40). The dissonance between narrative resolution of crimes against indigenous peoples present in Morgan's text and the real continuation of a historical process of expropriation and discrimination is also a common characteristic of indigenous detective fiction from other parts of the English-speaking world (see Libretti 1999, 62, and Stewart 1999, 170). In a genre once noted either for its indifference to sociopolitical questions or for its ideology of defense of middle-class order against a threat from below (see Benstock 1983, 189, and Knight 1980, 1–7), this aspect of indigenous detective fiction represents a radical rupture and demands a rethinking of the very notion of crime narrative. For all its importance as a milestone of contemporary indigenous literature, this profound ambivalence in *My Place*, paradoxically associated with the very terms in which the text endeavors to inform white Australians of their own past, complicates and hampers Morgan's project. Even when Morgan's autobiography confronts and revises earlier representations of crimes against the indigenous peoples, to be found for instance in Upfield's Bony narrative, such an undertaking appears to be trammeled by the broader discursive formations constraining the enunciation of indigenous discourses of activism and protest. Or, alternatively, to reformulate an issue addressed by John Irwin, the ethnic mystery story, once it has been unraveled, does not cease to hold the interest of the reader; it does this through its synecdochic refiguring of a social dilemma whose urgency as a nonfictional task remains insistently in the form of a "mystery to a solution," necessarily beyond the boundaries of the inevitably limited reach of the fictional project (see Irwin 1994, 2).

WORKS CITED

Anderson, Benedict. 1991. *Imagined Communities: Reflections on the Origin and Spread of Nationalism.* 2d ed. London: Verso.

ATSIC. Aboriginal and Torres Straits Islanders Commission Homepage. www.atsic.gov.au (10 August 2001).

Benstock, Bernard. 1983. "The Education of Martin Beck." In *Essays on Detective Fiction*, edited by Bernard Benstock, 189–209. London: Macmillan.

Benterrak, Krim, Stephen Muecke, and Paddy Roe. 1984. *Reading the Country: Introduction to Nomadology.* Fremantle: Fremantle Arts Centre Press.

Brewster, Anne. 1996. *Reading Aboriginal Women's Autobiography.* Sydney: Sydney University Press.

"Bringing Them Home: Report of the National Inquiry into the Separation of Aboriginal and Torres Strait Islander Children from Their Families." *Reconciliation and Social Justice Library Homepage.* April 1997. www.austlii.edu.au/au/special/rsjproject/rsjlibrary/hreoc/stolen/prelim.html (10 August 2001).

Chambers, Ross. 1991. *Room for Maneuver: Reading (the) Oppositional (in) Narrative.* Chicago: University of Chicago Press.

Donaldson, Tamsin. 1991. "Australian Tales of Mystery and Miscegenation." *Meanjin* 50:341–52.

Dunker, Michael. 1991. *Beeinflussung und Steuerung des Lesers in der englischsprachigen Detektiv- und Kriminalliteratur.* Frankfurt: Peter Lang.

Gilbert, Pam. 1988. *Coming Out from Under: Contemporary Australian Women Writers.* Sydney: Unwin Hyman.

Gilroy, Paul. 1993. *There Ain't No Black in the Union Jack: The Cultural Politics of Race and Nation.* London: Routledge.

Gosselin, Adrienne Johnson, ed. 1999. *Multicultural Detective Fiction: Murder from the "Other" Side.* New York: Garland.

Healy, J. J. 1989. *Literature and the Aboriginal in Australia.* St. Lucia: University of Queensland Press.

Hodge, Bob, and Vijay Mishra. 1991. *Dark Side of the Dream: Australian Literature and the Postcolonial Mind.* Sydney: Allen and Unwin.

Irwin, John T. 1994. *The Mystery to a Solution: Poe, Borges, and the Analytical Detective Story.* Baltimore: Johns Hopkins University Press.

Jaireth, Subhash. 1995. "The 'I' in Sally Morgan's *My Place:* Writing of a Monologised Self." *Westerly* 40, no. 3:69–78.

Knight, Stephen. 1980. *Form and Ideology in Crime Fiction*. London: Macmillan.

Langer, Beryl. 1991. "The Real Thing: Cliff Hardy and Cocacola-Nisation." *SPAN* 31:29–44.

Langford, Ruby (Ginibi). 1991. "Introductory Notes to 'Koori Dubays.'" In *Heroines*, edited by Dale Spender, 129. Ringwood, Victoria: Penguin.

Libretti, Tim. 1999. "Lucha Corpi and the Politics of Detective Fiction." In Gosselin 1999, 61–82.

Morgan, Sally. 1987. *My Place*. Fremantle: Fremantle Arts Centre Press.

Muecke, Stephen. 1992. *Textual Spaces: Aboriginality and Cultural Studies*. Sydney: University of New South Wales Press.

Napier, A. David. 1992. *Foreign Bodies: Performance, Art, and Symbolic Anthropology*. Berkeley and Los Angeles: University of California Press.

Narogin, Mudrooroo. 1990. *Writing from the Fringe: A Study of Modern Aboriginal Literature*. Melbourne: Hyland House.

O'Regan, Tom. 1996. *Australian National Cinema*. London: Routledge.

Roe, Paddy. 1983. *Gularabulu: Stories from the West Kimberley*, edited by Stephen Muecke. Fremantle: Fremantle Arts Centre Press.

Rowley, C. D. 1972. *The Destruction of Aboriginal Society*. Ringwood, Victoria: Penguin.

Rowse, Tim. 1993. *After Mabo: Interpreting Indigenous Traditions*. Melbourne: Melbourne University Press.

Shklovsky, Viktor. 1990. *Theory of Prose (1925/1929)*. Translated by Benjamin Sher. Elmswood Park, Ill.: Dalkey Archive Press.

Stewart, Michelle Pagni. 1999. "'A Rose by Any Other Name': A Native American Detective Novel by Louis Owens." In Gosselin 1999, 167–83.

Tani, Stefano. 1984. *The Doomed Detective: The Contribution of the Detective Novel to Postmodern American and Italian Fiction*. Carbondale: Southern Illinois University Press.

Todorov, Tzvetan. 1980. "Typologie du roman policier." *Poétique de la prose suivi de Nouvelles recherches sur le récit*, 9–19. Paris: Seuil.

———. 1987. "Les deux principes du récit." In *La Notion de littérature et autres essais*, 47–65. Paris: Seuil.

Upfield, Arthur. [1959] 1984. *Bony and the Black Virgin*. Sydney: Pan Books.

Part IV:
Interviews

An Interview with
Barbara Neely

ALISON D. GOELLER

6 APRIL 2001, TOURS, FRANCE

AG: I'd like to start off by asking a question about how you work, because I'm really interested in that. Perhaps you could just talk about how you work, what your work habits are. Do you write every day?

BN: I was trying to decide whether I should talk about the ideal days or the usual days; so let's see. I try to write every day; I can't say that I'm successful all the time, but I do try to write every day. I usually try to start my day by 7:30 in the morning, which allows me a couple of hours to fiddle around before I can finally settle down to my desk. I am now working on a first draft, and usually I write both in longhand and on the computer. I start in longhand and will go on writing in longhand if that's working; sometimes your mind is working faster than your head and I'll switch to a computer. I do write longhand and put it into the computer and, of course, revise those pages as I'm putting them into the computer. I print out a copy, revise it by hand, then revise it in the computer. I used to have a page count for myself, but I don't really do that anymore. I try to write at least half a day, then take a walk in the middle of the afternoon, read what I've written in the morning, that evening, throw half of it in the wastepaper basket, and wonder what was I thinking of when I wrote this.

Generally, when a manuscript is finished—not a first draft, nobody gets to see a first draft—but when I have a draft that I think is halfway presentable, I have a system of readers that I send the manuscripts out to; the people who are listed in the acknowledgments are generally the people who read the books for me, give me feedback; some of it I take; some of it I don't. Most of the books—all of the

300   ALISON D. GOELLER

books—have been revised at least seven times before they're finished and, of course, as far as I am concerned, they are never finished; every time I read the book it's like, "Oh gosh, how could I miss this, how could they have let me put that sentence in that way?" So I guess, really, it isn't so much when you're finished, but when it's time to just let it go. When you know it won't get any better.

AG: The other question along with that is do you write every day, more or less 365 days of the year, because I know that some writers feel like they have to write every day even if they don't use it—or do you work on a book and then take some time off?

BN: No, time off is a very bad thing for me. Because writing for me is still very much of a scary process, so any break in it makes it very difficult for me to come back. So I do try—I won't say that I succeed—but I do try to write every day, and if not, if I don't get anything written, then at least I revise a page that I've already done. I do something that is somehow related to the manuscript every day because I think that a book is really written in the revision. There are often huge holes in it. I haven't done all the research for my latest book, I know that certain scenes need to go someplace but I haven't written them yet, and I don't want to stop to think about them, so I just put a note in: I need to do X here and I just go on. So with each revision, this is where the books actually get written; when the humor gets put in, when the character gets more developed—all of this stuff happens after the first draft.

AG: Yes, somebody said writing is really rewriting.

BN: Absolutely.

AG: Who do you imagine your audience to be? Toni Morrison has said over and over again that she started out as a writer because there weren't books out there that she wanted to read. I'm sure you know this. So I can imagine you theorize who you're writing for, but I was wondering . . .

BN: Oh, tell me your theory.

AG: Well, I think you're definitely writing for women; that's pretty clear to me. And probably black women, although I love your books. I spent a couple of weeks in Sardinia reading Barbara Neely and thinking, "This is so interesting. Here I am in Sardinia reading Barbara Neely." So that's who I would say your audience is, but I don't know. Do men read Barbara Neely? Do you write with them in mind?

BN: Yes, actually it's pretty much the Morrison answer. I'm my reader: I write the books that I want to read. Because this, in fact, is how the series began. I was working on another novel and when I would get stuck on it, I would go off and read the book of somebody who

AN INTERVIEW WITH BARBARA NEELY 301

already figured out how to do it. And I got to the point where I didn't have anything I particularly wanted to read. I've always been interested in political fiction; I don't think you get a lot of good political fiction. Usually, the politics are over here and the story is over there and the reader is running back and forth between the two. So I decided to just play around with whether or not I could write a book that was political, about race and class—and that was also funny. What sort of character can carry a story about race, class, and gender with humor? Every time I got stuck on the real book that I was working on, I would pick this other thing up and play with it. The books really began for myself so that I could read them and I've kept that.

AG: So you are the main reader?

BN: I am the reader, yes.

AG: And then, the thing that I'm dying to know is how Blanche came to you; because she is just so wonderful.

BN: It would be wonderful to have a clear memory of exactly what that process was, but as I said, I do remember thinking when I knew that I was going to be playing with this thing about race, class, and gender, who would be the right person to tell this story. I wanted the worldview and the inner life of a poor working-class woman, I knew that. When I lived in North Carolina—I lived there for about four years—I met a woman whose name was Blanche. And the Blanche in the books looks pretty much like her. I remember when I met her thinking that we need a heroine who looks like this woman; these are not the women who ever get to star in anything. I was thinking about race, class, and gender, and remembering Blanche; what a perfect name for a book about race and what a perfect name for a really, really dark-skinned black woman.

AG: And then Blanche White.

BN: Right, and so that just seemed sort of logical. The thing that I have been accused of in the past in other work situations is telling people something, then telling them that I told them and then telling them what I told them, just doing that over again. So with Blanche White, it was, "Well, if you don't get that this is a book about race, let me give you this big black woman whose name means white—twice."

AG: So you really wanted to make that clear.

BN: Yes, I did.

AG: Even though I was thinking that in some ways she's like Aunt Jemima. Are you appropriating that image by your making her . . . ?

BN: No, actually, the Aunt Jemima has appropriated Blanche's image, because there are millions and millions of women who look like

302 ALISON D. GOELLER

Blanche. What I was trying to do more than to represent Aunt Jemima was to do an antidote to her. This is the real black woman. That woman that you see in the commercial with that smile who you think is this loving, passive mammy—let me introduce you to who she really is.

AG: You've actually already answered the question about social significance or political agenda. I've done a lot of work with Walter Mosley, and I would say that you're doing it in a different way; I don't know if subtle is the right word. His is pretty hard-hitting. You have this feminist element in there, which I love. I'm sure a lot of readers really appreciate that, because that doesn't happen very often, especially in detective fiction.

BN: Well, it was really important for me to do that. I was talking the other day, I think before you got here, about how I wanted Blanche to be what I've been calling a behavioral feminist. That is, one who does not come to feminism through an organization or the academy or reading books, but from her gut; her life experience has told her that it's in her best interest to behave like a feminist. Now, if somebody asked Blanche if she's a feminist, I don't know how she would answer that question. I am pretty sure that if they asked her, "What do you think of Gloria Steinem," she would ask them whether she is on a soap opera or something. She has no idea. But, of course, if you ask her all the questions about equality, she has all of the feminist's answers. As I said, a more behavioral way of approaching things.

AG: And I think that makes it more powerful; maybe that's why I was thinking of the word "subtle," because it is a natural consequence of who she is, and then that's connected to this idea that she is not married and she has no children, although she's got these adopted kids, and she doesn't want to marry Leo. I assume that was deliberate.

BN: Absolutely! I wanted her to be a woman who did not want to have biological children, because, of course, we still live in societies that tell us that if your womb has not been used, you cannot be a real woman; I wanted to deal with that. There are huge numbers of women who are not attached to a man, and they have wonderfully fulfilling lives—I wanted to demonstrate that. And there are people who don't think that marriage is the only way to make yourself happy. And I have friends who have lovers they don't want living in their house, which to me makes absolute sense. I really did want to demonstrate those things. I wanted her to be a black woman who did not process her hair; she is very comfortable and happy with what she looks like and doesn't understand why people don't find this beautiful. Also,

AN INTERVIEW WITH BARBARA NEELY 303

because big women do not get that kind of affirmation, I thought that this is a really important thing to do.

AG: And she does get affirmation in the novels.

BN: Yes.

AG: She is very attractive to various men.

BN: And that's another thing I wanted to bring out that in the black community a fairly large percentage of men are attracted to big women, and I'm assuming that this is very much a part of coming from African peoples. I remember recently hearing a man from Ghana talking about the fact that you want a woman who has some meat; this is an indication of health and strength. So the Twiggy look is not popular throughout the black community. As I said, there is a fair percentage of men who like big women, but the impression that those women get from the larger society is that they can't possibly be attractive because they're too big.

AG: I am still very interested in how Blanche came to you; I was wondering if you read detective fiction. You came to Blanche first and then decided to make her a sleuth or . . . ?

BN: When I was working on the first book, and I only intended for it to be one book, I thought that what I was doing was writing a novel that had a murder in it. I did not think about it as a mystery, and I still don't think about the books in that way. The mystery aspect of the books is the least important and interesting aspect for me. Once I decided that there would be more than one book (I've told the story to people a thousand times), my editor suggested that I might want to write a sequel to the first book, and I didn't. It was like, I've written this book. Why would I want to keep working on this? And then a couple of days after he made that suggestion, my bank statement came and I called him back and said, "You know, Michael, the sequel, that sounds like a good idea." Either that or I was going to have to get a real job. So that's how the series actually began, and because the first book did so well—it was a mystery, it won three of the four major mystery awards in the States—it was clear to me that this was the perfect place to write about serious social issues in a way that was accessible to a popular audience who wouldn't necessarily pick up a book that says, "This is a book about race" or "This is a book about class and gender and feminism," but who would read the book because they want to know who did what to whom and along the way get what I think are the important parts of the book and that is the development of the character and the social issues in the book.

AG: So you are sneaky.

BN: Exactly. I think about the books in a way almost as being subversive. Because you may not want to know about color within the black community, but if you read *Blanche Among the Talented Tenth*, you will get that. And I have had readers say, "This is interesting; I didn't know anything about this. I wouldn't have read this book if I knew it was going to just be about this!"

AG: That's great. And I'm also very interested in Blanche and Ardell, their relationship. Part of that is just exposition: Blanche gets on the phone and tells her what's going on. It's nice to see that friendship and it's a friendship where even if they're not geographically close to each other, they're always on the phone. How did that happen?

BN: I don't know any healthy women of any color who don't have girlfriends; I don't know how people get by without girlfriends, so that was just a logical thing. Of course, she would have somebody that she was close to. But in the fourth book, Blanche is back in her hometown and for the first time she and Ardell are in the same place and see the tensions in the friendship that weren't as obvious on the telephone. I have numbers of long-distance girlfriends and we just love each other and we e-mail and we phone—then you decide to take a vacation together and, oh, yes, now I remember the fifteen things I can't stand about her. So in that book there is some tension and they're logically in different directions. So I'm going to be very curious to see how their friendship develops from this point on. They will always be friends at some level because they have history together. But whether they'll be as close or whether there will be even more tension in the relationship—I don't know yet.

AG: In comparison to the hard-boiled detective who is always alone, a female sleuth really can't be alone, because, you're right, women— of course, there are exceptions—women just don't operate that way and so it would make sense. I really love that friendship.

BN: But you've asked me whether or not I read detective fiction. I did read detective fiction until I started working on that series and then I stopped; because I'm one of those people who learn best from books, I don't want to professionalize Blanche. I don't even think of her as an amateur sleuth, I think of her as an everyday black woman who deals with whatever problems life presents and I want to keep that. So I have stopped reading detective fiction, but when I did, I gravitated, of course, to people like Sarah Paretsky, who, at least when I was reading detective fiction, was one of the very few women who broke that hard-boiled thing. She has family; she has people that she cares about, people she's involved with; she seemed much more like a real person to me than the other female detectives out there.

AG: So will you keep writing Blanche books?

BN: I think that there will be at least two more, because I know that the way in which I decide about the books is: What is the issue that I want to write about? And I know that I want to write a book about ageism. And so I know that there will be at least that one. And I would like to do something, I think, around black land laws in the South. Black farmers in the United States were just losing their land at a huge rate. It may turn out that these book subjects are in the same book, so at least one, probably two, and I don't know beyond that. I'm now working on a book that is not a Blanche book, cannot in any way be construed as a mystery except in the sense that all novels are mysteries, because you want to know what happened. And I'm uneasy about it, I feel like a typecast actress; I don't know if anyone will buy another Blanche book.

AG: I don't know if you are familiar with Donna Leon, an American mystery writer whose books are set in Venice. Her books are very popular in German translation and, in fact, several have been televised. I think she's on her eighth or ninth novel and I imagine there is a lot of pressure on her to keep writing. She is only one example, of course. Might you at some point say, "I've had it with Blanche!"

BN: I'm sure I will at some point; this has got to happen eventually. Every time I've finished one and it's time to start the next one, I have this sinking feeling like, "Oh no, why have I done this?" But the fact that she is ageing, she is not the same person in every book. . . . I don't know how people write series in which their character is thirty-five years old for fifteen years; that's got to be boring at some level. So there's always an issue: I remember when I was out on tour, maybe it was after the second book, somebody was saying, "Wow, are you going to write more Blanche books?" I said, "Yes." She said, "Don't forget menopause!"

AG: Do you feel her presence when you're writing?

BN: What happens with me is that there are certain directions that I can't go because of who Blanche is. For example, at the end of the first book, what I had planned to happen was to have Blanche be rescued by Archibald, you know, the lawyer, and I tried for weeks and weeks to write that scene and it was just as flat as this floor; it wouldn't work. Finally, it was almost like I could hear Blanche saying to me, "I'm not a runner, I'm a fighter; when was the last time a white man ever saved me from anything?" So I realized that it didn't really work. There's a way in which she keeps me strict. The character is developed in such a way that she will not let me write her out of character.

306 ALISON D. GOELLER

AG: So she really is there at some point?

BN: Yes.

AG: This morning when you were reading, I was thinking about your ancestor altar. I hope this is not too personal a question, but I wondered if there was any autobiographical element, and that was the one I thought of: "Does Barbara Neely have an altar?"

BN: It's more related to the fact that there are lots of—I don't want to say lots—certainly a substrata of African Americans who are really uncomfortable with both Christianity and Islam, because they associate both religions with our oppression either in the United States or in Africa, but who also recognize that they want some sort of spiritual life. People talk about how they resent the fact that you can't get ritual unless you go to church. What would a person do, then, if they wanted a spiritual life and couldn't fit into that? And, of course, both religions fly right against Blanche's brand of feminism, because they're run by boys, and she wouldn't be interested in any of that. But I do think that there is a strain of a kind of ancestor worship that runs through me and probably all African American people. Once again, coming from African people, ancestor worship is an important spiritual aspect. I was saying to some black people recently that we do it without giving it a name: the numbers of women who get pregnant when somebody dies in their family, the number of children who are born who are not just named for someone but are told, "You have our Aunt Clara's personality." So I think it is something that runs through our community; we just don't call it that. In fact, I asked one young man about his tombstone dates on his arms and he said, "This is the day my grandmother was born and the day she died." So there's another kind of ancestor worship.

AG: But you don't have an altar?

BN: I'm not answering that.

AG: Is there anything else you can think of that you want to say about your craft? Can you speak about this other book that you're writing?

BN: Well, just a little bit. It is a book set in the 1950s in a small town and I started thinking about this book when I heard a black minister who'd been intimately involved in the civil rights movement say that he now feels as though integration is the worst thing that ever happened to us. And I started thinking about people for whom that literally would be true, and that's what the book is about, that integration is coming and half the community is for it, the other half is resisting, and how that plays out.

AG: That's great. I wonder about your translated books?

AN INTERVIEW WITH BARBARA NEELY 307

BN: I am concerned about translations, because it makes me wonder whether people who are reading the book translated into another language are in fact reading the same book that I've written. I've talked to German friends who read the book both in English and in German and said the German version loses a great deal through the translation. In fact, I wanted to ask the translator who spoke this afternoon, "What is the color of the person who does the translation?" It seemed to me that to use an American who is fluent in French, for example, would be the best possible way to go. So then it's somebody who at least understands the culture and can get closer to it than someone who, you know—all they do is translate books and don't really have any sense of the culture the books are coming out of.

AG: I can just imagine that would be a huge problem, but I can't imagine somehow that it would be successful unless there was somebody who . . .

BN: Or at least one of her readers should know the culture, because translators talk about the fact that they do the translations, somebody reads it, then they need to do more. I have a black American friend who lived in Germany for fifteen years, and I was thinking, somehow she ought to be involved in the translation. She could undoubtedly point out things that they will miss. Writing across cultures, across languages is a very exciting and challenging endeavor.

AG: Thank you very much for your time.

An Interview with
Valerie Wilson Wesley

DOROTHEA FISCHER-HORNUNG
and MONIKA MUELLER

7 DECEMBER 2000, COLOGNE, GERMANY

MM: Welcome to Cologne. Are you looking forward to your readings here in Germany?

VWW: Oh, it is very exciting to be here and I have much more time than I usually do—just one city a day. I once had a tour for *No Hiding Place* with three cities all in one day, Chicago, Detroit, and Atlanta. It was very exhausting. And you're reading with people and every reader in the audience is different. You owe your readers something. They bought the book; they're excited about the character—you owe them at least your attention. But it is exhausting.

DFH: How often do you do reading tours like this?

VWW: Well, it's getting to the point where actually I'm happy now about doing a reading tour at all. The publishing business is changing rapidly. They do these tours less and less often because they tend to be expensive. And you're happy if you get a tour because many writers don't get one at all. I toured for *No Hiding Place* but not for *Easier to Kill*. My tour for *Ain't Nobody's Business* was the longest; that was about a twelve-city tour. And then, of course, I'm touring here in Germany with *Easier to Kill*. The first few tours were kind of fun—good hotels, nice food. But you certainly have to work for it; you do have to sing for your supper.

MM: Are you going to any other places in Europe?

VWW: No, just to Germany. Diogenes is a really fine publisher. They are really top-notch.

AN INTERVIEW WITH VALERIE WILSON WESLEY 309

MM: What other languages have your books been translated into?

VWW: French and Polish. I haven't seen the Polish version, though. But publishing in Europe is so different from publishing in the States now. In the U.S.A. you never meet your publisher—you do meet your editor—maybe once. Very often there's no one person who guides you, a person like Ruth Geiger, who personally guides my books for Diogenes.

DFH: There are major differences between U.S. and European publishing. In Germany, for example, the price of books is fixed and people complain about the high prices. German books are, therefore, comparatively expensive, but it has helped prevent some of the extreme consolidation that you find in the U.S.A. Small publishers, unfortunately to a decreasing extent, can still survive. The volume possible in English is also much greater so the price can be lower. Often, the translation into English of a German book, for example, is cheaper than the original. There's simply a bigger market for books in English.

VWW: Another difference is how the audience is targeted. With my books in the States, they don't really target my audience as the mystery audience. All my mysteries are seen as "black" books. That's what they market them for—this is Penguin/Putnam—and I have a lot of mystery fans who are white. What they did on the last tour for *No Hiding Place*, which I thought was unconscionable, was that they sent me to Dallas—which has a really nice mystery bookstore whose owner I happen to know—but they didn't send me to that store, much less any mystery store. They just sent me to the black bookstore. I certainly have a very large African American audience, but I have a mystery audience as well. And they didn't seem to see that. They're really limiting the number of books I could sell.

MM: Does it surprise you that your books are so successful in Germany?

VWW: It just makes me feel so good! I can't tell you how important that is to me. I think it's the same feeling that African American musicians have when they play at home and they find that they're restricted. When they come to Europe, it's often like an emancipation. Music is for everybody and so are my books. My books are for everybody—I just write, share the experience, and would like other people to experience it, too. It's a very important feeling and it's a really important affirmation of myself as a writer. I can't tell you how much it means . . . Often in America—a personal prejudice—they just put you in a little box. Even with *Ain't Nobody's Business If I Do*. It's about women and marriage and men. Race is not even mentioned, you know. There's no reason to mention it. If you describe a character, you certainly might describe their skin tone, just like they might have blonde hair. It is simply part of how they look. Yet when it came out, some of the booksellers didn't put it with *new* books; they put it with *black* books. As a result, a lot of readers who were looking for it couldn't find it. Several readers even wrote to me because they couldn't figure out why they couldn't find the book. When I talked to a bookseller, the answer was, "Well, black people come into the store and they want . . ."

DFH: Isn't it possible to position a book in two places?

VWW: Well, in some stores, they do put it in the "mysteries" and in the "black" sections. One advantage of on-line ordering is that it kind of erases all that classification business. You just type in the title and up comes your book—no black, no mystery. For Diogenes, who markets my German translations, the fact that there is a problem not only with content positioning but also with language is somewhat difficult. They are selling the German versions to the people who come to the readings. But I have heard it is not hard to get the English versions on-line in Germany. But they're very generous in that respect, too.

DFH: There are the cases of Americans who have published and sold more outside of the United States—Chester Himes being a famous example, with many of his mysteries first published in French rather than English. Currently, Donna Leon sells many more books in German translation than in the original English and proportionally more of her books are sold in Great Britain than in the United States.

VWW: I know. Ruth Geiger was telling me that John Irving, for example, sells better in Germany than in the U.S. I really think it's the limitations in American publishing companies because they're under such financial pressure. Many of them have been sold; there've been so many changes so quickly that many of them are afraid to take chances. But there are examples of companies who do take chances: Scholastic, which is a family-owned company, took a great risk with the *Harry Potter* books. They probably would not have been published if they had not been a family-owned company. They have a certain kind of self-confidence, a vision about what books are about.

MM: There was an interview in the German version of *Rolling Stone* magazine that said that the German *Harry Potter* publisher, Carlsen in Hamburg, which is a really small publishing company,

AN INTERVIEW WITH VALERIE WILSON WESLEY 311

has made it really big. I guess they just can't believe what is happening. They took a risk and it worked.

DFH: How much influence does your publisher have on the content, on the themes in your books?

VWW: None, actually absolutely none! I'll tell you how that happened. It was a deal-breaker with my first book. The editor wanted certain changes, and I just felt I had to have control over the content. I explained that the whole structure of the book depended upon particular details. A particular thing happens and that's what sets my protagonist, Tamara, into action. That's what makes her realize what is happening; you can't simply change that. This was my first book and I was very uncertain about standing up for myself. I talked to my husband and I asked him what to do. And Richard said, "You know, if you compromise on this now, you will never have control over your work all the way down the line. You've got to face it!" And he was right. But I was really scared when I went to the publisher, so I said, "I don't know, let's just compromise, maybe we can find a way to make it work . . ."

DFH: That must have been terrifying the first time around.

VWW: Oh, it was scary . . . And my agent asked me what I wanted to do. I knew what I wanted and decided to stick to it. The thought of having to rewrite what I had done just made me ill. It went all the way to the top because the editor insisted on changes—and then on, and on, and on. But I stuck it out, thinking: "If you sell out that cheap in the first round, there's no limit."

DFH: At your reading last night, you mentioned the idea of selling the movie rights. I remember Doctorow once saying at a lecture in Heidelberg that he would never do another movie after the film version of *Ragtime* since you sell your soul when you sell the rights. But then there was the *Billy Bathgate* film made after his statement, wasn't there?

VWW: When they do the film script, they change so much and you have no say. You take the money and that's it! I did think about selling the movie rights. Walter Mosley actually approached me because he wanted to produce a film. He's probably the only one that I would trust. He would write the screenplay or my husband, who's a screenwriter, would do it, but I would have to have control. The difference between films and writing is that as a writer your work goes straight from the writer to the reader and there's no one in between. So it's just a complete, direct connection. You bring in somebody else with their own particular perception and the whole thing is distorted.

312   DOROTHEA FISCHER-HORNUNG AND MONIKA MUELLER

DFH: I guess that was part of the discussion surrounding Oprah Winfrey's film version of *Beloved*. How can you actually visualize the spirit of Beloved?

VWW: I know, I know. It's just beyond any kind of visualization. It can't be done. You can't capture it. No nuances are captured.

MM: How do you go about plotting your books?

VWW: In terms of plotting a book, you know where it ends, at least in general. You know who the murderer is and you know where it is going to end. And you also know there's a certain path which the character must take to get there—you know that road. There are a number of plot points that give the novel its structure, its form. I even go so far as to plot out each chapter individually. Chapter by chapter, I determine what's going to happen and who's going to be in it. Then you have to pace it because pacing is everything in a mystery. And you can pace it only if you have a sense of structure. A lot of writers don't use outlines. Walter [Mosley] doesn't use outlines, which is amazing

DFH: But he must have a sense of the structure in his head.

VWW: He's a brilliant guy . . . But I have to have something that I can look at and say, this is what is happening and where I am going. Even with the love story [*Ain't Nobody's Business If I Do*], it's the same thing. I thought that I would be able to just write it, but I had to have a structure for it. As an author you then take that structure and use it as a general framework.

MM: Well, obviously, you're using some of the conventions of detective fiction. Which generic rules do you use?

VWW: There are a couple—I always have the murderer appear in the first two or three chapters. I mean, he's always there or she's always there. You've got to grab the reader. And you may not know where he or she is, but they're there. Like the parking attendant, Johns, in *Easier to Kill*. How that came to me was because I was actually in a parking lot with a guy like that. You know, I never noticed him; he was invisible. You don't really notice these guys; you don't have to see them. They come over and want you to pay money—the usual. But you never know; what if this person were somehow involved in something like this? But for example, I also had to make sure that Mandy Magic never actually sees him, because she would recognize him. So someone else parks her car. You have to establish things like this early in the plot. Later, it has to be obvious to the reader that this unrecognized person is guilty, but it can't be obvious from the beginning. You have to

AN INTERVIEW WITH VALERIE WILSON WESLEY   313

cover every single point. It has to be obvious, but not obvious at the same time. To make it subtle you have to connect it with something else, for example the reason why the parking attendant kills, which is the dead baby.

MM: And, of course, you have to put in some false clues. You have to lead the reader off the track.

VWW: Absolutely, throughout the novel.

MM: It seems to me that with women writers, you get less of that hard-boiled style, that sort of careless, tough attitude of the classic noir. Something we started calling semihard-boiled and you called medium hard-boiled in your lecture last night.

VWW: Yes, it's not really hard-boiled; well, it's softer than that.

MM: It seems to me that when females are the heroines, they are more connected to the community, more connected than the men in the genre are. Often they have more responsibility than the guys, who can stay sort of aloof as loners.

VWW: This is important. I think as women we simply *are* more connected to our community. The same holds true for women who are divorced: they still have time for the community—we belong to the church; we have parents . . .

DFH: Women's ethnic crime fiction seems to be characterized by this connection to a personal and ethnic community. But Mosley's characters are also embedded in their community, even if somewhat differently.

VWW: Mostly, I think it comes down to being a member of the black community. We do have those kinds of ties.

DFH: Well, but that's what I liked about Johns, the parking lot attendant character, because he reminds Tamara of her father, of her own father's invisibility. He is an ancestor, but he turns out to be such a dangerous one. Or turning around Rufus Greene. I love that character . . .

VWW: I had to turn him around. I couldn't have him just be a pimp, because I'm not going to have a man who beats women and who is all bad. He really does care for his daughter. And when he talks about Mandy, you know, he says she's gorgeous and red. But he isn't just the bad guy, the guy with absolutely no feelings. He isn't just the pimp. I wanted to do that because he is the girl's father. I cannot abide men who beat up women—as the girl's father, there had to be more to it.

MM: Another thing I noticed about women's writing is that food seems to take the position of drinking in the men's novels. This is also

314 DOROTHEA FISCHER-HORNUNG AND MONIKA MUELLER

characteristic of Barbara Neely's books. You know, I always want to eat when I read these books. Are you familiar with Garcia-Aguilera's books?

VWW: Yes, I haven't read her, but I know who she is.

MM: The Cuban food and the coffee and all that . . .

DFH: I had a Cuban American student in my class who's been away from Cuba for a long time. Now she's in Germany and when we · read Aguilera's books, she said she got very homesick for the food. I remember her reaction was, "Yeah, that's really what it is like! I get so hungry when I read those books. It's exactly what we eat on Sundays." For her eating *is* the community and a way of communicating.

VWW: With Jake in *No Hiding Place*, for example, it is sort of the same thing. He fries oysters for Tamara, something which I personally find terribly hard to do well. My idea there is that he is also a very nurturing man, a man who cooks and who kind of feeds Tamara.

DFH: Spiritual and physical feeding seem to be connected in a woman's consciousness.

VWW: Absolutely! We are the nurturers. We are the ones who feed.

DFH: But nurturing is not only about people in your novels. Newark seems to be very much like a character in your books, a character that needs nurturing. The city is like a person—an individual who has problems, who grows, who's constantly shifting, changing. Tamara has a difficult relationship with the police in Newark, for example. And, of course, the police are a part of Newark. And the African American community is also part of Newark. Tamara's difficult relation with the police seems to be connected with the problems between the city's police and the community.

VWW: It's such a difficult connection. On the one hand, well, I have had terrible things happen with the police. About ten years ago, my oldest daughter gave a party. We live in a racially mixed neighborhood, partly black and partly white. We knew she was giving a party and we were in the neighborhood, but not at home. The party was without alcohol—but the cops came to our house. My daughter told them they didn't have the right to come in, but the police saw that there were a lot of kids there—they were white and black. When the kids challenged them, they came in and beat up the kids. It was horrible! I wrote about it for *Essence* with one of my daughter's friends who was also at the party. I wrote it as a parent, she as a daughter.

This experience really fundamentally changed how I look at the police. I mean, they were terrible. My other daughter, who

AN INTERVIEW WITH VALERIE WILSON WESLEY 315

was sixteen at the time, at one point asked me, "What do we do if someone tries to break in. Who do I call? —Not the police!" I said, "Call the fire department." She was devastated and asked, "But Mom, the police have done this to us; what happens now? Who protects us?" Tamara knows this about the police. But, of course, there are good police . . . Actually, a friend who is a police officer called us and told us that we should go home because the situation at our house with the police was out of control.

DFH: Structurally, the police seem to have a problem.

VWW: I think the problem is being taught in certain things in certain ways about black people—it's the structure. And what happened with Tamara—she isn't comfortable with going to the police about anything. None of my characters want to go to the police.

DFH: That is an old generic feature of detective fiction. Then tension between the police and minorities is a specific example. Orson Welles's film *A Touch of Evil* plays with that fundamental structural problem of corruption as well as profiling as a specific example of minority oppression. But if you read the original novel by Whit Masterson, it's very interesting because Welles moved the plot to the Mexican border, the border between the first and the third world. The film totally politicizes the plot.

MM: Let me change the subject: male bashing. Do you think you bash men in your novels?

VWW: I hope not. I've tried to create men who are nice, rounded, strong . . .

MM: Jake is nice, but unavailable.

VWW: Yes, that's true. But there's Jamal.

DFH: Rufus Greene is . . .

VWW: I didn't bash Rufus Green even though he's got a very shady side. Actually men have been very positive about my male characters and have told me that I do a good job . . . And I try to.

MM: Tamara does not seem to be able to find a marriageable man. Do you want her to remain unattached?

VWW: Eventually, in the next Tamara book that I'm working on now, she's going to find a guy who is really OK. And that's going to go on for a couple of books.

MM: But then they'll split . . .

VWW: Well, I think what it comes down to is that he really can't accept what she does for a living. She's tough, and it's dangerous, but it's part of who she is. And that's what ultimately forces the couple apart. She's an independent soul.

DFH: But for many people it is sort of the modern condition. Even if

	you find a good relationship at some point, you change, the other person changes.
VWW:	That's the reality. Even in a good marriage, you have to be prepared. I mean, it's like, you can't sell your soul. Respecting each other's independence and having a sense of humor, that's what it often comes down to . . .
DFH:	Is there any author who's particularly important to you?
VWW:	In terms of PIs, I like John McDonald and his Travis McGee. But I guess Walter Mosley is my favorite, because he was out there doing it first. He took a genre and he made it his own. His stories take place in the thirties and forties, but in a way that I could connect to. I like the way he perceives the world, and the way he writes about it.
MM:	Who do you read outside of mystery fiction?
VWW:	Margaret Atwood. I love her and I've been reading her continuously most of this past year. Every book is different. She's been a real inspiration to me—what you can do, the chances you can take. I also like Iris Murdoch. I like a lot of different writers.
MM:	Sometimes it is important to reread a book years after a first encounter. I think Toni Morrison is an author like that.
VWW:	I reread *Sula* recently and I was astonished. It's still a revelation. But I can't get into *Paradise*.
DFH:	The problem is, what do you write after *Beloved*?
VWW:	I liked *Jazz*. It wasn't *Beloved*, but she took a lot of risks. The way she would change rhythms—it was like solos and duets and trios. It was jazz!
MM:	Do you ever read any academic criticism of your writing? One thing that critics often argue is that the detective formula doesn't really go with feminism—that you can't do both. Or that one genre takes precedence. It's either you're doing the feminist thing, or you're doing the detective thing. I was wondering what you think about that, and if it also applies to race and ethnicity? What's more important to you?
VWW:	Well, I don't know. I guess just telling a good story is uppermost; then comes getting points across. I think you can do them all if the character is strong enough, but I'm not sure.
DFH:	I think one of the advantages of writing African American detective fiction is that you don't have to spend as much time on the groundwork on explaining culture. That is not to say that there aren't any cultural differences between African American culture and the mainstream; that's not what I'm getting at. But if you take someone like Tony Hillerman—he's not Native American

AN INTERVIEW WITH VALERIE WILSON WESLEY 317

himself but he's done his homework—he has to spend much more time on explaining aspects of Navajo culture, because many people outside of and perhaps even in the Southwest have no access to it.

VWW: I think you're basically right. But also I think feminism is different for black women and white women. In her book *Women, Race, and Class*, Angela Davis really talks about how in some ways there are the same struggles but in other ways the struggle is different—there is a different sense of woman in a black community, for example. In Herbert Gutman's *Black Family in Slavery and Freedom*, he explains that when you had the choice between sending your daughter or your son to Harvard, you sent your daughter because you didn't want her working in the kitchen because she could be raped. And there was no recourse. That was the choice and it was such a fundamental choice. The same things didn't play out in the same way in white families. In my family, for example, my uncle took care of us because my mother was working and his wife was working. So there was a different struggle because racism oppressed everyone. In the sixties and seventies, the "problem with no name" was not an issue for black women. That is where a lot of the anger came from.

DFH: When I came to Germany in the early seventies, one of the fundamental differences between what I experienced in the U.S. and the German women's movement was the lack of consciousness about ethnic minorities. Race and ethnicity was, in many cases, a reality check for activist white women in the U.S.A. In Europe the emphasis was on class. Of course, the two are not unrelated, but the emphasis is different in the U.S.A. and Europe. The ethnic factor came into European thinking later through the migration of foreign workers and later the influx of refugees—but it came into the discussion of feminism for very different reasons.

MM: But if you think of the young Turkish women now. In my freshmen class, there are so many. I mean, people in my classes are from all over the world. Germany has become a multiethnic society even if there are still some people who deny it. There have been and will continue to be fundamental changes in European society due to this.

DFH: But Angela Davis, who studied in Frankfurt, emphasizes both class and race within the African American community.

VWW: Oh, absolutely, which is another thing that I write about. I think in my books it's especially reflected in the color consciousness within the community.

MM: Barbara Neely certainly emphasizes this point in her books.

VWW:	You know, I look at this in my latest book—I talked about color a lot more in *The Devil Riding* than in my previous books. It really talks a lot about color, in terms of the way it's a big thing with black people. That is the reality. So, if you make a lot of money, you marry "lighter"—a lot of times it's men who make a lot of money and they tend to marry women who have white skin, because that looks like the ruling class.
MM:	In Germany, if you think of Boris Becker and people like that, paradoxically it seems almost to be the other way around.
DFH:	It's trendy to have a "café au lait" partner.
VWW:	It's happening a little bit in the States; my oldest daughter went with a white guy, but it's not much of a question of being trendy. It's certainly not the same feelings they have for "mixing" that my generation had. They're very comfortable together. They don't talk about race; it's not the same. It's a real change. And if they talk about race, they talk about it freely. And then I think, "Thank God!" The United States is a country of great opportunity. The dream of it is there, of course, and people have died for that dream. Therefore I think in some ways Tamara is a very American character.
DFH:	You have written several children's books, for example, *Afro-Bets Book of Black Heroes from A to Z,* and *Where Do I Go from Here?*, which seems to be a young adult novel . . .
VWW:	And in that book I actually deal with race and class a lot. *Where Do I Go from Here?* is a story about a girl from Newark, who goes to a high-class private school. There's another girl from Newark, a young white Italian girl who goes to the same school, and they have this big fight. It's about working-class kids in an environment where there is a lot of money.
DFH:	So, you actually have two young adult characters, one who's African American, one who's Italian American. Both are from a lower-class background, and they go to this upper-class school?
VWW:	The story in a nutshell is, Lea goes to this posh school and there's this other kid there named Marcus Garvey Williams. He is the star of the school, but he also is from a working-class environment in Harlem. You know, he is one of those kids who is simply an absolute star. He has it all under control and he kind of takes her under his wing. One day, he leaves the school without any explanation and Lea is left by herself. She can't understand where he went and why he left. She feels deserted.

There's an Italian girl from north Newark who has never been kind to her. There's a kind of hostility between the two girls, be- |

AN INTERVIEW WITH VALERIE WILSON WESLEY

cause north and central Newark have a kind of hostility. Anyway, the two get into a big fight—hair-pulling, etc.

The story revolves around Lea's search for Marcus. She finds that he left because he apparently fathered a child over the summer and he's had to take care of this child. But he's still basically got it together because he's enrolled in his local school. He's going to graduate; he's going to be OK.

Lea ends up going back to her posh school. It ends with her and the Italian girl coming to a sort of resolution after the week they spent searching for Marcus. The book ends where it begins with a better life for both. They discover they should try to work out their differences because they have more things in common than things that separate them.

DFH: Did you see this ending as an attempt to convince young people that education is important?

VWW: It is not as pat as its sounds in my summary. I saw it as an attempt to say that sometimes you can't take color as the standard—it's not everything. And at the end of the book they could say something like: "Oh, I don't know if we're going to be friends or not, but I know that there's more to this than I thought."

DFH: So, don't judge a book by its cover!

VWW: Exactly. The long way of saying, "Don't judge a book by its cover!"

DFH: And the *Afro-Bets*?

VWW: Oh, this is just a little book of heroes and heroines done with Just Us Books, which is a small black publishing company.

DFH: So you feel a commitment to the next generation?

VWW: Oh, yes. I really do. I've also written *Freedom's Gifts: A Juneteenth Story,* which is a picture book for children. It's a beautiful book about Juneteenth.

Right now I'm doing a children's series called *Willimena and the Cookie Money* and *Willimena and Mrs. Sweetley's Guinea Pig*. My inspiration for that was the *Ramona* series. And it takes the same age girls—seven, eight, nine—as its target audience. There were no picture books, no chapter books for young black girls in that age group—like the *Babysitter Club* series. I was approached by Hyperion to write the series because there's nothing; it's an absolute lack. And the feeling was that there should be something because black girls are reading and there's no connection. They need something they can relate to. So these books for young people are my commitment to the next generation.

Afterword

DOROTHEA FISCHER-HORNUNG
and MONIKA MUELLER

WHEN WE STARTED OUT ON OUR ENDEAVOR, WE WERE A SMALL GROUP OF SCHOLARS who got together for a session of workshops in which we attempted to define how ethnicity is explored and expressed in the genre of detective fiction—how the performance of ethnicity is affected by the genre as well as how the genre is affected by the performance of the ethnic detective. What are the conclusions we can draw at the end of our endeavor? And what significant questions remain unanswered?

A key question is why ethnicity and the detective novel genre seem to fit together so well. Certainly one explanation could be that ultimately both address the question of identity, spanning the arch from "Whodunit?" to "Who am I?" Both questions emphasize the unity of subject and object that is entailed in the crime fiction genre: exploring the self and other, the borderlands of minority and majority relations, dominance and alterity, as well as marginality and centrality.

But an even more fundamental question—one implicit in the exploration of all these concerns—is precisely what ethnicity is and what constitutes an ethnic detective? And does an author have to "be one" to write about an ethnic group? This question is deeply connected to the issues associated with identity politics as they have been discussed over the past two decades. How does whiteness factor into the question of ethnicity? This is a particularly important question in postcolonial and American studies, whereas linguistic barriers seem to be a greater concern in European studies.

The novels by Tony Hillerman, the Thurlos, and Arthur Upfield, for instance, exemplify how very limiting to the life of human imagination it would be to not be able to slip into someone else's skin, so to speak, and to try out what it feels like—and then write about it. If to "be one" were a requirement in creating fictional characters, literature would be the poorer for it, indeed.

The pleasure of assuming another ethnic identity by exploring worlds that are outside one's personal experience certainly accounts for one aspect of the popularity of the ethnic crime fiction genre. The appeal of the "exotic" is also a factor that should not be underestimated. However, minorities (ethnic/racial/gender) fulfill a special role, especially by adding to the self-consciousness of a society. Therefore, it is essential that minorities speak for themselves. We cannot deny the special perspective that members of a specific ethnicity can and do have.

In the past the scholarly exploration of the ethnic detective genre has been primarily within the context of anglophone detective fiction; therefore, we have expanded and internationalized our approach. Ethnicity, as we have seen, factors into the crime genre very differently in various countries: in France with immigrants from the Maghreb, in Germany with Turkish migrants, in Great Britain with its historically difficult relationship to Scotland, in Australia with its Aboriginal population, and in the United States with its various ethnic and racial groups. In the anglophone and francophone countries a common language enables majority/minority communication, despite the linguistic domination implicit in the process of colonization. This unified dominant language, however, has often been unavailable to first-generation immigrants and migrants—a fact that is exemplified in this volume by the discussion of early U.S.-Italian crime fiction, where the move from immigrant consciousness to that of an American one is marked in the move away from Italian-language writing to English. Further, the dominant language is modified, honed, and cast in a somewhat different form by minority languages and cultures within a given country.

Ethnicity is often marked very differently in the European situation, where it is not necessarily—but still frequently—associated with skin color. Language or regional dialects as well as customs usually play a more significant role in the European context. As the example of Jakob Arjouni's German Turkish detective, Kemal Kayankaya, who does not speak a word of Turkish, indicates, culture and language—or the lack thereof—significantly complicate the matter. Although he is visually identified as a Turk by his German environment and even by Turks, he is simultaneously a member and not a member of both cultures. It has also become evident that to focus exclusively on ethnicity severely limits interpretation; the intricate interplay of race and ethnicity, ethnicity and gender, class and history, as well as a multitude of combinations of these and other factors, makes for the specific shadings and nuances of the genre.

Paradoxically, internationalization and cosmopolitanism are often at odds with the ethnic detective novel's focus on ethnicity. Books travel across borders in translation—to our great pleasure—in that these translations open up worlds that would otherwise be inaccessible to us. In the process of traveling, these books change. For example, Grangé's *Blood-Red Rivers* loses its ethnic, class, and subcultural markers when translated into English. Barbara Neely, in the interview included in this volume, expresses her skepticism about the translation of her own Blanche White novels, noting her German translator's potential lack of familiarity with the African American cultural context. The erasure of ethnicity is even more drastic in the film adaptation of *Blood-Red Rivers*, where all ethnic markers such as appearance, language, and names are erased and flattened into "Frenchness." A different but related phenomenon is exemplified by the marketing of Rudolfo Anaya's mysteries across genres, where a "translation" process occurs in reviews and criticism that mediate publications to readers, marketing the novels exclusively either as mysteries or ethnic fiction.

One significant recognition that has emerged from a number of contributions to this volume is that a fractured sense of identity is not limited to the margins, but rather is something shared by society as a whole, defining postmodern transnationalism. The question arises if the concept of a consolidated identity characterized by closure is outdated. While some contributors feel that an "authentic" identity can indeed be accomplished, others argue that identity is an ongoing process, something that can never be fully achieved—nor even should be.

Some have declared the end of the era of racism, but the detective fiction discussed in this volume indicates quite the opposite. Race and ethnicity—and they are not the same—remain defining factors in our lives. Cities the world over often "feel like" a collection of disparate ethnic tribes. This applies equally to Los Angeles, Chicago, and New York; Frankfurt, Paris, and London; and Bombay, Lagos, and Jakarta.

Global urbanization and migration contributes deeply to the current boom in the crime fiction genre. Ethnic crime fiction in particular provides a forum for the staging of contemporary fears concerning ethnic and urban conflict. The intricate intersection of varied histories of migration, occupation, and colonization defines what is considered ethnic and in turn alters the definition of dominant cultures. It is the interplay of class, race, gender, ethnicity, and migratory and colonial histories that keeps readers turning the pages in an attempt to solve the crime in the book as well as to explore the mysteries of our increasingly globalized world. While ethnic detective fiction is a booming segment of the popular fiction market, it remains a relatively unexplored field of scholarly endeavor—we hope we have made a small contribution to changing this.

Contributors

CARMEN BIRKLE is Associate Professor of American Studies at the University of Mainz, Germany. She has published numerous articles on American literature and her dissertation, "Women's Stories of the Looking Glass: Autobiographical Reflections and Self-Representations in the Poetry of Sylvia Plath, Adrienne Rich, and Audre Lord," was published in 1996. With Jochen Achilles she has co-edited *(Trans)Formations of Cultural Identity in the English-Speaking World* (1998) and she has recently completed another book *(habilitation), Writing Multicultural America: Migration, Miscegenation, Transculturation.* She is assistant editor of the journal *Amerikastudien/American Studies* and associate editor of the journal *Feminist Europa.*

STEPHANIE BROWN holds a Ph.D. in American literature from Columbia University with a dissertation entitled "Constructing and Contesting Authenticity in the Postwar African American Voice." She has published articles on popular culture and African-American literature and is currently Assistant Professor of English at Ohio State University at Newark.

MARINA CACIOPPO holds a D.Phil. from the School of English and American Studies at the University of Sussex, England. Her thesis addressed the representation and construction of ethnic identity in Italian American literature. She has published articles on Italian American detective fiction and immigrant autobiography and presently works for the Humanities Computing Unit at the University of Oxford.

THEO D'HAEN studied languages and literatures in Belgium, the United States, and France. He is Professor of English and American Literature at Leiden University, The Netherlands, and Academic Director of the Onderzoekschool Literatuurwetenschap/Netherlands Graduate Research School for Literature. He has published extensively on modern literature in European languages, particularly on postmodernism and postcolonialism. His and

Hans Bertens's *Contemporary American Crime Writing* is forthcoming with Palgrave.

KATRIN FISCHER holds a degree in American Studies, English, and German from Chemnitz University of Technology, Germany. She has completed a Ph.D. thesis on the representation of Native Americans in contemporary crime and detective fiction at the University of Paderborn, Germany. She has published articles on American literature and teaching English as a foreign language. Her compilation of Shakespeare quotations, *Reclams Lexikon der Shakespeare-Zitate*, will be published by Reclam in 2002.

DOROTHEA FISCHER-HORNUNG is Senior Lecturer at the University of Heidelberg, Germany. She has published on the works of Ralph Ellison, *Women in the United States* (1990), and coedited *Women and War* (1991) with Maria Diedrich, *Holding Their Own: Perspectives on the Multi-Ethnic Literatures of the United States* (2000) with Heike Raphael-Hernandez, and *EmBODYing Liberation: The Black Body in Dance,* with Alison Goeller, (2001). She is a member of the Executive Board of MESEA, The Society for Multi-Ethnic Studies: Europe and the Americas.

CARMEN FLYS-JUNQUERA is Associate Professor of English at the University of Alcalá, Spain, where she also serves as Assistant Director of the Center for North American Studies. She has published articles on Chicano and African American fiction, coedited *El Poder Hispano* and *El Nuevo Horizonte: España/Estados Unidos* (forthcoming), and is in the process of coediting an anthology on representations of the contemporary American family in literature and the media. She is Executive Editor of the journal *Revista Española de Estudios Norteamericanos (REDEN)* and critical editor for the *Journal of Caribbean Literature* and *Atlantis*.

ESTHER FRITSCH holds master's degrees from the University of Rochester and from the University of Cologne. She teaches courses in American Studies at the University of Cologne and has completed a Ph.D. thesis on the functions of gossip in novels by contemporary U.S. ethnic women writers. Her research interests include Native American, African American and Caribbean literatures, and postcolonial theory.

ANN-CATHERINE GEUDER studied Latin American and German literature at the Free University of Berlin, Germany, where she received her M.A. in 1997. She is currently writing a dissertation entitled "Opportunities and Challenges in Publishing Chicano/a Literature."

CONTRIBUTORS 325

ALISON D. GOELLER teaches ethnic literature and women's studies for the University of Maryland/European Division in Heidelberg, Germany. She holds a Ph.D. in American literature from Temple University in Philadelphia and has published articles on American literature and coedited a collection of articles on African American dance with Dorothea Fischer-Hornung: *EmBODYing Liberation: The Black Body in American Dance* (2001).

MARION GYMNICH holds a Ph.D. in English literature from Cologne University, Germany. Her dissertation on concepts of female identity in twentieth-century British novels by women, "Entwürfe weiblicher Identität im englischen Frauenroman des 20. Jahrhunderts," was published in 2000. She is currently working on a book on metalinguistic reflections in contemporary novels and short stories written in English. She has published articles on twentieth-century women writers and Restoration drama and linguistics, as well as an introductory textbook on English linguistics. She teaches at the University of Giessen, Germany.

SAMANTHA HUME studied English language and German in Canterbury and earned an M.A. specializing in contemporary German writing. She now teaches English and women's writing at the University of Cologne. Her research interests focus on women's sexuality as well as violence against women in British detective and crime fiction.

KONSTANZE KUTZBACH received her degree in English from the University of Cologne with a thesis entitled "A Narratological Analysis of the Depiction of Female Experience in Contemporary Youth Literature." She is a Ph.D. candidate at the University of Cologne and is currently writing a dissertation entitled "The Representation of Liminal Experience(s) in Contemporary Literature and Film."

MONIKA MUELLER is Assistant Professor of English at the University of Cologne, Germany. She received her Ph.D. from the University of Alabama and has published *"This Infinite Fraternity of Feeling": Gender, Genre, and Homoerotic Crisis in Hawthorne's* The Blithedale Romance *and Melville's* Pierre (1996) as well as articles on American and British fiction. She has completed a book *(habilitation)* on George Eliot and American literature. Her research and teaching interests include gender and cultural studies.

SABINE STEINISCH has taught in the Department of English at the University of Würzburg, Germany, and participated in research projects at the Universities of Potsdam and Cologne. Her research interests include postcolonial literatures and theory, as well as cultural and gender studies. She has published on the cultural history of marriage and is currently working on a dissertation on Angela Carter.

RUSSELL WEST is Professor of English at the Free University of Berlin, Germany. He has published *Conrad and Gide: Translation, Transference, and Intertextuality* (1996), *Figures de la maladie chez André Gide* (1997), and *Spatial Representations and the Jacobean Stage* (2002); he coedited *Marginal Voices, Marginal Forms: Diaries in European Literature and History* (1999) and *Subverting Masculinity: Hegemonic and Alternative Versions of Masculinity in Contemporary Culture* (2000).

Index

Aboriginal/s, 321; culture, 287; detective, 13, 18, 285; full-blooded, 282; half-caste, 282; half-caste children, 284–86, 288; identity, 18; storyteller, 280
Adorno, Theodor, 75, 79n
African American/s, 136, 318; cinema, 164, 170; community 31, 100, 102–3, 112, 133, 135, 142, 144, 156, 161, 178, 303, 306, 313–14; cultural identity, 110; detective, 16, 28, 32n, 172, 177; detective fiction, 15, 33, 97, 141, 316; female detective, 16, 136; female PI, 144–45; history, 176; Miss Marple, 114; vernacular, 111; woman sleuth, 303. *See also* black
Alexie, Sherman, 17, 204, 213, 220
Algeria, 271, 276
alienation, 190, 200, 241, 254
alterity, 190, 240, 253–54, 257, 264, 276, 278
Arab, 18; ethnic, 241, 245–46
alternative belief systems, 99, 102
Anaya, Rudolfo, 15, 81, 84, 86, 88, 99, 101, 107–8, 111, 322
ancestralism, 84, 99, 105; Native American, 207, 286
Anglo-American/s: culture, 107, 193, 196–97, 201n; descent, 188; identity, 214; society, 189; tradition, 188; value system 189, 193
animism, 98–99, 105
Anzaldúa, Gloria, 183
Arab, 18, 261–62, 264, 266, 271, 276; detective, 14, 18
Arjouni, Jakob, 13, 240, 243, 245
Asian American/s: culture, 43; community, 44–45; detective, 38, 50; detective fiction, 14; women, 51

assassin, 242, 246, 249, 251, 253, 255, 257–58; hard-boiled, 249, 251, 257
assimilation, 54–55, 59, 70, 73, 99
Atwood, Margaret, 316
autoethnography, 54, 76

Baker, Nikki, 115
Baldwin, James, 167, 171
Bhabha, Homi, 53, 55, 151, 194, 262, 271–72
bildungsroman, 81, 91
black: magic, 89; masculinity, 168–69; police officer, 172n; private dick, 164, 167; women, 300–302. *See also* African American/s
Black Hand, 27, 33
blaxploitation, 164, 166, 171, 172n
Bogart, Humphrey, 38
Bond, James, 11
"Bringing Them Home" report, 281, 290, 294
brujería, 81, 97, 99, 102, 107–8, 111
Buranelli, Prosper, 14, 25, 27–28, 30, 32
Butler, Judith, 117, 122

capitalism, 176, 177, 179
Cawelti, John G., 188
Chandler, Raymond, 24, 36–37, 74, 121, 135, 194
Chesterton, G. K., 78n
Chicano/a: community, 86, 112; culture, 82; detective, 101; detective fiction, 15, 97; folk belief, 107; literature, 86, 90; movement, 86; vernacular 108, 111
children's literature, 318–19
Chinatown, 25, 29–30, 33, 45, 153, 155

328 INDEX

Chinese American/s: culture, 153; community, 25, 30, 44–45; detective fiction, 14, 24; identity, 151; Italian Chinese Americans, 181; women, 153
Christie, Agatha, 128, 131n, 134, 201
CIA, 83–84
class, 119, 122, 125, 230, 301, 317–18, 321–22
communism, 176, 178
community: ethnic, 44, 97, 157, 272. *See also entries for individual ethnicities*
contact zone, 54, 59, 68, 76–77
Corpi, Lucha, 15, 99, 101, 111
Cross, Amanda, 116
crosscultural: detective, 190; initiation, 194; themes, 189
Cuban American/s: identity, 119, 121; lady dick, 114
curanderismo, 98–99, 107–8, 111

Daly, Carroll John, 36–37
Davis, Angela, 317
de Lauretis, Theresa, 117
detective: ethnic, 11–12, 14, 17–18, 111, 129, 165, 175, 190–91, 204, 241, 262, 275, 277, 320; female, 144–45, 190, 200, 201n, 304; hard-boiled, 29, 39, 42, 65, 75, 144–45, 165, 170, 177, 183, 205, 217, 240, 243, 245, 256–57, 274, 304; as loner, 16, 33, 77, 83, 100, 139, 179, 191–95, 199, 217, 264; medium-boiled, 145n; multiethnic, 43, 100, 128, 149; postcolonial, 277; rabbi, 57, 63, 77
detective fiction: classical, 97, 111, 148, 155, 162; ethnic, 14, 18, 25, 48, 97, 111, 129, 175, 204; formula, 85, 116, 189, 220; genre of, 76, 90–91, 188, 200, 232, 312, 320; golden age of, 188, 201; hard-boiled, 25, 36, 43, 51, 73–75, 77, 78n, 97, 99–100, 110, 112, 115, 117–18, 123, 134, 136, 140, 172n, 175, 194, 240, 257, 267; lesbian, 235; medium-boiled, 140; women's, 12, 54, 116, 134, 213, 275, 302. *See also* mystery fiction; novel
diaspora, 16, 152
difference: cultural, 248, 250; gender, 121; racial, 193
Dische, Irene, 14, 240, 241, 245, 257
discourse, 238n, 240, 247–49, 253, 256

Doctorow, E. L., 311
doppelgänger, 18, 104, 109, 264–66, 273–75
double consciousness, 241, 246, 254, 256–57, 265
Doyle, Arthur Conan, 61
D'Souza, Dinesh, 171
Du Bois, W. E. B., 30–31, 241

Ellison, Ralph, 178
English: cultural values, 237; identity, 13, 227, 283
essentialism, 51, 171; ethnic, 42
ethnicity, 11, 121, 189, 317, 321; post-ethnicity, 55, 164
eugenics, 267, 270, 274–77
European Americans, 187

fabula, 283, 286–89
Fanon, Frantz, 148
FBI, 83–84, 176, 178, 182–83, 190–91, 195; agent, 192–94, 198, 201n
feminism, 115, 235, 302–3, 306; socialist lesbian, 228, 237
feminization, 251, 253
femme fatale, 121, 206, 273–75
film: African American, 164; noir, 172n, 277
Fisher, Rudolph, 11, 14, 25, 28, 31
Flynn, Errol, 11
folk: belief/s, 15, 97–99, 102, 104–5, 107, 109–12; healing, 99, 103, 108
formula: detective, 189, 220; genre, 87; hard-boiled, 99–100, 257; mystery, 81, 85, 89
Foucault, Michel, 117, 242, 249, 255
Freese, Peter, 56–57, 62, 149, 188, 190, 275
French detective, 262, 273
French-Arab detective, 14, 18
Frenchness, 263–64, 271, 276
Furutani, Dale, 13–14, 19n, 38–39, 45, 50–51

Garcia-Aguilera, Carolina, 15, 114, 116–23, 129, 314
Gates, Henry Louis, 117, 130n
gender, 64, 77, 119, 121, 127, 129, 187, 191, 237, 301, 317, 321–22; performativity, 122; stereotype, 58, 61, 116

INDEX

genre, 87, 129, 188, 200, 218–19, 313, 316; modification, 116–17, 131n. *See also* detective fiction

German culture and identity, 243, 245, 248

German-Turkish detective, 321

Ghost Dance, 218–19, 221, 222n

ghosts, 143, 204–7, 209, 212, 220

globalization, 53, 55, 265, 272

Goldberg, Ed, 15, 56–57, 69–77

Gosselin, Adrienne Johnson, 149

Grangé, Jean-Christophe, 14, 18, 260–79, 322

Grant, Cary, 11

Gruesser, John Cullen, 117, 130n, 131n, 177

Guy, Rosa, 16, 150, 156–59, 162

Hall, Stewart, 156–57, 185

Hammett, Dashiell, 24, 36–37, 74, 134–35, 138–39

hard-boiled. *See* detective; detective fiction; private investigator; sleuth

Harlem, 24–25, 27–33, 37, 161–62

Hillerman, Tony, 12–13, 16, 88, 175, 181, 185, 189, 201n, 219, 316, 320

Himes, Chester, 265, 172n, 271, 276, 236–37, 134–35, 138–39, 310

Hollinger, David, 54–55

Holocaust, 67–76, 78–79n, 265, 269

hoodoo, 97–99, 101–2, 107

Hudson, Rock, 11

hybridity, 14, 48, 64, 148, 151

identity, 13, 15, 17, 115, 161, 162, 179, 182, 230, 235, 320, 322; aboriginal, 18; black, 165–66; crisis, 192, 245; cultural, 185; English, 13, 227, 283; ethnic, 12, 150, 157, 162; formation, 16, 204, 242, 256; fractured, 244, 247, 252, 254–56; German, 245; hard-boiled, 251; hybrid, 48; Japanese, 42, 46; Jewish, 67, 70, 72; Kurdish, 248; lesbian, 235; multiple, 183; Navajo, 190, 194; postmortem, 185; racial, 129, 192; Scottish, 227, 229, 232, 238n; sexual socialist, 232; subversive, 17; transnational, 148, 150

immigration, 11, 27–28, 30, 103, 150, 153, 156

Indo-Hispanic culture, 15, 81, 88–90

Irish Americans, 32

Irving, John, 310

Italian American/s, 23–28, 136–37, 181, 318; community, 26, 28, 32–33; detective fiction, 14, 33

Jackson, Samuel L., 166–69

Japanese: community, 40; culture, 41–42, 46

Japanese American/s, 38–39; detective, 13, 38; detective fiction, 14

Jewish American/s, 54, 67, 69–70, 72, 137, 178, 260, 275; community, 58–59, 65–66; detective fiction, 14, 54–56, 58, 76–78; women, 64

Jones, Manina, 116–17, 121, 130n, 144

Jung, Carl Gustav, 81

juvenile ethnic detective fiction, 13, 16

Kellerman, Faye, 15, 56–57, 62–68, 70, 73, 76–77, 78n

Kemelman, Harry, 15, 56–63, 70, 74, 76–77, 78n

killer: contract, 241–42, 246; serial, 213, 216–18, 266, 277

King, Martin Luther, 171

Klein, Kathleen Gregory, 54, 115–16, 123, 171, 238n

Komo, Dolores, 136, 144, 146n

Korean Americans, 41

Kristeva, Julia, 250

Kurdish: ethnicity, 245; identity, 248

Kurdish-Turkish identity, 249

Lacan, Jacques, 262

Langford, Ruby, 289, 293

Lapolla, Mato, 14, 25, 29–30, 32

Leon, Donna, 310

lesbian: detective fiction, 235; feminist, 17, 227, 235–36; identity, 235; sleuth, 235

Little Italy, 24–25, 28, 33

Maghreb, 277, 321

Marple, Miss, 128–29

marginalization, 50, 148, 150, 152, 157, 161, 163, 175, 190

marketing, 309; strategies, 13

masculinity, 251; black, 168–69

Massey, Sujata, 43, 46, 50–51

Masterson, Whit, 315

McDermid, Val, 13, 17, 227, 231, 234, 236–37
McDonald, John, 316
McGee, Travis, 316
melting pot, 53, 59, 71, 188
Mercer, Kobena, 168
MESEA, 12, 19n
Mexican American/s, 183; identity, 90
migration, 18, 150, 151–52, 154, 156, 157–58, 160, 317, 321–22
minority: cultural, 149; ethnic, 148; racial, 156
miscegenation, 271
Morgan, Sally, 18, 280–81, 285–86, 288, 290–94
Morrison, Toni, 105, 110, 316
Mosley, Walter, 15–16, 99, 104, 111, 135–36, 175, 185, 311–12
multicultural: detective fiction, 43, 100, 128, 149; literature, 51; society, 184
Munt, Sally, 116–17, 128, 130n
murder: fetishized, 261, 266, 275; ritual, 267; serial, 210, 212
Murdoch, Iris, 316
mystery fiction: classical, 25; domestic, 15n; plot, 129, 131n. *See also* detective fiction

nagual, 107–8
Namias, June, 187, 201
narrative: captivity, 187; detective, 110; epistemological, 290; gnoseological, 290
Native American/s, 187–89, 192, 316; ancestors, 207; beliefs, 212; church, 211, 221n; community 115, 213; culture, 204, 215, 219; detective fiction, 12, 219; identity, 192, 214–15; investigator, 191, 220; private investigator, 190; sleuth, 16, 189, 216; stereotypes, 187

Navajo: belief/s, 182, 184, 196, 198; community, 176, 183, 189, 193, 198; culture, 176, 182, 184, 189, 199; detective, 176, 182; female detective, 200; identity, 190, 194; police, 182–84, 194, 200; religion, 196, 198; tradition, 193–97
Neely, Barbara, 13, 15, 99, 101, 104, 111, 114, 116–17, 123–29, 141, 299–307, 314, 317

novel: classical detective, 155, 162; ethnic detective, 175; hard-boiled detective, 51, 75, 78n, 99, 112, 123, 240. *See also* detective fiction
Nuevo Mexicano: community 83, 85, 88; culture, 83, 86–87; spirituality, 91

order: patriarchal, 234; symbolic, 254–57
outlaw, 264–65
Owens, Louis, 17, 115, 204, 209, 215, 220, 221n

Paretsky, Sarah, 304
Parks, Gordon, 165, 173n
patriarchal: discourse, 238n; norm, 116; social structure, 234–36
Pocahontas, 222n
Poe, Edgar Allan, 26, 60, 61
police: behavior, 233; brutality, 139
Portuguese Americans, 137
postcolonial: detective, 277; situation, 18, 272; studies, 320; theory, 16
postethnicity, 55, 164
Pratt, Mary Louise, 53–54
private eye, 38, 44, 100
private investigator (also abbreviated as PI), 75, 99, 101, 114, 118, 123, 133, 137–38, 141–42, 144, 243, 246, 316; African American female, 144, 201n; American Indian, 190; as loner, 77, 83. *See also* detective; sleuth
publication strategy, 82, 89, 91
publishing business, 308–11
Pueblo Indians, 88–89
pulp fiction, 188, 278

race/racial, 12, 97, 124, 187, 191, 301, 317–18, 321–22; conflict, 141; consciousness, 125; difference, 193; discrimination, 118, 175; identity, 129, 192; injustice, 237; minority, 156; prejudice, 192; relations, 127
racism, 138, 144
rap music, 278
reader: perception, 82, 91; response, 292
Reed, Ishmael, 15, 99, 101, 108, 111
Riefenstahl, Leni, 268, 278
Roe, Paddy, 280, 282, 293
roots, 193; African, 159; Asian American, 43; Indo-Hispanic, 15; Navajo, 194
Roundtree, Richard, 164, 167, 169

Rowland, Laura Joh, 14, 43, 48, 50–51
Rozan, S. J., 14, 43, 45, 51
Rushdie, Salman, 151–52

Said, Edward, 192, 272
Sayers, Dorothy, 134
Scotland, 227, 321
Scottish: cultural values, 237; detective, 227, 231; identity, 13, 227–29, 232, 238n
sexism, 118, 234
shamanism, 82, 84
Silko, Leslie Marmon, 184
skinwalker, 195, 198
sleuth: amateur, 304; female, 304; hard-boiled, 42; lesbian, 235; loner, 179. *See also* detective; private investigator; sleuth
Smith, John, 222n
socialism, 229–30
socialist: identity, 232; lesbian feminism, 228, 237; lesbian identity, 237; value system, 231
society: capitalist, 177; multicultural, 184; multiethnic, 317
Soitos, Stephen, 29, 108, 115, 131n, 133, 135, 141–42
spiritual: bildungsroman, 81, 91; guide, 84–85; power, 82
Stolen Generation, 281, 294
subalternity, 240–41, 246, 258
subject position, 148, 151, 156
sujet, 283–89
supernatural, 17, 198; elements, 220

superstition, 15, 98
syncretism, 97–98, 221n

third space, 53, *55*
Thurlo, Aimée and David, 12, 17, 187, 189, 320
Todorov, Tzvetan, 283, 286, 289–90
transculturation, 53–55, 76
trickster figure, 108, 177, 182, 213
Turkish: cultural identity, 243, 248; detective, 11; ethnicity, 245; identity, 13; migrants, 321
Turkish-German investigator, 17

value system: Anglo-American, 189, 193; dominant, 110; mainstream, 112; socialist, 231
Vechten, Carl Van, 24, 30
visions, 106–7

Walton, Priscilla, 107, 116–17, 121, 130n, 144
Welles, Orson, 144, 277
Wesley, Valerie Wilson, 16, 133–40, 144–45
Wiesel, Elie, 75, 78n
Wiesenthal, Simon, 72
Winfrey, Oprah, 312
Wright, Richard, 167, 171, 178

xenophobia, 23

Yep, Laurence, 16, 150, 153, 155–57, 162

Zangwill, Israel, 53, 77n